Taxing Capital Income in the European Union

Taxing Capital Income in the European Union

Issues and Options for Reform

Edited by SIJBREN CNOSSEN

OXFORD
UNIVERSITY PRESS

OXFORD
UNIVERSITY PRESS

Great Clarendon Street, Oxford OX2 6DP

Oxford University Press is a department of the University of Oxford.
It furthers the University's objective of excellence in research, scholarship,
and education by publishing worldwide in

Oxford New York

Athens Auckland Bangkok Bogotá Buenos Aires Calcutta
Cape Town Chennai Dar es Salaam Delhi Florence Hong Kong Istanbul
Karachi Kuala Lumpur Madrid Melbourne Mexico City Mumbai
Nairobi Paris São Paulo Singapore Taipei Tokyo Toronto Warsaw

and associated companies in Berlin Ibadan

Oxford is a registered trade mark of Oxford University Press
in the UK and certain other countries

Published in the United States
by Oxford University Press Inc., New York

British Library Cataloguing in Publication Data

Data available

Library of Congress Cataloging-in-Publication Data

Taxing capital income in the European Union: issues and options for reform/Sijbren Cnossen [editor].
p. cm.
Papers presented at a conference.
1. Capital gains tax—European Union countries—Congresses. 2. Income tax—European
Union countries—Congresses. I. Cnossen, Sijbren.
HJ4706.5 .T385 2000   336.24'3—dc21   99-086733

ISBN 0-19-829783-1

1 3 5 7 9 10 8 6 4 2

Typeset by Newgen Imaging Systems (P) Ltd., Chennai, India
Printed in Great Britain on acid-free paper by
Biddles Ltd
Guildford & Kings Lynn

Acknowledgements

The papers in this volume grew out of a conference organized under the auspices of the International Seminar in Public Economics (ISPE) and the Research Centre for Economic Policy (OCFEB) of the Economics Faculty of Erasmus University Rotterdam. Financial support was provided by the Dutch Ministry of Economic Affairs, Nippon Hosei Gakkei, the Netherlands Organization for Scientific Research (NWO), and the Royal Netherlands Academy of Arts and Sciences (KNAW).

The organization and execution of the conference and the subsequent production of this volume were greatly facilitated by the extensive and able co-operation received from all the contributors, commentators, and referees. Judith Payne's help was truly indispensable in preparing the manuscript for publication.

Sijbren Cnossen

Contents

Participants: ISPE and OCFEB Seminar

[Affiliation at time of Conference]

Julian Alworth, *University Luigi Bocconi*
Krister Andersson, *Skandinaviska Enskilda Banken*
Richard Bird, *University of Toronto*
Stephen Bond, *Institute for Fiscal Studies* and *Nuffield College, Oxford*
Lans Bovenberg, *Netherlands Bureau for Economic Policy Analysis*
Stephen Clark, *OECD*
Sijbren Cnossen, *Erasmus University Rotterdam*
Michael Daly, *OECD*
Michael Devereux, *Keele University* and *Institute for Fiscal Studies*
Antonio DiMayo, *University of Firenze*
Ruud van den Dool, *Erasmus University Rotterdam*
Malcolm Gammie, *Linklaters & Paines*
Silvia Giannini, *University of Bologna*
Roger Gordon, *University of Michigan*
Rachel Griffith, *Institute for Fiscal Studies*
Robert Glenn Hubbard, *Colombia University*
Bernd Huber, *University of Munich*
Harry Huizinga, *University of Tilburg*
Hiromitsu Ishi, *Hitotsubashi University*
Flip de Kam, *University of Groningen*
Gerold Krause-Junk, *University of Hamburg*
Charles McLure, *Hoover Institution*
Jack Mintz, *University of Toronto*
Peggy Musgrave, *University of California, Santa Cruz*
Richard Musgrave, *University of California, Santa Cruz*
Scott Newlon, *US Department of the Treasury*
Søren Bo Nielsen, *Copenhagen Business School*
Satya Poddar, *Ernst & Young*
Jarig van Sinderen, *Erasmus University Rotterdam*
Bernd Spahn, *Goethe University*
Emil Sunley, *International Monetary Fund*
Eiji Tajika, *Hitotsubashi University*

Servaas van Thiel, *European Commission*
Henk Vording, *University of Leiden*
Joann Weiner, *US Department of the Treasury*
Scott Wilkie, *Ogilvy Renault*

Figures

Tables

1

Taxing capital income in the European Union: summary and discussion

SIJBREN CNOSSEN

Following the introduction of the euro, the European Union (EU) has started to debate the desirability and feasibility of more co-ordination in the field of capital income taxation. In contrast with product taxes, the EU Treaty does not provide for explicit authority to harmonize income taxes. So far, little co-ordination has taken place, even though the capital income tax base is much more mobile and hence more difficult to tax than is, for instance, consumption (and labour). There is much discussion on a minimum withholding tax on interest and on a code of conduct for business income taxes, but in practice little real progress is being made in aligning the various capital income taxes. More fundamentally, a broad, tax-policy type of discussion on whether, where, and how capital income should be taxed is lacking.

The papers in this volume try to fill this void. Roger Gordon addresses the question of whether or not capital income should be taxed. Subsequently, Peggy Musgrave and Richard Bird/Scott Wilkie try to come to grips with the question of where capital income should be taxed—in the member state of source or the member state of residence. Michael Devereux and Harry Huizinga/Søren Bo Nielsen then analyse various issues that arise in taxing equity income and imposing a withholding tax on interest. Next, Stephen Bond and Sijbren Cnossen discuss specific comprehensive proposals for taxing capital income in open economies. Finally, Scott Newlon and Charles McLure/Joann Weiner look at the difficulties of and alternatives to maintaining separate corporate income taxes in the EU. This introductory chapter summarizes the various papers and briefly discusses the basic issues and solutions.

1. Should capital income be taxed?

Roger Gordon begins his provocative paper by pointing out that existing personal and corporate income tax structures honour the requirements of comprehensive income taxation largely in the breach. Although statutory tax rates are high, effective tax rates are low on account of tax preferences for pension plans and owner-occupied housing. Perhaps this should not surprise theorists who for a long time have pointed out that taxes on capital income not only lose revenue but also generate large efficiency costs and have distributional effects of dubious appeal.

Equity is violated because the comprehensive income tax discriminates against late consumers. Efficiency is compromised because (anticipated) capital income taxes reduce capital accumulation, thereby shifting the burden of the taxes on to labour income. Furthermore, the allocation of capital is distorted because effective tax rates typically differ across assets and across investors, offering opportunities for wasteful tax arbitrage. The equity and efficiency case against capital income taxes is even stronger in open economies. Residence-based taxes that affect saving can easily be avoided or evaded. But source-based taxes impinge on investment which can obtain a higher net-of-tax return elsewhere. In this situation, before-tax returns can only be raised by paying lower wage rates.

According to Gordon, three hypotheses may be suggested for why open-economy countries none the less continue to impose source-based taxes on the capital income of foreign investors: implicit co-ordination of tax policy across countries through use of crediting arrangements, market power in capital markets, and immobility of capital across countries. These hypotheses forecast taxes on the capital income received by non-residents, as a form of tariff. However, the hypotheses cannot so easily explain any continuing high statutory taxes on the capital income accruing to residents. In practice, though, there may not be much that needs explaining. The symbiosis between interest deductibility and the existence of tax-exempt investors, such as pension funds, means that effective average tax rates may be close to zero.

Thus existing theory forecasts little or no tax on capital income in an open economy. In any case, it is more efficient to tax labour directly than to tax it indirectly through a capital tax. Accordingly, tax policies should focus on the appropriate taxation of labour income. In Gordon's view, there are three likely approaches: a payroll tax, a cash-flow income tax (with expensing and no taxation of income from financial assets), and a value added tax.

In an open economy, all of these taxes would face enforcement problems. These problems are worst under the payroll tax, because firms would have a strong incentive to shift to some form of compensation other than wages and salaries to avoid the tax. The income tax scores better. In effect, it supplements the payroll tax with a cash-flow tax on business income, neutralizing the avoidance opportunities through, say, stock options, available under a payroll tax. The income tax remains vulnerable, however, to transfer pricing and other mechanisms for shifting income between subsidiaries in different countries. These problems disappear under a destination-based value added tax. Since the tax is due on the price paid by the final consumer, it is unaffected by transfer pricing within the producing firm. But the value added tax is vulnerable to cross-border shopping. These arguments point towards some mix of income tax and value added tax. Preferably, the (progressive) income tax should also be made border-adjustable to eliminate transfer pricing problems.

2. Residence or source principle?

As Gordon points out, co-ordination permits countries to view their economies as closed when setting tax policy. This would enable them to continue to tax capital income, say, for distributional reasons. This policy prescription is very much at the heart of *Peggy Musgrave's* paper, which deals with company taxation with particular emphasis on the EU. When a company carries out its profit-generating activities across two or more member states, a process of fiscal co-ordination is essential to meet a satisfactory trade-off between the following principal criteria: (1) the assignment of company profits based on some concept of interjurisdictional equity, (2) tax neutrality with respect to investment among the member states, and, particularly relevant for the EU, (3) consideration for the principle of subsidiarity whereby each member state should be free, so far as possible, to design its tax system in line with its own standards of taxpayer equity and economic objectives.

Musgrave believes that there does not appear to be any objective, single answer to the question of how company profits should be divided in a multijurisdictional setting. Recourse must be made to international practice, which is based on the principle that source entitlement is applicable to the taxation of company profits, with residence taxation merely determining how the income remaining after the source tax has been paid is divided between the Treasury and the taxpayer of the resident country. Source taxation of company profits at different rates but without the protective overlay of residence taxation would be non-neutral, because residence taxation controls the degree of neutrality with respect to EU-wide capital resource allocation. Co-operation is therefore needed to achieve neutrality either through general application of the enterprise-based residence entitlement principle (with use of a full foreign tax credit) or, more likely, by adoption of equal or approximately equal effective rates of tax in all member states under the activity-based source principle.

Although Musgrave believes that there is much to be said for central-ization of the company tax, in light of developments so far company taxa-tion in the EU will most likely remain the prerogative of the individual Member States. In this setting, the issue of inter-nation equity can be resolved only by source taxation of primary profits at reciprocally equal rates under a common definition of taxable profits. Interest paid and per-haps royalties should be non-deductible. Personal income taxes could then be allowed to vary, including whatever degree of corporate–individual tax integration at the recipient-shareholder level is chosen by each Member State. Equally, a reasonable degree of tax neutrality calls for convergence of effective rates. In short, in Musgrave's view, a substantial degree of har-monization of company tax bases and rates is needed, even though this allows little autonomy in policy choice.

Richard Bird and *Scott Wilkie* challenge the usefulness of the traditional 'source vs. residence' paradigm as a framework for making neutrality and equity choices. In their view, the pragmatic issue of establishing nexus—the economic connection between an activity and a jurisdiction—is prior (as well as common) to the question of source or residence. The resolution of this issue requires intelligent mutual co-ordination and case-by-case accom-modation of competing national tax claims, basically without regard to source or residence (which anyway are not, and, even in theoretical terms, never have been, alternatives). In this context, any procedure adopted is inherently arbitrary and purpose-driven—simply a construct, with no intrinsic or other significance except to approximate some verifiable corre-spondence between economic and financial, or tax, income arising in more than one tax jurisdiction. In a real sense, the rules precede the principles.

From this perspective, 'source' and 'residence' are simply guidelines to help in assigning and assessing tax jurisdiction. The emphasis on rules rather than principles implies that a gradualist approach instead of a hol-istic approach should be adopted. Policymakers should be advised to grap-ple for incremental changes in existing fiscal institutions that may be acceptable, workable, and an improvement. In fact, the EU's approach to the problems of multinational corporations (as addressed in the Merger Directive, the Parent–Subsidiary Directive, and the Arbitration Convention) mirrors this approach very closely. In this context also, the problem is not so much one of designing an appropriate system of international tax rules but one of ensuring that the process by which such rules are established is as open and as well informed as possible. For this reason, Bird and Wilkie urge that more attention should be paid to the process by which resolutions to international tax issues are reached and less to the alleged, and often dis-putable, normative principles (such as 'source' and 'residence') to which such resolutions may nominally adhere.

3. Issues in taxing equity income and debt income

Traditionally, as Bird and Wilkie point out, all EU Member States operate hybrid source–residence systems of income taxation. Foreign direct investment income (FDI) is usually taxed on a source basis, while foreign portfolio investment income (FPI), whether dividends or interest, is generally taxed on a residence basis. The following two contributions examine the divergent treatment of these forms of income and the implications for tax harmonization.

The first contribution, by *Michael Devereux*, explores the implications for optimal tax policy of the distinction in equity income between FDI and FPI and its relevance to the appropriate specification of forms of integration of corporate and personal income taxes in the EU. Devereux notes that the natures of the two flows are inherently different. It is reasonable to suppose that the expected rate of return on portfolio investment is the normal or minimum required rate of return (asset prices will adjust until this is true), implying that the impact of the tax on investment can be analysed using the effective marginal tax rate—the difference between the normal returns pre-tax and post-tax. Distortions can then be avoided by targeting the tax base precisely towards economic rent; the tax rate would not be relevant. By contrast, direct investment will frequently expect to earn an economic rent over and above the normal return, reflecting a situation of imperfect competition. If direct investment does earn an above-normal return, the decision about the location of the investment is primarily affected by the effective average tax rate, which is the product of the tax base *and* the tax rate.

None the less, conventional theory would still suggest that the effective marginal tax rate is important in determining the size of the investment, once the location is given. In the context of co-operative tax policy, the distinction between FDI and FPI then leads to two conditions: effective marginal tax rates on direct investment should be the same for any given company, and differences in such tax rates across member states should be offset by differences in personal tax rates. A feasible way of applying these conditions would be to set all effective marginal tax rates on direct investment equal (and to give integration credits at the rate of the shareholder's country of residence) and to set effective marginal tax rates on portfolio investment on a residence basis. If effective marginal tax rates on direct investment are not equal, then integration credits must be used to offset differences in the underlying corporate tax rates, implying that they should be the same for all shareholders of a given corporation. Finally, at the level of the corporation, foreign-source income should either be exempted or taxed with a deduction for foreign tax and an integration credit in the same way as for domestic income.

The next paper, by *Harry Huizinga* and *Søren Bo Nielsen,* analyses the role and effects of a minimum withholding tax on interest in the EU. Such a withholding tax might be useful in putting a floor under the taxation of capital income and in combating tax evasion. A simple model with three countries—a typical EU country, an 'inside' tax haven, and an 'outside' tax haven—permits the authors to stress the connection between minimum withholding taxes in the EU and the competition for financial business activity between tax havens inside and outside the EU. In line with economic intuition, the simulations indicate, generally, that it is welfare-improving for the typical EU Member State to have the inside tax haven raise its tax on interest. The inside tax haven, by contrast, generally loses from the requirement to raise its tax (due to loss of banking business to the outside tax haven and to the EU partner), but then it can be compensated.

The analysis casts a mildly positive light on the proposal to introduce a minimum withholding tax in the EU. The authors believe that an interest-reporting system, already used by five EU Member States, is not a viable alternative to a common withholding tax, because it would run afoul of bank secrecy and blocking laws in many EU Member States. Of course, an EU-wide reporting system would allow Member States to continue to adhere to the residence principle in taxing interest. The authors note that a common withholding tax would not be easy to enforce, particularly if residents from third countries would be exempted (giving an impetus to 'triangular arbitrage'). Equally serious, a host of new derivative financial instruments do not lend themselves well to withholding taxes. An alternative would be to tax interest at the level of the producer instead of the saver. This could be done through the EU-wide adoption of a comprehensive business income tax (CBIT) under which interest would not be deductible in determining taxable company profits and hence taxed implicitly at the corporate income tax rate.

4. ACE, CBIT, or DIT?

As the papers by Devereux and Huizinga/Nielsen note, in all EU Member States corporate income taxes treat debt and equity differently. While interest is deductible in the computation of profits and often is not taxed subsequently, the opportunity cost of using equity finance (nearly exclusively retained profits) is taxed at company level (as are economic rents). The result is that investment financed by debt is treated more generously than investment financed by retained profits. This diverse treatment is distortionary and appears difficult to justify.

Stephen Bond observes that two principal proposals have been made over the last decade that share the aim of equalizing the treatment of

debt and equity but have suggested that this should be achieved in diametrically opposed ways. The allowance for corporate equity (ACE) proposal advocates the introduction of a new tax allowance to reflect the
opportunity cost of using equity finance, whilst the comprehensive business income tax (CBIT) proposal advocates the elimination of interest
deductibility. The ACE tax would tax only profits that constitute economic
rents and would exempt the normal return on equity. Its effect would be to
reduce the user cost of capital for investment financed by retained profits.
The CBIT, on the other hand, would approximate to a tax on accounting
profits before interest. Its effect would be to raise the cost of capital for
investment financed by debt.

However, as Bond argues persuasively, for a small economy in a world
with increasing mobility of physical capital between countries, the user cost
of capital may no longer be the only route through which corporate taxes
influence the level of domestic investment. If, as is likely, multinational companies dominate in the earning of economic rents (on account of their
market power), their discrete location decision would also be influenced
directly by the statutory or average tax rate. Under an equal-yield
assumption, this rate would have to be higher under the ACE tax, which
would distribute corporate tax payments towards relatively profitable companies. By contrast, a lower-rate CBIT would leave profitable multinational
companies with lower tax bills. In this situation, a government in an open
economy may achieve a higher level of domestic investment by lowering
the statutory rate and accepting a broader tax base, even though this
results in a higher cost of capital.

In light of these considerations, the implication for future corporate tax
reforms clearly favours changes in the direction of the CBIT proposal rather
than the ACE proposal. The increase in the statutory rate to achieve revenue
neutrality and the redistribution of corporate tax payments towards the
more profitable companies may be considered too prejudicial to inward
investment for the ACE proposal to gain acceptance in a small open economy—and, in a world context, the EU should be considered a small open
economy. Finally, the analysis suggests an unfortunate trade-off between
attracting inward investment (with a low statutory or effective average tax
rate on profitable companies) and promoting investment by smaller domestic firms (with a low cost of capital). As Bond points out, one way of alleviating this trade-off would be to target investment incentives at smaller
companies, which are more likely to be domestic and relatively immobile.

The paper by *Sijbren Cnossen* attempts to pave the way for a CBIT by
levelling the playing field for capital income taxation. Cnossen reports on
the Nordic experience with a dual income tax (DIT) which separates the
tax treatment of capital income from the treatment of labour income. Tax

arbitrage and capital mobility considerations have led the Nordic countries, most notably Finland and Norway, to conclude that all income from capital should be taxed at a single, uniform rate equal to the corporate tax rate (while labour income should continue to be subject to progressive tax rates). Under the DITs currently in force, double taxation of distributed profits is avoided through a full imputation system (alternatively but equivalently, dividend income could be exempted at shareholder level). In Norway, double taxation of retained profits is also avoided by allowing shareholders a write-up of basis with retained profits net of corporate income tax.

In the domestic context, the DITs achieve substantial uniformity of the overall effective tax rates on the return to equity, whether retained or distributed, and the return to debt. Compared with existing arrangements, the equal treatment of equity and debt reduces the cost of equity-financed investment and increases the cost of debt-financed investment. In particular, this should benefit small, newly starting firms which face difficulties in attracting debt because they do not yet enjoy a high credit rating, they own mainly non-liquid assets (such as firm-specific machinery) against which it is difficult to borrow, or they generate insufficient taxable profits to be able to deduct interest. Furthermore, the DITs treat the corporate and non-corporate form of doing business on a par. An ingenious yet simple scheme separates capital income from labour income when these two forms of income accrue jointly in proprietorships and closely held companies. Beyond that, the uniform rate, in conjunction with source withholding taxes (which can represent the final income tax liability if, as in Finland, there is no basic exemption for capital income), minimizes the potential for tax avoidance and evasion, and lowers the compliance and enforcement costs of the income tax regime.

The existing DITs, however, do not counter international tax arbitrage. So far, the Nordic countries have been reluctant to impose comprehensive withholding taxes on interest and royalty payments made abroad for fear that these taxes would deter inward investment. Also, the withholding taxes that are imposed are waived with respect to treaty countries. Existing arrangements, moreover, enable residents to behave as non-residents and shield their capital income from the DIT (subject to the limitations imposed by controlled foreign company legislation). Clearly, this hole in the DIT bucket can only be plugged by imposing non-refundable withholding taxes on interest and royalty payments on inward investment. But this conversion of the DIT into a fully source-based tax on capital income requires consultation and agreement with treaty countries, as well as approximation of capital income tax rates. Cnossen recommends that existing corporate and personal capital income taxes in the EU should be converted into DITs, but that current international tax rules should be left intact for the time being. Following this levelling of the domestic playing field for capital income taxation, EU-wide (and international) agreement could be reached on imposing minimum non-refundable withholding taxes on domestic as well as inward investment.

5. Separate accounting or unitary taxation?

Basically, the CBIT, suggested by Bond, and the DIT, proposed by Cnossen, proceed from the separate-entity or separate-accounting approach—applied according to the arm's-length principle—in determining the taxable profits of affiliated companies located in different member states. Separate accounting requires the allocation of joint income and expense items between the related parties. This process, known as transfer pricing, constitutes an incentive for income shifting from high-tax to low-tax member states. Income shifting can erode national tax bases and distort the financial and real investment decisions of multinational enterprises. Even if the normal return to capital were taxed—either implicitly under the CBIT or explicitly under the DIT (through non-refundable withholding taxes on interest payments to non-residents)—there would still be an incentive for income shifting with respect to economic rents.

The paper by *Scott Newlon* reviews the pressures and distortions created by income shifting within multinational enterprises and examines how various policies may ameliorate or exacerbate these problems. To begin, there are various practical and conceptual obstacles to applying the arm's-length principle, mainly due to lack of information. Examples are the valuation of intangibles and intermediate goods within integrated production units. In many cases, there is not even a conceptual solution. The arm's-length principle, moreover, is of limited usefulness as a guide for determining the appropriate financial structure, and therefore interest expense, for affiliates within a multinational enterprise. A number of studies reviewed by Newlon provide evidence consistent with income shifting by multinational enterprises, although the absolute magnitude of the estimates does not indicate substantial tax-base erosion. Interestingly, the pressures to shift income depend not only on differences in statutory rates, but also on how the home country taxes the foreign income of resident companies—namely, world-wide taxation with a foreign tax credit or exemption of foreign-source income. Newlon concludes that exemption systems, found in most EU Member States, provide benefits from income shifting to low-tax affiliates in a broader class of cases than do credit and deferral systems.

Subsequently, Newlon surveys the various policies that could be used to reduce the incentive for income shifting. These policies include better enforcement (higher penalties, more information reporting and exchange between countries, and co-ordination of the application of transfer pricing rules), the current taxation of the income earned by foreign affiliates of domestic companies, the approximation of company tax rates, thin-capitalization measures, and formula apportionment (see below). Newlon notes that all of these policies for reducing income shifting would raise problems of their own. In his view, the need for more radical policies—formula apportionment, tax rate approximation, the replacement of income taxes with destination-based consumption taxes—remains to be proven. Instead, the emphasis should be on greater co-ordination and co-operation between countries, preferably through binding multilateral agreements. The EU offers a suitable opportunity for such an agreement, since the mechanisms for policy co-ordination exist and, given the economic integration of the Member States, the gains from co-ordination are likely to be substantial.

The final paper, by *Charles McLure* and *Joann Weiner*, examines one of the more radical policies for dealing with income shifting—namely, the abandonment of separate accounting in favour of formula apportionment (used by the US states and Canadian provinces for companies operating in more than one state or province). Formula apportionment would attribute a fraction of the total income of a multinational company to each member state in which the company carries out its business. This fraction is equal to the weighted average of the member state's share in various economic activities of the company, represented by such factors as its payroll, property, and sales (apportionment factors). Obviously, the incentive for income shifting would not be eliminated unless the members of an affiliated group of companies that are found to be part of a unitary group are combined and effectively treated as a single entity for tax purposes (unitary combination). Formula apportionment in conjunction with unitary combination is referred to as unitary taxation.

From the outset, McLure and Weiner make clear that formula apportionment is conceptually inferior to separate accounting *if* separate accounting can be applied. In contrast with reality, formula apportionment assumes, for instance, that profitability is uniform across related companies operating in different member states. Furthermore, the application of uniform formulas to all industries, although very different in terms of production technology and financial structure, could create inequities and distortions. Beyond that, the adoption of unitary taxation may complicate relations with non-EU countries. In addition, the introduction of formula apportionment would give rise to serious policy-sequencing and transition problems for EU Member States. Accounting conventions and institutional structures would have to be harmonized. All of these problems would be exacerbated by complex technical questions, such as defining a unitary business, choosing the apportionment formula, and measuring the factors in the formula.

The authors evaluate formula apportionment in light of the political constraints the EU faces in undertaking company tax reform at the EU level—namely, subsidiarity and fiscal autonomy. They observe that, so far, EU efforts at harmonizing company tax systems have been unsuccessful. While some minor aspects of company taxation have converged, substantial variation is likely to be a permanent feature of company taxation in the EU. Therefore formula apportionment must consider the demonstrated reluctance of Member States to cede corporate tax issues to the EU level. Not surprisingly, McLure and Weiner stop short of giving a definitive answer to the question of whether it makes policy sense to adopt formula apportionment. Instead, they conclude with what the EU should not do if it decides to adopt formula apportionment. First, if wide variations in tax rates continue to exist, formula apportionment should not be introduced without unitary combination. Second, formula apportionment should be limited to the water's edge of the EU and not be applied on a world-wide basis. Third, there should be substantial conformity in definitions of tax bases, apportionment formulas, measures of apportionment factors, and definitions of a unitary business. Finally, the only way to make a move to unitary taxation, if one is to be made, is multilaterally, by all members of the EU.

6. Discussion

Most papers in this volume envisage a continued role for capital income taxes in a co-operative EU setting. Gordon's paper is the exception. He concludes that theory forecasts little or no tax on capital income in an open economy and that it would be more efficient therefore to tax labour directly rather than indirectly through a capital tax. Most papers also share common ground with regard to their recipe for tax policy. First, primarily for administrative reasons, source taxation of debt as well as equity income should be accorded a greater role. However, neutrality considerations would then require closer approximation of tax rates which would conflict with subsidiarity. Second, the papers indicate a preference for treating interest (and royalty) payments in the same way as dividend payments. In other words, the payments should not be deductible at company level as prescribed under the comprehensive business income tax (CBIT) or, equivalently, subject to a non-refundable withholding tax under the dual income tax (DIT). Third, for the time being, the separate-accounting approach should probably remain in place; unitary taxation seems a bridge too far.

These recommendations also echoed through the final round-table discussion of the conference. Commenting on whether or not capital income should be taxed, *Richard Musgrave* expressed a strong preference for the comprehensive accretion type of income tax with capital income included in the tax base. He also believed that taxes should be personal and visible, both as a matter of equity and as a matter of fiscal discipline. Personal taxation is needed in the Wicksellian spirit to establish a link between taxes and citizens' control over expenditures. He emphasized that it was highly important not to separate the problem of what the tax base should be from the question of how that tax base would be used—for an impersonal or a personal tax. The choice of the tax base and the use to which it would be put, in combination, had important implications for equity, efficiency, and implementation.

Leaving aside the implications of optimal taxation (which focuses on dead-weight losses), the choice of the tax base could be made in favour of income, consumption, or wages—broadly defined for reasons of horizontal equity. Normatively speaking, the choice was not obvious. In Musgrave's view, the consideration that an income tax discriminates against future consumption was relevant but not decisive, because account should be taken of the triangular substitutability between surrendering leisure, present consumption, and future consumption. Much depended on the elasticity of substitution between these three possibilities. Furthermore, consumption is not the only purpose of saving: holding wealth is also pleasant. Beyond that, not all saving leads to consumption, because bequests are left. So the minimization of the dead-weight loss of a consumption tax required a supplementary wealth tax, as well as the inclusion of bequests in the donor's tax base. Musgrave much preferred this approach to a consumption tax to the approach that, in effect, taxes wages by exempting capital income. In his view, someone who has to surrender leisure to obtain consumption should not be penalized as compared with someone who can use capital income for consumption purposes.

Summing up his position, Musgrave would give an A to a comprehensive personal income tax (with full integration of the corporate income tax) and a personal Kaldor-type consumption tax, a B to the DIT and the CBIT, a C to the VAT, a D to the cash-flow tax (which is misleadingly represented as a business tax and which unjustifiably includes entrepreneurial income in the base), and an E to the no-tax case. In doing so, he noted that tax policy prescriptions, including his own, often tended to be based on what a 'good' tax should look like in a first-best closed-economy setting. But in the real world, trade-offs must be made between equity, efficiency, and feasibility, and allowance must be made for the effects of openness.

Next, *Gerold Krause-Junk* proposed two working rules in trying to answer the question of who should tax capital income. His first rule would be that whoever taxes capital income should tax all forms of capital income—profits as well as interest and royalties (possibly by making payments non-deductible). If this were done, equal treatment and tax neutrality would gain compared with the present confused mix of source–residence rules.

His second rule would be that whoever it is agreed should tax capital income should be entitled to do so to the exclusion of all others. There should be no residual entitlement of others to tax capital income. If these two rules could be agreed to, he believed that the source principle emerged as the preferred tax-base allocation rule. Effective and neutral taxation then required agreement among the large producing regions of the world—North America, Europe, the Far East—to impose minimum taxes, collected at source, on all forms of capital income. Double taxation could be avoided simply by exempting capital income that had already been taxed elsewhere. In Krause-Junk's view, it is easier to establish and implement sourcing rules than to trace capital income under the residence principle. If source taxes are in place, most tax havens would vanish. To induce countries to join the agreement, the capital income of residents of countries signatory to the agreement arising in countries not signatory to the agreement should be taxed.

Lans Bovenberg then dwelt on the rate at which capital income should be taxed. He believed that the world would be moving in the direction of flat taxes on capital income, because flat taxes can be levied at source and limit opportunities for tax arbitrage. He noted that this would be less of a change in comparison with prevailing practice than some people might think, because the progressivity of the current capital income taxes is more apparent than real. Under flat taxes, progressivity at the bottom end of the income distribution would still be possible through tax allowances and tax credits. Income distribution issues, moreover, could largely be taken care of through the expenditure side of the budget. If desired, some progressivity at the upper end of the income distribution could be achieved through progressive labour income taxes and net wealth taxes.

Bovenberg pointed out that there was a conflict between domestic and international considerations. On the domestic scene, much could be said for taxing all capital income at a single flat rate, but inward investment might be deterred if the same rate were imposed on internationally mobile capital. This conflict could only be resolved through multilateral co-ordination. In this connection, he thought that the major industrial countries would probably be able to reach agreement on abolishing interest deductibility as proposed under the CBIT, but that they might have to replace deductibility by immediate expensing. A CBIT would promote equal treatment and limit opportunities for tax arbitrage by applying the same flat (top) rate of tax to labour and capital income. But this rate might be too low to meet revenue requirements if international agreement on minimum tax rates on capital income were not forthcoming. Also, countries might be reluctant to lower progressivity at the upper end of the income distribution. Thus it was not surprising that countries with high revenue needs, keen on progressivity, but aware of the danger of taxing capital income at high rates, had opted for the DIT. On balance, he favoured the Norwegian DIT which taxes capital income at a flat rate of 28 per cent.

Finally, *Charles McLure* tried to formulate an answer to the question of to what extent capital income taxes should be co-ordinated. In his view, the case against co-ordination rested on the benefits of decentralized decision-making and in protecting people from Leviathan. None the less, tax competition imposed costs: revenue is eroded through market forces rather than by explicit decision. On balance, therefore, he favoured more co-ordination. In the EU, the alternatives to tax harmonization, in the sense of uniformity, would be improved exchange of information between the Member States to shore up residence-based income taxes, and an EU-wide system of (minimum) withholding taxes creditable against the income taxes levied by the residence states. Even if these measures were in place, the level of capital income tax rates in the EU would still be limited by the rates levied by third countries. The unanimity requirement in the EU, which creates free-riding problems, was also an obstacle to greater co-ordination. Furthermore, consideration should be given to the role of the European Court of Justice, which might impose greater uniformity through the judicial system.

In McLure's view, in the end, much could be said in favour of a corporate income tax levied at the EU level. This tax could either replace the current corporate income taxes (with the revenue returned to the Member States) or act as an umbrella to the 15 separate corporate income taxes levied by the Member States. The latter combination, found in the US, would also smooth out tax differences between the Member States. More generally, in his view, the time seemed to be ripe to negotiate a GATT for income taxes. The problem is that the bench-mark under the current GATT for product taxes is a zero tax. Obviously, this would not be possible for an agreement on capital income taxes. Furthermore, the real GATT stipulates that countries have to refrain from taking specified measures, whilst the GATT for income taxes would prescribe positive action, such as disallowing interest deductibility. This would be much more difficult to define and monitor. None the less, the point was that greater co-ordination within the EU could not be separated from greater co-ordination between the EU and third countries, such as the US and Japan.

2
Taxation of capital income vs. labour income: an overview

ROGER H. GORDON

The existing personal and corporate income tax structures in most European Union (EU) and other OECD countries are still heavily influenced by the idea of a comprehensive income tax, as first proposed by Schanz (1986) over a hundred years ago and later by Haig (1921) and Simons (1938). Under their proposals, each individual should be taxed annually on the sum of all their real incomes from labour and capital, regardless of source. More recent support for this basic structure for the income tax includes the Royal (Carter) Commission on Taxation (1966) in Canada, the Campbell Committee (1981) in Australia, and the US Department of the Treasury (1984), many of whose proposed reforms were in fact enacted in 1986.[1]

In theory, under a comprehensive income tax, there would be no need for a separate tax on corporate income. The perceived role of the corporate tax in this system is to offset administrative problems faced in taxing accruing capital gains. The practice has been to impose a direct tax on corporate retained earnings[2] to supplement whatever personal tax is imposed on capital gains at the personal level so that the two together tax accruing capital gains on corporate equity at roughly the same rate as applies to other forms of capital income.[3]

The author would like to thank the participants at the ISPE conference, and especially Lans Bovenberg, Jack Mintz, and Søren Nielsen for comments on an earlier draft, and to acknowledge National Science Foundation Grant no. SBR-9422589 for financial support during the writing of this chapter.

[1] The Meade Committee (Institute for Fiscal Studies, 1978) in the UK, in contrast, favoured a move towards some form of an expenditure tax.

[2] Since corporate income paid out as dividends is taxed as ordinary income at accrual, there is no need to impose any surtax on dividends. Most countries in fact have provisions that in effect rebate corporate taxes on income paid out as dividends.

[3] If the combined tax rate differs from this level, then individuals face an incentive to shift income between the personal and the corporate tax bases to reduce their overall tax liabilities, creating a variety of economic distortions—for example, to a

While many elements of existing tax structures continue to resemble those under a comprehensive income tax, an increasing number of deviations have been introduced over time. Pension plans and other savings plans subject to cash-flow tax treatment are becoming an increasingly important part of total individual savings, but the return earned on capital held in these plans faces a zero or even negative effective tax rate in present value.[4] The real returns to owner-occupied housing (in many countries), consumer durables, life insurance, and some specifically tax-exempt assets (for example, municipal bonds in the US) are subject to much lower effective tax rates than are other sources of income. These, together with pensions, comprise most of household savings. In addition, the value added tax and the payroll tax are now major sources of revenue in most developed countries. The payroll tax is a tax on most forms of labour compensation, while the value added tax collects no taxes in present value on marginal investments but does tax labour income (plus rents). On net, therefore, the effective tax rate on an individual's return to capital is likely to be far below that on the return to labour, in sharp contrast to the normative views under a comprehensive income tax.

The academic literature dealing with the taxation of labour income vs. capital income has evolved over time even more dramatically than actual tax policy, as described in Section 1. Substantial questions have been raised about the equity of taxing capital income, even assuming that the incidence of the tax falls on capital owners. This is particularly the case, given that the forecasted incidence of taxes on capital falls mostly on labour. In addition, there has been substantial research documenting a wide variety of distortions to economic behaviour generated by current taxes on capital income. These distortions imply that capital taxes cause much larger efficiency losses than taxes on labour income. The loss in revenue from these behavioural responses is large enough that some papers even question whether the existing taxes on capital income succeed in raising any revenue. The academic literature suggests that tax rates on capital income at best should be much lower than tax rates on labour income, if capital income should be taxed at all.

firm's choice of organizational form, to corporate financial policy, and to forms of employee compensation. See, for example, Gordon and MacKie-Mason (1994), Auerbach (1985), or Gordon and MacKie-Mason (1995) for recent work on these distortions.

[4] The effective tax rate is zero if contributions to the plans are fully deductible and receipts are fully taxable, subject to the same tax rate. If the tax rate on receipts is lower than that on contributions, as is likely in practice, then the effective tax rate in present value is negative.

The question then is not why effective tax rates on capital have declined over time, but why tax rates on capital income have remained as high as they have,[5] and why the basic tax structure continues to contain important elements of a comprehensive income tax. Is the explanation simply that practice evolves slowly and will eventually match the theoretical forecasts, or has the theory failed to account for important practical considerations that drive current policies? Section 2 explores several potential explanations for why taxes on capital income remain in use and examines their consistency with the evidence. The leading hypotheses are: implicit co-ordination of tax policy across countries through use of crediting arrangements, market power in capital markets, and immobility of capital across countries. These hypotheses forecast taxes on the capital income received by non-residents, as a form of tariff. Such taxes are in fact observed, as are some negotiated attempts to reduce these tariffs through bilateral tax treaties. The hypotheses cannot so easily explain any continuing taxation of the capital income accruing to residents, however. Given that existing taxes on the capital income of residents appear to collect little or no revenue, there may not be much that needs explaining.

Section 3 then explores briefly the range of options countries have if they continue to shift the tax burden from capital income to labour income, as forecast. Among the principal means for taxing labour income—payroll taxes, cash-flow income taxes, and value added taxes—the existing literature suggests that value added taxes have proven to be more robust to the pressures faced in an open economy.

1. Changing views on the taxation of labour income vs. capital income

A comprehensive income tax calls for *equal* tax rates on labour income and capital income on equity grounds. Even if we accept the equity arguments for equal tax rates, recent papers have raised serious concerns about the efficiency costs of equal tax rates. In particular, Chamley (1985) and Judd (1985) both note that the tax-induced change in the capital stock in response to an increase in the tax rate on capital income depends critically on how far ahead this tax increase is anticipated. If a tax increase is totally unexpected, then individuals have no opportunity to alter the size of the existing capital stock and the tax becomes a lump-sum tax, generating no efficiency cost at all. But if a tax increase is expected, individuals have an incentive to consume

[5] The lack of correction for inflation when calculating interest income, capital gains income, and depreciation deductions can even imply tax rates on some forms of capital income that exceed those on labour income.

some of their existing assets in order to avoid the higher future tax rate. Chamley and Judd show that the resulting drop in the capital stock, and the resulting efficiency cost of a tax on capital income, grow dramatically the longer ahead of time individuals anticipate a tax increase.[6] The resulting drop in the capital stock shifts the burden of the tax on to labour income, reducing the appeal of capital taxes on both equity and efficiency grounds.[7] In particular, if the shifting of the burden on to labour is complete, then labour bears the entire burden of both capital income taxes and labour income taxes, so both distort labour supply decisions. Capital income taxes, however, also distort savings decisions, so are dominated by labour income taxes.

Within the Chamley (1985) and Judd (1985) models, unanticipated taxes on capital income would still be appealing. One problem with such unanticipated taxes is that they are time inconsistent—the government would gain if it could make a commitment not to impose such taxes in the future. In addition, when effective tax rates vary both by asset and by investor,[8] as is inevitable, a capital income tax (even if unanticipated) can generate sufficient arbitrage between investors in different tax brackets that it collects little or no revenue at substantial efficiency costs.[9] In fact, Boadway and Keen (1998) argue that these arbitrage opportunities are intentionally built into the tax law as a form of precommitment not to impose windfall taxes on existing capital owners.[10] Therefore, unless these arbitrage possibilities can be eliminated, governments may not have much incentive to impose even unanticipated taxes on capital income.[11]

---

[6] Their argument also implies that taxes on capital income are time inconsistent. A government *ex post* has the incentive to use 'unexpected' taxes on capital even if it would choose not to do so *ex ante*, taking into account the effects on savings behaviour.

[7] When capital taxes are fully anticipated in their model, the burden falls entirely on labour income.

[8] Typically, the nominal return to bonds is taxable and a rough approximation to the real return on equity is taxable, while the returns to owner-occupied housing and pension holdings are normally tax exempt.

[9] See Stiglitz (1985) for a theoretical discussion of the many arbitrage possibilities inherent in current tax law. Gordon and Slemrod (1988) find that the US income tax has been losing revenue on net from its attempts to tax capital income, due to such arbitrage.

[10] This assumes that the provisions opening up arbitrage possibilities are harder to change than capital income tax rates.

[11] Arbitrage requires unequal tax rates both across assets *and* across investors. If all investors faced the same set of tax rates, as, for example, occurs domestically under a dual income tax, then domestic arbitrage should be eliminated. This ignores, however, the remaining variation in tax rates *across* countries.

The equity grounds for equal tax rates on labour income and capital income have also been much debated. To begin with, Kaldor (1955) among others[12] questioned whether equity considerations justify taxing individuals based on their capital income as well as their labour income. Ignoring bequests, how much capital income individuals receive depends on whether they prefer to spend their earnings early or late in life. If two individuals have the same earnings stream from labour, why should the one who chooses to be frugal when young deserve a heavier tax burden than the one who consumes relatively more early in life, given that both had the same choices available to them? On equity grounds, the tax rate on capital income should be zero.

This argument ignored bequests. If one of these individuals receives a bequest, he is made better off. On horizontal equity grounds, he should therefore pay a larger share of the tax burden than someone without such a bequest who is otherwise identical.[13] However, otherwise equivalent potential donors then face different tax rates depending on whether they consume their wealth themselves or instead donate it to others, a differential treatment among donors that can be viewed to be horizontally inequitable. Another complication is that bequests generate externalities, so should be subsidized on efficiency grounds.[14] Even the sign of the optimal tax rate on bequests is therefore unclear.

A variety of other approaches might be taken to justify non-zero taxes on capital income. Corlett and Hague (1954), for example, argue on efficiency grounds that goods that are complementary to leisure should be taxed more heavily.[15] This would justify a positive tax rate on capital income if those who work less tend to consume relatively more later in life, so accumulate more assets and therefore earn more capital income. Empirically, however, hours of work and retirement ages tend to be higher for the more

[12] For a related view, see Musgrave (1976) and Gordon (1984).

[13] When bequests occur in an illiquid form such as a business, it may make sense to defer the tax payment. For example, the tax could be imposed only when funds (both principal and interest) are withdrawn from the bequest. But there is no reason to increase the present value of the tax to the extent that consumption of the bequest is postponed in time.

[14] In particular, the donor is indifferent at the margin to an additional donation, but the recipient clearly benefits from more donations. See Stiglitz and Bevan (1979) for further discussion.

[15] The same argument can be made on equity grounds. A case can be made that a person's potential consumption, holding wealth fixed, should include purchases of leisure as well as purchases of goods and services. Observed income therefore understates potential consumption, and more so for those who take more leisure.

able, suggesting a subsidy rather than a tax on capital income based on Corlett–Hague considerations.

Another argument, made, for example, by Arrow and Lind (1970), is that taxes on risky income result in lower net costs of risk bearing, so are desirable on efficiency grounds. Their intuition is that individuals cannot easily diversify the risks they face,[16] particularly on the income from their own businesses, yet these risks are largely idiosyncratic from a national perspective. Governments can therefore absorb these risks at little cost. This argument may justify higher marginal tax rates on the cash flow from riskier activities,[17] but does not justify depreciation rather than expensing of new investments.

There may also perhaps be some market failures that can be alleviated through some forms of taxes on capital income. If firms cannot easily borrow from outside investors due to asymmetric information problems,[18] then a subsidy to use of debt has the potential to generate efficiency gains on net. A general tax on capital income would be justified, if there is too much savings or investment on efficiency grounds due to some form of market failure. If anything, however, there is likely to be too little savings and investment on efficiency grounds (taxes aside) due to 'lemons' problems arising from asymmetric information between savers and investors, justifying a subsidy rather than a tax on capital income.

A quite separate challenge to the use of non-zero taxes on capital income arose in recent years due to the implications of economies being open. In a closed economy, the primary effect of a tax on capital income is to reduce the return to savings for domestic residents. This is true whether domestic savings are taxed under the personal income tax or domestic investment is taxed under the corporate income tax, since domestic savings and domestic investment are equal in a closed economy. In an open economy, however, investors can easily invest in financial securities issued throughout the world, and will invest in domestic securities only if the net-of-tax return is as attractive as that available elsewhere. In this setting, a tax on domestic savings and a tax on domestic investment have totally different effects. If the country is small relative to world capital markets, then a tax on domestic investment should have no effect on the net-of-tax return to savings received by investors, since opportunities abroad remain unaffected by the tax. If firms are to continue to attract investors, then they must

[16] As noted in Diamond (1967), if securities markets are working well, then risk is allocated efficiently without government intervention, eliminating the need for such taxes.

[17] See Varian (1980) for further discussion.

[18] See Myers and Majluf (1984) for further discussion.

raise the before-tax return they pay investors by enough that investors continue to receive the same net-of-tax return as elsewhere. Since firms cannot raise their output prices, given the competition from abroad, they can raise their before-tax return only by paying lower wage rates. As a result, in a small open economy, a tax on the return to domestic investment ends up reducing the return to labour, while leaving unaffected the net-of-tax return to capital.

Even though a tax on the return to domestic investment ends up being paid by labour through lower wage rates, it is not equivalent to a direct tax on labour income since it introduces a variety of extra distortions that are not created by direct taxes on labour income. The amount of taxes a company owes depends on its capital income, whereas the amount of compensating savings it receives through paying lower wages depends on its labour costs. As a result, labour-intensive firms need a smaller drop in their wage rate to compensate for any given tax rate on the return to domestic capital. A tax on domestic capital therefore induces the country to specialize in more labour-intensive commodities, thus distorting trade patterns. Multinationals based in the country are at a particular disadvantage in world markets. Parent firms based in the country in principle owe domestic taxes on their world-wide capital income. As a result, they will have particularly high capital income relative to their *domestic* labour costs. Since a capital income tax and a labour income tax both reduce the net wage of domestic workers, yet the capital tax introduces all of these other distortions as well, small open economies should not tax or subsidize the return to capital accruing to domestic firms. This result follows quickly from the work of Diamond and Mirrlees (1971), as shown, for example, by Dixit (1985).

On equity grounds, countries may still want to tax the return to the savings undertaken by domestic residents. The existing theory—for example, Diamond and Mirrlees (1971)—suggests that such taxes can, in principle, be part of an optimal tax system even in an open economy. The problem is that a tax on savings is very difficult to implement.

Consider first the feasibility of taxing dividend and interest income. The primary mechanism for enforcing domestic taxes is to obtain information directly from domestic firms and domestic financial intermediaries regarding the amounts paid out to each domestic resident. But governments cannot obtain equivalent information from foreign firms and foreign financial intermediaries on the amounts they paid to each domestic resident. As a result, individuals can evade domestic taxes on any investments they make through foreign financial intermediaries. They can even avoid tax on income from domestic securities if they purchase them through foreign financial intermediaries, since the information the tax authorities can acquire simply indicates that the security is held in the name of this foreign intermediary.

Countries do attempt to learn more through signing bilateral tax treaties with other countries, which promise some exchange of information about the taxable income accruing to each other's residents. In theory, however, such information-sharing agreements can be effective at eliminating avoidance only if the agreements are universal. Even if one country (say Switzerland) were omitted from the agreements, investors world-wide can acquire anonymity by funnelling their investments through Switzerland.

As a result, if there are no added costs in making use of foreign financial intermediaries, individuals can entirely avoid paying any domestic taxes on their dividend and interest income.[19] Shifting savings abroad certainly does involve some added costs, particularly learning costs, so not all taxes on dividends and interest will be avoided. Small savers, and those whose savings are largely for transactions purposes, are much less likely to find the costs of capital flight low enough to make tax avoidance attractive. As a result, only those with substantial assets may in fact choose to avoid domestic taxes on dividends and interest. While some revenue may still be collected from small savers and from transactions balances, these considerations make the tax much less attractive on equity grounds.

What about taxes on accruing capital gains on foreign securities owned by domestic residents? In a closed economy, capital gains are taxed in part at realization under the personal tax, but mainly they are taxed indirectly through a corporate tax on retained earnings. In an open economy, countries would need to tax the retained earnings accruing to residents on both foreign and domestic shares that they own, in order to tax the full return to savings. Under international tax conventions, however, they do not even have the nexus required to tax the retained earnings of foreign firms accruing to domestic residents as a result of their portfolio investments.

International tax conventions do allow countries to tax the retained earnings accruing abroad to domestic firms,[20] and countries commonly tax on accrual the retained earnings of foreign branches of domestic firms. The retained earnings of foreign subsidiaries of domestic firms, however, have in practice been subject to domestic taxes only when funds are repatriated, if then.[21,22] Partly this may reflect the administrative costs of monitoring foreign-source earnings year by year. Partly it may reflect the

---

[19] Razin and Sadka (1991) then conclude that there are no feasible taxes on the return to savings.

[20] Countries are required, however, to use some acceptable means to avoid having profits subject to double taxation in both the host and the home country.

[21] The US, the UK, and Japan are examples of countries that tax at repatriation these foreign-source retained earnings of domestic firms. The Netherlands and

ease with which domestic investors can avoid any domestic corporate sur-tax on retained earnings abroad by acquiring foreign capital through port-folio investment rather than through investments abroad by domestic multinationals.[23] According to the evidence in Hines and Hubbard (1990), the income earned abroad by US multinationals largely seems to avoid domestic corporate taxes, even though the US has expended much more effort than other countries to enforce its tax on foreign-source income. In fact, existing dividend imputation schemes can result in a net domestic subsidy to the foreign-source earnings of domestic firms, since the rebate of corporate taxes on dividends paid to domestic investors can occur in practice for dividends financed by foreign-source as well as domestic-source income, even though domestic taxes have been paid (in full) only on the domestic-source income.[24]

Under a tax on the return to savings of domestic residents, income accru-ing to foreign residents would not be subject to tax, implying not only that dividends and interest paid to foreign residents should be free from domes-tic taxes but also that taxes collected on the retained earnings of domestic firms should be proportional to the fraction of the shares owned by domes-tic residents. It is common, however, for countries to impose a withholding tax on at least dividend if not interest payments to foreign residents, at rates that approximate or even exceed rates that apply to domestic residents. Also, no country has exempted firms from corporate taxes in proportion to their foreign ownership. In fact, when dividend imputation schemes provide rebates only to domestic shareholders, the corporate tax on income paid out as dividends applies exclusively to foreign shareholders.[25] The tax treatment

France are among the countries that exempt these earnings from domestic tax. New Zealand is the only country that taxes these earnings at accrual.

[22] Since multinationals have the choice whether to treat foreign operations as a branch or a subsidiary, they have an incentive to organize operations as branches only if they normally generate tax losses.

[23] Only to the extent to which portfolio and foreign direct investment abroad are imperfect substitutes can any domestic taxes be collected on foreign retained earnings. See Gordon and Jun (1993) for further discussion.

[24] Eligible dividends are in practice limited to domestic earnings. Since dividend pay-out rates are normally of the order of only 50 per cent, however, this means that this constraint would not be binding in a given year unless the multinational is earning more than about half of its income abroad. (The domestic book capital of the firm is reduced as a result, however, with potential tax consequences in the future.) See Boadway and Bruce (1992) for further discussion.

[25] Domestic tax-exempt organizations may also not be allowed a rebate. Two exceptions are the UK and Ireland.

of foreign investors in domestic firms is therefore another important difference between existing income taxes and a comprehensive income tax.

Thus, although a comprehensive income tax would tax the return to savings by domestic residents, existing taxes on capital income are in large part taxes on the return to domestic investments. Foreign-source earnings can easily avoid domestic taxes, while domestic earnings are largely subject to tax regardless of the nationality of the owner. Yet the theoretical literature argues that the incidence of a tax on the return to domestic investment should be mainly on labour income and, as a result, that such a tax would be dominated by direct taxes on labour income.

The efficiency costs of existing taxes are likely to be even higher than those from a tax on domestic investment, since arbitrage and transfer pricing reduce tax payments yet further.[26] Under existing tax provisions, multinationals can easily shift their domestic accounting profits into a subsidiary located in a country with a low corporate tax rate. This can be done through the choice of location in which the multinational borrows, through the location of its patents, and also through the choice of transfer prices.[27] On net, Hines and Rice (1990) estimate that a third of the earnings of US multinationals abroad accrued in tax havens even though only 4.3 per cent of their employees are located there. Therefore existing tax provisions not only collect little, if any, revenue from foreign investments, but they also enable firms to avoid considerable domestic taxes on their income from domestic investments.

Of course, many of these theoretical arguments about the incidence and efficiency costs of existing taxes lack empirical confirmation. They depend on plausible assumptions, but ones that can easily be debated. There is only limited empirical evidence, for example, that taxes on domestic investments leave net-of-tax rates of return to capital unaffected, instead causing a fall in domestic wage rates. Some evidence is provided by Huizinga (1996) and Huizinga and Demirguc-Kunt (1995), who find that developing countries that impose withholding taxes on foreign investors end up paying roughly an unchanged net-of-tax rate of return to these investors. Even if before-tax

---

[26] The efficiency cost of a tax can be approximated by half of the revenue loss resulting from behavioural changes in response to the tax. Under a tax on all income from domestic investment, the revenue and efficiency loss comes primarily from the fall in real investment, whereas, under existing taxes, revenue falls much further due to financial responses linked to tax arbitrage and the shifting of income abroad. That the revenue fall comes from financial vs. real adjustments does not matter for efficiency calculations, unless there are some market failures.

[27] For further discussion of such income shifting, see, for example, Altshuler and Mintz (1995), Hines and Rice (1990), or Grubert and Slemrod (1998).

Table 2.1 Changes in personal and corporate tax liabilities per return from shifting to a cash-flow tax base (1983 dollars)

Labour income group	Change in personal tax liabilities	Change in corporate tax liabilities	Change in total tax liabilities
<$20,000	−143	49	−94
$20,000–$40,000	258	49	307
$40,000–$70,000	956	135	1091
$70,000–$100,000	1424	479	1903
>$100,000	−1775	1916	141
Age>65	−1965	646	−1319
Dependants	−360	110	−250
Total	−159	143	−16

Note: The shift to a cash-flow tax eliminates interest, dividend, and capital gains, and allows expensing rather than depreciation of capital for both corporate and non-corporate businesses. The investment tax credit is also eliminated.

Source: Gordon and Slemrod, 1988, table 6.

rates of return do not rise nor domestic wage rates fall in response to taxes on the return to domestic capital, however, the incidence of existing taxes on capital income is still rather unappealing on equity grounds. For example, Gordon and Slemrod (1988) compare the tax payments that would be made by investors with different reported amounts of labour income in the US in 1983 under the existing tax treatment of the return to capital in that year with tax payments under a system that exempts all financial income from capital and allows immediate expensing rather than depreciation for new investments. The changes in taxes that would result if the existing treatment of capital income were replaced by such a cash-flow tax are reported in Table 2.1.[28] If market wage rates and interest rates do not change in response, these figures approximate the welfare effects of the tax change on each group.[29] According to the numbers in the table, aggregate tax payments are

[28] Here, the reported income categories do not include those over age 65, given that their reported labour income does not well approximate their lifetime earnings. The average figure for the elderly is reported separately. The figures do include changes in corporate rates of return that result from changes in corporate tax liabilities.

[29] While individual behaviour will certainly change in response, individuals would have been indifferent at the margin to changes in behaviour, implying that these changes have no first-order effect on their welfare.

left almost entirely unchanged when the existing tax on the return to capital is replaced by a cash-flow tax, ignoring any resulting changes in behaviour, but the tax burden shifts heavily from the retired to individuals in middle income brackets, with the richest and the poorest groups both left largely unaffected. These figures ignore, however, not only the efficiency gains that would arise from such a shift, but also the distributional effects of any resulting increase in real wage rates and fall in the pre-tax rate of return to capital. Taking into account plausible sizes of these factor price changes, the distributional effects of the shift to a cash-flow tax should be quite progressive. Given the efficiency gains and the rise in wage rates, tax revenue should also rise on net as a result of the shift to a cash-flow tax.

2. Why then do taxes on capital income still exist?

The results from the academic literature therefore suggest that existing taxes on capital income lose revenue yet generate large efficiency costs and have distributional effects of dubious appeal. The formal models for a small open economy forecast that the optimal tax rate on capital income is simply zero. Yet existing income taxes in OECD countries continue to incorporate many elements of a comprehensive income tax. Is the explanation simply that actual practice adjusts slowly to the added pressures created as economies become more open? Or is the explanation instead that the theories omit important considerations that explain the use of capital income taxes? In this section, we explore several such explanations, to see to what degree each is consistent with the evidence.

2.1   Implicit co-ordination across countries

The strongest conclusions above regarding the lack of appeal of taxes on capital income were derived from models of optimal policy in a small open economy, where the government takes as given the required after-tax rate of return to investors and where governments cannot effectively monitor the income that domestic investors earn abroad. In contrast, models of optimal policy in a closed economy can potentially yield non-zero taxes on capital income.

One reason why governments might view economies as closed when setting tax policy is co-ordination among governments in policy setting. The world as a whole is a closed economy, so if countries can co-ordinate their policies with respect to taxes on capital income, then they would jointly be setting policy in a closed world economy.

Casual observation does suggest the possibility of such co-ordination. For example, in the mid-1980s, many of the major OECD countries more or less simultaneously cut their statutory corporate tax rates and broadened their tax bases. If co-ordination has been occurring, however, it is certainly not explicit. While there are explicit international agreements with respect to tariff rates, none exist concerning tax policy.[30] Even within the EU, the co-ordination to date has mainly been limited to the imposition of minimum value added tax and excise tax rates. There are a number of bilateral tax treaties, dealing with withholding tax rates and information sharing. However, if any two countries together remain small with respect to the world capital market, the theory forecasts that a bilateral tax treaty will result in no change in tax policies. In any case, these treaties have attempted to reduce withholding tax rates, whereas the forecasted effect of co-ordination should be to raise rather than reduce tax rates relative to those chosen without co-ordination.

Co-ordination does not require explicit treaties, however. Implicit agreements can instead be enforced through the threat of some form of punishment in case of defection. There have been many cases of countries publicly announcing such punishments in response to perceived defections from agreements on tariff or non-tariff barriers to trade. However, I know of no instance of any such threat in response to changes in tax policy.

One limited form of international co-ordination has occurred through the requirements for membership in the OECD. OECD members must agree to adopt an acceptable mechanism to avoid double taxation of the profits of multinationals. Among the acceptable methods is either exempting foreign-source profits of domestic firms from corporate tax or else granting a credit against domestic tax liabilities for any taxes already paid in the host country.

Under the first rule, countries can impose taxes only on the corporate profits earned on capital physically located in their country. The theory continues to forecast that such taxes will be unattractive in a small open economy.

Gordon (1992) argues, however, that the second rule can in theory result in enough co-ordination to yield non-zero capital income tax rates in equilibrium.[31] In particular, given the use of the second rule, each capital-importing country can tax the foreign subsidiaries that choose to invest in

---

[30] Given the many complex aspects of the tax code that are important in determining the effective tax rate on capital income, such agreements would not even seem feasible if individual governments are to be left any flexibility in setting tax structures.

[31] As noted below, this conclusion requires several strong assumptions, among them: (1) profits are taxed in the home country on accrual; (2) the credit is calculated separately for each subsidiary; (3) successful evasion requires some real expenditures; and (4) the home country acts as a Stackelberg leader.

the country at a rate equal to that faced by these subsidiaries in their home country without affecting the firms' after-tax profits.[32] Firms simply offset dollar for dollar any extra taxes they pay to the host government with reduced tax payments to the home government. As a result, when a capital-exporting country raises its tax rate, it induces its clientele of capital-importing countries to raise their tax rates by equal amounts.[33] In setting policy, the exporting country should take this reaction into account. An exporting government would then no longer take the after-tax rate of return available elsewhere to domestic investors as given, but instead recognize that the return available abroad will fall as the domestic tax rate is increased. As a result, domestic labour no longer bears the entire burden of the tax, so that, on distributional grounds, some use of a tax on capital income might seem appropriate. The outcome is not equivalent to a tax on the return to domestic savings, however, since the extra taxes collected on savings invested abroad go to the host rather than the home government. As a result, the equilibrium tax rates should be lower under the crediting scheme than under a tax on savings.[34]

This explanation for capital income taxes runs into several problems, however. For one, taxes in practice are due in the home country on profits earned by subsidiaries abroad only when these profits are repatriated. As a result, any corporate tax in the host country does raise the cost of capital for the subsidiary, since the tax must be paid immediately while any offsetting credit is postponed to some point in the future when the profits are repatriated. If repatriations are postponed indefinitely, we know from Diamond and Mirrlees (1971) that the country is made worse off by an increase in its corporate tax on capital. In general, only if repatriations are fast enough will the host country have an incentive to impose a corporate tax on these subsidiaries. Withholding taxes imposed in the host country on repatriations, in contrast, do not raise the cost of capital for subsidiaries, since the parent firm receives an immediate credit against its

---

[32] When tax rates differ among the capital-exporting countries, the theory forecasts that capital-importing countries would, in equilibrium, divide into clienteles, with each clientele importing capital from only one of the capital-exporting countries. In equilibrium, the relative size of each clientele would adjust so that no capital-importing country would gain from changing clienteles.

[33] In addition, more countries may join its clientele.

[34] In particular, under a crediting scheme, the exporting country ignores the benefits to importing countries when it raises its tax rate. Other exporting countries, however, would potentially be harmed by this change in tax rate, since their clienteles could shrink. Under reasonable assumptions, however, it is possible to show that the country raising its tax rate makes a net transfer to other countries as a group, so underestimates the net efficiency gain from raising its tax rate.

home-country taxes for these payments. When home-country taxes are due only at repatriation, the model therefore forecasts that host countries will impose withholding taxes rather than corporate income taxes on foreign-owned subsidiaries. Even if withholding taxes are ruled out (for example, by tax treaty), host governments would still prefer not to use corporate taxes if repatriations are deferred for long enough.

Another omitted complication is the common availability of world-wide averaging when calculating the available credits for a multinational repatriating profits. If a firm would owe surtax when it repatriates profits from a country with a low corporate tax rate, for example, then it can avoid this surtax simply by repatriating enough profits as well from countries with high corporate tax rates so that, on average, no further domestic taxes are due on the combined repatriations.[35] If the available rate of return net of local taxes is the same in each country,[36] then there would be no costs to the multinational from maintaining enough subsidiaries in high-tax countries to enable it to avoid any surtaxes on profits repatriated from low-tax countries. The outcome is then equivalent to a setting in which corporate taxes apply only to profits from domestic capital; we know that, in this setting, corporate taxes are dominated by labour income taxes.

In principle, multinationals may have a high enough demand for subsidiaries in high-tax countries to drive down the net-of-local-tax rate of return there below the value available elsewhere.[37] Multinationals owing a surtax on profits accruing in low-tax countries would still gain by investing in high-tax countries as long as the pre-tax rate of return there remains above that available in the home country.[38] If the net rate of return to capital in high-tax countries falls, however, then avoiding surtaxes on profits repatriated from low-tax countries does have some real cost to firms. As a result, less investment would occur in low-tax countries.

---

[35] This forecast is consistent with the evidence in Hines and Hubbard (1990), who report that US multinationals pay effectively no domestic taxes on their foreign-source earnings.

[36] This would be true in equilibrium if each country's corporate tax applies only to domestic capital.

[37] In this case, local firms in high-tax countries would not be able to earn a high enough rate of return to survive, given the cost of funds they face.

[38] If the firm would be paying a surtax on profits accruing in a low-tax country, then the effective tax rate on any investment in a high-tax country is the home-country rather than the host-country rate. Investment in the high-tax country is then attractive as long as the pre-tax rate of return exceeds that in the home country.

In this case, the pressures determining tax rates do change. Capital-exporting countries face yet more pressure to reduce their tax rates, in order to raise the rate of return their multinationals earn before domestic tax on their investments abroad. In contrast, the incentive faced by capital-importing countries to reduce their tax rates is now somewhat less, since doing so attracts less additional investment. It seems implausible, however, that the resulting differences in net-of-tax rates of return are large enough to fully offset the gains that capital-importing countries would otherwise receive from cutting their corporate tax rates.

On net, therefore, it does not appear that the use of tax credits can explain the survival of taxes on capital income, given that profits from foreign subsidiaries are taxed only at repatriation and with world-wide averaging.

2.2   Countries are not price takers in world capital markets

If countries are not price takers in world capital markets, then tax policies that affect the amount of domestic investment can affect the equilibrium net-of-tax rate of return received by investors. In this case, the burden of the tax on domestic capital falls in part on capital owners, rather than entirely on domestic workers, so may be attractive on equity grounds.

One reason why countries may not be price takers is simply that they are large enough to affect market rates of return to capital. The tax cuts in the US under Reagan, and the resulting sharp increase in capital imports, do seem to have increased world interest rates.[39] Similarly, interest rates, at least in Europe, seem to have risen noticeably in response to German reunification. If a country is large enough to affect world interest rates, then, by an optimal tariff argument, it has an incentive to restrict net capital flows:[40] if a large country is a capital exporter, it gains from reducing these exports in order to drive up the rate of return it earns on the remaining exports, while if it is a capital importer, it gains from reducing its imports. One way it can reduce exports is to tax domestic savings and subsidize domestic investment. To reduce imports, these respective tax rates would change sign. This forecast is entirely inconsistent with the pattern of tax rates seen historically, however. Capital importers and capital exporters have very similar taxes on savings and investment, contrary to the argument, and tax policy seems largely unaffected by changes in the sign of a country's net trade flow, as occurred in the US in the early 1980s.

[39] See, for example, Sinn (1988).
[40] See, for example, Gordon and Varian (1989) for further discussion.

Gordon and Varian (1989) argue, however, that countries may have market power over the price of equity in domestic firms, even if they cannot affect rates of return to capital more generally. If rates of return are uncertain and the return pattern for equity from any country cannot be duplicated by investments elsewhere, then investors gain from diversifying their portfolios, implying a downward-sloping demand curve for any one country's equity. As a result, the optimal tariff on domestic equity may be non-zero. Countries do choose to impose positive withholding taxes on dividends, consistent with this story.

If these withholding taxes are being used to take advantage of market power, however, then there would be mutual efficiency gains if countries jointly reduced their withholding tax rates. As with agreements reducing tariffs, such agreements can be among subsets of countries. We do see frequent bilateral agreements reducing withholding tax rates. These agreements are inconsistent with the previous hypothesis of co-ordinated *increases* in tax rates, and seem hard to explain through other means.

These treaties deal with withholding tax rates only. Yet the effects of withholding taxes can be replicated in various ways. For example, granting a rebate of corporate taxes on income paid out as dividends to domestic but not foreign shareholders is equivalent to making dividends deductible under the corporate tax but then imposing a withholding tax on dividends paid to foreigners at a rate equal to the corporate rate. Similarly, increasing the corporate tax rate on the return to domestic capital and reducing the personal tax rate enough to leave the return to domestic investors on domestic investments unaffected is again equivalent to imposing a tax on foreign investors. Given that these alternatives are unrestricted by international agreements, existing agreements are probably largely ineffective at reducing barriers to cross-border investment.[41]

Another approach to restricting use of tariffs is to require that domestic investors face tax rates on their income from domestic capital at least as high as those faced by foreign investors. Under this restriction, equilibrium tax rates would still be positive.[42] The optimal tariff rate will now be

[41] Note that, even if personal taxes on the entire real return to domestic equity were feasible, they generate positive externalities to foreign owners—by discouraging domestic investment, they raise the pre-tax rate of return to all owners. A particular combination of corporate and personal taxes on domestic investments would therefore be needed to leave foreign investors unaffected, making it difficult to design a set of rules that prevents taxes from generating externalities across countries.

[42] There is a first-order gain from raising the tariff rate from zero, and only a second-order loss from imposing a non-zero tax on domestic residents.

lower, however, assuming the optimal tax rate on residents is below that on foreigners. This restriction is embodied in current OECD restrictions on tax policy.

Capital owners rather than workers bear the burden of a tax on capital income under this hypothesis only to the degree to which the demand curve for domestic equity is downward sloping, which depends on the degree to which the return on domestic equity is uncorrelated with the returns available elsewhere. Adler and Dumas (1983) found quite low correlations across stock markets. Even assuming returns are entirely independent, however, Gordon and Varian (1989) found that the optimal tariff would be very small. As a result, while this hypothesis can explain non-zero tax rates on foreign investors, it cannot explain the order of magnitude of the tax rates actually seen.

2.3   Capital is relatively immobile across countries

The gains from portfolio diversification may not be the only reason, however, why investments located in different countries are not perfect substitutes for investors. If the demand curve for shares in domestic equity is more downward sloping than is implied by portfolio diversification reasons alone, then the optimal tariff rate is higher, and perhaps as high as is in fact seen.

There certainly is substantial empirical evidence implying capital immobility. Feldstein and Horioka (1980), for example, find that countries with a high savings rate systematically have a high investment rate, suggesting that most extra savings is invested at home. Adler and Dumas (1983) and French and Poterba (1993) both provide clear evidence, if any is needed, that individual portfolios are heavily specialized in domestic assets, contrary to the forecasts from a standard portfolio model in an open economy which would forecast full international diversification.

The implications of capital immobility for tax policy can vary substantially, however, depending on the explanation for this immobility. Gordon and Bovenberg (1996) hypothesize that the reason for capital immobility is that foreign investors are at an informational disadvantage when buying domestic financial securities, and as a result tend to buy the 'lemons'. The resulting drop in trade under their story represents a loss to the domestic economy. As a result, governments have an incentive to subsidize foreign investors to buy domestic financial securities, to offset the overpayments these investors make due to their poorer information. This story forecasts negative rather than positive tax rates on capital imports, however, contrary to the evidence.

Other explanations for the observed immobility, however, can forecast positive taxes on capital income. For example, firms with unique technologies may find particular local inputs essential.[43] Such firms would not abandon their local production unless local tax payments become large enough to offset the gain they receive from access to these local inputs.[44] In this situation, Huizinga (1992) shows that countries will tax foreign subsidiaries, and that the resulting tax rates will be too high from a global perspective, since no country takes adequate account of incentives for research and development.[45]

Other stories suggest that domestic investors may specialize in domestic equity in order to hedge against risks that they face from other sources. For example, Eldor et al. (1988) and Bottazzi et al. (1996) argue that the return on domestic equity is negatively correlated with the earnings of domestic workers, giving these workers an incentive to hedge against their labour risks through investments in domestic equity.[46] Hartley (1986), in contrast, hypothesizes that the returns to domestic publicly traded and closely held firms are negatively correlated, giving owners of closely held firms an incentive to hedge through investing as well in publicly traded domestic firms. Since most closely held firms are owned by domestic residents, these domestic owners would tend to specialize in domestic publicly traded equity.[47] Yet another such hedging story is presented in Gordon and Gaspar (1997), who hypothesize that the value of domestic equity is positively correlated with the price of domestic consumption goods,[48]

[43] Given their unique technology, they would not necessarily face enough outside competition to bid up the price of these inputs to the point where the firms just break even.

[44] Mintz and Tulkens (1986) use this story to explain the taxation of foreign-owned subsidiaries.

[45] While a cash-flow tax is the most effective means of taxing rents accruing to the local subsidiaries of foreign multinationals, multinationals likely would not be able to receive a credit for local cash-flow tax payments against their home-country income tax liabilities. Given that some key countries (for example, the US and Japan) tax their multinationals on their foreign-source income and offer a credit for *income* taxes paid abroad on this income, it is understandable that rents are subject to income rather than cash-flow taxes.

[46] This story would forecast, however, that wealthy individuals with little labour income—for example, the elderly—gain little from hedging so should hold internationally diversified portfolios.

[47] Most domestic individuals do not have ownership claims in such non-traded firms, however, so have no such incentive to specialize. Pesenti and van Wincoop (1996) report evidence that any such hedging gains are minor.

[48] Not only should both be affected similarly by inflation, but changes in the relative demand and therefore relative price of domestic vs. foreign goods should

giving domestic consumers an incentive to protect their purchasing power by holding domestic equity.

Among these papers, only the paper by Gordon and Gaspar explores the implications for tax policy of inelastic demand for domestic equity. Their model implies that taxes on capital income continue to serve mainly as a tariff on foreign investors. Their model does not so clearly forecast positive tax rates on the income from domestic investments accruing to domestic owners.

As before, the fact that tax policy is serving as a tariff on foreign investors suggests that countries together would gain from reducing the taxes on foreign investors. The same problems described above remain in finding an effective means to accomplish this.

2.4   Capital income taxes: forecasts vs. policies

The above theories forecast taxes on the income accruing to foreign owners from domestic capital, as an implicit tariff. In contrast, the theories cannot easily explain positive taxes on the income accruing to domestic owners from this capital. How consistent are these forecasts with the evidence?

To begin with, countries do tax foreign owners of domestic capital. Not only do countries impose withholding taxes on dividend, interest, royalty, and realized capital gains income paid to foreign owners, but also a variety of other tax provisions implicitly serve to tax foreign owners. In particular, dividend imputation schemes that grant tax rebates to domestic but not foreign owners impose implicit taxes on these foreign owners. Corporate taxes on the income accruing to foreign owners can also serve as an implicit tariff.

What about existing tax rates on domestic owners? Statutory tax rates on capital income under both the corporate and the personal tax in most OECD countries are quite high. Using US data, however, Gordon and Slemrod (1988), Kalambokidis (1992), and Shoven (1991) all find that the average tax rate on capital income is zero or negative. In particular, they find that tax revenue would go up slightly in present value if the US eliminated all taxation of income and deductions for payments on financial securities and allowed expensing rather than depreciation for physical capital.[49] In large part, the erosion of tax revenue from real investments occurred through use of debt finance to reduce substantially the taxable income of

cause comparable changes in the relative value of shares of the producers of these domestic vs. foreign goods.

[49] Sørensen (1988) found similar results for Denmark.

both firms and individuals in high tax brackets, with the resulting interest income accruing largely to tax-exempt organizations (for example, pension funds or municipal governments).[50] If the average tax rate on domestic capital approximates the marginal tax rate on new domestic investment, once all the various complications in the law are taken into account, then practice and theory may not be that different.

The theory does very much forecast a corporate (cash-flow) tax in addition to a personal tax on labour income. Without a corporate tax, individuals can avoid the personal labour tax by accepting compensation in a form that shows up as corporate rather than personal income for tax purposes.[51] The theory also provides a variety of reasons why the corporate (cash-flow) tax rate should be below at least the top personal tax rate, as is in fact the case in most countries. For one, countries face pressure to keep their corporate tax rate low to lessen the degree to which firms shift their domestic earnings into foreign subsidiaries. In addition, when asymmetric information between firms and outside investors results in credit constraints, there is an efficiency gain from reducing corporate tax payments and instead taxing non-wage compensation through personal taxes on the resulting capital gains. Gordon (1998) also argues that having a low corporate tax rate relative to at least the top personal tax rate creates a subsidy to entrepreneurial activity, helping to internalize the positive spillovers presumably created by such activity.

There still remain important differences between existing taxes and those forecast from the theory, however. The key difference is undoubtedly the deductibility of interest payments, which creates a variety of arbitrage opportunities lowering both economic efficiency and tax revenue. Rather than converging to a cash-flow tax, with expensing of new investments but no deductibility of interest payments, the tax system instead may be converging to one that allows a set of deductions that are equivalent in present value to expensing but that are deferred in time, as occurs, for example, with the ACE proposal by Gammie (1992).[52] Why it has not converged already is

---

[50] The reported calculations are not able to measure the amount of transfer pricing and other means used to shift earnings abroad. The tax change that is analysed, however, would do nothing to change the incentives to engage in income shifting if statutory rates are held fixed.

[51] Qualified stock options would be one example in the US relevant for publicly traded firms. In a closely held corporation, many other approaches are possible.

[52] Such a deferral of deductions has advantages and disadvantages. For a credit-constrained firm, expensing lessens the need for outside financing compared with deferred deductions of equal present value. Conversely, when investors are in different tax brackets, any variation over time in taxable rates of return opens up

still a question, however. Perhaps the explanation is simply that countries are slow to understand the nature of the pressures created in an open economy, and that tax structures will, in due course, converge to those forecast by the theory. The recent shift towards a dual income tax in the Scandinavian countries, with a lower tax rate on capital income than on labour income, is an example of such a convergence. So is the recent substitution of a cash-flow tax for various taxes on profits and payroll in Italy.

3. Taxation of labour income in an open economy

The above theories forecast little or no taxes on capital income in an open economy. But there are many alternative ways to implement a tax that is confined to labour income. The approaches that would involve the least change from current law are: (1) a payroll tax; (2) an income tax, but with depreciation deductions replaced by expensing and no taxation of income from financial assets; and (3) a value added tax. As economies become more open, each of these alternatives would also be subject to added enforcement problems.

The payroll tax faces the worst problems. Under this tax, individuals are taxed on their wage and salary income. Firms then have a strong incentive to shift to some form of compensation other than wages and salary, to avoid the tax. The alternatives are many, including: offering discounts to the employee on purchases of goods from the firm; paying other firms (for example, financial intermediaries) to provide discounts to employees on their products (for example, on insurance, loans, or other financial transactions with employees); and offering equity as compensation in a form that is not subject to payroll tax (for example, as qualified stock options). The opportunities for owners of a business are even greater—they can simply retain earnings within the firm rather than paying themselves wages and salaries.

In contrast to an income tax or a value added tax, the payroll tax does not tax the return to existing assets, as emphasized by Auerbach and Kotlikoff (1983). Time variation in payroll tax rates therefore does not result in the types of windfall gains and losses on existing assets that occur with variation in income tax or value added tax rates. This is one compensating advantage of a payroll tax.

arbitrage possibilities—for example, through tax shelters. This time variation should be much smaller when deductions are deferred so as to coincide in time with the resulting income.

The income tax in effect supplements a payroll tax with a cash-flow tax on business income.[53] Because of this supplementary tax, the income tax is less vulnerable than the payroll tax to income shifting. In particular, some of the alternative forms of compensation (for example, qualified stock options) that avoid the payroll or personal income tax do not provide the firm a deduction from its corporate taxable income, unlike wage and salary payments. If the corporate tax rate equals the personal tax rate, then there are no net tax savings from such a shift in compensation for the firm and its employees together. The easier this shift in form of compensation, the more pressure is faced to equate corporate and personal tax rates.[54] Assuming that compensation of all but the top executives would take the form of wages and salaries, taxes aside, the main pressure is to raise the corporate tax rate towards the top personal tax rate. This is consistent with several of the proposals for implementing a labour income tax.[55]

The income tax remains vulnerable, however, to transfer pricing and other mechanisms for shifting income between subsidiaries in different countries. Multinationals make use throughout the world of the ideas and technologies created by their domestic employees. The domestic tax law would need to impose the same effective tax rate on the resulting earnings, regardless of location, to avoid both exempting some part of the labour income of these domestic residents from tax and opening up the opportunity for the firm to use transfer pricing to avoid tax on the remaining labour income. An effective labour income tax then requires that foreign subsidiaries of domestic firms be subject to a cash-flow tax at the same rate that applies to the cash flow generated from domestic activities.[56]

Note that, in theory, the deferral of tax until repatriation creates no problems as long as repatriations face the same tax rate that applied to funds sent abroad and as long as repatriations eventually occur. The

---

[53] The payroll tax is then a special case of an income tax, in which the supplementary tax has a zero rate.

[54] These tax rates are automatically equated under a value added tax.

[55] See, for example, McLure (1991), Bradford (1986), and Hall and Rabushka (1995).

[56] Such a cash-flow tax can be imposed year by year, as occurs currently with foreign branches. Alternatively, the multinational can face a cash-flow tax on any funds that flow between the parent and the subsidiary—it could receive a deduction when funds are transferred to the subsidiary and then pay tax on all funds repatriated from the subsidiary regardless of their form. The latter approach approximates the current tax treatment of subsidiaries.

problem is that firms are potentially of infinite life, so can postpone indefinitely any tax liability on income accruing abroad in the hope that the tax rate on repatriations may eventually fall (even for only a brief period) or that opportunities may arise to repatriate profits without tax. When foreign earnings potentially face a lower effective rate in present value, then transfer pricing and other means can be used to shift domestic earnings abroad for tax purposes, leaving many of the same enforcement problems in place even without a tax on capital income.

The labour income tax faces other enforcement problems even in a closed economy. For example, sales can take the form of a discounted price and a loan with an artificially high interest rate—unless all receipts are subject to tax, evasion opportunities arise. Yet another example would be the sale of use of the firm's ideas or technology to others. The resulting revenue should be taxable even if it takes the form of a sale of shares. Revenue from some financial assets therefore needs to remain taxable, even if the return to passive investments in financial assets is exempt from tax.[57]

Another complication is that, with expensing of investment, new businesses are more likely to have tax losses. The availability of refunds invites the creation of businesses that run fictitious losses—for example, by hiring relatives—in order to receive such tax refunds.

In almost all cases, these enforcement problems exist under current income taxes as well. A number of them disappear, however, under a destination-based value added tax. As long as individuals are immobile even if their ideas are not, they will spend their earnings within the home country. This allows the government to monitor and enforce a tax on these earnings at the time they are spent, even if it cannot monitor all sources of income at the time they accrue.[58] The tax due simply depends on the price paid by the final consumer, so is unaffected by transfer pricing within the multinational that may have produced the good or by the source of the funds being spent. If individuals' foreign-source income is unreported, then the country's reported imports will be larger than would be expected,

---

[57] A related problem is the taxation of the return to effort expended managing one's financial portfolio. This form of labour income can again be taxed through use of a cash-flow tax on the financial transactions involved. Where to draw the line between active investments, where the return includes labour income, and passive investments, which can be exempt from tax, will not be clear-cut.

[58] Note, however, that an attempt to tax individual consumption by measuring the individual's income less net additions to savings suffers from the same enforcement problems as the labour income tax, since foreign-source earnings remain difficult to monitor.

given its observed exports, implying that the border corrections under a value added tax should raise revenue in present value.[59]

While destination-based value added taxes continue to face many of the other enforcement problems that exist under a labour income tax (for example, dealing with the underground economy), one new source of tax avoidance or evasion can arise when individuals purchase goods abroad. While in principle countries can use border controls to detect the repatriation of consumption goods and impose tax at that point, in practice these border controls are sufficiently disruptive that at least the EU countries have abandoned them on their internal borders. Another new problem deals with measuring the location of consumption rather than production of financial services. With the growing ease of electronic communications, these problems will become more important in the future.

Of the three commonly used means of taxing labour income, the payroll tax seems to have strong disadvantages relative to the income tax. Both tax wages and salaries, yet the income tax imposes a tax as well on any compensation not taking the form of wages and salaries. This supplementary tax lessens or eliminates a variety of income-shifting opportunities.[60] Why then is the payroll tax so commonly used? Its main use is to finance various social insurance programmes—for example, Social Security, Disability Insurance, or Unemployment Insurance. Under these programmes, there is commonly a link between the generosity of benefits an individual receives and the amount of taxes he or she paid, leaving little *net* tax on labour income.[61] Such a link between individual taxes and benefits would not be straightforward if an income tax were used instead, given the lack of information concerning whose non-wage compensation generated the taxable corporate cash flow.

The income tax and the value added tax both have their weaknesses. In particular, the income tax is vulnerable to transfer pricing while the value added tax is vulnerable to cross-border shopping. Since the nature of the avoidance activity and its sensitivity to tax rates are very different under

[59] For the world economy as a whole, trade should be exactly balanced year by year, but, according to the International Monetary Fund's *International Financial Statistics*, for the period between 1950 and 1993, reported imports on average were 3.1 per cent larger than reported exports. Among the industrialized countries, imports were 4.7 per cent larger than exports. While this is consistent with the industrialized countries being net debtors, the reverse is more likely to be the case.

[60] See Gordon and Slemrod (forthcoming) for evidence on the empirical importance of income shifting in the US.

[61] See, for example, Feldstein and Samwick (1992) for evidence.

the alternative tax bases, overall efficiency costs from evasion for a given net tax revenue would, in general, be minimized when both tax bases are used. Intuitively, the efficiency loss from evasion of either tax grows roughly in proportion to the square of that tax rate, providing an incentive to make use of both taxes. The less the evasion that occurs under one type of tax, the higher this tax rate should be relative to the other rate. Gordon and Nielsen (1997) attempted to measure the relative amounts of under-reporting of value added vs. labour income in Denmark, using detailed data for 1992, and found much more under-reporting of labour income. Their estimates suggested that, based on this consideration alone, the tax system would have been more efficient if much more weight were put on the value added tax relative to the income tax.

One likely response, therefore, to the increasing pressures countries face in enforcing their income taxes is to shift domestic tax systems more towards destination-based taxes. Note that a destination-based tax can, in theory, preserve the progressive rate structure commonly used in income taxation.[62] In particular, any progressive tax on labour income can, in principle, be supplemented with border corrections to shift it towards a destination-based tax. These border corrections impose a positive tax on imports and offer a tax rebate at the same rate on exports. The present value of imports and exports is zero, ignoring any non-zero initial capital account. Ignoring enforcement problems as well, therefore, a tax on imports and a rebate on exports collect no revenue in present value and create no distortions, regardless of tax rate—they simply induce an offsetting re-adjustment of the exchange rate. Opportunities for evasion through income shifting drop, however, as the tax rate on net imports moves closer to that faced by entrepreneurs on their domestic income. The difficulty countries face in practice in enacting such a progressive destination-based tax is that existing GATT rules allow border corrections only for 'indirect' taxes. Basing tax liabilities in part on individual wage income would be likely to force the tax to be labelled as a direct tax. Since GATT rules do not allow border corrections for a tax with a progressive rate structure, it appears that any progressivity will need to be concentrated in the income tax component of the overall tax structure. Changes in GATT rules may therefore be needed to facilitate a shift towards greater use of destination-based taxes.

If other countries continue to use labour income taxes, the incentives for any one country to shift towards greater use of a value added tax are

---

[62] As in the SAT proposal by McLure (1991), firms can be allowed a deduction for wage payments and then individuals can be taxed subject to a progressive rate schedule on their labour income.

even larger. If one country eliminates its income tax and replaces it with a destination-based value added tax, then firms have a strong incentive to use transfer pricing to shift their accounting profits into that country away from others that continue to have a corporate income tax. As a result, firms will be attracted to the country relying on the value added tax, in order to facilitate their evasion of corporate taxes elsewhere.[63] This type of tax competition is an inherent part of an income tax system when foreign-source income is more lightly taxed, but would be avoided if countries relied instead on value added taxes.

References

Adler, M., and Dumas, B. (1983), 'International portfolio choice and corporation finance: a synthesis', *Journal of Finance*, 38: 925–84.

Altshuler, R., and Mintz, J. (1995), 'US interest allocation rules: effects and policy', *International Tax and Public Finance*, 2: 7–35.

Arrow, K., and Lind, R. C. (1970), 'Uncertainty and the evaluation of public investment decisions', *American Economic Review*, 60: 364–78.

Auerbach, A. J. (1985), 'Real determinants of corporate leverage', in B. M. Friedman (ed.), *Corporate Capital Structures in the United States*, Chicago: University of Chicago Press.

——and Kotlikoff, L. J. (1983), 'National savings, economic welfare, and the structure of taxation', in M. S. Feldstein (ed.), *Behavioral Simulation Methods in Tax Policy Analysis*, Chicago: University of Chicago Press.

Boadway, R., and Bruce, N. (1992), 'Problems with integrating corporate and personal income taxes in an open economy', *Journal of Public Economics*, 48: 39–66.

——and Keen, M. (1998), 'Evasion and time consistency in the taxation of capital income', *International Economic Review*, 39: 461–76.

Bottazzi, L., Pesenti, P., and van Wincoop, E. (1996), 'Wages, profits and the international portfolio puzzle', *European Economic Review*, 40: 219–54.

Bradford, D. F. (1986), *Untangling the Income Tax*, Cambridge, MA: Harvard University Press.

[63] Offsetting this, consumers would have an incentive to buy abroad. The results in Gordon and Nielsen (1997) suggest that such cross-border shopping is minor, however.

Campbell Committee (1981), *Final Report of the Committee of Inquiry into the Australian Financial System*, Canberra: Australian Government Publishing Service.

Chamley, C. (1985), 'Efficient tax reform in a dynamic model of general equilibrium', *Quarterly Journal of Economics*, 100: 335–56.

Corlett, W. J., and Hague, D. C. (1954), 'Complementarity and the excess burden of taxation', *Review of Economic Studies*, 21: 21–30.

Diamond, P. A. (1967), 'The role of the stock market in a general equilibrium model with technological uncertainty', *American Economic Review*, 55: 1126–50.

—— and Mirrlees, J. (1971), 'Optimal taxation and public production, I: production efficiency; II: tax rules', *American Economic Review*, 61: 8–27; 261–78.

Dixit, A. (1985), 'Tax policy in open economies', in M. S. Feldstein and A. J. Auerbach (eds), *Handbook of Public Economics*, Amsterdam: North Holland.

Eldor, R., Pines, D., and Schwartz, A. (1988), 'Home asset preference and productivity shocks', *Journal of International Economics*, 25: 165–76.

Feldstein, M. S., and Horioka, C. (1980), 'Domestic savings and international capital flows', *Economic Journal*, 90: 314–29.

—— and Samwick, A. (1992), 'Social security rules and marginal tax rates', *National Tax Journal*, 45: 1–22.

French, K. R., and Poterba, J. M. (1993), 'Investor diversification and international equity markets', in R. H. Thaler (ed.), *Advances in Behavioral Finance*, New York: Russel Sage Foundation.

Gammie, M. (1992), 'Corporate tax harmonization: an "ACE" proposal', *European Taxation*, 31: 238–42.

Gordon, R. H. (1984), *Essays on the Causes and Equitable Treatment of Differences in Earnings and Ability*, New York: Garland Publishing, Inc.

—— (1992), 'Can capital income taxes survive in open economies?', *Journal of Finance*, 47: 1159–80.

—— (1998), 'Can high personal tax rates encourage entrepreneurial activity?', *IMF Staff Papers*, 45: 49–80.

—— and Bovenberg, A. L. (1996), 'Why is capital so immobile internationally? Possible explanations and implications for capital income taxation', *American Economic Review*, 86: 1057–75.

—— and Gaspar, V. (1997), 'Taxation of asset income: implications of monetary union', University of Michigan, mimeo.

—— and Jun, J. (1993), 'Taxes and the form of ownership of foreign corporate equity', in A. Giovannini, R. G. Hubbard, and J. Slemrod (eds), *Studies in International Taxation*, Chicago: University of Chicago Press.

——and MacKie-Mason, J. K. (1994), 'Tax distortions to the choice of organizational form', *Journal of Public Economics*, 55: 279–306.

——and——(1995), 'Why is there corporate taxation in a small open economy? The role of transfer pricing and income shifting', in M. S. Feldstein, J. R. Hines, Jr., and R. G. Hubbard (eds), *The Effects of Taxation on Multinational Corporations*, Chicago: University of Chicago Press.

——and Nielsen, S. B. (1997), 'Tax evasion in an open economy: value-added vs. income taxation', *Journal of Public Economics*, 66: 173–98.

——and Slemrod, J. (1988), 'Do we collect any revenue from taxing capital income?', in L. H. Summers (ed.), *Tax Policy and the Economy*, 2, Cambridge, MA: MIT Press.

——and——(forthcoming), 'Are "real" responses to taxes simply income shifting between corporate and personal tax bases?', in J. B. Slemrod (ed.), *Atlas Shrugged*.

——and Varian, H. (1989), 'Taxation of asset income in the presence of a world securities market', *Journal of International Economics*, 26: 205–26.

Grubert, H., and Slemrod, J. (1998), 'The effects of taxes on investment and income shifting to Puerto Rico', *Review of Economics and Statistics*, 80: 365–73.

Haig, R. M. (1921), 'The concept of income: economic and legal aspects', in R. M. Haig (ed.), *The Federal Income Tax*, New York: Columbia University Press.

Hall, R. E., and Rabushka, A. (1995), *The Flat Tax*, Stanford, CA: Hoover Institution Press.

Hartley, P. (1986), 'Portfolio theory and foreign investment: the role of non-marketed assets', *Economic Record*, 62: 286–95.

Hines, J. R., Jr., and Hubbard, R. G. (1990), 'Coming home to America: dividend repatriations by US multinationals', in A. Razin and J. Slemrod (eds), *Taxation in the Global Economy*, Chicago: University of Chicago Press.

——and Rice, E. M. (1990), 'Fiscal paradise: foreign tax havens and American business', National Bureau of Economic Research, Working Paper 3477.

Huizinga, H. (1992), 'The tax treatment of R&D expenditures of multinational enterprises', *Journal of Public Economics*, 47: 343–59.

——(1996), 'The incidence of interest withholding taxes: evidence from the LDC loan market', *Journal of Public Economics*, 59: 435–51.

——and Demirguc-Kunt, A. (1995), 'Barriers to portfolio investments in emerging stock markets', *Journal of Development Economics*, 47: 355–74.

Institute for Fiscal Studies (1978), *The Structure and Reform of Direct Taxation*, London: George Allen & Unwin (the Meade Report).

Judd, K. (1985), 'Short-run analysis of fiscal policy in a simple perfect foresight model', *Journal of Political Economy*, 93: 298–319.

Kalambokidis, L. T. J. (1992), 'What is being taxed? A test for the existence of excess profit in the corporate income tax base', Ph.D. thesis, University of Michigan.

Kaldor, N. (1955), *An Expenditure Tax*, London: Unwin University Books.

McLure, C. E., Jr. (1991), 'Tax policy for economies in transition from Socialism', *Tax Notes International*, 27 (March): 347–53.

Mintz, J., and Tulkens, H. (1986), 'Commodity tax competition between member states of a federation: equilibrium and efficiency', *Journal of Public Economics*, 29: 133–72.

Musgrave, R. A. (1976), 'ET, OT, and SBT', *Journal of Public Economics*, 6: 3–16.

Myers, S. C., and Majluf, N. S. (1984), 'Corporate financing and investment decisions when firms have information that investors do not have', *Journal of Financial Economics*, 13: 187–221.

Pesenti, P., and van Wincoop, E. (1996), 'Do non-traded goods explain the home-bias puzzle?', National Bureau of Economic Research, Working Paper 5784.

Razin, A., and Sadka, E. (1991), 'Efficient investment incentives in the presence of capital flight', *Journal of International Economics*, 31: 171–81.

Royal Commission on Taxation (1966), *Report*, Ottawa: Queen's Printer (the Carter Report).

Schanz, G. (1986), 'Der Einkommensbegriff und die Einkommensteuergesetze', *Finanzarchiv*, 13: 1–87.

Shoven, J. (1991), 'Using the corporate cash flow tax to integrate corporate and personal taxes', *Proceedings of the 83rd Annual Conference of the National Tax Association*, 19–26.

Simons, H. (1938), *Personal Income Taxation*, Chicago: University of Chicago Press.

Sinn, H-W. (1988), 'US tax reform 1981 and 1986: impact on international capital markets and capital flows', *National Tax Journal*, 41: 327–40.

Sørensen, P. B. (1988), 'Wealth taxation, income taxation, and savings', University of Copenhagen, Institute of Economics, Blue Mimeo 163.

Stiglitz, J. E. (1985), 'The general theory of tax avoidance', *National Tax Journal*, 38: 325–37.

—— and Bevan, D. (1979), 'Intergenerational transfers and inequality', *Greek Economic Review*, 1: 8–26.

US Department of the Treasury (1984), *Tax Reform for Fairness, Simplicity, and Economic Growth*, Washington, DC: US Government Printing Office.

Varian, H. (1980), 'Redistributive taxation as social insurance', *Journal of Public Economics*, 14: 49–68.

3

Interjurisdictional equity in company taxation: principles and applications to the European Union

PEGGY B. MUSGRAVE

The issue of internation or interjurisdictional equity (hereinafter referred to as IJE) in the context of company taxation (CT) arises when a company carries out its profit-generating activities across two or more jurisdictions. The question then arises as to how the entitlement to tax those profits is to be assigned between the jurisdictions and, further, what tax share of the assigned base each jurisdiction should claim. The answer to these questions involves the principle of IJE, or fair tax shares in the profits of multijurisdictional companies. This is a matter of particular importance and complexity as groups of economies become more closely integrated, or as devolution occurs in once unitary countries. In these circumstances, a process of fiscal co-ordination has to take place founded on the following principal objectives: (1) tax neutrality with respect to investment among the member jurisdictions; (2) the attainment of IJE; (3) administrative feasibility and integrity; and, depending on the degree of cohesion among member states, (4) consideration for the principle of subsidiarity.[1] The same issues arise, but with different priorities and degrees of difficulty, in shaping tax agreements between independent nation states.

Section 1 explores the conceptual underpinnings and principles of IJE, while Section 2 considers their application to economic unions of nation

While solely responsible for the final product, the author wishes to acknowledge helpful comments and suggestions by Sijbren Cnossen, Gerold Krause-Junk, Richard Musgrave, Paul Bernd Spahn, and the anonymous referees.

[1] Subsidiarity, as specified in Article 3(b) of the Treaty for the Foundation of the European Community (1 January 1995), does not call for devolution of tax authority in general, but leaves that authority to Member States where not specifically assigned to, or not better performed by, the Union. Thus space is left for Union action.

states differentiated by the centralization or decentralization of the CT. In Section 3, these models are applied specifically to the European Union (EU) and to proposals for CT co-ordination that have been made to date.

1. Nature of the problem

Beginning with a conceptual framework to the problem, we first consider the broadly accepted basic entitlements to tax in a multijurisdictional setting.

1.1 Jurisdictional entitlements to tax

It has been traditional practice, and expressed in international tax treaties, to recognize two entitlements to tax income earned from cross-border factor movement.[2] One is source entitlement, which permits a jurisdiction to tax income arising within its geographical borders but accruing to non-residents. The other is residence entitlement, which recognizes the right of a jurisdiction to tax all income of its residents including that earned in other jurisdictions.

Various committees of experts were sponsored by the League of Nations in the 1920s to consider problems of international taxation (Seligman, 1928), among them the assignment of different taxes to each of the two entitlements. It was recommended that property taxes on tangible wealth, as well as impersonal taxes on income derived from such wealth, be assigned according to the *situs* of property and source of income. Taxes on movable and intangible property, as well as the personal income tax, in turn were to be assigned to the country of domicile. Thus a schedular approach was taken to international entitlements to tax income, with the implication that company income should be taxable only in the country of source. With the important exceptions of the US, the UK, and Japan, most countries to this day obey this rule. Largely under US influence, however, the Draft Double Taxation Convention on Income and Capital drawn up by the Fiscal Committee of the OECD (1963) recognized residence taxation of corporation income tax along with relief from double taxation via deduction or credit for foreign tax.

1.1.1 Entitlement to tax primary income

International practice is thus based on the principle that source entitlement is applicable to the taxation of primary income generated in the productive activity of physical factors of production, largely capital and labour. It follows that taxes appropriate to capture a share for the country of source in this

---

[2] For a fuller discussion of this topic, see Musgrave and Musgrave (1972) and Brean (1992).

primary income are impersonal (*in rem*) income taxes such as the company income tax and payroll taxes that do not require the reporting of the taxpayer's global income as under the residency principle. Since, historically, capital displays greater mobility, the CT on profits has been seen as an essential instrument for the exercise of source entitlement. The income tax on individuals, on the other hand, is assigned to the country of residence and applies to wages and derivative income such as dividends, interest income earned on financial investments, and royalties earned from the use of intangible assets.

Exercise of the source and residence entitlements involves different policy norms.[3] Taxation at source establishes the share of the taxing jurisdiction (JS) in the income earned by non-residents, irrespective of whether the jurisdiction of residence (JR) chooses to tax that income under the residence principle. Taxation by JS thereby determines its share in the tax base provided by income accruing to non-residents and the share left for JR, and therefore involves the issue of IJE. Exercise of the source entitlement plays the greater role in the issue of IJE, with residence taxation merely determining how the income remaining after the JS tax is paid is divided between the Treasury and the taxpayer resident in JR.

Where exercise of source entitlement is of primary importance for IJE, that of residence entitlement is of major concern with regard to efficiency, since it controls the degree of tax neutrality with respect to interjurisdictional capital resource allocation. Specifically, tax neutrality in this context is defined as equal overall tax burdens imposed on residents whether they invest at home or abroad, often referred to as capital export neutrality. Such neutrality requires that JR impose a tax (whether positive or negative) on foreign-source income such that, combined with JS's tax, it results in the same total tax burden on that income as the JR tax on domestic-source income. In practice, this requires JR to apply its tax to income earned by its residents in JS with a full refundable credit for the tax paid at source.[4] Alternatively, JR may aim to achieve national efficiency by maximizing its national returns from the foreign investment of its residents by allowing only a deduction for JS taxes (Richman (P. Musgrave), 1963; Musgrave, 1969; Feldstein and Hartman, 1979; Slemrod, 1995). However, governments are reluctant to take this approach since it results in heavier tax burdens on

---

[3] For a fuller discussion, see Musgrave (1969 and 1996).

[4] Unless company tax rates are everywhere the same, capital export neutrality will nevertheless leave companies of differing residencies but operating in the same country to be subject to different tax rates. Although this may put the higher-taxed firms at a competitive disadvantage, this does not violate neutrality conditions for the choice of location but merely reflects how each country of residence chooses to tax its residents.

investment made abroad than on that made at home. Source taxation alone, without the protective overlay of residence taxation, will, however, be non-neutral except in the unlikely event that tax rates are universally equal. Furthermore, without this 'umbrella effect' of residence taxation, jurisdictions are exposed to tax competition resulting in possible inefficiency in the fiscal conduct of the public sector (Musgrave, 1991). Interjurisdictional co-operation is therefore needed to achieve neutrality either through general application of the residence entitlement with use of a full foreign tax credit or by adoption of equal or approximately equal effective rates of tax in all countries.

Residence taxation is also required to protect the equitable tax treatment of JR's residents. Although taxpayer equity clearly requires JR to tax income comprehensively including the foreign-source income of its residents, this may leave an excessive double taxation of such income. In practice, JR accedes to the primary tax claim of JS but alleviates the double burden by exempting foreign-source income or by allowing a deduction or credit for the JS tax. In principle, there is no single answer to how the JS tax is to be treated—whether as a credit against JR tax, as a deduction from taxable foreign-source income, or to be ignored with full double taxation applied (Musgrave, 1969). It also follows that exercise of the residence entitlement allows JR to use this tax instrument to deter, encourage, or remain neutral in relation to capital outflow. A refundable foreign tax credit will create a neutral tax environment, and anything less than that (such as partial credit for or deduction of JS taxes) will discourage capital outflow, while deferral of tax until repatriation or any other form of exemption, whether temporary or permanent, will provide an incentive to outflow. A country that applies the residence principle to investment income earned by its residents abroad (provided that they do not leave the jurisdiction) can thereby protect itself against loss of investment through tax competition of other countries, without losing its taxing sovereignty by having to follow suit.

There is little doubt that JS is in a more favourable position to tax income accruing to non-residents, and source entitlement is generally regarded as the primary right to tax and is more emphatically asserted in tax agreements and model tax treaties (Head, 1997). The residence entitlement in practice has been notoriously difficult to implement since it requires the reporting of foreign-source income, a process inviting evasion. Residence taxation thus calls for a strong administration backed up by co-operation between tax authorities in JS and JR and resistance to political pressures. There is also the problem of defining 'residence', particularly in the case of company taxation. Is JR in this case to be defined as the jurisdiction where the company is registered (a rule followed by the US), where it is headquartered, or where its seat of management and control is (applied by the UK and Australia)? These legal tests may each give different results in terms of where the residence entitlement is to be exercised and thus where JR tax revenue is received. It is a further reason why application of the residence principle is appropriate only for central governments, for at lower levels companies may too easily select whatever residence location gives them the greatest tax advantage. Company tax revenue would then be concentrated in the jurisdictions where registration customarily occurs. There are also practical difficulties, such as assigning a residence status to joint ventures. A question also arises as to whether the concept of residence entitlement should apply not only to the income earned directly by the unincorporated foreign branches of a parent corporation but also to all income earned indirectly by subsidiaries of the parent that are incorporated in outside jurisdictions and therefore perhaps subject to residence taxation there. As tax lawyers put it, should the 'corporate veil' be pierced?

There is another way in which the legal form of doing business plays an important role in the implementation of the source and residence entitlements, and in turn in interjurisdictional tax relationships. The residence principle, in its application to the company tax, is *enterprise*-based, i.e. it applies to the global income of a company judged to be resident (by way of registration, management, or other test) in the taxing jurisdiction. It is derived from the tenet that residency carries with it a tax allegiance to JR. But whereas the residence principle is applicable to individuals or corporations, the source principle is *activity*-based since it involves the right to tax income arising from economic activity carried out within the borders of JS, and therefore calls for an impersonal activity-based tax. A CT is therefore not entirely compatible with the source-based approach. The US, for instance, which taxes according to both source and residence principles, defines residence as country of incorporation and therefore, under the residence principle, taxes the global income of those enterprises that are incorporated within the US. At the same time, application of the source principle requires it to tax all profits earned within its borders, whether those profits are attributable to US incorporated enterprises or not. Here the concept of 'permanent establishment' enters, which allows the profits earned by unincorporated branches of foreign corporations to be taxed. The source principle in its application to the company tax has therefore to be applied on a permanent establishment basis, a definitionally imprecise concept.

1.1.2 Tax treatment of derivative income

The case for both source and residence entitlements to tax profits as a primary form of income is well established and clear-cut. But what of other investment income flows such as dividends, interest, and royalties received by a corporation, and how does their treatment differ under the two entitlements?

With regard to dividends, the applicability of the source and residence principles depends on whether taxation of the underlying profits at source fulfils the IJE criterion. Let us suppose that it does. Then there is no justification for the dividends paid from those profits to be retaxed by JS, for further taxation via, for instance, a withholding tax would result in an excessive tax share. On the other hand, if profits have not been appropriately taxed by JS under whatever IJE standard is chosen, a further compensatory withholding tax on the dividends might be called for.[5] These conclusions apply whether the dividends are paid to non-resident firms both related and unrelated to the paying company, or whether they are paid to non-resident individual shareholders. Furthermore, if the dividends are paid to a corporation resident in another jurisdiction, JR, which taxes only on the source principle, the dividends should not in principle be taxed. Were they to be taxed by JR, this would result in double taxation, since the underlying profits have already been taxed at source. On the other hand, if JR applies the residence principle, the dividends may be taxed to the receiving corporation by JR, presumably with an allowance for the underlying company tax. In principle, the same rules should apply if the dividends are paid to a non-resident individual shareholder. In this case, the dividends would be taxable under the individual income tax in JR according to the residence principle, but with whatever allowance for the underlying CT in JS that JR chooses to permit.

The question of whether a company's interest payments should be deducted and taxed to the recipient under residence entitlement, or whether they should be non-deductible and taxed at source, is somewhat more complicated. Prevailing practice is to permit interest to be treated as a cost and therefore deducted from taxable income of the paying firm. If paid to a non-resident firm or individual, a low withholding tax may be applied. This then leaves the interest to be taxed under the residence principle to the receiving taxpayer in JR. However, if JR does not apply the residence principle, such interest may go virtually untaxed. For this and other reasons in an interjurisdictional setting, many tax experts advocate that interest not be deductible in JS to ensure that it does not escape tax or that tax avoidance by disguising profits as interest is prevented (Cnossen, 1996). Non-deductibility of interest then subjects interest payments to company tax at source. Again, the jurisdiction, JR, in which the interest is received may or may not then apply its company or personal income tax with allowance for the tax in JS. In view of the fact that the residence principle is not universally applied (especially by sub-units of a federation), the application of source entitlement to interest through non-deductibility seems reasonable. There is, however, one controversial aspect to such a rule, for it assumes that interest has its

---

[5] See Section 1.5.

source where the profits are generated rather than where the financial capital is provided. It might be claimed that the income generated by financial capital, as distinct from the 'primary' income created by real investment, does not readily lend itself to the principle of taxation at source.

Royalty payments are subject to the same considerations as is interest. That is to say, there is a case to be made that royalties should not be deductible from taxable profits and therefore, along with those profits, be taxed at source. However, the source of some forms of royalties, including payments for specialized technologies, is again not readily identified, and leaving them to be taxed by the JS where the profits arise may not be satisfactory.

1.2 Basis for claims to taxation at source

Since source entitlement is central to the implementation of IJE, we now examine the basis for that entitlement, and the form of tax that is called for.

1.2.1 Benefits provided

One of the most readily understood arguments on behalf of source entitlement is based on the benefit principle. Each jurisdiction should charge for the services that it has rendered. This calls for CT to be applied by the jurisdiction in which the production process occurs and the benefits are received. Such benefits may be seen in either of two ways. First, they might be looked at as being in the nature of intermediate goods which therefore lower the cost of production. In this case, a company profits tax is not as well suited to reaching those benefits as would be a more broad-based tax reaching a variety of inputs, such as a value added tax. Alternatively, the benefits might be seen as arising from the government provision of part of the company's capital stock (in the form, for instance, of transportation facilities and other infrastructure) which, together with the firm's own capital, generates the profits. In this case, a company profits tax might be seen as a means of sharing in the firm's profits by the government corresponding to its provision of part of the productive capital. There is a further complication. The benefits (of whatever kind) provided to the firm may emanate from the jurisdiction of residence as well as from that of source, even in the absence of current profits arising in the former. In all, the company tax is not a satisfactory vehicle for implementing a standard of IJE based on the benefit rule.

1.2.2 National rental

From the economist's perspective, perhaps JS's entitlement to tax is best justified as a national rental charge for the use of its investment environment and natural resources by residents of another jurisdiction. This cross-border investment results in increased profits and reduced labour income in JR, with the opposite occurring in JS, and with an overall net gain. JS might argue that it should be able to share, through tax participation, in JR's increased profits, with the tax acting as a rental or royalty charge. This might call for deductibility of both interest and cost of equity capital, along with inclusion of royalties, but leaves open the question of how high this charge should be, a matter discussed in Section 1.5.

1.2.3 Territorial sovereignty and reciprocity

Company taxation imposed at source does not appear to be a suitable vehicle for achieving IJE based on the above standards. As a matter of historical precedent, however, there is a generally accepted basis for source-based CT which simply derives from the notion of territorial sovereignty. Without further justification, this notion merely asserts the right to tax income of non-residents arising within own borders and leaves open the questions of at what rate such income should be taxed to achieve IJE and of how it should be defined. But inasmuch as CTs do not generally correspond to benefits provided by the host government, nor can they be regarded as forms of rental charges, those rates have to be set as a matter of interjurisdictional agreement based on mutually agreed notions of fairness. In this context, it seems reasonable to conclude that, in order to resolve conflict, the principle of reciprocity should apply. Reciprocity suggests that each pair of jurisdictions should tax the profits earned by residents of the other at equal rates and contrasts with the more generally applied rule of non-discrimination, which requires that each jurisdiction tax the income earned by investors from abroad at the same rate that income accruing to domestic investors is taxed. Reciprocity, imposed in a pure form as a standard of IJE, would call for JS to tax profits accruing to investors resident in different jurisdictions at different rates, each rate being equal to that imposed by the other. A limited reciprocity rule has, in fact, been adopted in a number of international tax treaties whereby withholding taxes are applied at equal rates by each treaty partner to investment income but this rule has not been applicable to CTs at source.

1.3 Significance of IJE

How to define a jurisdiction's tax share in the income earned within its borders by non-residents is a matter of universal concern and is a problem addressed in international tax treaties and in compacts among constituent states in federations. The question takes on major importance when a significant proportion of operating capital in that jurisdiction is owned by non-residents. Then the share of national income claimed by non-residents and, in turn, taxes on that income as a share of total tax revenue may be substantial. This is the case especially for members of a federation within which businesses are highly mobile and their activities spread widely across jurisdictions. By the same token, the larger the share of non-resident income claimed by JS, the smaller the after-tax returns to JR, whether that jurisdiction chooses to tax outside income of its residents or not.

Interjurisdictional equity, as it relates to base shares, involves two issues. The dominating issue concerns the share by jurisdiction JS in the income created by the activities in JS of factors of production owned by residents of another jurisdiction, JR. In the context of the company income tax, the issue of IJE may arise from direct investment by JR's resident investors (whether corporations or individuals) in JS. Then IJE involves the tax share of JS, mutually considered to be fair, in the investment returns accruing to the residents of JR. The situation is further complicated when the profit-generating activities of the company extend across more than one JS, in which case the tax share claimed by each JS will also depend on how the profits are divided for tax purposes among those jurisdictions. A second dimension to IJE concerns the previously noted definition of 'residence', which in turn determines which JR receives a tax share in after-tax income received from JS.

Before taking a closer look into the determination of tax shares, it is important to recognize their place in the context of IJE. In fact, the significance of these tax arrangements for IJE goes beyond the mere revenue share. As capital moves from one jurisdiction to another, this not only affects tax bases but also has its impact on factor earnings in both host and home jurisdictions. For developing countries in particular, the gain to labour from a capital inflow may outweigh in importance any revenue to its Treasury. At the same time, allowance for these secondary effects in determining an equitable distribution of tax bases would be administratively unmanageable, so, for practical purposes, IJE has to be confined to revenue shares.

1.4 Base share: determination of source

Interjurisdictional equity is defined in terms of (1) tax base share among jurisdictions of source and (2) tax shares of source jurisdictions in those assigned bases. The means by which income is assigned to its source must now be considered.

1.4.1 Separate entity vs. formula apportionment

The problem of CT base division arises wherever companies transact with their affiliates across jurisdictions, whether the latter be autonomous nations, associations of nations, or political units within a federation, so long as one or more of those jurisdictions has taxing authority. There are two ways of approaching the determination of source of primary profits. One is to take a separate entity approach, which utilizes normal accounting procedures to assess the profits of each business entity operating within a given jurisdiction, cutting off the accounts at the border or 'water's edge'. The accounts of related business entities operating within that jurisdiction may be consolidated, but transactions with related business units outside must be separated. Usual international practice is to establish base share by this means of water's-edge separate accounting whereby all permanent establishments within a country determine their profits through accounts that terminate at the border. However, the very nature of multijurisdictional enterprises is a condition of interdependence between parts of the firm doing business in different jurisdictions.[6] Such an integrated enterprise has been named 'unitary'. This interdependence presents great difficulties for the process of separate accounting which requires the assignment of shared costs and returns to parts of the firm located in specific jurisdictions. In practice, these difficulties are addressed by requiring intra-firm transactions to be valued at arm's-length prices, or, in the extreme, by rules of thumb prescribed by the revenue service.[7] Furthermore, multijurisdictional activities of the firm provide opportunities for profit shifting for tax advantage through transfer pricing and strategic intra-firm borrowing.[8] This is clearly a severe problem at the international level, but even more so at the subnational level where enterprises become highly interjurisdictional in nature, markets are closely integrated, and separate accounting is rarely possible. Indeed, in some federal systems, such as the US and Canada, profits are assigned among member states by a process of formula apportionment.[9]

Given these difficulties, many economists have reached the conclusion that this approach should be followed more generally and that the assignment of profits to jurisdictional source should be carried out by formula apportionment applied to groups of multijurisdictional firms related by

---

[6] McLure (1984) describes these interdependencies as arising from 'shared expenses, economies of scale or scope, intra-group transactions, vertical integration, or other economic interdependencies'.

[7] Examples of such methods are the 'cost plus margin' and 'price less margin' approaches to valuation.

[8] As one analyst has described it, 'the allocation of profits within a multinational enterprise is thus inherently and unavoidably arbitrary since such businesses are, as a rule, inevitably "unitary" in character' (Bird, 1986).

[9] The formula may be applied by individual states to unitary enterprises (as in the US) or the revenue may be distributed to members from the central government by formula (as in Canada) or according to collection points (such as in Germany).

ownership and control (the unitary enterprise).[10] As Bird (1986) has put it, 'the unitary approach has in its favor the economic reality that the income of a multinational enterprise is the fungible product of a set of integrated income-producing factors that are essentially under common control, regardless of location'. The unitary approach is activity- rather than enterprise-based, for it takes the unit of apportionable profits to arise from the total activities of a unitary group of businesses and assigns those profits by a formula that is judged to indicate their geographical source. Thus a CT may have to be applied to profits of a business group that includes activities undertaken by enterprises that would not normally be subject to company taxation. The determination of what is 'unitary' is, of course, a somewhat judgemental procedure and, like other elements in the division of tax base, should be subject to generally acceptable rules that satisfy notions of reasonableness and fairness.

1.4.2   Alternative formulas

Formula apportionment is applied to the pooled profits of a group of multijurisdictional business activities related through ownership, management, or control and is designed to assign profits to their territorial origin. The obvious place to begin is to assign profits according to the location at which the actual operation of the capital occurs. Thus profits would be assigned according to the location of capital use, including fixed capital as well as working capital. But this approach implicitly assumes that the rate of return to capital is the same in all locations in which a unitary business group operates. Furthermore, profits are not generated by capital alone, but other co-operative factors of production are involved, primarily land and labour. The three factors of production—capital, land, and labour—all represent the supply side in the creation of value, and it can be argued that the demand side should also be allowed for in the form of sales. This raises the further question of whether it should be sales at origin or destination, and, beyond that, there is the practical question of where the sale was actually consummated.

The next question is how these elements in the formula are to be measured. Land might well be combined with fixed and working capital as a 'property' factor. Consistent with the inclusion of property as a stock, labour input might enter the formula via average working capital needed for wage payments. For the same reason, sales would enter via investment in sales establishments. Alternatively, each factor might be put in the form of

---

[10] For a critical view of formula apportionment, see, for example, Kopits and Mutén (1984); for problems in implementing it, see Chapter 10 by McLure and Weiner.

a current input, with payroll combined with depreciation of fixed capital and natural resource rent.

Finally, what weights are to be attached to each element in the formula? With regard to the contribution of the factors of production, this depends on the form of the production function for each unitary business. The underlying analysis suggests such a cumbersome administrative task and complex compliance requirements to be impractical and that the answer in practice has to be a rather crude and uniform formula that nevertheless satisfies participating jurisdictions as being reasonable and equitable. For instance, sales might reasonably be given even weight with combined property and labour input. For example, the weights might be $\frac{1}{6}, \frac{1}{3}$, and $\frac{1}{2}$ for property, payroll, and sales, respectively. Application of a uniform formula across firms assumes that production functions are everywhere the same and that each factor contributes the same share of total profits. This is clearly not the case, but differentiation of formulas by type of activity would not seem practicable. The assignment of profits among jurisdictions by formula apportionment, while avoiding some of the problems associated with separate accounting, is nevertheless by necessity a somewhat arbitrary procedure that has to be determined by common agreement rather than objective economic rules; and uniformity of formula is a standard of IJE that is more likely to render the system mutually acceptable.[11]

Table 3.1 gives a numerical illustration of the very different outcomes that are possible between separate accounting and formula apportionment, and in turn between different formulas. Three jurisdictions—J1, J2, and J3— are considered, with one unitary enterprise, the accounts of which reveal a distribution among the jurisdictions as shown in the top block of the table. The lower part of the table shows how the profits tax base is divided among the jurisdictions, first with separate accounting (lines 1a and 1b) and then with various three-factor, two-factor, and one-factor formulas. The three-factor apportionment includes equally weighted sales, property, and payroll and is shown with both a destination-based and an origin-based sales factor. The two-factor formula includes equally weighted property and sales, while the one-factor example is shown for destination-based sales and for property. The internal interest payments of the unitary firm are offsetting in the combined profit report, so that with formula apportionment the problem of the treatment of such interest does not arise as it does with separate accounting.

---

[11] As noted by Bird (1986), 'there is, even in principle, no clear objective economic basis on which to allocate revenues and costs to the particular units that comprise parts of a multijurisdictional enterprise'.

Table 3.1 Numerical illustration of alternative apportionment formulas

	Jurisdiction			ΣJi
	J1	J2	J3	
Firm's annual accounts				
Sales (product)				
Destination	0	50	50	100
Origin	50	50	0	100
Property	100	150	50	300
Payroll	35	25	10	70
Interest paid	5	5	0	10
Interest received	0	0	10	10
Profits	—	—	—	30
Profits tax base				
division (% of total)				
1. Separate accounting[a]				
a. Interest deductible	33.3	33.3	33.3	100.0
b. Interest non-deductible	50.0	50.0	0.0	100.0
2. Formula apportionment[b]				
a. Three-factor formula (sales at destination)	27.8	45.2	27.0	100.0
b. Three-factor formula (sales at origin)	44.4	41.9	13.7	100.0
c. Two-factor formula	41.7	42.8	15.5	100.0
d. One-factor formula (sales at destination)	0.0	50.0	50.0	100.0
e. One-factor formula (property)	33.3	50.0	16.7	100.0

[a] It is assumed here that, if interest payments are deductible, interest receipts are includable.
[b] In this example, intra-firm interest payments are assumed to be offsetting in arriving at combined profits.

In the real world, formula apportionment of profits takes a variety of forms. The federal government of Canada, for instance, assigns profits among the provinces on the basis of a formula including 50 per cent each on sales and payroll (Smith, 1976). Most member states of the US that apply a corporation income tax follow a unitary combination approach and employ different combinations of factors in the formulas and different weighting systems. The most prevalent formula in use, however, includes property, payroll, and sales, each with a weight of one-third (as in line 2a).

One conclusion is clear: all participating jurisdictions should follow the same rules in applying formula apportionment—from taxable nexus and definition of permanent establishment, to scope of unitary combination and to the formula that is used. Thus a high degree of continuing co-operation, not only in reaching agreement on the formula, is required to implement the apportionment approach if it is to be applied correctly. This requires a good deal of political will, but the alternative of separate accounting can be the loss of integrity of company tax systems. Similar and more subtle application of separate accounting in the presence of unitary, multijurisdictional enterprises also requires considerable co-operation for it to be well implemented.

1.4.3 Conclusions for tax base division

There does not appear to be any objective, single answer to the question of how company profits should be divided in a multijurisdictional setting. The rules governing such division have to be arrived at by mutual agreement based on a shared sense of what constitutes IJE.

1.5 Choice of tax rates

Previous attention was given to tax base shares in income accruing to non-residents, but final tax shares are the product of tax base division and the tax rates applied to base shares. Both are matters of IJE. What arrangement of rates might be considered reasonable and equitable?

1.5.1 Interjurisdictional redistribution

One approach is to think of IJE in terms of the interjurisdictional redistribution that company taxation at source permits. For instance, the tax share in profits earned by non-residents might be allowed to rise inversely to the level of per capita income in JS and directly in relation to per capita income in JR (Musgrave and Musgrave, 1972). Such a scheme would be of particular interest in the relation between developed and developing countries, an important issue not to be considered here.

1.5.2 Non-discrimination vs. reciprocity

International rules expressed in tax treaties as well as common practice call for the principle of non-discrimination to apply to company taxation. This means that the country of source should apply the same rate of CT to income accruing to non-residents as to income earned by its own residents. On the other hand, the withholding tax rates on remitted dividends and on other income payments are generally set below the standard rate but are required to be reciprocally equal. The quid pro quo approach embodied in the principle of reciprocity seems in line with an acceptable standard of IJE, but it makes little sense to confine it to the low-rate withholding taxes only. The argument can be made that the reciprocity rule should apply to the company tax in combination with withholding taxes, so that each pair of countries take the same share of profits earned by residents of the other.[12] This would mean a replacement of the prevailing non-discrimination rule for CTs with that of reciprocity and require a major change in traditional international rules of the game. The tax rate applied to non-resident profits would then be determined by considerations of IJE, whereas that applied to profits earned by residents should be determined by considerations of domestic tax policy, such as resident taxpayer equity. If such a scheme could be implemented with interest and royalties included in the tax base, there would be little justification for withholding taxes. Once JS has taken a fair share of primary profits, no further share by JS in income derived from those profits as dividends, interest, and royalties is appropriate on IJE grounds.

Alternatively, the present system of non-discriminatory company taxation might remain in place, but reciprocity be implemented by the use of compensatory withholding taxes, as will be illustrated in the models of Section 2.

2. Models of IJE in economic unions

One objective of company tax harmonization within an economic union, whether explicit or implicit, is that of fair tax shares in company profits accruing to non-resident taxpayers. In addition, and consistent with one of the basic purposes of an economic union, is a tax environment that is neutral in its treatment of capital flows, presenting no incentives or disincentives to the free flow of capital within the union. Beyond these two basic objectives, the principle of subsidiarity is recognized whereby each member jurisdiction should be free, so far as possible, to design its tax system as it applies to its resident taxpayers in line with its own standards of taxpayer equity and economic objectives. Since IJE with respect to the company tax cannot be evaluated without allowance for these other policy considerations, the discussion that follows is set in the broader framework of CT harmonization.

In this section, various models of CT harmonization are proposed that meet the criteria of IJE while at the same time allowing each member a substantial degree of sovereignty in shaping its income tax system as it applies to its resident taxpayers. Much will depend on the institutional framework—in particular, whether the CT continues to be applied as a decentralized tax as federalization proceeds, or whether it is transferred in whole or in part to a central tax authority. In the case of a hitherto unitary state devolving into a federal system, the same consideration applies, i.e. whether the central government transfers the CT in whole or in part to

---

[12] This was first proposed in Musgrave (1974); the concept is discussed in Sato and Bird (1975).

member jurisdictions. In both cases of integration and devolution, if the central authority is responsible for all or part of the company tax, a further consideration is whether it acts merely as a collection agent returning revenue to 'source' or whether it collects the tax to finance its own expenditures. In all cases, intra-union co-operation will be essential to meet a satisfactory trade-off between the three criteria of tax neutrality, IJE, and the subsidiarity principle.

All models assume the source principle to be justified in terms of territorial sovereignty. All models also assume that IJE be given expression through agreements on reciprocity of tax rates rather than by way of non-discrimination. We begin, in Model I, with the case of a fully decentralized company tax, while Model II considers a fully centralized tax with attention given to the advantages and disadvantages that centralization brings. Both cases are modified in Model III to a dual system (such as in the US) where the tax is applied by both constituent states and the central government.

2.1 Model I: company tax fully decentralized

How might a decentralized system of company taxation among members of an economic union be designed to meet the above-mentioned three criteria?

Implementation of the source principle calls for an activity-based, impersonal tax on profits. The company tax fits this requirement so long as taxable business entities include all corporate-connected permanent establishments, with at least a threshold level of activity in the source jurisdiction.

Within a unified market, profit-earning activities of companies will be dispersed widely across borders. In consequence, there will be many intra-firm, cross-border transactions. Because of this, as noted in Section 1.4.1, each jurisdiction's share in the company tax base cannot readily be determined by taking a separate-entity—separate-accounting approach. Formula apportionment is needed to assign taxable profits to source. Furthermore, as was suggested earlier, there is no single formula that can be judged to be economically correct in apportioning the profits on a geographical basis. It is essential, however, that the formula applied and measurement of its components be uniform for all jurisdictions. Exactly which formula is chosen, however, must be a matter of what seems reasonable and acceptable to member states as part of their harmonization agreements, as well as administratively feasible. Leading options most likely would be one or more of the components property, payroll, and sales, with the choice of sales preferably measured at destination. The apportionable base should at least include all profits from the activities of each company throughout the union. In principle, it should also extend to the company's world-wide operations to include sources outside the union. Political considerations may preclude this and require a water's-edge approach, in which case foreign profits of foreign companies operating within the economic union would be excluded from the apportionable base, through an accounting process that records intra-firm transactions across the union's external borders.

Interest payments by firms would not be deductible, for reasons discussed in Section 1.1.2. Since the CTs of member states are source-based with respect to profits arising within the union, dividends received by companies from other member states should be excluded from the apportionable base to avoid double counting. Failure to impose residence taxation on profits arising within the union should not cause a serious breach of tax neutrality for capital flows within the union since there will be agreement on reciprocity of tax shares (see below), and the range of effective CT differentials will be limited by general agreement. However, it would be desirable to protect tax neutrality with respect to capital outflow to non-members by applying residence taxation to company profits earned outside the union. This may partly be achieved by taxing dividends received from outside the union, grossed up by the foreign tax, and with a foreign tax credit, although accrual taxation of foreign profits without deferral is preferable to protect the union's investments from tax competition by outside tax haven jurisdictions.

With company profits apportioned among member states, IJE calls for reciprocally equal rates among member jurisdictions' CTs as applied to profits of capital owned by other members. However, the rates applied to such cross-border company investments in principle need not be the same as those chosen to apply to domestically owned investments. Indeed, in the interests of the subsidiarity principle, each member state would have the right to apply a rate of company tax to profits accruing to its residents that is determined by domestic tax policy considerations, and these rates may differ.[13] However, administrative and other considerations may preclude the use of different rates as applied to resident and non-resident investors and mandate application of a single non-discriminatory rate. In this case, non-uniform withholding taxes may be applied to profits distributed outside each member state to adjust the effective combined rate (on profits and dividends) to the common source rate, as illustrated in Table 3.1.

---

[13] Some might argue that an agreement among member states to apply the same rate of tax to their intra-union flows of income represents some surrender of tax autonomy, i.e. violation of subsidiarity. However, failure to do so opens the union to tax competition in which subsidiarity can be said to be violated by the workings of the private capital market. One analyst has described the alternative to international agreements on taxation as a situation of 'increasingly outflanked national tax administrations in this age of financial and technological international interdependence' (Bird, 1986).

Although second best, since undistributed profits would carry the resident rate only, this policy would nevertheless go some way to achieving reciprocity. Consideration might also be given to the application of the adjustable withholding tax to all profits as they accrue to non-residents, whether distributed or undistributed, on a prepaid basis without deferral until time of distribution. This, however, might present formidable imputation difficulties. The use of compensatory withholding taxes on a prepaid basis would also doubtless run into opposition from countries outside the union, but the principle of reciprocity has much logic and should be firmly adhered to in the treaty bargaining process.

Such a system is illustrated in the numerical example of Table 3.2. JA and JB are member states of the union while JC is a non-member country. Suppose the reciprocally equal tax rate on intra-union company profits to be 30 per cent. The rate chosen for resident investors, however, is 20 per cent in JA and 40 per cent in JB. There is no agreement on a common rate between union members and outside countries, represented here by JC, the CT rate in which is 35 per cent. Reciprocity is achieved by use of a compensatory withholding tax rate, *tw*, imposed on profits accruing to non-residents. If *tp* is the company tax rate, then the adjustable withholding tax rate, *tw*, is determined by the following equation:

(3.1) $$tp + (1 - tp)tw = t^*,$$

Table 3.2 Model I: company and withholding tax rates in member states for IJE

	Recipients of profits resident in:		
	JA	JB	JC
Source jurisdiction JA			
Company tax rate, *tp*	0.20	0.20	0.20
Withholding tax rate (prepaid), *tw*	0.0	0.125	0.309
Combined rate, t^*	0.20	0.30	0.447
Source jurisdiction JB			
Company tax rate, *tp*	0.40	0.40	0.40
Withholding tax rate (prepaid), *tw*	(0.167)	0.0	0.079
Combined rate, t^*	0.30	0.40	0.447
Source jurisdiction JC			
Company tax rate, *tp*	0.35	0.35	0.35
Withholding tax rate (on dividends), *tw*	0.15	0.15	0.0
Combined rate, t^*	0.447	0.447	0.35

where t^* is the common rate chosen for each pair of countries of source. In this example, t^* equals 0.30 within the union. Between the union and outside countries, t^* will be determined as equal to the tp imposed by JC plus its withholding tax on dividends, or 0.447. It is assumed here that tw in JC reflects past practice without mutual adjustments for purposes of IJE. It may be noted that the tw applied by JA to profits accruing to residents of JB will be positive, while that applied by JB to profits accruing to residents of JA will be negative (i.e. in the form of a refund).

In this model of a decentralized CT within an economic union, which incorporates harmonizing rules among member states, two objectives are attained. First, an IJE standard is met since, with the application of a compensatory withholding tax, each member as a jurisdiction of source takes an equal tax share in company profits accruing to other members of the union. The model also equalizes the tax share that members of the union and non-members take in the company profits earned by resident investors of the other. Interest payments are not deductible and therefore included in the apportionable base, while receipts of dividends are excluded since they are derived from already apportioned profits. Income received from outside the union is taxed under the residence principle, with dividends received from outside grossed up by foreign tax, then submitted to separate company taxation in each member state with a credit for foreign tax. Thus neutrality is achieved with respect to investment flows to countries outside the union. This is important in order to create a shield of neutrality around the union to protect members from tax competition of outside tax havens.

Second, the model conforms with the subsidiarity principle by allowing each member to set its own rate of tax applicable to its own resident investors, both corporate and individual. Furthermore, this model goes further in permitting each jurisdiction to choose its own method of dividend relief (for residents only) provided it is given in a 'dividends received' rather than a 'dividends paid' form. The reader is reminded that this decentralized model allows for different rates of company tax with compensating withholding taxes to equalize the burden on income accruing to other members of the union, and agreement has to be reached on what that combined burden is to be.

It is assumed that individual income taxes in member states are differentiated according to their own preferences, with the same applying to their relationship to the CT. The principle of subsidiarity also allows each member to choose for itself whether to have partial or full crediting, to have no integration at all, or to follow the so-called 'classical' method whereby the company tax is effectively deducted from taxable dividends of the individual shareholder. The choice will depend on each state's view of taxpayer equity, a matter best left to them under the subsidiarity principle.

The only stricture required for reasons of IJE is that any relief from the company tax on dividends be extended on a 'dividends received' rather than a 'dividends paid' basis since, as noted before, the latter would interfere with the IJE principle of reciprocity. It is true that, depending on what degree of integration (0 to 100 per cent) is chosen by each member, individual shareholders resident in each state will be subject to differing effective rates of tax on their equity investments. This raises the problem of non-neutralities with respect to choice of residence by individual investors. However, this is not likely to be a major problem since individuals are less likely to shift their place of residence than are companies, and it is a necessary price to pay for the greater degree of subsidiarity that this allows.

2.2 Model II: company tax fully centralized

There is much to be said for centralization of the company tax, for the following reasons, and some would maintain that a CT does not belong at the subnational level in a federation of the US type at all (McLure, 1983); similar considerations are also of interest in the European context:

1. The central tax authority has access to more complete and co-ordinated information on the activities of companies within the union and tax administration is thereby strengthened.[14]
2. Provided that the revenue is used to finance central government functions, or for inter-member grants that do not involve return of revenue to source, the problems involved in determining source of profits of a decentralized tax are avoided.
3. To the extent that the company tax is a central tax, issues of IJE within the union do not arise since tax rates will be equalized across union members. With regard to achieving IJE between the union and outside countries, the central tax authority is in a more advantageous position to impose compensatory withholding taxes on profits accruing to residents outside the union along the lines suggested earlier, so as to achieve reciprocally equal tax shares in company profits flowing into and out of the union.
4. Centralization of the company tax can promote more neutral tax treatment of union investment and thus greater efficiency in its allocation.

---

[14] This fact has been stated as follows: '...separate national (let alone subnational) governments are not really in a position to monitor adequately the intragroup transactions characteristic of multinational enterprises. Even the U.S. experience with sections 482 (transfer pricing) and 861 (income allocation) has been far from satisfactory, as has been extensively documented in recent official reports—and the U.S. has both had more experience with, and devotes more resources to, the taxation of multinationals than any other country.' (Bird, 1986.)

This is so within the union, first, since all company profits arising within the union will be taxed at the same rate, and, second, because a central tax authority is in a better position to tax capital income received from outside the union on the residence principle. This allows the inclusion of foreign-source income with foreign tax credit, so that investments made by union residents will be taxed at the same total rate whether located within or outside the union.

While there is much to be said for full centralization of the company tax (Plasschaert, 1996), a major drawback is that it compromises the principle of subsidiarity. Whether or not centralization of the tax is acceptable to member states will depend on the degree of political solidarity they share, for fiscal independence is a key element of subsidiarity. The company tax is more closely associated with issues of IJE than most taxes since it involves the tax shares in income earned by non-resident capital, the most mobile of factors of production. On these grounds, it can be said that subsidiarity is an especially important issue with respect to the company tax. In harmonizing the tax, therefore, consideration should be given to partial centralization, whereby some of the advantages of centralization might be gained while maintaining some decentralized control over member states' shares in the base and revenue. We now consider various forms that such sharing of CT autonomy might take.

2.3 Model III: company tax partially centralized

Partial centralization of the company tax can mitigate some of the administrative and economic disadvantages of the decentralized system while maintaining some degree of subsidiarity. Central and member state governments may share responsibility for CT and, in so doing, provide alternative trade-offs between subsidiarity and other criteria.

2.3.1 Company tax at both levels

One approach is exemplified by the US system in which each level of government applies its own corporation income tax independently. Member states operate the tax on the source principle while the federal government applies its own tax on both source and residence principles. Profits are assigned among member states by use of unitary combination and apportionment based on a uniform formula (in theory if not in practice). In the US, the federal tax is dominant, the statutory rate being nearly three times that of the state with the highest rate, and state rates varying from 0 to 12 per cent. But such need not be the case. Although this model involves two levels of tax administration, the administrative cost can be lowered if the member states use the federal base with adjustments, such as unitary combination, as need to be made. Such combination may, however, stop at the water's edge (as it does for most US states), excluding foreign profits from the apportionable base.

The fact that, in this model, there is a double layer of taxation of company profits, with member states applying source-based company tax at varying rates overlaid by a residence-based central company tax, has both advantages and disadvantages. Compared with a fully decentralized system, such degree of centralization as occurs has the advantages attributable to centralization of the tax as discussed above. The centralization of part of the tax also serves to moderate effective tax rate differentials between member state taxes, provided the latter are deductible from the tax base of the central authority.[15] This deductibility acts as a kind of umbrella sheltering member states from undue tax competition. Such differentials among states that remain after allowing for deductibility will cause non-neutralities but are likely to be smaller than they would be in the absence of the central tax, and fiscal competition is likely to reduce them still further. With regard to IJE, the lower rates made possible by sharing of the tax with the central government moderate such inequities as result from differential rates placed on non-residents, and these can be removed by a system of compensatory withholding taxes as discussed in Model I. In addition, there is the potential administrative advantage of sharing with member states information available to the central tax authority. This is of particular importance in establishing water's-edge accounts or the foreign income to be included in the apportionable base, depending on which method is used to establish domestic-source income by member states.

2.3.2 Central government as collection agent

One modification to the fully decentralized model would have the central government act as the CT collection agent on behalf of member states, with the latter selecting their own rules and rates (but not base); Canada comes closest to this model. The degree of subsidiarity, neutrality, and IJE present in the fully decentralized model would remain largely unchanged but administrative costs would be reduced and stronger enforcement would result from the pooling of information. Most important, there are potentially large gains to be had in this centralized collection model from the uniform base, source rules, rules of taxable nexus, and unitary combination, in terms of administrative and compliance costs, although there is some loss of economic efficiency due to the differentiation in provincial rates.

---

[15] For instance, if tax rates in member states JA and JB are 0.20 and 0.30, respectively, and the central rate is 0.40, then the combined effective rate in JA will be $0.20 + 0.40(1 - 0.20) = 0.52$, while that in JB will be $0.30 + 0.40(1 - 0.30) = 0.58$, a differential of 0.06 rather than the differential of 0.10 between JA's and JB's rates.

2.3.3   Revenue returned to source

An alternative model of company taxation in which both central and state governments participate provides for the central tax authority to apply the tax at a uniform rate with a share of the proceeds distributed among member states according to a source-of-profits formula in the same manner as the base might be apportioned in the fully decentralized model. Such a system carries all the advantages of the fully centralized CT, while subsidiarity is not entirely lost since presumably the member states as a group have some influence on the choice of apportionment formula as well as their (equal) tax shares applied to the apportioned base. Moreover, with a uniform CT rate, each member state may also allow a uniform imputation credit for dividends received by union residents, at anywhere from 0 to 100 per cent, in line with their standards of individual taxpayer equity. Indeed, if the CT is seen as merely a conduit for capital income originating in the corporate sector, this plan does not involve any loss of subsidiarity, since autonomy over the individual income tax is preserved. Neutrality is sustained within the union since all company profits are subject to the same rate of tax, and capital export neutrality prevails since the central government taxes on the residence principle with credit for foreign tax. Furthermore, the central government may also achieve equity with respect to non-union jurisdictions by the application of compensatory withholding rates to dividends paid abroad in line with the reciprocity principle of IJE. The advantages of this model include the substantial reduction in administrative costs, uniform standards and greater efficiency of tax enforcement, more uniform and therefore more efficient and equitable apportionment of profits, and protection of the integrity of the company tax by deterring tax competition with outside nations by the central government's use of the residence principle. This latter point may become of great significance if other major players in the market for direct investment should adopt the kinds of tax structure changes that are under discussion.

This model corresponds, in some respects, to the company tax system prevailing in the German federation, except that the practice there is for a (negotiable) share of company tax revenue to be distributed to *Länder* according to where the revenue was collected rather than according to a source-of-income formula.

A modified version of this plan would leave the administration of CT in the hands of member states, but the latter would apply their own rates of tax to the tax base as defined at the central level. This would secure a uniform definition of base, and yet preserve member states' autonomy with respect to the choice of rates, but, otherwise, results are similar to those described in the fully decentralized model.

Table 3.3 Evaluation of alternative company tax models

	Model I: fully decentralized	Model II: fully centralized	Model III: partially centralized		
			[a] Tax at both levels	[b] Central government collects tax	[c] Revenue shared
IJE within union	Yes	Yes	Yes	Yes	Yes
IJE with non-members	Yes	Yes	Yes	Yes	Yes
Neutrality within union	No	Yes	Partial	No	Yes
Capital export neutrality	No	Yes	Partial	No	Yes
Subsidiarity	Yes	No	Partial	Partial	No
Administrative advantage	No	Yes	Partial	Yes	Yes

2.3.4   Evaluation of alternative company tax models

Comparison of the various models with regard to IJE as well as other criteria such as neutrality, subsidiarity, and administrative cost and quality is summarized in Table 3.3. All models are designed to yield IJE, but trade-offs are involved in selecting one model over another to achieve other objectives.

3. The case of the European Union

How do these models, aimed at the three objectives of IJE, locational neutrality, and subsidiarity, fit the case of company tax harmonization in the EU? Much will depend on the degree of cohesion among the members of the Union and the extent to which they share the same values, for these will determine the amount of co-operation that can be expected. Different models call for differing degrees of administrative co-operation and willingness to surrender sovereignty to a central taxing authority or to reach compromises on those elements of the company tax that call for uniformity. The future of the CT in the EU will therefore depend on the extent to which a centralized tax authority will develop and the form that any such transfer of tax sovereignty from member nations to a central fisc will take.

3.1   Developments to date[16]

Although the removal of regulatory restrictions on factor flows within the EU has greatly increased the potential for tax-induced misallocations of capital with ensuing downward pressure on company tax rates as tax competition takes place, progress towards harmonization of the company tax has been slow. Indeed, a greater official emphasis on the desirability of 'subsidiarity' or tax autonomy for Member States has emerged in recent years, reflecting resistance to uniformity rules and centralization of tax authority.[17]

A directive, proposed by the European Commission in 1975, aimed to equalize statutory rates of company tax between 45 and 55 per cent, with a uniform partial imputation system similar to the French *avoir fiscal* with a single rate of credit for distributed dividends. It is interesting that the proposal called for the dividends credit to be provided at the source country's end. The proposal was not approved by the European Parliament since it was believed that harmonization of the tax base should precede the equalization of statutory rates, and in 1991 it was withdrawn.

Subsequently, the Commission indicated its support for a single, but lower, statutory rate with full imputation and prepared a draft directive to

---

[16] For a fuller presentation of harmonization proposals, see Easson (1992).

[17] Unanimous consent of the Council is required for adoption of tax harmonizing measures.

harmonize the determination of taxable profits by setting guidelines for depreciation allowances, capital gains, inventory valuation, reserve provisions, valuation adjustments, and overhead costs. Tax incentives to investment were to be explicit, in the form of cash grants, investment tax credits, or preferential statutory rates rather than through the less transparent device of accelerated depreciation (Kopits, 1992). This draft directive has not been formally issued or adopted.

In 1991, two directives were adopted to alleviate 'double taxation' of EU investment income. One allows member countries to choose between residence-country exemption of foreign-source income or a credit for foreign host-country taxes on foreign-source branch income or remitted subsidiary income. It also abolishes withholding taxes on dividend remittances to the parent company in a member country of residence, except for those countries (Germany and Greece) that have a split-rate system for distributed earnings.

The Ruding Committee, appointed in 1991 to advise the Commission on the shape of future proposals, proposed harmonization of the definition of company tax base and a 30 per cent minimum statutory company tax rate (Commission of the European Communities, 1992). No basic reforms of the company tax and no change in the existing degrees of integration of company and personal income taxes in each country were included in the recommendations.

Based on the discussion of Sections 1 and 2, these proposals invite the following comments:

1. The various proposals all proceed on the assumption that the company tax is a fixture on the European fiscal scene. That is consistent with the principle of IJE, which calls for each country of source to share in the primary profits generated by non-resident investors.
2. The proposals have all been made within the framework of decentralized, source-based company taxes.[18] Since IJE calls for a system of reciprocity in tax shares in non-resident profits, either effective rates of company tax should be equalized or a system of compensatory withholding taxes should be applied to income paid to non-residents to bring about that reciprocity. The latter would require a rather elaborate set of agreements between members of the EU and non-members alike. The proposals point in the direction of harmonization of both base

---

[18] A company statute was proposed by the Commission in 1988 which would give multinational enterprises in the EU a supranational legal status. Centralization of the company tax as it applies to such enterprises would be a natural corollary to this measure, if adopted.

rules and statutory rates, or at least a minimum rate of tax as a cushion against tax competition among members. This is helpful, but again IJE will not be fully implemented until either full equalization of rates is achieved or compensatory withholding rates are applied.

3. None of the proposals envisages a departure from the current practice of separate accounting for the division of tax base. But as the internal market becomes ever more closely integrated, with the removal of non-tax barriers to cross-border investment flows, it remains to be seen whether this traditional approach is viable or whether a formula apportionment method will become necessary, as in other federal systems. Adoption of a common currency will undoubtedly render the application of formula apportionment more feasible.

4. The proposal to harmonize company tax bases and rates is helpful in promoting tax neutrality for company investment within the EU. However, capital export neutrality for direct investments made by EU residents outside the Union would require residence taxation with foreign tax credit. This may become a matter of concern to the EU in the future should the US move from income- to consumption- or wage-based taxation. Residence taxation with respect to non-EU investment is needed as a shield of neutrality around the EU in much the same manner as the common external tariff. European Union directives allow each country to tax foreign-source income with a foreign tax credit as an alternative to exemption, but this should be made mandatory to achieve neutrality for outgoing investment.

5. The issue of the tax treatment of interest paid has not been satisfactorily addressed in the EU context. Deductibility of interest from taxable company profits is evidently a widely used avenue for tax avoidance and evasion and, in the view of one analyst [Head, 1997], threatens the survival of capital income taxation in a global setting. Disallowance of interest deduction would close this loophole, render the tax more neutral, and be consistent with IJE.

6. The proposal to harmonize (i.e. make more uniform) the degree of integration of company and personal income taxes would seem to require an undue surrender of subsidiarity which is evidently very important to Member States at this stage of their historical process of integration. Income tax integration should be seen as a matter for each member to decide for itself since it relates to each member's concept of taxpayer equity under the personal income tax. Moreover, placing the revenue cost of the imputation credit on the source country's shoulders might reduce that country's tax share in non-resident profits to a level below that which is consistent with IJE. Variations in the degree of integration of CT and personal taxation may have differential effects on

the rate of personal saving among countries but should not affect the allocation of investment among them. It may affect individual investors' choice of residence, since residence taxation may be avoided by emigration. However, residence mobility is far less than investment mobility, and non-neutrality with respect to residence may be seen as a price for subsidiarity in this tax policy area.

3.2 Conclusion

It will not be an easy task to attain IJE (based on reciprocity in tax treatment of cross-border direct investment) as well as standards of economic efficiency in reforming and harmonizing the company tax within the EU, while at the same time maintaining an acceptable degree of tax autonomy for member countries. All this will require a substantial degree of co-operation—a concept, however, quite compatible with the principle of subsidiarity.[19] What are the options for harmonization of company taxes open to the EU, taking into consideration the principle of subsidiarity (calling for action by the Union only where functions cannot be performed adequately by the Member States), along with the achievement of fairness in tax shares in cross-border investment and the need to improve tax neutrality?

3.2.1 Uniformity vs. diversity

In an economic and political union that involves a fiscal role for a central government with taxing powers of its own, the company tax should be a prime candidate for centralization. In the absence of a major fiscal role for a central government, there is a strong case to be made for equalizing company tax rates at lower levels. This is so for reasons of both efficiency and IJE, while allowance for subsidiarity can be made by allowing for diversity in the personal income tax structure as well as in the degree of integration between the two taxes. There is little doubt that the high degree of uniformity in rates of tax within federal systems such as Canada, the US, and Germany, which emanates from the largely centralized nature of the tax in those countries, is likely to yield gains in terms of efficiency, IJE,

---

[19] This author does not agree with the notion that co-operation among Member States, not only in setting common rules of interjurisdictional taxation, but also in terms of exchange of information for tax administration purposes, is something to be deplored, for it is through mutual co-operation that jurisdictions can protect themselves against destabilizing, beggar-my-neighbour practices and can strengthen the integrity of their own tax systems. Many of the problems in taxing interjurisdictional capital flows efficiently and equitably arise from a dearth of co-operation among jurisdictions in prisoner's dilemma situations.

and administrative effectiveness. However, the EU does not appear at present to have the necessary degree of cohesion to make such centralization likely. It is therefore to be assumed that, for the time being, a decentralized model is more relevant to the EU case. Provided members can reach agreement on a number of key provisions with regard to the company tax, a degree of tax autonomy may be preserved while achieving some measure of neutrality and IJE for the company tax.

Since decisions by companies on investment locations are much more sensitive to tax differentials than are the residence choices by individual investors, there seems to be no reason to require all members to offer the same degree of dividend relief. Since residence mobility by individuals is as yet limited, personal income taxes may well be allowed to vary in a decentralized system. In that spirit, the relationship of company and personal income taxes is a matter of each country's preferences regarding equitable treatment of their resident individual taxpayers and therefore need not be the same for all members. Indeed, selective adoption of a schedular CT (the Nordic tax) need not be ruled out.

3.2.2   Interjurisdictional equity

It has been suggested in this chapter that the issue of interjurisdictional or inter-nation equity for the company tax be resolved by source taxation of primary profits at reciprocally equal rates. This calls for a common definition of taxable profits. Interest paid and perhaps royalties should be non-deductible. The EU may well find it increasingly difficult to determine source by the present system of separate accounting, as non-tax barriers to direct investment flows are removed. At the least, rules may have to be developed to assign profits to divisions of a unitary business located in different states. The time may indeed come when profits of unitary businesses have to be apportioned by formula. There is no single formula that is appropriate, even for a single industry, and the choice must be based on common agreement that it is reasonable and equitable.

The concept of a unitary business to which the formula is applied needs to include all activities of the unitary business, whether or not in corporate form, and for this purpose the definition of 'permanent establishment' needs to be addressed. To achieve the condition of reciprocity, it has been suggested that compensatory withholding taxes be applied at either positive or negative rates so that, together with the company tax, the effective rate on profits accruing to non-residents equals that of the recipient state. It is further suggested that this 'reciprocity rate' for the EU be set at a common level, which might be equal to the lower limit agreed on for the company tax.

It is obviously important for reasons of IJE that, whatever degree of integration between company and personal taxes is chosen by each member, it be provided at the recipient shareholder level so as not to interfere with reciprocity. Of all the EU members, it appears that only Germany and Greece, with their split-rate company taxes, would need to change their practices in this regard. Although the principle of reciprocity has hitherto only been applied with respect to withholding taxes in international tax treaties, extending the concept as a matter of IJE to primary profits, with withholding taxes used for compensatory purposes, has a compelling logic. In this spirit, it would seem easier for member countries to make those tax concessions required of them for harmonization purposes when their tax shares in non-resident profits are set at reciprocally equal levels.

3.2.3 Allocative efficiency

Contrary to the view that tax competition is desirable, the Treaty of Rome (1957), affirmed by the Single European Act (1986), correctly put the emphasis on allocative efficiency as a primary purpose of the integrated EU market. To achieve this, tax neutrality through tax harmonization is needed. Achieving a reasonable degree of tax neutrality with respect to locational choices of direct investment calls for a convergence of effective rates through limitations on the range of effective company tax rates within the EU. It also requires the residence principle to be applied to profits earned by EU investors (corporate and individual) outside the Union, while the source principle alone is applicable within the Union. Uniformity of tax rules and definition of base are important, with nominal rates allowed to range between the limits set.[20] There might, however, be a certain flexibility permitted to allow investment tax credits or grants for development purposes in lagging regions. Thus analysts have urged that reform of each Member State's CT should be a condition for co-ordination between them. Foremost among those reforms, it is suggested, is the non-deductibility of interest, to counter tax avoidance and evasion which account for many of the distortions in the present system. In this connection, it might be noted that if unitary combination with formula apportionment were adopted for determining source, it would make no difference if intra-firm interest payments were deductible or non-deductible because of the consolidation of accounts.

---

[20] Sinn (1990) has suggested that effective rates should lie in a band sufficiently narrow to make gains from tax arbitrage lower than transportation and transaction costs.

3.2.4   Administrative co-operation

Maintenance of a decentralized CT will require substantial agreement on harmonizing measures (reformed and uniform tax base, tax rules, limits on rates, reciprocity rules, and adoption of residence principle for outside profits). Administrative co-operation will also be needed, particularly for exchange of information to prevent tax evasion and generally facilitate enforcement. Such forms of co-operation with other members of the Union should not be seen as incompatible with the principle of subsidiarity. In fact, it is needed to protect fiscal independence and necessary to avoid a prisoner's dilemma brought about by unbridled fiscal competition among nations. Furthermore, fiscal co-operation should be welcomed as a forerunner of closer political ties and social solidarity in the future. Co-operation in tax matters is surely not beyond the capabilities of a group of nations that have already shown they can agree on a monetary union and common currency.

References

Bird, R. M. (1986), 'The interjurisdictional allocation of income', *Australian Tax Forum*, 3: 333–54.

Brean, D. J. S. (1992), 'Here or there? The source and residence principles of international taxation', in R. M. Bird and J. M. Mintz (eds), *Taxation to 2000 and Beyond*, Toronto: Canadian Tax Foundation.

Cnossen, S. (1996), 'Company taxes in the European Union: criteria and options for reform', *Fiscal Studies*, 17(4): 67–97.

Commission of the European Communities (1992), *Report of the Committee of Independent Experts on Company Taxation*, Luxemburg (the Ruding Report).

Easson, A. (1992), 'Harmonization of direct taxation in the European Community: from Neumark to Ruding', *Canadian Tax Journal*, 40: 600–38.

Feldstein, M. S., and Hartman, D. (1979), 'The optimal taxation of foreign source investment income', *Quarterly Journal of Economics*, 93, 613–29.

Head, J. G. (1997), 'Company tax structure and company tax incidence', *International Tax and Public Finance*, 4: 61–100.

Kopits, G. F. (ed.) (1992), *Tax Harmonization in the European Community*, Occasional Paper 94, Washington, DC: International Monetary Fund.

——and Mutén, L. (1984), 'The relevance of the unitary approach for developing countries', in C. E. McLure, Jr. (ed.), *The State Corporation Income Tax: Issues in Worldwide Unitary Combination*, Stanford, CA: Hoover Institution Press.

McLure, C. E., Jr. (1983), 'Assignment of corporate income taxes in a federal system', in C. E. McLure, Jr. (ed.), *Tax Assignment in Federal Countries*,

Canberra: Centre for Research on Federal Financial Relations, Australian National University.

——(1984), 'Defining a unitary business: an economist's view', in C. E. McLure, Jr. (ed.), *The State Corporation Income Tax: Issues in Worldwide Unitary Combination,* Stanford, CA: Hoover Institution Press.

Musgrave, P. B. (1969), *United States Taxation of Foreign Investment Income: Issues and Arguments,* Cambridge, MA: Harvard Law School International Tax Program.

——(1974), 'International tax differentials for multinational corporations: equity and efficiency considerations', in C. S. Shoup (ed.), *The Impact of Multinational Corporations on Development and on International Relations,* Technical Papers (Taxation), New York: Department of Economic and Social Affairs, United Nations.

——(1991), 'Fiscal coordination and competition in an international setting', in L. Eden (ed.), *Retrospectives on Public Finance,* Durham, NC: Duke University Press.

——(1996), 'Current proposals for tax reform in a globalized setting', paper presented to the 52nd Congress of the International Institute of Public Finance, Tel Aviv.

Musgrave, R. A., and Musgrave, P. B. (1972), 'Inter-nation equity', in R. M. Bird and J. G. Head (eds), *Modern Fiscal Issues: Essays in Honour of Carl S. Shoup,* Toronto: University of Toronto Press.

OECD (1963), *Draft Double Taxation Convention on Income and Capital,* Paris: Fiscal Committee, Organization for Economic Co-operation and Development.

Plasschaert, S. (1996), 'A European-Union tax on the consolidated profits of multinational enterprises', unpublished manuscript.

Richman (Musgrave), P. B. (1963), *Taxation of Foreign Investment Income,* Baltimore, MD: Johns Hopkins Press.

Sato, M., and Bird, R. M. (1975), 'International aspects of the taxation of corporations and shareholders', *IMF Staff Papers,* 22: 384–455.

Seligman, E. R. A. (1928), *Double Taxation and International Fiscal Co-operation,* New York: Macmillan.

Sinn, H-W. (1990), 'Tax harmonization and tax competition in Europe', *European Economic Review,* 34: 489–504.

Slemrod, J. B. (1995), 'Free trade taxation and protectionist taxation', *International Tax and Public Finance,* 2: 471–90.

Smith, E. H. (1976), 'Allocation to provinces of the taxable income of corporations: how the federal–provincial allocation rules evolved', *Canadian Tax Journal,* 24: 545–71.

4

Source- vs. residence-based taxation in the European Union: the wrong question?

RICHARD M. BIRD and J. SCOTT WILKIE

> Historical rules based on geographic source of income and nationality of taxpayers, and jurisprudential concepts that emerged in the early twentieth century, are simply not adequate in today's world.
>
> Ross, 1992, p. 947

> As technological change weakens the links between economic activity and a particular location, traditional tax concepts, such as 'residence' and 'source' become difficult to apply.
>
> Owens, 1997, p. 594

Observations such as these raise questions about the usefulness of the traditional 'source' and 'residence' principles as devices to define the framework of neutrality and equity choices. Indeed, are these principles alternatives, or do they rather establish limits of a continuum on which the optimal position is in increasing doubt, owing to contemporary economic developments? We suggest in this chapter that 'source' and 'residence' are best understood as proxies for a practical paradigm to allocate world-wide income (and tax base) in line with underlying economic income and that we may need a new paradigm to achieve this goal more adequately in the world of today and, even more, that of tomorrow.

The authors are associated with the International Centre for Tax Studies (ICTS) of the University of Toronto and are especially grateful for support extended to ICTS through the assistance of Albert J. Radler by three European tax firms—Francis Lefebvre (France), Loyens & Volkmaars (the Netherlands), and Oppenhoff & Radler (Germany)—which initially led them to work on this subject. They are also grateful for helpful comments on an earlier version of this chapter received from participants at the ISPE conference, in particular Sijbren Cnossen and Henk Vording, as well as those by an anonymous reviewer.

In Section 1, we consider whether 'source vs. residence' is really the question at issue in this discussion and conclude that it is not. In Section 2, we briefly review the current European Union (EU) debate from this perspective, broadening the discussion in Section 3 to consider the issue in a more general context. We conclude with some preliminary thoughts on potentially more productive ways to focus the discussion of how to determine who gets how much in the international tax world.

The waters of international tax policy explored in this chapter are troubled, murky, and deep. We do not pretend to have found our way successfully to the promised land that may, or may not, lie on the other side. All we have attempted to do is to suggest a potentially more useful starting-point than the essentially sterile 'source vs. residence' question from which to begin to explore some of the critical problems currently confronting those interested in international tax policy.

1. Is 'source vs. residence' the question?

In essence, the 'source vs. residence' debate concerns the legitimacy and practicality of asserting tax jurisdiction by members of a community of nations whose economic relations with each other require acknowledgement of intersecting fiscal claims. Jurisdictions always have a choice: to recognize and accommodate competing tax claims grounded in some legitimate connection of an income-earning activity to a jurisdiction, or to go it alone and let others worry about overlapping tax claims. By convention—though importantly not in accordance with any systemic or normative international tax principle—most countries have adopted a regime that acknowledges and accommodates competing claims, for the most part with substantial international agreement as to both the underlying objectives and the means to achieve them. The foundation of this conventional regime is economic. Its essential purpose is to allocate world-wide tax base among jurisdictions based on the economic connection of the activity to the competing jurisdictions. All modes of international tax allocation, whether they take the form of domestic foreign tax credit systems or contractual arrangements in tax treaties, in effect attempt to establish a correspondence (historically transactional) between economic income in this sense and financial income as reflected in information available to tax authorities. The fundamental question at issue is thus how countries can best assert inherently territorially-based claims to income in a global context.

Viewed in this way, both the source and residence principles as traditionally discussed may be viewed as theoretical guidelines intended to explain and test the utility of particular allocative or jurisdictional decisions. The decisions in question, however, are (1) inherently economic in concept and commercial in practice, (2) unlikely to accord fully with any pure expression of either underlying principle, and (3) necessarily influenced, both in practice and in theory, by the specific circumstances to which they are applied. As the world has developed, and is developing, however, we suggest that confining discussion of the fundamental tax jurisdiction issue within the limits of the traditional 'source vs. residence' paradigm no longer provides a useful framework. The 'source or residence' dichotomy does not deal adequately with the core problems confronting international tax policy today.

These problems include: (1) increased international commercial activity of a sort not clearly associated in economic terms with national jurisdictions; (2) lack of co-ordination between jurisdictions with respect to rules separating the taxation of corporate income at the corporate and shareholder levels; (3) the absence of a coherent basis for distinguishing between payments or distributions by corporations, some of which are deductible for corporate tax purposes and some of which are not; and (4) pressures arising from what may be called fiscal 'free-riding' when some recipients of income are not taxable owing to their tax-exempt status within a particular jurisdiction's tax system (or, more generally, because the jurisdiction as a whole is a 'tax haven').

Such problems are, in a way, the tax policy analogues to many of the broader issues arising as a result of economic liberalization (Slemrod, 1995). In the fiscal literature, 'globalization' is little more than an imprecise code word for the fact that national tax authorities everywhere are in trouble owing to the increasing irrelevance of national borders with respect to determining the location of economic activity in traditional tax policy terms.[1] The problems have always been there, but increased global economic activity has raised the stakes in allocating a finite world tax base among competing national claimants whose relative claims are adjudicated at most by convention and contract or unilateral concession—devices that establish or reflect the limits of disagreement as much as they do principles of agreement.

As the recent discussion of the taxation implications of electronic commerce has emphasized, more explicit attention needs to be paid to what intersecting open economies (and tax jurisdictions) have in fact always been trying to do through the jurisdictional and allocative judgements

---

[1] It is easy to overdo the scale and scope of 'globalization', however: see, for example, the interesting empirical analysis of the continuing great importance of borders with respect to trade even between the US and Canada (post-NAFTA) in McCallum (1995) and Helliwell (1996). None the less, the issue is clearly with us, and seems much more likely to intensify in the future than to go away.

that have traditionally been expressed in the income tax sphere by the notions of source and residence.[2] The distortionary effects created by the interaction of direct capital income tax systems can, we suggest, realistically be ameliorated only by intelligent mutual co-ordination and case- by-case accommodation of competing national tax claims. Since we do not think that national tax systems, even within the EU, will soon be harmonized in any significant sense, solutions that require such harmonization to succeed have a low probability of success in dealing with these problems.[3] In the circumstances, a more pragmatic (though perhaps less 'principled') approach seems the only feasible way to deal with international tax conflicts.

Of course, in a sense, there is little new in our arguments. Virtually everyone writing on this subject recognizes that neither a 'pure' source nor a 'pure' residence principle exists. In fact, source and residence are not, and, even in theoretical terms, never have been, alternatives. These so-called 'principles' are best considered as constructs intended to guide the evaluation in any particular context of the relative desirability and justifiability of taxation on a territorial or personal basis. The source principle has not dominated tax policy decisions concerning jurisdiction in part because of the difficulty of satisfactorily identifying (and meaningfully describing in legislative terms) the source of income. In addition, for obvious reasons, governments tend to be more concerned with maximizing national welfare and the fair treatment of their residents than with the fate of non-resident recipients of income generated within their borders. Consequently, almost everywhere some form of hybrid residence–source system is in operation, with the source approach given primacy in the taxation of direct investment income (supported by the foreign tax credit system of major residence-based capital exporters) and the residence principle taking primacy with respect to passive (portfolio) capital income (though, in practice, the hold of the residence principle is, despite repeated international

[2] See the interesting discussion in Warren (1994). As in the original European discussion, much of the recent US literature on electronic commerce has focused on consumption tax issues (origin/destination)—see, for example, McLure (1997b) and the report of the National Tax Association Internet Tax Study Panel (1997)—but of course similar problems arise to an even greater extent with respect to income taxes.

[3] Systemic uniformity may still be required to cope with the free-riding problem noted above, but this problem is, to a large extent, separable from the more basic problems caused by the 'dematerialization' of economic activity (King, 1996). Moreover, the solutions major countries, acting independently or in concert, are likely to adopt to the latter problems will almost certainly significantly reduce free-riding in any case (see Section 4).

declarations to the contrary, weak even in this area owing to the persistence of withholding taxes, particularly on cross-border flows of dividends).[4]

Economists tend often to favour the residence principle because of the undesirable allocative effects (from a world-wide perspective) of the source principle if statutory tax rates differ between countries. Many legal scholars tend to favour it also as a logical component of achieving horizontal equity among domestic taxpayers.[5] Administrators and those more concerned with what *can* be done than with what *should* be done have, on the other hand, tended to favour the source principle for pragmatic reasons, reflecting the considerable practical difficulties of extending the residence principle beyond national borders without hard-to-secure co-operation from foreign tax authorities. In practice, exactly how this balance has been struck has, over time, reflected the outcome of the ongoing (and sometimes overt) conflict between countries that inevitably lies at the root of the international tax policy conundrum.[6]

The emphasis on these various factors varies substantially from author to author—contrast the stress on allocative efficiency as a goal in Frenkel et al. (1991), for instance, with the more balanced assessment of other policy objectives and administrative constraints in Tanzi (1995). But in recent years all seem to agree that these issues have come back into the centre of tax policy discussion owing to the rise of new thoughts and dark forebodings about the future, if any, of corporate taxation in the emerging global world of financial innovation (Warren, 1993; OECD, 1997; Avi-Yonah and Swartz, 1997; Alworth, 1998) and electronic commerce (US Department of the Treasury, 1996; Glicklich et al., 1996; Dunahoo and Carlisle, 1997). As the OECD (1991, pp. 175–6) puts it:

The removal of non-tax barriers ... to international capital flows and the globalisation of financial markets, has focused attention on the effect of taxation on foreign direct investment. Governments and others are concerned about how taxation may influence inward and outward direct investment flows and the ways in which these investments are financed. They are also concerned with the ways in which the revenues from international transactions are shared between countries and the new avenues opened up by globalisation for the avoidance of tax. These factors suggest that governments may need to re-evaluate the traditional criteria

---

[4] Owing to fears of increasing business costs, similar taxes are seldom imposed on interest income, which gives rise to considerable problems in a world in which it is not always easy to characterize a flow as interest, dividends, royalties, or whatever. See, for instance, the Canadian system discussed in Brean et al. (1991).

[5] See Kingson (1981) for a classic statement; also Musgrave (1969). For a contrary position, see Vogel (1990).

[6] See, for example, Head (1997) and Slemrod (1995).

used to assess domestic tax policies. An examination of these issues requires an analysis of not only the domestic tax regimes but also how these regimes interact in the context of existing international agreement.

The villain, of course, is 'globalization'—an imprecise term that to some degree has become the mantra of analysts captivated and confused by challenges to the relevance and effectiveness of national tax and trade policies arising from transnational activity, particularly in contexts such as the EU and North America (NAFTA), in which such activity is encompassed in a new(ish) institutional framework.[7]

Globalization implies the increased intersection of national or regional economies, in a setting in which fewer intrinsic characteristics of economic activity associate it with (or locate it in) any particular political jurisdiction ('dematerialization', as King (1996) calls it). Free trade areas and economic unions increase the importance of addressing impediments to the efficient allocation of resources within those zones. In principle, nationals and aliens are, as a rule, supposed to be treated in essentially the same way by political jurisdictions within such zones: the ideal is a kind of economic unity within which economic activity is directed by market factors. In this setting, it is important to determine whether and how there should be greater integration of national tax policies and practices towards harmonization or even uniformity.[8]

As suggested above, such problems arise in part because the existing system of taxing international capital flows is fundamentally inadequate to deal with the reality of the modern economic environment. Whether one thinks the source or the residence principle is more desirable on efficiency or equity or administrative grounds is secondary to the more basic choice of how countries are to tax companies (and, more broadly, capital income) in the world of the twenty-first century. Once that choice is made, we argue that the source—residence choice will essentially be settled without ever having to be decided explicitly along the lines of the traditional debate.

The real issue is thus how to establish a meaningful correspondence between measurable economic income associated with a tax jurisdiction and the financial income that can be reached by that jurisdiction's tax rules on a basis that compels respect for that claim by other jurisdictions that have an interest in the activity, its outcome, or the actors engaged in the activity.[9]

---

[7] See McDaniel (1994) and other authors in the same journal on the tax aspects of NAFTA.

[8] See, for example, Daly (1997) on these issues in the context of the pending Multilateral Agreement on Investment.

[9] As Rosenbloom (1994, p. 595) put a similar argument in the context of NAFTA, 'Of course, taxes impede and interfere with activities, if one compares a

The existing 'system' of international income taxation is posited on a set of facts that no longer holds, if indeed it ever did. The gap between economic reality and the assumptions underlying the existing international tax system needs to be bridged before the source—residence question can be insightfully considered—and, if it is bridged, that question will be answered without recourse to the usual discussion of the source and residence principles.

2. The EU debate

The EU is an interesting laboratory—a kind of world tax base in microcosm—in which to evaluate issues of tax jurisdiction and co-ordination.[10] The debate over source vs. residence is by no means confined to the EU context,[11] but the EU furnishes a unique opportunity to consider this discussion because at its core is a degree of economic uniformity, and a corresponding subordination of Member State policies impinging on borderless economic interchange, that in a sense create the ideal economic world in microcosm. The Member States have widely divergent tax systems, particularly in the areas of company taxation (Cnossen, 1996). To some extent, the reform of company taxation in the EU has been closely identified with the question of the choice of source- vs. residence-based taxation. For example, Cnossen (1996, p. 80) argues that '...most practical considerations imply that the choice is not between the source principle and the residence principle for taxing company profits, but between the source principle and no tax at all'. None the less, the residence principle

world in which taxes exist with one in which they do not....But short of dispensing with government functions altogether...there really are not alternatives. There are poor, better and still better tax systems, and their nature may change over time and from country to country, but some tax system, impeding some activity, is inevitable....The argument over whether, and to what extent, source basis taxation should be reduced in the name of avoiding double taxation is a tax policy argument. It does not yield easy and immutable answers. Rather, it calls for judgment on a case-by-case basis, and it may well produce the sort of complex division of revenues found in the US treaty arrangement with Canada.'

[10] Since one of us is a lawyer, we should perhaps note explicitly that our discussion of the EU case is not intended as a commentary on the legal characteristics of EU law but rather simply to note some points that, from our comfortable distance, seem to raise important questions about how the source vs. residence debate should be perceived, and perhaps resolved, in the EU.

[11] See, for example, Brean (1992) for a strong argument in favour of the source approach and, more recently, US Department of the Treasury (1996) for a statement in favour of the residence approach.

clearly remains, for many, an important and relevant concept with respect to the proper final allocation of European tax base among competing national claimants. Even the Ruding Committee seems not to have stepped beyond the basic source–residence divide as an expedient or precondition to the effective implementation of its specific recommendations to achieve a degree of harmonization bordering, perhaps, on unification of members' corporate tax systems.[12]

Apart from the typical ways countries now recognize multiple tax claims (foreign tax credits and income tax treaties), there is no mechanism to require or effect any degree of modification of domestic tax systems in deference to the overriding objectives of the EC Treaty.[13] The basic notion of transnational equality of treatment is reflected in Article 6 of the Treaty, which provides that 'Within the scope of application of this Treaty, and without prejudice to any special provisions contained therein, any discrimination on grounds of nationality shall be prohibited'. The principles of 'freedom of movement', 'freedom of establishment', 'freedom of provision of services', and 'freedom of capital movements' are considered to be outgrowths of this basic principle. Article 48 provides for the '... free movement of workers ... within the Community ...'. Article 52 states, in its entirety, that 'Companies or firms formed in accordance with the law of a Member State and having their registered office, central administration or principal place of business within the Community shall, for the purposes of this Chapter, be treated in the same way as natural persons who are nationals of Member States'. Article 59 states that 'Within the framework of the provisions set out below, restrictions on the freedom to provide services within the Community shall be progressively abolished during the transitional period in respect of nationals of Member States who are established in a State of the Community other that of the person for whom the services are supplied'. And Article 73b, an outgrowth of the Treaty of Maastricht, provides, in material part, that 'Within the

---

[12] See Radler and Blumenberg (1992).

[13] As Tirard (1996) notes, 'If the harmonization in indirect tax matters is almost achieved, on the contrary the harmonization of direct taxation in Community Law is still in the embryo stage [reference is made to the Parent–Subsidiary Directive, in Council Directive 90/434/EEC, and to the Merger Directive, in Council Directive 90/435/EEC], since the Treaty does not give any directions to Community authorities to harmonize Member State's (*sic*) direct taxes. Indeed, direct taxation is under the sole jurisdiction of Member States.

'This said, even in the fields which come under their sole jurisdiction (i.e., direct taxation), Member States cannot adopt measures which would have the effect of unjustifiably blocking the free movement of persons, services or capital or infringe the fundamental principles laid down in the Treaty.'

framework of the provisions set out in this Chapter, all restrictions on the movement of capital between Member States, and between Member States and third countries shall be prohibited'.[14]

Despite this apparently sweeping assertion, however—and also introduced by the Treaty of Maastricht—Article 73d of the EC Treaty seemingly subordinates the freedom of capital movements otherwise offered broadly in Article 73b by confirming (1) '... the right of Member States: (a) to apply the relevant provisions of their tax law which distinguish between taxpayers who are not in the same situation with regard to their place of residence or with regard to the place where their capital is invested'; (2) the sustainability of restrictions on the freedom of establishment 'compatible with this Treaty';[15] and (3) that the qualifications in (1) and (2) '... shall not constitute a means of arbitrary discrimination or a disguised restriction on the free movement of capital and payments as defined in Article 73b'.

Strictly, the non-discrimination prescription in the EC Treaty is cast in terms of nationality.[16] However, the European Court of Justice (ECJ) has been willing to interpret the Treaty with an eye to both overt and less obvious, or indirect, forms of discrimination, notably in the context of Article 52, leading, for example, to a determination that refusing a national of one state access to another on the basis of freedom of establishment because of the national's residence was prohibited[17]—although, more generally, if discrimination is on the basis of residence rather than nationality, the non-discrimination prohibition may be of more limited effect.[18] Indeed, on at least one occasion, the ECJ explicitly asserted that discrimination otherwise prohibited by the EC Treaty could be justified to sustain

[14] Restrictions on payments between Member States and between Member States and third countries are also prohibited.

[15] Gammie and Brannan (1995) note that the freedom of establishment (Article 52) is subject to the capital movement Article, which in their view implies that (1) above is likely to apply to portfolio rather than direct investment, in the expectation that the circumstances of portfolio investors are more likely to be distinguishable by their residence.

[16] This is frequently a difficulty with non-discrimination provisions in tax treaties, even those finding their pedigree in the Model Tax Convention of the OECD (Lewin and Wilkie, 1993). Generally, in the OECD context, resident and non-resident taxpayers are not considered to be in comparable circumstances. Consequently, as generally understood, applying tax rules differently to non-residents on the basis of non-residence and not nationality is not encompassed within the prescription of nationality non-discrimination (Avery Jones, 1995).

[17] Case C-80/94 *Wielockx v. Inspecteur der Directe Belastingen*, CJEC, 11 August 1995, *Wielockx.*

[18] *Finanzant Koln-Alstadt* v. *Schumacker*, ECJ Case C-279/93, *Schumacker.*

the coherent application of a Member State's tax system, given underlying public policy reasons grounded in maintaining an effective coherent national tax system.[19] We cannot consider the complex and difficult discussion that these and other pertinent decisions have inspired.[20] But it does seem fair to say that it is not at all clear from the current legal position what degree of direct income tax co-ordination may be anticipated, let alone required, in the EU in the future.

To sum up, the EC Treaty does not directly address the harmonization or co-ordination of direct income taxation, but it contains two main principles relevant to this issue—non-discrimination and freedom of establishment.[21] Some see these principles as implying that a certain degree of direct income tax harmonization is needed (or, indeed, even anticipated) to avoid distortions in the achievement of the Treaty's overriding goal to establish an economic, commercial, and monetary union. It might even be suggested that the existence and context of the Treaty make it unnecessary to introduce any specific rules on direct income tax harmonization.[22] This line of thought implies that the Treaty establishes an expectation of supranational co-operation that transcends national jurisdictions that would otherwise be pre-eminent. If so, the tax policy of Member States would clearly be subordinated to the achievement of EU goals and effectively to something in the nature of a supranational tax order that imposes its own standards of tax policy coherence and co-ordination.[23]

[19] *Bachmann v. Belgian State*, ECJ 28 January 1992 Case Rs.C-204/90, *Bachmann.*

[20] Gammie and Brannan (1995), for example, note that '...the fact that a company may be non-resident does not entitle the Member State to apply arbitrary tax rules of a discriminatory nature—there must be some justification for the differential treatment'.

[21] These concepts are reflected principally in Articles 6, 48, 52, 58, 59, and 73 of the Treaty (Tirard, 1996).

[22] As Tirard (1996) may be read to suggest, the broad context of a treaty contemplating the elimination of barriers distorting economic, commercial, and monetary circumstances, and indeed designed to create a union, implies that all barriers, including those induced by tax systems, are in play. On the other hand, the Treaty of Maastricht enshrines the subsidiarity principle, which would seem consistent with unlimited tax sovereignty, subject to the traditional ways of international tax co-ordination (Hinnekens, 1992).

[23] The Ruding Committee's findings (Commission of the European Communities, 1992) could be interpreted consistently with this perception of the Treaty. While the Ruding Committee did not recommend a European tax system as such, its harmonization recommendations show an awareness of how deeply co-ordinated the member national tax systems may need to be in order to serve the overriding objectives of the Treaty of Rome.

On the other hand, the Treaty of Maastricht in effect enshrines in the EC Treaty the hegemony of national tax jurisdiction and national tax policies of countries within the Union—while at the same time appearing to mandate free capital flows.[24] Specifically, the Treaty of Maastricht seemingly entrenched the principle of subsidiarity, or what Cnossen (1996) has called the 'operational independence' of member tax systems.[25] But this principle must be understood in the context of broad principles of long standing in the EC Treaty that appear to imply that distortions arising from the inconsistent formulation and application of national tax policies should be mitigated. The apparent conflict may perhaps be resolved in various ways without requiring the imposition of a uniform 'Union tax'. Consistent domestic rules with respect to company taxes and corporate group finance may, for example, suffice to achieve the apparently mandated level of EU-wide agreement.[26] Subsidiarity could then be interpreted as, in effect, simply an accounting device to determine who gets how much of the group income, thus recasting the issue in terms of the source vs. residence debate, as Cnossen (1996) to some extent does.

This approach, however, tends to lose the real issues with respect to company income tax in an international context. We suggest that the collision between ultimate economic co-ordination (i.e. a comprehensive economic union) and the maintenance of a substantial degree of tax sovereignty raises even more compelling tax policy issues. For example, a country's choice to deliver and finance public goods either through the tax system (tax expenditures) or as direct expenditures should presumably be made without undue influence or intervention from choices made by

[24] Gammie and Brannan (1995) consider the interaction of these issues arising from the Treaty of Maastricht in an article evaluating the implications for the (then) UK corporate tax imputation regime.

[25] In this connection, however, consider also the earlier discussion with respect to Articles 73b and 73d of the EC Treaty.

[26] Cnossen (1996) instructively draws a parallel to the value added tax (VAT) system in the EU, suggesting that something similar may emerge with respect to company taxation. The parallels may be even stronger than he suggests, given the emerging extension of the concept of 'location of supply' in reaction to changes in electronic commerce and financial innovation. This extension of the destination principle of VAT to define the source of supply as the location of the consumer is interestingly parallel to the recent US Department of the Treasury (1996) proposal to, in effect, extend the concept of residence to encompass a wide variety of transactions clearly not carried out in the US under the usual concept of residence. For further discussion of these issues in the US context, see the references in note 2.

other jurisdictions.[27] How public goods and services are delivered should not depend upon international tax interactions. On the other hand, in the EU context, the concept of non-discrimination suggests the need to extend what might be perceived as national tax preferences to outsiders (Tirard, 1996). Tentative, controversial steps to bridging the divide between union and separation have been made by the European Court of Justice, which has, as noted above, considered whether discriminatory tax treatment of non-nationals should be permitted on the basis of the coherence of domestic tax policy. Such 'coherence', if it is indeed a relevant policy concern, would provide a basis within the EC Treaty for asserting what the principle of subsidiarity suggests is pre-eminent: the ability of national tax jurisdictions to use tax policy as an instrument of social and economic design unimpaired by the choices or policy imperatives of others.[28]

On the whole, the present situation in the EU appears to be a precarious balance of the competing principles of union and subsidiarity. Several directives and a convention dealing with the taxation of corporations have targeted the most prominent economic actors—multinational corporations—within the Union, allowing them to reorganize their operations and to consolidate without income unsupported by a real economic accretion giving rise to tax (the Merger Directive) as well as to recognize both the reality of the allocation questions implied by complex transnational economic activity (the Parent–Subsidiary Directive) and the need to allocate the income of multinational enterprises in a definitive manner (the Arbitration Convention).[29] Such measures accept the existence of a comprehensive economic union but acknowledge the reality of the subsidiarity of tax

---

[27] See, for example, Ip and Mintz (1992), who postulate this as one of the objectives of tax policy in a federal union. Of course, one may think that countries often overdo the use of tax expenditures (Surrey and McDaniel, 1985), but that is a quite different issue.

[28] For a strongly expressed view advocating limits on any principle of 'coherence' that undermines the effective application of the non-discrimination principle in the Treaty, see Knobbe-Keuk (1994). In her view, while Member States have jurisdiction to devise their own rules, they may not apply them in defiance of the overriding Community law in the Treaty, reflected in the Articles of the Treaty noted above. The view of 'coherence' we imply in the text is broader, recognizing the various ways in which Member States can deliver public goods or finance national infrastructure and programmes. We do not see why accomplishing these goals using the tax system—i.e. through tax expenditures—justifies intervention based on extranational principles that would be mitigated (or at least muted) if direct expenditures were used instead.

[29] See Council Directives 90/434/EEC and 90/435/EEC of 23 July 1990 and EC Convention 90/436/EEC.

policy and administration. They set a limited but nevertheless meaningful scope for co-ordination that does not require explicit harmonization, and they focus on the correspondence between economic and tax, or financial, income in a practical way, notwithstanding a certain degree of expediency. This is, we suggest, exactly the right way to deal with the basic problems that lie at the heart of the 'source vs. residence' debate.

Consider, for example, the current EU debate on the apparently conflicting goals of neutrality and subsidiarity. At some level, this argument is meaningless since no tax system anywhere exists in isolation. *All* domestic tax systems are, to paraphrase Cnossen (1996), simultaneously both operationally independent (subsidiarity) and, so to speak, operationally co-ordinated (neutrality) through existing international tax arrangements. Free trade, the removal of restrictions on factor movements, and (perhaps) monetary union may make this situation more apparent, but they do not fundamentally change it.[30]

From one perspective, what the EU is attempting to do is, as it were, to rewrite the current international tax system in EU terms. Currently prevailing international tax rules, however, essentially presume that there is a rough correspondence between financial flows across borders and the economic reality of the territorial base of economic activity. Such correspondence no longer holds for the world as a whole, let alone for the EU. The old rules of the international tax game—separate-entity arm's-length pricing, permanent establishment, non-discrimination, source, residence, etc.—decreasingly serve to carve up the international tax base in a reasonable and sustainable way, whether in the EU or more generally. At the very least, something has to be done to shore up these constructs through measures such as source taxation of interest (Huizinga, 1994) if national tax systems are to retain any coherence in the face of the new reality. More boldly, we suggest that it is useful to put these constructs aside and reconsider more fundamentally the nature of the basic problems with which they try to deal.

Of course, theory and reality have already been reconciled to some extent in most OECD countries by, in essence, applying source tax to direct foreign investment and (in principle, if not so much in practice) residence tax to portfolio investment. But this solution depends for its implementation on (1) distinguishing between these two types of investment, (2) establishing some nexus for taxation for each jurisdiction (for example, by way of the concept of permanent establishment), and

---

[30] See Slemrod (1995) for a thought-provoking treatment of the parallels and differences between 'free trade' and 'protectionist' taxation in both commodity and factor markets.

(3) measuring the taxable income attributable to each jurisdiction with nexus. These are the building blocks of any meaningful international tax system.

The basic problem that we see arises because the nature of each of these problems is such that they can only be resolved in practice in the modern economic world by applying an essentially arbitrary procedure. Whether that procedure is a straightforward agreed split (as in a formulary approach) or a more complex, but equally arbitrary, detour through the byways of permanent establishment, source vs. residence, separate-entity arm's-length pricing, and so on is an important, but secondary, issue. The *central* issue is that *any* procedure adopted is inherently arbitrary: it is simply a construct, with no intrinsic or other significance except to approximate some verifiable correspondence between economic and financial, or tax, income in respect of competing national claimants. As Surrey (1978) said years ago, adherents of the comprehensive income tax principle are logically required to attempt to match income and expenses rationally on a transaction-by-transaction basis that is internationally coherent. But as Surrey also recognized, there may come a point at which further stretching of reality on this arbitrarily constructed logical rack is no longer feasible, and a more straightforward look at the core problem—determining the size of the pie and how to divide it—is required. We suggest that the time has come for such a look, not just in the context of the EU but by the international tax community as a whole.

3. The broader context

Perhaps the most fundamental rule of international taxation is that there *are* no rules of international taxation—just domestic tax rules applied to cross-border flows taking into account (or not) that such flows may be subject to taxation in more than one jurisdiction. If income (in some sense) arises (somehow defined) within a jurisdiction, that jurisdiction is likely to tax it. Bilateral tax treaties, for example, are international agreements on how to allocate income among jurisdictions with which the taxpayer arguably has a sufficiently strong connection for them to assert their right to tax. The overt purpose of such arrangements is to limit 'double taxation'. But their effect is that the countries involved admit that other countries are, in some sense, entitled to impose tax. In other words, international tax rules are essentially an attempt to work out a division of economic income between two political jurisdictions: they are inherently pragmatic and they are purpose-driven. Normative rationalizations of particular sets of operational rules may come along later and become widely accepted. But it is important to understand that, in a real sense, the rules precede the principles.[31]

That the objective of international tax rules is to achieve some degree of measurable and administrable correspondence between economic and financial or tax income is evident, for example, in the concept of 'permanent establishment' and the embedded companion notion of 'carrying on a business in a place'. At a time when factor inputs were more clearly associated with political (and therefore tax) jurisdictions because of their physical characteristics, traditional expressions of financial income or profit generally approximated some meaningful measure of economic income. Increasingly, however, important factor inputs contributing to the earning of income are not, and do not need to be, closely tied to particular political jurisdictions. Neither political divisions nor the formal characteristics of corporate organization and commercial activity any longer serve necessarily to indicate the location of economic activity or the 'source' of economic income.[32]

From this perspective, 'source' and 'residence' are simply guidelines intended to help in assigning and assessing tax jurisdiction in the sense discussed above, attaching income either to the jurisdiction with which

---

[31] As Edmund Burke once said, 'Circumstances (which some gentlemen pass for nothing) give in reality to every political [or, we suggest, economic, or legal] principle its distinguishing color and discriminating effect. The circumstances are what render every civil and political scheme beneficial or noxious to mankind' (*Reflections* (1790), as cited in Bredvold and Ross (1967, p. 72)).

[32] Consider Article 9 of the OECD Model Tax Convention. This is the well-known 'transfer pricing' article. Despite what some discussion of transfer pricing may imply, this article is not transactional but rather deals with the problem of attaining a reasonable allocation of 'profit'—a net income concept—among members of a controlled group. This is intrinsically an economic problem. As the 1995 guidelines of the OECD on transfer pricing (OECD, 1995), and the evolving transfer pricing experience of other countries (notably the US), demonstrate, more attention is now being paid to the imperfections of measuring economic income using legal and financial accounting precepts that may bear no relationship to economic reality. Increasingly, economic analysis is being used to evaluate whether there is a sustainable correspondence between economic and financial income with respect to the locations in which a multinational enterprise conducts activities through its legal components. In effect, the functions performed by (value contributed by) and the risks assumed by particular components must be assessed in the context of the economic whole which is the enterprise. Recognition of the reality of the inherently unitary nature of most multinational enterprises has, it seems, arrived by the back door—despite the vehement denials still posted on the main entrance in most countries.

the economic activity may be most clearly associated or to that in which the owner (if identifiable) resides. The key question is not whether one or another principle should be applied, but whether the times have changed sufficiently that the rules need to be changed also to secure fair (acceptable, workable) results. At a more fundamental level, what is at issue here is the difficult and controversial concept of 'fairness' in an international context—that is, 'fair shares' for all relevant claimants to the tax pie—as indeed earlier writers (for example, Musgrave and Musgrave (1972)) explicitly recognized. When two countries have such different concepts of what is fair that the claims of one seem to the other to be beyond the realm of plausible fairness, agreement is unlikely to be reached. On the other hand, as a recent survey of the growing literature on such self-serving biases suggests, '... there are many problems that people are unable to solve in the abstract, but are able to solve when placed in a real-world context' (Babcock and Loewenstein, 1997, p. 122). That is, what principle cannot resolve, practice sometimes can—which is one way of looking at our argument in this chapter.

Since the first League of Nations efforts in the 1920s (Carroll, 1978; Picciotto, 1992), the international tax community has developed a set of rules and principles that have served it moderately well in devising and implementing tax regimes that can both identify taxable international flows and collect taxes. The existing rules—and the principles derived from them—were designed to divide income between jurisdictions in a fashion that roughly proxied economic reality. But the reliability and the relevance of these jurisdictional markers are increasingly called into question as high-value intangible property and various manifestations of financial property or money increasingly dominate international economic flows, since the existence and exchange of such property is inherently difficult to tie to national territories either conceptually or in practice. The neutrality vs. subsidiarity version of the residence vs. source debate that has recently been emphasized by some in the EU context does not alter the reality that, in *both* cases, what are at issue are two different, and more fundamental, questions: (1) 'what is the best way in principle to "map" financial flows to the underlying economic activity?' and (2) 'what can actually be done?'[33]

The fundamental problem is that an economic solution is needed to assess and divide the tax base. *Any* attainable solution will inevitably be somewhat artificial. But it need not be as artificial as the present system, rooted as it is in a simpler day in which there was, on the whole, a much

---

[33] The similarity of this way of framing the question to much of the discussion with respect to the conceptual and administrative aspects of formulary taxation is, of course, not a coincidence: see, for example, McLure (1984) and Bird (1988).

closer correspondence between financial flows and economic activities, when a bond was a bond, a dividend a dividend, and a foreign investment was physical—a hole in the ground or a building on top of it. Times have changed in all these respects.

To date, recognition of the inadequacy of national income tax systems in the face of globalization has largely been cast in terms of the opposing principles of neutrality and subsidiarity and their apparent tax policy analogues of residence and source. Putting the question in these terms, however, in effect presumes that either source or residence is, or should continue to be, the primary approach to the determination of appropriate national taxes on international flows. This approach side-steps the central problem, which is not one of whether source or residence is the better normative or operational principle, but rather one of (re)defining the much more difficult 'nexus' questions common to both source- and residence-based tax systems.[34] Both source and residence in effect allocate tax base and revenues on the assumption that identifiable actors are carrying out identifiable and measurable economic activities that may be assessed to tax in accordance with flows attributable to a particular jurisdiction. These principles are really ways of dividing up the pie in accordance both with some notion of what is going on where *and* with some concept of who has what right to share in the fruits of international economic activity.[35]

[34] As mentioned in note 32 above, this is what is at the heart of the debate over transfer pricing guidelines which culminated, in 1995, in the publication of the first stage of the OECD's revised guidelines, following on the heels of extensive discussion internationally about initiatives in the US to achieve a closer approximation of economic and financial income.

[35] There are various ways of looking at the legal emanations of these principles. In the course of a commentary on the efficacy of an international network of bilateral tax treaties, for example, Vann (1991) effectively criticized the relevance and utility of separate-entity financial-accounting devices to identify and allocate income among members of a controlled group according to a standard—the venerable if grossly imperfect arm's-length standard—that is antithetical to the basic characteristics of the taxpayers whose income it is meant to assist in evaluating. Vann would favour a much more economic, indeed formulary, approach to the division of the international tax base.

Similarly, state taxation in the US has presented many of the same issues as arise in the EU. Interestingly, the analytical focus in this discussion has been on discerning a 'substantial nexus' between the relevant activity or income, and achieving a 'fair apportionment' of tax among competing claimants. As a rule, substantial nexus typically requires some degree of physical presence, although recently the notion has been extended to include the 'presence' of intangible property in a state as a result of certain licensing arrangements (Gordon, 1995). Such analysis is

The narrow question of source- vs. residence-based taxation, whether in the EU or more broadly, is thus the wrong question. Even the best answer to the wrong question is not likely to be worth much. Framing the debate along these lines almost inevitably leads economists concerned primarily with allocative efficiency to conclude that the most desirable outcome is the harmonization of direct capital taxation, regardless of the principle adopted. If the residence principle is chosen, in effect the residence-country system is extended to cover the relevant world. If the source principle is chosen, then still stronger harmonization—indeed, uniformity—is called for from an allocative perspective. The debate about jurisdictional guidelines thus becomes confused with the more important issue of the fundamental inadequacy of *either* traditional approach as a method of establishing a meaningful correspondence between the financial flows that can be observed by taxing authorities and the economic activities to which they correspond. The gap between what either principle is supposed to accomplish and what the application of these outdated notions actually yields in today's world is great, and growing greater daily.

The prior question, accordingly, relates to why, whether, and how any nation asserts tax jurisdiction over international capital income. Essentially, it does so by associating some financial flow of which it is aware with some economic activity that can reasonably be asserted to fall within its political jurisdiction. Establishing nexus—the economic connection between

grounded in the recognition that the tax base to be allocated is itself a finite resource: there ought to be taxation of the tax base only once among all contending claimants.

Finally, Palmer (1989) is particularly direct in translating the economic qualities of nexus and apportionment into justifications to impose taxation on an economic basis that is source-driven or fundamentally territorial: 'An approach for establishing a priority of tax claims must be aimed at an equitable division, among nations, of the world tax base. It is submitted that such a division of the world tax base best would be accomplished by initially focusing on the relationship between the individual national economies and the world economy. It follows from this view that rules for fixing income tax jurisdiction should be based on the principle that each nation should have an exclusive primary claim over the income produced by that nation's economy. More specifically, primary jurisdiction to tax an increment of income should be assigned by determining which nation's economy was the greatest causative factor (or, in different terminology, which nation's economy was to the greatest extent exploited) in producing the income. For any given nation, the sum of these increments would constitute its national tax base. ... Under the national tax base theory, however, what is important is the interaction of the taxpayer *with the economy* of a given nation in a manner resulting in the production of income.'

an activity and a jurisdiction—is prior to the question of source or residence. Unless there is some means of reliably associating economic activity with transactional flows, there is no way of knowing whether any rebalancing of the source–residence scale in the EU (or in any economic grouping) will be meaningful, let alone desirable in any sense. Implicitly, some of the authors noted earlier seem to recognize this point—for example, when they suggest that completely revising the system in some way, such as adopting some form of consumption taxation or some form of formulary allocation, may be the only means of dealing with the potentially devastating implications of globalization for conventional income taxation. Globalization has not created the problems with the present system to which such proposals are supposed to be solutions; it has just made them more evident.

The central issue is thus how best to deal with the inevitable inadequacy of *any* system that may be applied in practice to divide up the international tax base. Contrary to the natural academic bias towards establishing principles and judging practice by how well it accords with principle, we suggest that what matters is not the extent to which any particular solution accords with some presumed normative principle, but rather how well it works and how likely it is to prove acceptable to most major players in the international tax game.[36] That is, in our view, although the rules in place have traditionally been rationalized to some extent in terms of how well (or how ill) they accord with some pre-established principle, this gets matters backwards in the sense that the 'principles' themselves, to a considerable extent, derive from the rules.[37] From this perspective, the source–residence question is, essentially, 'who gets how much tax?'.

[36] For simplicity, we have conducted most of this discussion on the assumption that we know the tax base and are determining how to allocate it. But, of course, it must always be remembered that, in practice, critical issues are (1) that only the taxpayer really knows and (2) that how we divide up the pie may affect both the size of the pie and the size of the piece of it of which we are aware.

[37] Perhaps this admittedly subtle point may be better understood as follows. One of the referees of this chapter suggested that 'norms' such as the residence and source principles were needed to protect the interests of those with less power, such as small states, and that our apparent abandonment of principle opened the doors to tax grabs by the strong. On the contrary, we suggest that the extent to which such 'norms' prevail—or are advocated—itself reflects the realities of power: see, for example, the classic argument of Kingson (1981) for the residence principle in terms of the inherent and obvious justice (from a US point of view) of rewriting international tax rules to accord with US concepts—and interests. For further discussion of the extensive literature of the extent to which self-serving biases are commonly hidden in the guise of 'norms' and 'principles', and the obstacles such concepts may pose to the attainment of mutually beneficial solutions, see Babcock and Loewenstein (1997).

Answering this question in the context of the EU (or the world) essentially requires answering the more fundamental and difficult questions posed above (at note 33) first—and, as we have emphasized, once these questions are answered, the source–residence question as such no longer arises.[38]

The source–residence debate is therefore largely irrelevant. In all likelihood, very similar results may be achieved in practice with similar efforts under either approach. Indeed, depending upon the underlying assumptions adopted about the extent to which there is some degree of integration of company and shareholder taxation (or a surrogate of some sort in the absence of such integration), this is evident in Cnossen's (1996) excellent analysis of the comprehensive business income tax (CBIT) and the dual income tax (DIT). If, for example, one (1) limits the deductibility of charges in the nature of interest, rents, and royalties, and (2) assumes away 'free-riding' (as defined earlier),[39] the result is an economic approach to direct income taxation based on allocative assumptions that could be expressed in an appropriate formula.[40] On these assumptions, the only

[38] The complexity of factor and capital flows that makes it difficult to measure and tax capital income is the Achilles' heel of *both* source and residence principles. The view taken by many authors that the source approach is more feasible is simply a pragmatic recognition that it is easier, in practice, to tax income where it is earned. But the underlying problem remains: how can one determine that in fact the income is 'earned' in any particular jurisdiction, short of applying such increasingly tenuous conventions as SEAL (separate-entity arm's-length) accounting?

[39] We do not want to downplay the importance of this problem, as evidenced, for example, in Tanzi (1995). All we suggest here is that the competitive 'race to the bottom' that worries some tax policy analysts (for example, Bird and McLure (1990)) need not govern whether practical degrees of co-ordination are undertaken. Most economic activity still requires some kind of economic or commercial infrastructure and hence will be anchored, in some real economic sense, in one or more non-tax-haven jurisdictions. As noted below, if this (perhaps optimistic) assessment is true, most instances of 'free-riding' can be dealt with directly without requiring systemic integration of national tax systems.

[40] McLure (1997a) has recently argued that we should abandon labels that have guided the income measurement debate—formulary vs. arm's-length separate accounting—in favour of other more flexible strategies. His approach to this issue to some extent mirrors the view we take with respect to the utility of debates in which the reality of economic circumstances has been less the focus of discussion than academic constructions based on assumptions of dubious practical relevance. To those who may think our approach to norms and principles is too Machiavellian, we would note, with a recent commentator, that although 'Machiavelli is most notorious for his repudiation of conventional ethics,...his readers have too often failed to notice the exact grounds for this move: the problem with those who would do good is that they fail to recognize the condition of contingency' (Hariman, 1995, pp. 30–1).

material determinant of where and why income is taxed is the connection of the income-earning activity to the primary earning location, and, as Cnossen (1996) shows, the traditional approach leaves only two meaningful contenders as corporate tax systems, each of which is source-based.

The result thus turns on the more basic question of how to measure economic activity on a territorial basis—that is, how to associate income and the activity that generated it with a particular source. The basic problem is how to avoid base distortion and erosion as a result of the disparate treatment within and between countries of specific financial flows, such as interest, rather than the decidedly secondary source–residence issue. Neither the source nor the residence concept provides very useful guidance on how to assign economic income to a particular territorial jurisdiction.[41] Before debating tax technique, one must be clear what the objectives of international tax policy are. We suggest that, in general, as in the EU debate, the main objective may usefully be considered to be to assign taxing power to each jurisdiction as required to meet national needs (subsidiarity) without unduly impeding market decisions (neutrality). To do this, of course, one must first be able to relate financial flows to territorially-based economic activity in an acceptably reliable way. As we have emphasized, this task precedes, and is more fundamental than, the source–residence discussion, and its resolution is not affected by that discussion.

4. Approaches to a solution

The leading question that forms the title of this chapter has thus been answered. 'Source vs. residence' is indeed the wrong question. But how can the more fundamental questions of what can and should be done be answered? As the title of this final section implies, we do not think that there is or can be any one definitive answer to these questions. Rather, we suggest that much more attention needs to be paid, not so much to the substantive content of any particular answers, but rather to the *process* by which they are reached.

Both academic authors and tax officials and practitioners are, of course, well aware of the problems to which globalization, financial innovation, and electronic commerce are giving rise, as evidenced by the outpouring of writings on these various subjects and the connections between them. Some have seen a possible solution in a revamping of company taxation, for example, in the form of the dual income tax system (Cnossen, 1996) or

---

[41] Distortions arising from differential treatment of corporate and shareholder income may result in undesirable overtaxation or undertaxation of international capital flows, but this matter can be dealt with separately. It is not further discussed here: see, for example, Sato and Bird (1975), Bird (1989), or Ault (1992).

some form of cash-flow or consumption tax (King, 1996). Consumption (cash-flow) taxes in their various forms simplify the problem by both eliminating timing problems and defining financial flows as the relevant economic activity to be taxed.[42] Formulary approaches cut through the obfuscation of conflicting principles to the pragmatic resolution of who gets what in a mutually agreed fashion.[43] Others have suggested that the only solution may be the creation of some form of *de facto* world-wide fiscal authority, at least in the form of greatly intensified and improved information exchange (Tanzi, 1995). Despite valiant attempts to pretend that the fiscal dam can be maintained by patching up holes here and there—for instance, maintaining the fiction that improved transfer pricing rules can do the job—even those who uphold the existing system most strenuously, on the understandable ground that it has taken so much time and argument to get to where we are that we should stick with it lest worse disagreement and fiscal chaos ensue, seem uncomfortable with the present system. One result is the proliferation of conferences and the growing flood of papers on various aspects of the problem.

Two broad approaches toward a solution of the fundamental problem arising from the broader span of economic enterprise than of political jurisdiction may be discerned. One is holistic, attempting to resolve the problem by some grand design, either to restructure the form of capital taxation (cash-flow taxes) or to turn over the problem to some higher, and presumably wiser, authority (imposed EU uniformity: a 'Eurotax'). The other approach is a more gradualist approach—sometimes unattractively labelled as 'muddling through'—that is, grappling for incremental changes in existing fiscal institutions that may be (a) acceptable, (b) workable, and (c) an improvement. Most discussion to date has focused on the first of these approaches, which is obviously more attractive to the logical thinkers who dominate the literature. None the less, we suggest that not only is the

---

[42] Of course, consumption taxes have their own problems when it comes to determining where transactions take place!

[43] Two common criticisms of formulary approaches are (1) that they will result in intractable 'tax-grabbing' conflicts between jurisdictions to the detriment of both international comity and allocative efficiency and (2) that they are terribly difficult and arbitrary in implementation. The first criticism assumes unilateral action (the California approach, or more broadly the US situation with respect to the allocation of subnational corporate tax bases); it is clearly not an essential component of the approach but a local peculiarity. The second is simply wrong: it is no more difficult (or easy) to implement an agreed formulary approach than any other internationally agreed approach. (For further discussion of experience in federal countries and the relevance for the EU, see Daly and Weiner (1993) and the earlier discussion in Bird and Brean (1986).)

second, gradualist, approach more likely to be the way to go,[44] but also that in fact the EU has already—as noted in Section 2—laid some of the necessary foundations for a roughly satisfactory solution along these lines, and that such a solution seems to be about as good as one can realistically expect.

Holistic approaches are overly ambitious. All that are really needed in the international tax context are rules upon which there is agreement (Shelton, 1997). The mere existence of 'borderless' transactions does not mean that the only answer is for everyone to do the same thing. But it does mean that, because the actions of one impinge on others, we are more likely to come closer to maximizing joint welfare if each acts taking into account the actions of others to some extent.[45] The need for agreement does not mean that what is, must be. On the contrary, what it means is that although change is needed, it is critical to ensure that any changes made are agreed upon by all major players.[46]

One holistic approach—favoured by Tanzi (1995), for example—would be to formalize and multilateralize international tax information exchanges through what used to be called 'a GATT for taxes' or what may perhaps now be called a 'World Tax and Trade Organization (WTTO)'. In the absence of international tax police—that is, an overriding sovereign jurisdiction—it seems unlikely that this approach will prove to be much more productive than the current unsatisfactory experience with information exchange. No country's tax administration will ever be willing to give a high priority to enforcing another country's taxes, nor indeed should it.

Another holistic approach, much favoured in the European discussion as well as by economists focusing on world-wide allocative efficiency as the most relevant international tax policy objective, is some form of imposed

---

[44] Contrary to what many academics seem to believe, there are excellent philosophical and practical grounds supporting the incremental approach we suggest, although this is not the place to go into such matters. Those who seek a more general justification of this approach, and some relevant references (Simon, Lindblom, Popper, etc.), may consult Bird (1970), for example.

[45] Note that our discussion does not take into account the positive side of tax competition stressed by such authors as McLure (1986) and Brennan and Buchanan (1980). From this perspective, measures facilitating the building and maintenance of governmental tax cartels are just as perverse in welfare terms as any other cartel activity: the task of the wise tax analyst is to restrain Leviathan, not to bolster him!

[46] The parallel with an unduly neglected strand in the literature of fiscal federalism emphasizing issues of process is obvious but cannot be further developed here: see Dafflon (1977), Wiseman (1987), and Bird (1986). Writers on international tax issues perhaps have more to learn from the federal finance literature than they seem to think (see, for example, Bird (1984 and 1989)).

harmonization or uniformity. At one level, this implies international tax policing again, or the cession of national sovereignty. It therefore seems about as unlikely as the first approach to be successful, absent the complete unification of Europe. At another level, this approach perverts the meaning of harmonization from the achievement of common goals to the imposition of uniform rules, which again denies the reality of national differences and Member State sovereignty.[47] Imposed harmonization with respect to company taxation seems thus to be either unworkable or undesirable.

This leaves the second broad approach mentioned above—namely, accretionary and voluntary harmonization from below. This is the approach implicit in EU directives with respect to parent–subsidiary relations and to mergers and take-overs, and in the transfer pricing convention. It is obviously partial, transitory (in some sense), and conceptually unsatisfactory in some respects. But it is also not only happening but workable. Two aspects of EU experience in this regard are noteworthy. First, this solution is limited to the activities and income of the main economic actors in the Community—the multinational enterprises. No attempt has been made to follow the intellectually tantalizing but likely unproductive path of mandating systemic change to domestic company taxation. Second, and more interesting, what has been done has established considerable co-ordination aimed at precisely what jurisdictional principles are intended to accomplish—namely, providing a basis for a measurable correspondence between economic and financial income.

The Parent–Subsidiary and Merger Directives facilitate the organization and financial consolidation of complex enterprises across national borders without the intervention of costs traceable to the taxation of 'phantom' income— income that is not an outgrowth of an economic accretion—in two important aspects of their existence: organization or reorganization, and the distribution of net income. In effect, these directives implement a notion of unitary (EU-wide) economic enterprise. This inherently economic approach accords well with why company groups are constructed the way they are, and with the reality of their income-earning activities. The convention on transfer pricing and arbitration is similarly economic and is pragmatic. It acknowledges the difficult reality of assigning economic income to competing jurisdictions and establishes a finite mechanism for resolving multiple taxation of enterprise profit. The principles adopted in the convention reflect familiar international taxation precepts aimed at relieving double taxation of the income of associated enterprises. Ultimately, there is a binding determination.

The main gap, and the main problem in many ways, continues to be the treatment of interest (Huizinga, 1994)—together with the equally fundamental problem of the existence of tax-exempt providers of capital such

---

[47] Compare Dosser (1966), Krauss (1971), and Bird (1989).

as pension funds (Alworth, 1998). So long as some capital suppliers are tax exempt and some flows of capital income are privileged, tax arbitrage will persist, and neither administratively nor allocatively can a fully satisfactory solution be reached. It thus remains a long way from here to there (Brean, 1992). None the less, some progress is being made in the right direction. If flows between countries are roughly equal, and their treatments in the different countries are roughly similar, the results of the prevailing rules may continue to be (roughly) allocatively acceptable. But if one country is a low-tax jurisdiction (tax haven), whether in general or with respect to some form of capital income, trouble looms and 'free-riders' will multiply. Moreover, even if there is no tax haven problem, the problems arising from tax-exempts are likely to increase in the future, given the apparent current propensity to privatize public pension plans[48] and to shelter corporate income through trusts and similar devices.[49] So long as tax arbitrage is possible, whether between countries, entities, or flows, it will occur.

The problem in the real world, however, is not how to achieve the tax collector's nirvana of no arbitrage, but rather how to co-ordinate the limits of disagreement between jurisdictions. One approach may be, as some have suggested, to get rid of the income tax as we know it and to shift to a cash-flow basis. This solution has the great advantage of eliminating the problems arising from the tax treatment of interest and especially the problems arising from interest deductibility. But we do not think it will soon be adopted in major countries (Munnell, 1992; Cnossen and Bird, 1990). Another approach may be to deal directly with low-tax jurisdictions and tax-exempt entities by a system of advance corporate tax which in effect 'ring-fences' free-riders (or those operating within 'free-riding' states) rather than contemplate a more

[48] Almost none of the voluminous discussion on the need to reform public pension plans in the direction of privatization mentions the possibly profound implications for tax policy of thus increasing the scope for tax arbitraging.

[49] In this regard, it is interesting to note the recent proliferation of income unit trusts in Canada. Their effect, assuming substantial investment in them is by tax-exempts, is effectively to make the payment of corporate-level tax elective. Ordinarily, corporate income is taxed at the corporate level, and distributed income in the form of dividends is taxed at the shareholder level, with a degree of over- or under-integration depending upon the circumstances. But if a trust earns the stream of income otherwise constituting taxable revenue of a corporation, no tax is paid at the corporate level or perhaps at all. The originator of the income deducts it, and therefore pays no tax. The trust receives the income but is not taxable on it since it distributes it to unitholders. And if the unitholders are preponderantly tax-exempts (such as pension plans and retirement savings plans), the income is not taxed (at least for a considerable period, until distribution to the beneficiaries of the plan investors). The result is that the corporate tax otherwise applicable disappears.

intrusive (of national tax sovereignty) redesign of international tax conventions. The dual income tax approach (Cnossen, 1996) in effect does this to some extent, though in an indirect fashion that avoids direct evaluation of the basic international issue: establishing jurisdictional nexus.

So long as there is a rough correspondence between economic and financial realities, it may not matter too much how one determines the territorial tax base, whether on the basis of the characteristics of transactions, or entities, or whatever. But when there is no longer such a correspondence—as is increasingly likely to be the case—rough proxies such as permanent establishment and non-discrimination are unlikely to suffice. Like the source and residence principles, such concepts should be understood primarily as guidelines as to how to carve up the tax base, given the economic reality. When one is no longer sure of that reality, new guidelines are needed. The question is not whether change is needed. It is. The question is, rather, whether it is reasonable to expect the needed new guidelines to arise from voluntary co-operation.

This is not a question of principle but of fact, similar to the much-discussed question of whether a Coasian solution can be reached with respect to a variety of externality problems. Although this issue cannot be discussed in detail here, the answer depends very much upon the level of transaction costs relative to the level of externalities, as well as upon the distribution of both sorts of costs among the players in the game and how often the game is played (Cornes and Sandler, 1996). We do not know enough about these costs with respect to international taxation to say whether it is plausible to expect such a solution, or whether countries will voluntarily decide that the most efficient way to resolve externality problems would be to cede some authority to a central authority as in a federation, or as may perhaps ensue in the EU, or even in the perhaps future WTTO.[50]

What we do know is that each country must respond to common economic influences, that the response of each affects others, and that the overall outcome of such actions is likely to be better if they are carried out with mutual critical awareness both of the underlying influences and of the policy responses of others. The problem is not so much one of designing an appropriate system of international tax rules. Rather, it is one of ensuring that the process by which such rules are established is as open and as well informed as possible.[51] In other words, discussions such as that in this chapter are not

[50] Given the centrality of this issue, it is a bit surprising that so little has been done along these lines by analysts of the EU. An interesting early starting-point for such discussion was provided by Meade et al. (1962) but seems seldom to have been noted or discussed (see, however, Bird (1966)).

[51] For examples of how this might work, see Dafflon (1977) and Wiseman (1987).

academic frills but, in a sense, constitute part of the essential discursive process of reaching a viable solution to the inherently intractable problems facing the international fiscal community.

All approaches to the difficult problems of international tax policy are inevitably deficient. Perfection is not attainable. But a feasible pragmatic solution should be. With relatively open economies, even if not in perfect balance, the application of different company tax regimes should not be unduly distortive, provided—and this is a major proviso—that productive activity is not easily located in jurisdictions that do not also have developed tax systems that, in principle, approach taxation in a similar manner.

This conclusion follows provided that (1) legal acts of the primary international actors that do not produce economic income are not considered to produce taxable income and (2) corporate profit is taxed only once as between the corporation and its shareholders and may otherwise be distributed within the zone free of border tax impediments—a condition which, in turn, requires (3) a basic reconsideration of the deductibility of periodic charges (such as interest) paid by corporations. If such charges are not deducted, and if an 'advance corporation tax' approach is followed for corporate payments, free-riding is much less of a concern since the taxation (or not) by the destination jurisdiction of distributed corporate income is irrelevant.

No doubt, even in these circumstances, many imperfections will remain, and it will still be possible for the unscrupulous, the clever, and the well-advised to locate intangible or financial property in places with limited taxation. Ultimately, however, such property generally gets used, one way or another, in countries that have a real tax system: taxes, like death, may take a long time to come, and they are not as inevitable as death, especially with respect to international flows. In the end, however, most of the international tax base seems likely to be caught, one way or another—or, at least, so an optimist might conclude.[52]

---

[52] For instance, focusing on transnational company operations, as in the various EU directives discussed earlier—while it of course will not deal with individuals holding offshore bank accounts, for example—will, if the net is cast widely enough and its mesh is fine, in the end catch most cross-border flows at some stage. As Gordon (1995) notes in the US state context, so long as charges for the use of money or intangible property are not deductible, the supplier effectively has a taxable presence in the taxing jurisdiction: see, in particular, his discussion of *Geoffrey, Inc. v. South Carolina Tax Commission*, 437 S.E.2d (1993), cer. denied, 114 S.St. 550 (1993), in which he observes that the required nexus of intangible property to a US state was created by the use of the property in that state by a related party licensee.

In short, like a number of other recent authors (McLure, 1996 and 1997a; Head, 1997; Slemrod, 1995; King, 1996; Tanzi, 1995), we conclude that, in practice, there is unlikely to be any one best way to deal with the problem. But there are several promising approaches, ranging from a drastic revision of company taxation, to a drastic revision of the international tax system, to a more modest strategy of continued evolution from where we now are to where, we suggest, we are going to have to go, at least if taxes on capital income are to be maintained.[53] What all these approaches have in common is that they require either voluntary agreement or some international enforcement mechanism. Since the latter does not, and is not likely to, exist, it appears that, unless voluntary agreement can be attained by at least the major players, in the end the corporate income tax may not be sustainable. Experience suggests, however, that when it is sufficiently in the interests of most players to reach agreements, agreements are in fact generally reached, albeit often in a gradualist manner that is difficult either to conceptualize or to operationalize. None the less, pragmatic modesty seems more advisable than normative righteousness in such matters. In the end, the fundamental problems in taxing capital income in a global economy seem unlikely ever to be resolved except by the application of arbitrary solutions, and the only way we know to make such solutions tolerable—fair, if one will—is by ensuring that those affected agree to them. For this reason, we urge that more attention should be paid to the process by which resolutions to international tax issues are reached and less to the alleged, and often disputable, normative principles (such as 'source' and 'residence') to which such resolutions may nominally adhere.

References

Alworth, J. S. (1998), 'Taxation and integrated financial markets: the challenges of derivatives and other financial innovations', *International Tax and Public Finance*, 5: 507–34.

Ault, H. (1992), 'Corporate integration, tax treaties and division of the international tax base', *Tax Law Review*, 47: 565–608.

Avery Jones, J. F. (1995), 'Carry on discriminating', *British Tax Review*, 525.

[53] As mentioned earlier, our position is in some respects very close to that of Cnossen (1996). His argument, however, is directed primarily to suggesting a system that (a) will be close to traditional concepts and practices and (b) will work better. In contrast, what we want to emphasize is not so much any particular substantive 'solution' but rather the importance of looking at the questions in a more basic way. Moreover, we suggest that what is most fundamental in the long run may be less *what* is decided than *how* it is decided.

Avi-Yonah, R. S. and Swartz, L. Z. (1997), 'US international tax treatment of financial derivatives', *Tax Notes International*, 14 (3 March): 787–800.

Babcock, L. and Loewenstein, G. (1997), 'Explaining bargaining impasse: the role of self-serving biases', *Journal of Economic Perspectives*, 11: 109–26.

Bird, R. M. (1966), 'Regional policies in a common market', in C. S. Shoup (ed.), *Fiscal Harmonization in Common Markets*, two volumes, New York: Columbia University Press.

——(1970), 'The tax kaleidoscope: perspectives on tax reform in Canada', *Canadian Tax Journal*, 18: 444–73.

——(1984), 'Tax harmonization and federal finance: a perspective on recent Canadian discussions', *Canadian Public Policy*, 10: 253–66.

——(1986), *Federal Finance in Comparative Perspective*, Toronto: Canadian Tax Foundation.

——(1988), 'Shaping a new international tax order', *Bulletin for International Fiscal Documentation*, 42: 292–9, 303.

——(1989), 'International aspects of tax reform in Australia', in J. G. Head (ed.), *Australian Tax Reform in Retrospect and Prospect*, Sydney: Australian Tax Research Foundation.

—— and Brean, D. J. S. (1986), 'The interjurisdictional allocation of income and the unitary tax debate', *Canadian Tax Journal*, 34: 1377–416.

—— and McLure, C. E., Jr. (1990), 'The personal income tax in an interdependent world', in S. Cnossen and R. M. Bird (eds), *The Personal Income Tax: Phoenix from the Ashes?*, Amsterdam: North-Holland.

Brean, D. J. S. (1992), 'Here or there? The source and residence principles of international taxation', in R. M. Bird and J. M. Mintz (eds), *Taxation to 2000 and Beyond*, Toronto: Canadian Tax Foundation.

——, Bird, R. M., and Krauss, M. (1991), *Taxation of International Portfolio Investment*, Ottawa: Centre for Trade Policy and Law and the Institute for Research on Public Policy.

Brennan, G. and Buchanan, J. (1980), *The Power to Tax*, Cambridge: Cambridge University Press.

Bretvold, L. I. and Ross, R. C. (eds) (1967), *The Philosophy of Edmund Burke*, Ann Arbor, MI: University of Michigan Press.

Carroll, M. B. (1978), *Global Perspectives of an International Tax Lawyer*, Huntsville, NY: Exposition Press.

Cnossen, S. (1996), 'Company taxes in the European Union: criteria and options for reform', *Fiscal Studies*, 17(4): 67–97.

—— and Bird, R. M. (eds) (1990), *The Personal Income Tax: Phoenix from the Ashes?*, Amsterdam: North-Holland.

Commission of the European Communities (1992), *Report of the Committee of Independent Experts on Company Taxation*, Luxemburg (the Ruding report).

Cornes, R. and Sandler, T. (1996), *The Theory of Externalities, Public Goods and Club Goods*, Cambridge: Cambridge University Press.

Dafflon, B. (1977), *Federal Finance in Theory and Practice with Special Reference to Switzerland*, Berne: Paul Haupt.

Daly, M. (1997), 'Some taxing questions for the Multilateral Agreement on Investment (MAI)', *The World Economy*, 20: 787–808.

—— and Weiner, J. (1993), 'Corporate tax harmonization and competition in federal countries: some lessons for the European Community?', *National Tax Journal*, 46: 441–61.

Dosser, D. (1966), 'Economic analysis of tax harmonization', in C. S. Shoup (ed.), *Fiscal Harmonization in Common Markets*, two volumes, New York: Columbia University Press.

Dunahoo, C. and Carlisle, J. F., Jr. (1997), 'Cybertax 1.0: the US Treasury paper on electronic commerce', *Tax Notes International*, 14 (24 February): 693–9.

Frenkel, J. A., Razin, A., and Sadka, E. (1991), *International Taxation in an Integrated World*, Cambridge, MA: MIT Press.

Gammie, M. and Brannan, G. (1995), 'EC law challenge to the UK corporation tax: the death knell of UK imputation?', *Intertax*, 8/9: 389–405.

Glicklich, P. A., Goldberg, S. H., and Levine, H. J. (1996), 'Internet sales pose international tax challenges', *Journal of Taxation*, 84: 325–30.

Gordon, S. L. (1995), 'Taxation issues in a federal state and economic groupings with concurrent taxing authorities', paper presented to International Fiscal Association, Geneva, September.

Hariman, R. (1995), *Political Style*, Chicago: University of Chicago Press.

Head, J. G. (1997), 'Company tax structure and company tax incidence', *International Tax and Public Finance*, 4: 61–100.

Helliwell, J. F. (1996), 'Do national borders matter for Quebec's trade?', *Canadian Journal of Economics*, 29: 507–22.

Hinnekens, L. (1992), 'The Tax Arbitration Convention: its significance for the EC based enterprise, the EC itself, and for Belgian and international tax law', *EC Tax Review*, 70.

Huizinga, H. (1994), 'International interest withholding taxation: prospects for a common European policy', *International Tax and Public Finance*, 1: 277–91.

Ip, I. K. and Mintz, J. M. (1992), *Dividing the Spoils: The Federal–Provincial Allocation of Taxing Powers*, Toronto: C. D. Howe Institute.

King, M. A. (1996), 'Tax systems in the 21st century', paper presented to International Fiscal Association, Geneva, September.

Kingson, C. (1981), 'The coherence of international taxation', *Columbia Law Review*, 81: 1151–289.

Knobbe-Keuk, B. (1994), 'Restrictions on the fundamental freedoms enshrined in the EC Treaty by discriminatory tax provisions: ban and justification', *EC Tax Review*, 1994/3: 74.

Krauss, M. (1971), 'Two approaches to tax harmonization: a rejoinder', *Public Finance,* 26: 607–10.

Lewin, R. and Wilkie, J. S. (1993), 'Non-discrimination rules in international taxation', in *Cahiers de droit fiscal international,* Deventer: Kluwer.

McCallum, J. (1995), 'National borders matter: Canada–US regional trade patterns', *American Economic Review,* 85: 615–23.

McDaniel, P. (1994), 'Formulary taxation in the North American Free Trade Zone', *Tax Law Review,* 49: 691–744.

McLure, C. E., Jr. (1984), 'Defining a unitary business: an economist's view', in C. E. McLure, Jr. (ed.), *The State Corporation Income Tax: Issues in Worldwide Unitary Combination,* Stanford, CA: Hoover Institution Press.

——(1986), 'Tax competition: is what's good for the private goose good for the public gander?', *National Tax Journal,* 39: 341–8.

——(1996), 'Tax policies for the 21st century', paper presented to International Fiscal Association, Geneva, September.

——(1997a), 'US federal use of formula apportionment in the taxation of income from intangibles', *Tax Notes International,* 14 (10 March): 859–71; also in US Department of the Treasury, *Conference on Formula Apportionment,* 12 December 1996, Washington, DC.

——(1997b), 'Electronic commerce, state sales taxation, and intergovernmental fiscal relations', *National Tax Journal,* 50: 731–49.

Meade, J. E., Liesner, H. H., and Wells, S. J. (1962), *Case Studies in European Economic Union: The Mechanics of Integration,* London: Oxford University Press.

Munnell, A. H. (1992), 'Taxation of capital income in a global economy: an overview', *New England Economic Review,* September–October: 33–52.

Musgrave, P. B. (1969), *United States Taxation of Foreign Investment Income: Issues and Arguments,* Cambridge, MA: Harvard Law School International Tax Program.

Musgrave, R. A., and Musgrave, P. B. (1972), 'Inter-nation equity', in R. M. Bird and J. G. Head (eds), *Modern Fiscal Issues: Essays in Honour of Carl S. Shoup,* Toronto: University of Toronto Press.

National Tax Association Internet Tax Study Panel (1997), report, *State Tax Notes,* 18 (17 November): 1236–8.

OECD (1991), *Taxing Profits in a Global Economy,* Paris: Organization for Economic Co-operation and Development.

——(1995), 'Transfer pricing guidelines for multinational enterprises and tax administrations. Part II: applications', *Intertax,* 6/7: 312–65.

——(1997), 'Taxation of global trading of financial instruments: a discussion draft', *Tax Notes International,* 14 (17 February): 597–623.

Owens, J. (1997), 'Tax reform for the 21st century', *Tax Notes International,* 14 (17 February): 583–95.

Palmer, R. L. (1989), 'Toward unilateral coherence in determining jurisdiction to tax income', *Harvard International Law Journal*, 30: 1–64.

Picciotto, S. (1992), *International Business Taxation*, London: Weidenfeld & Nicolson.

Radler, A. J., and Blumenberg, J. (1992), 'Harmonization of corporate income tax systems within the European Community', Annex 10A in Commission of the European Communities, *Report of the Committee of Independent Experts on Company Taxation*, Luxemburg.

Rosenbloom, H. D. (1994), 'What's trade got to do with it?', *Tax Law Review*, 49: 593–8.

Ross, S. G. (1992), 'International taxation: a 20-year view', *Tax Notes*, 57 (12 November): 945–8.

Sato, M., and Bird, R. M. (1975), 'International aspects of the taxation of corporations and shareholders', *IMF Staff Papers*, 22: 384–455.

Shelton, J. R. (1997), 'Emerging issues in taxing business in a global economy', *Tax Notes International*, 14 (20 January): 221–3.

Slemrod, J. B. (1995), 'Free trade taxation and protectionist taxation', *International Tax and Public Finance*, 2: 471–90.

Surrey, S. (1978), 'Reflections on the allocation of income and expenses among national tax jurisdictions', *Law and Policy in International Business*, 10: 409–60.

——and McDaniel, P. (1985), *Tax Expenditures*, Cambridge, MA: Harvard University Press.

Tanzi, V. (1995), *Taxation in an Integrating World*, Washington, DC: Brookings Institution.

Tirard, J. M. (1996), 'The European Community's solutions', paper presented to International Fiscal Association, Geneva, September.

US Department of the Treasury (1996), *Selected Tax Policy Implications of Global Electronic Commerce*, Washington, DC: Office of Tax Policy, US Department of the Treasury.

Vann, R. (1991), 'A model tax treaty for the Asian-Pacific region?', *Bulletin for International Fiscal Documentation*, 45(3): 99–111 and 45(4): 151–63.

Vogel, K. (1990), 'World-wide vs. source taxation of income: a review and re-evaluation of arguments', in *Influence of Tax Differentials on International Competitiveness*, Deventer: Kluwer.

Warren, A. C., Jr. (1993), 'Financial contract innovation and income tax policy', *Harvard Law Review*, 107: 461–92.

——(1994), 'Alternatives for international corporate tax reform', *Tax Law Review*, 49: 599–614.

Wiseman, J. (1987), 'The political economy of federalism: a critical appraisal', *Environment and Planning C: Government and Policy*, 5: 383–410.

5

Issues in the taxation of income from foreign portfolio and direct investment

MICHAEL P. DEVEREUX

Since the Neumark Committee reported in 1963, there has been an unresolved debate about harmonizing the taxation of corporate income in what is now the European Union (EU). A central issue has been the importance of, and the perceived need for harmonization of, the statutory corporation tax rate and the definition of the corporation tax base. Closely related to this is the relationship between taxation at the level of the company and at the level of the shareholder, especially where the company and the shareholder are resident in different countries.

This chapter aims to shed light on these issues, both for the collective welfare of a group of countries such as the EU and for the welfare of an individual country. The main theme of the chapter is that, in identifying the 'optimal' taxation of international investment flows, using corporate and personal taxes, it is useful to make a distinction between portfolio and direct investment.

The definition of these two forms of investment is usually in terms of the degree of control maintained by the investor over the investment activity. In this chapter, however, I assume that, in practice, this definition can be mirrored by the distinction between individual investors (or financial intermediaries) who undertake portfolio investment and are subject to personal taxes, and companies funded by such investors that undertake direct investment and are subject to corporation taxes.

This distinction immediately makes it possible to address the two issues raised above. First, although there are well-known results concerning the overall taxation of international investment flows in the economics literature, the implications for optimal corporate-level and optimal personal-level taxes separately have not been examined. Yet the political debate frequently

The author is grateful to the Leverhulme Trust for financial support for this research in the form of a Leverhulme Research Fellowship.

concerns the potential harmonization of corporation taxes, rather than the overall tax rates on investment. Making reasonable assumptions about how rates of return are determined for portfolio and direct investment permits an analysis of each form of taxation separately.

This is, of course, closely related to the second issue: the relationship between corporate and personal taxes. The existence of a tax on company profits and a separate tax on personal income or capital gains from companies constitutes so-called double taxation of corporate-source income. The impact of such double taxation is uncertain, but it may lead to lower investment and lower dividend payments than would otherwise be the case. As a result, there are, and have been, many different forms of integration of corporate and personal taxes in Europe. These include a 'classical' system— actually a lack of integration, as income is taxed once at the corporate level and again at the personal level when it is distributed; a 'split-rate' system— where the corporation tax rate is lower on distributed earnings than on retained earnings; a 'shareholder relief' system—where dividend income is subject to a lower income tax rate than other forms of income; and an imputation system—typically where dividends received carry an associated tax credit, reflecting corporation tax already paid.[1] Below, I use the general term 'integration credits' to apply to any of these specific systems (with the exception of the classical system).

The relative merits of these systems have been much debated in a domestic setting.[2] However, in an international context, there are two additional important issues, relating to which forms of income and hence double taxation are relieved. Consider a shareholder resident in country A, who owns shares and receives dividends from a company resident in country B. First, should integration credits be available for the shareholder in country A, as well as for shareholders resident in country B? If so, which country should give the credit? And should the credit be available at the rate of integration credit in force in country A or in country B? Second, suppose the company resident in country B has a wholly-owned subsidiary in a third country, C, from which it receives dividends. Should integration credits on dividends paid by the parent company in country B be available for both its domestic-source income and its foreign-source income from country C? And how is this issue related to how the foreign-source income is taxed at the level of the company?

The most recent proposals concerning at least some of these issues in the EU were made by the Ruding Committee (Commission of the European

---

[1] A fuller taxonomy of such integration systems is provided in OECD (1991), Chennells and Griffith (1997), and, in more detail, Harris (1996).

[2] For a survey, see Mintz (1996).

Communities, 1992).[3] With regard to the corporation tax regime, the committee proposed a minimum corporation tax rate and a much more closely harmonized corporation tax base. With regard to the integration of corporate and personal taxes, it proposed that Member States that already give some relief for double taxation of dividend income received from domestic companies should, on a reciprocal basis, also give tax relief to dividend income received by its residents from companies resident in another Member State. The committee explicitly rejected the idea that Member States should give relief to non-resident shareholders. That is, it proposed that country A should provide an integration credit for its shareholders on the dividend income from country B at the same rate as it gives to purely domestic dividend income.

The debate on integration has not been limited to Europe. In 1992, the US Treasury considered introducing a form of integration in the US. In its January 1992 report (US Department of the Treasury, 1992a), the Treasury proposed that the integration credit should be given only to domestic shareholders and should apply only to domestic-source income of the corporation. However, in December 1992 (US Department of the Treasury, 1992b), it considered a form of integration that applied only to domestic shareholders but for all income of the corporation.

The second important distinction between portfolio and direct investment concerns the taxation of economic rent. I assume that individuals purchase shares at the market price. They purchase only a small proportion of the total number of shares and therefore do not have active control over the activities of the company. Further, if the firm is expected to earn an economic rent, then this will be reflected in the share price, so that shareholders only expect to earn a normal—or the required—rate of return. It is conventional to measure the impact of tax on the required rate of return by the effective *marginal* tax rate—the difference between the required returns pre-tax and post-tax; there have been numerous studies that have attempted to measure such tax rates.[4]

---

[3] There has been a long history of such proposals. In 1963, the Neumark Committee recommended that corporation taxes should be harmonized along the lines of a split-rate system, with a lower tax rate on dividends than on retained earnings. In 1971, the van den Tempel Report recommended instead a classical system throughout the European Communities, with no compensation for the 'double taxation' of corporate profits. In 1975, the European Commission proposed a common partial imputation system, with a tax credit available to dividend recipients, irrespective of in which Member State they resided.

[4] The most well known is King and Fullerton (1984). This was extended to various forms of cross-border investment by Alworth (1988), Devereux and Pearson (1989 and 1995), and OECD (1991).

However, this may not be the relevant measure for analysing direct investment. Companies undertake investment in real activities, which I assume are undertaken directly by the company or through a foreign subsidiary that is controlled by the parent firm. This direct investment may frequently take place in the context of imperfect competition, where the firm expects to earn an economic rent over and above the minimum required return.[5] Further, it is likely to be the case that a multinational chooses between alternative locations for a single investment project. The preferred location will be the one that yields the highest post-tax profit; this implies that it is the effective *average* tax rate, rather than the effective *marginal* tax rate, which affects the location decision. Given a particular location, however, conventional theory would still suggest that the effective *marginal* tax rate is important in determining the size of the investment.

These considerations play an important role in choosing the corporation tax regime. For example, it has frequently been argued that a tax with a zero effective marginal tax rate would be optimal, since decisions as to whether to undertake any individual investment project would not be affected by the tax. There are several examples in the economics literature of such a tax, including a cash-flow tax (Institute for Fiscal Studies, 1978) and the ACE tax (Institute for Fiscal Studies, Capital Taxes Group, 1991). These taxes are levied *only* on economic rent and therefore leave marginal investment projects unaffected. The tax *rate* is not relevant to this result, but the definition of the tax *base* is crucial. However, in determining the effective *average* tax rate, and hence the location choice of multinationals, *both* the rate and base are important. To avoid distorting investment decisions, it is therefore not enough simply to harmonize the tax base to be equal to economic rent; it is necessary also to harmonize the tax rate.

---

[5] In the context of foreign direct investment (FDI), the economics literature on multinational corporations has identified a number of factors that are likely to be present, which are incorporated into the so-called OLI framework: see Dunning (1977 and 1981), Cantwell (1994), Krugman (1991), and Markusen (1995). This starts from the premiss that operating in a foreign country is costly; companies would not undertake such activity unless there were some offsetting gains from doing so. The OLI framework identifies three groups of possible advantages to a multinational firm undertaking FDI. First, there must be *ownership* advantages to the multinational that give it a competitive advantage over domestic firms operating in the same market. These could take many forms but would include, for example, the possession of a patent. Second, there must be some *locational* advantage that induces the multinational to produce in one location rather than another. Third, there must be some *internalization* reason why the multinational chooses to produce itself, rather than licensing some third party to undertake production.

It is necessary to make two further comments before proceeding. First, in analysing the welfare-maximizing policy either of a group of countries or of a single country, I take the tax policy of all other countries as given. Although there is a large and growing literature on tax competition between countries, involving the strategic interaction of tax setting, I leave such issues to one side.

Second, flows of capital across borders—either in the form of foreign portfolio investment (FPI) or foreign direct investment (FDI)—and real investment projects may be almost completely unrelated. For example, much FDI takes the form of acquisitions of other companies. This may have no impact on the level of capital in the country that receives the FDI—it is simply a transfer of ownership. On the other hand, multinationals may undertake greenfield investment, which is partly financed locally. This would constitute new investment, but only part of it would be FDI, even though it was completely controlled by the foreign multinational.[6] This chapter examines the taxation of cross-border flows rather than new investment.

The remainder of the chapter is organized as follows. Section 1 briefly reviews the typical definitions of portfolio and direct investment and summarizes the development of each over the last twenty years. Section 2 briefly summarizes the lessons for the optimal taxation of cross-border investment from existing economic theory. An important distinction made in the literature, reflected in the discussion in this chapter, is the nature of the optimization; that is, there is a difference between the optimal tax policy of a jurisdiction operating in its own interests without any co-operation with other countries and the optimal policy of a group of countries that co-operate with each other. However, this literature has not addressed the issue of the optimal treatment of relief for double (i.e. personal and corporate) taxation in a cross-border context.[7] Also it has only recently begun to examine the implications of imperfect competition for optimal tax rates on FDI. We therefore explore these two issues in Sections 3 and 4. Section 5 briefly concludes.

1. The nature of portfolio and direct investment

This chapter concerns the taxation of income from foreign portfolio investment and the taxation of income from foreign direct investment. Investment is usually labelled as 'direct' when the investor has some degree of control over the investment activity itself. In official statistics, there are International

---

[6] Auerbach and Hassett (1993) develop these distinctions in more detail, especially in the context of the US.

[7] Several papers have addressed the possible 'double corporate taxation' of a parent company and its foreign subsidiary. See, for example, Bond and Samuelson (1989).

Monetary Fund guidelines which reflect the proportion of an investment that a particular investor owns or controls. Thus, for example, official US statistics consider international investment as 'direct' if the investor owns or controls at least 10 per cent of an enterprise's voting securities.[8] By implication, all other forms of investment are 'portfolio'.

The volumes of both direct and portfolio capital flows have increased substantially over the last twenty years, particularly during the 1980s. For example, world outflows of FDI rose from around $35 billion p.a. in the second half of the 1970s to $226 billion in 1990, before falling back a little in the early 1990s.[9] The proportionate increase in FPI was even more substantial—from around $12 billion p.a. in the second half of the 1970s to $274 billion in 1991, again before subsequently falling a little. There was therefore a marked shift in the composition of total flows, with the share of FPI in total flows rising from 25 per cent to nearly 70 per cent. Most of the direct flows were between developed countries, although flows to developing countries increased in the early 1990s.[10]

A 'typical' FDI is probably undertaken by a multinational corporation which either acquires an existing firm, or sets up a greenfield investment, in another country. The expansion in FDI has been marked by a shift away from raw materials towards services and high-technology sectors (the latter rising from 25 per cent to 40 per cent of the total). By contrast, a 'typical' FPI is rather more difficult to define. However, the recent growth in FPI has been marked by four features: the expansion of securities markets; the growth of institutional savings; the internationalization of institutional savings; and the development of broad markets for derivative financial instruments.[11] These developments are related. For example, there has been a shift from bank lending to transactions in securities, mostly in the form of debt instruments, but also in shares; this at least partly reflects the growth of institutional investors which have a preference for securities over bank intermediated assets. Increased foreign diversification by institutions appears to be driven partly by the increased understanding of the benefits of such diversification and partly by closer integration of financial markets.

The reasons behind the explosive growth in both FPI and FDI are beyond the scope of this chapter, although they include such factors as the expansion of telecommunications, the spreading of computer technology,

---

[8] The UK uses a minimum figure of 20 per cent. Other countries—for example, the Netherlands—do not set a minimum at all.

[9] These, and subsequent, statistics are taken from Slemrod et al. (1996).

[10] These were primarily flows to the newly industrialized countries in Asia and debt finance to Latin America.

[11] See the discussion in Slemrod et al. (1996).

and the improved sophistication of pricing financial instruments. Whatever the reasons, however, the growth raises a number of important practical issues for tax policy—for example, the additional opportunities for tax-minimizing strategies and the difficulty in relying on traditional distinctions such as capital and income, equity and debt, interest and other payments, and realizations and accruals. These issues are discussed at more length in Alworth (1998) and Slemrod et al. (1996).

This chapter instead concentrates on a small number of narrower issues. Specifically, it is mainly concerned with applying the results of the optimal tax literature—which has traditionally made no distinction at all between types of international capital flows—to a world that at least acknowledges the existence of separate FPI and FDI. Before doing so, however, we briefly review the existing literature, which largely ignores this distinction.

2. Review of conditions for optimal tax rates

A central result in the theory of optimal taxation of international income is essentially an application of the Diamond–Mirrlees (1971) production efficiency theorem. As shown by, for example, Razin and Sadka (1991), under the conditions of the Diamond–Mirrlees theorem, it is optimal for the international tax system to preserve production efficiency—essentially that pre-tax rates of return to capital should be equated across different uses. The intuition behind this result is straightforward: if two projects have different pre-tax rates of return, total wealth could be increased by switching resources from the project with the lower return to the project with the higher return. However, this result leads to different policy prescriptions depending on whether the analysis applies to a group of countries that co-operate with each other (if necessary reallocating post-tax income between them) or to a single country that does not co-operate.

In the co-operative case, the requirement for production efficiency applies to all projects in all countries; this implies that the rate of return on projects in every location before all taxes should be equated. It is well known that this can be achieved by pure residence-based taxation: any individual investor must face the same effective tax rate on all investment, whether at home or abroad. This could be achieved if the source country does not apply any tax, or if the residence country offers a full credit (including the possibility of a rebate) for any foreign tax paid. It is reasonable to suppose that any individual investor will seek to earn the same post-tax rate of return on all investment projects, whatever their location. If the tax rate is the same on all investment projects for any investor, this is equivalent to equalizing the pre-tax rate of return from all investment projects—as would be the case in the absence of tax. Thus if all investors are taxed according to the residence principle, then location decisions will not be distorted by tax. This is known as capital export neutrality (CEN).

However, if the production efficiency result is applied by a single capital-exporting, non-cooperating country, then the relevant rate of return on outward investment is that which accrues to residents of that country; the social rate of return to that country is the rate of return net of any foreign tax. In this case, the country should seek to equate the pre-tax rate of return on domestic investment with the post-foreign-tax rate of return on outward investment. In standard models, this implies that the domestic tax system should allow foreign taxes paid to be deducted from earnings on outward investment in computing domestic tax; under such a system, the same tax rate would apply to all income due to domestic residents. This has been shown formally by Feldstein and Hartman (1979).

Similar analysis concerns a small capital-importing, non-cooperating country. Under the same conditions as the other results, such a country should not tax the income from capital imports—at least unless the capital-exporting country offers a credit for taxes paid in the capital-importing country. If no credit is given, a tax in the capital-importing country will drive a wedge between the pre- and post-tax rates of return. But if the investor can earn a given rate of return elsewhere, he will expect to earn that same rate of return in the capital-importing country. The impact of taxation will be to drive up the required pre-tax rate of return, by reducing capital imports and hence the capital stock in that country. The effective incidence of the tax must be on the immobile factors in that country. Given that the immobile factors bear the incidence, it would be better to tax them directly and avoid the distortion created by the tax.

As Razin and Sadka (1991) pointed out, combining these two results under non-cooperation leaves all countries applying a residence-based tax—exactly the same position as if they had co-operated. This implies that—in these simple models, at least—if all countries behaved optimally, and if residence taxation is feasible, there would be no gain from co-operation.

These results apply to countries that either export or import capital but not both. In fact, in the simplest models, countries will not both export and import capital. However, Slemrod et al. (1997) examine a simple extension in which, since capital exports are costly, countries do both import and export capital. In addition, they consider the case in which, for some reason, it is impossible not to tax capital imports.[12] In this case, the optimal setting of tax rates turns out to be a 'see-saw', under which a higher tax on capital imports implies a lower tax on capital exports and vice versa.

---

[12] The see-saw relationship is slightly changed if one of the other taxes is fixed.

All of these models are defined in terms of a single tax rate—an effective marginal tax rate—which applied to a single type of investment project. Section 3 discusses the relationship of personal and company taxes in the context of these simple models.[13] The aim is to explore the implications of there being two forms of investment and two layers of taxation. It therefore considers the effective marginal tax rate separately for each of FPI and FDI. Section 4 investigates the extent to which the effective marginal tax rate is adequate in summarizing the impact of taxation on FDI. That section investigates the role of the effective average tax rate.

Before doing so, however, it is worth mentioning some caveats to these simple models. The Diamond–Mirrlees production efficiency theorem critically relies on two assumptions: that there are no restrictions on the use of other tax instruments available to the government and that any economic rent is fully taxed at 100 per cent[14] (or there is no economic rent). These are not innocuous assumptions, but only recently have attempts to relax them been introduced into models of the optimal taxation of international income.

Keen and Piekkola (1997) analyse the optimal tax rates between co-operating countries when economic rents exist but are constrained to be taxed at a rate less than 100 per cent. In this case, the optimal tax system depends on similar factors to those identified by Horst (1980), namely the elasticity of the supply of savings and the elasticity of the demand for capital in each country. In addition, Keen and Piekkola show that the optimal structure depends on the rate at which economic rents are taxed. The precise relationship between these factors is complex. However, when these elasticities take extreme values (but economic rent is not taxed at 100 per cent), Horst's results continue to hold: residence taxation is optimal if savings are completely inelastic, while source-based taxation is optimal if the demand for capital is completely inelastic. The latter case achieves capital import neutrality (CIN) by taxing all investment—and hence investors—in a particular location at the same rate; it clearly distorts the choice of location for individual investors, but if the demand for capital is completely inelastic, then its allocation across countries is unaffected.

---

[13] Gordon and Jun (1993) investigate the degree to which differences in the tax treatment of FPI and FDI affect their relative use. They find that taxes appear to explain part of the composition of equity flows across borders, but that much variation depends on other factors; part of the difficulty in testing for the effects of tax were the existence of capital controls in many countries in the 1980s and the fact that tax policy itself is endogenous. The issue of the optimal tax treatment of direct and portfolio flows is also addressed by Slemrod (1995).

[14] Shown by Stiglitz and Dasgupta (1971).

Huizinga and Nielsen (1996 and 1997) investigate optimal international tax policy in the absence of co-operation, when economic rents are taxed at less than 100 per cent. Among other results, they show that while capital-importing countries should not tax capital income if economic rents are fully taxed, there is a role for such taxation when they are not fully taxed. If the economic rents are partly owned by foreign residents, then source-based investment taxes can be used to shift income from these foreign owners to domestic residents. They also show that, in these conditions, there will be a gain from a co-ordinated increase in the tax rate on investment.

The next section abstracts from the issue of possible constraints on the tax rate on economic rents. Instead, it is assumed that the conditions under which production efficiency is optimal hold. Rather than developing alternative optimal tax policies in more complex environments, the section concentrates on examining implications for optimal tax rates of there being two forms of international investment, FPI and FDI. Section 4 does investigate the role of taxes on economic rents, but falls short of developing optimality conditions.

3. Optimality conditions for personal and corporate tax rates on international investment

Consider two countries, A and B, each of which is the place of residence for one representative investor and one representative corporation. Each investor can purchase shares or lend to either corporation. Each corporation can undertake real investment in each country. This section explores the conditions for the taxation of these flows that are consistent with production efficiency; thus it is assumed conditions hold such that production efficiency is optimal. To begin with, we examine the conditions for global efficiency—that is, maximizing welfare when countries co-operate with each other. We then turn to the case of the optimal tax system for individual non-cooperating countries. First, however, consider a simple extension of existing models to incorporate two forms of investment.

In models with only one type of investment, there are two possible locations of taxation—in the source country, where the investment takes place, or in the residence country, where the investor resides. The tax rates in the two countries are not necessarily independent of each other. In particular, the tax rate charged in the residence country frequently depends on the tax rate charged in the source country; this would be true under a partial credit system, for example. However, we introduce two forms of investment—portfolio and direct—and allow both source- and residence-country taxation on each form of investment. To begin with, the tax rates are composite—that is, they incorporate all source- and residence-country taxes on the income from the portfolio investment, and similarly for the direct investment; they do not distinguish which country levies the charge. In analysing the optimal integration of corporate and personal taxes, however, the personal tax rates are split to identify whether integration credits are available for domestic and foreign portfolio investment separately. In analysing non-cooperative behaviour, it is also necessary to split the composite corporate tax rates according to which country levies the tax.

We proceed by considering a number of no-arbitrage conditions, which reflect the investment behaviour of each investor and each company. Suppose that the post-tax rate of return earned by the investor in country A from portfolio investment in each company is s^A and that earned by the investor in country B from portfolio investment in each company is s^B. The investor in country A will invest in both companies only if the post-tax rate of return earned from each is the same. Let the pre-personal-tax rate of return paid by the company in country A be r^A and that paid by the company in country B be r^B. The effective personal tax rates are of the form t_j^i where $i = A,B$ represents the country of residence of the investor and $j = A,B$ represents the country of residence of the company.

Ruling out short positions, the investor in country A will invest in both companies if and only if

$$(5.1) \qquad s^A = (1 - t_A^A)r^A = (1 - t_B^A)r^B,$$

and the investor in country B will invest in both companies if and only if

$$(5.2) \qquad s^B = (1 - t_A^B)r^A = (1 - t_B^B)r^B.$$

If only one of conditions (eqn 5.1) and (eqn 5.2) holds, then that defines which of the two investors is the marginal investor, holding both assets and hence determining r^A and r^B. The other investor must specialize, holding only the asset that yields the higher post-tax return.

The companies earn post-corporation-tax rates of return on their direct investment of r^A and r^B respectively. This is achieved by earning a pre-tax rate of return on investment in each country of p_j^i where $i = A,B$ represents the country of residence of the investor and $j = A,B$ represents the country of residence of the company. We therefore do not constrain the corporations to earn the same rate of return as each other in a single location. This may reflect, for example, differences in production technologies. We also make the stronger simplifying assumption that the rates of return earned by each company in the same location are independent of each other. That is, a rise in, say, inward direct investment to country A from country B does not affect the pre-tax rate of return on domestic investment in country A.[15] Finally, we also assume that FDI is wholly financed by the parent corporation; we do not allow the foreign subsidiary to be partly financed in the foreign location.[16]

Define the effective marginal tax rates faced by the company as T^i_j where again $i=A,B$ represents the country of residence of the investor and $j=A,B$ represents the country of residence of the company. Again, these tax rates are likely to incorporate elements of the tax systems of both countries—the corporation tax system of the country where the investment takes place and any further tax charged by the residence country on foreign-source income. It is reasonable to assume that each company will invest in each location up to the point at which[17]

$$(5.3) \qquad r^A=(1-T^A_A)p^A_A=(1-T^A_B)p^A_B$$

and

$$(5.4) \qquad r^B=(1-T^B_A)p^B_A=(1-T^B_B)p^B_B.$$

3.1 Co-operative behaviour

Within this simple framework, we can consider the combinations of tax rates that imply production efficiency. To begin with, consider the optimal tax structure when the two countries co-operate with each other. As noted above, it is already well known from the existing literature that the optimal tax structure in this case will exhibit capital export neutrality—the effective marginal tax rate facing each investor will be the same on all investments, although it may differ between investors. To investigate how that applies in this context, we set out the requirements for production efficiency, first in a co-operative setting:

$$(5.5) \qquad p^A_A=p^A_B=p^B_A=p^B_B.$$

Since the pre-tax rates of return on individual investments may differ from each other, production efficiency can only hold if (eqn 5.3) and (eqn 5.4) hold and at least one of (eqn 5.1) and (eqn 5.2) holds. To begin with, consider the case in which all the expressions (eqn 5.1) to (eqn 5.5) hold

---

[15] The implications of relaxing this assumption are analysed by Devereux (1998).

[16] Frisch (1990) and Hufbauer (1992) point out that, if, at the margin, each foreign affiliate of the multinational raises funds locally from portfolio investors, then multinationals would not play a decisive role in allocating capital across countries; this would imply that (eqn 5.3) and (eqn 5.4) may not hold.

[17] It should be noted that this formulation implies that corporate-level taxes are deductible for the purposes of determining personal-level taxes. The role of integration credits is explored below.

simultaneously. This implies the existence of an 'international capital market' in which investors from both countries invest in the corporations in both countries. Expressions (eqn 5.1) to (eqn 5.5) hold if the following two conditions are true:

(5.6) $$T^A_A = T^A_B \quad \text{and} \quad T^B_A = T^B_B$$

and

(5.7) $$\frac{1-t^A_A}{1-t^A_B} = \frac{1-t^B_A}{1-t^B_B} = \frac{1-T^B_B}{1-T^A_A}.$$

Expression (eqn 5.6) states that the corporate tax rate facing any corporation must be independent of the location in which the investment is undertaken: this is clearly a form of capital export neutrality, although it applies only at the level of the corporation.

If (eqn 5.6) holds, then the remaining requirements of the tax system to achieve production efficiency are summarized by expression (eqn 5.7). This is a slightly more complex requirement; it implies that any difference in the corporate tax rates faced by the two corporations must be offset by the personal taxes faced by all investors. Suppose, for example, that the corporate tax rate in country B exceeds that in country A, i.e. $T^B_B > T^A_A$. Then all investors must face a lower tax rate when supplying funds to the corporation in country B than when supplying funds to the corporation in country A, i.e. $t^A_A > t^A_B$ and $t^B_A > t^B_B$. This implies, for example, that the government in country A would need to set the personal tax rate on outward FPI lower than the personal tax rate on domestic portfolio investment, in order to offset the effect of the higher corporate tax in country B.

This offsetting effect is clearly unlikely in practice. However, one combination of tax rates that would satisfy both (eqn 5.6) and (eqn 5.7) is as follows:

(5.8) $$T^A_A = T^A_B = T^B_A = T^B_B$$

and

(5.9) $$t^A_A = t^A_B \quad \text{and} \quad t^B_A = t^B_B.$$

Expression (eqn 5.9) requires residence-based taxes on portfolio investment; this might be termed *portfolio capital export neutrality.* With such a tax system, it is clear from (eqn 5.1) and (eqn 5.2) that $r^A = r^B$: the post-corporation-tax rate of return must be the same for both corporations. Expression (eqn 5.8) then requires *all* corporate tax rates to be equal— given that the post-corporation-tax rates of return are the same, then all the corporation tax rates must also be equal. This condition goes beyond the requirement for capital export neutrality at the corporate level.

Instead, it can be seen as a requirement for both capital export neutrality and capital import neutrality at the corporate level; these might be termed *direct capital export neutrality* and *direct capital import neutrality*.

This distinction goes some way towards explaining the apparently divergent views on the relative importance of CEN and CIN expressed by McLure (1992): 'economists have generally favored CEN because it maximises global welfare ... but businessmen generally favor the "level playing field" provided by CIN'. The conditions set out here are essentially requirements for achieving CEN on total investment. But by splitting the relevant tax rates into two, it is understandable that businessmen focus primarily on corporation tax rates. If personal taxes are levied on a residence basis, then competing companies must earn the same post-corporation-tax rate of return. Any difference in the corporate tax rate faced by two corporations competing in the same location will give one a competitive advantage. Not surprisingly, then, businessmen are concerned with direct CIN; the analysis here shows that this is entirely consistent with CEN on total investment.

As noted above, this discussion has been based on the assumption that both (eqn 5.1) and (eqn 5.2) hold—that is, that tax rates are such that both investors invest in both corporations. This is not a necessary condition for production efficiency. Suppose, for example, that country B charges a very high tax rate on outward FPI (t_A^B), which leaves the investor resident in country B investing only in the corporation resident in country B. In this case, expression (eqn 5.2) will not hold and r^A and r^B will be determined from (eqn 5.1). The condition for production efficiency is then modified; the middle term in (eqn 5.7) disappears. It remains the case that the personal tax rates facing the investor resident in country A must offset any differences in the corporate tax rates in countries A and B; however, the personal tax rates faced by the investor resident in country B play no role.

3.1.1 Integration of corporate and personal taxes

The analysis so far has abstracted from any precise definitions of the tax rates. This has left an important issue unresolved: the role played by integration credits. Boadway and Bruce (1992) and Devereux and Freeman (1995) analyse the likely impact of introducing various forms of integration on domestic saving and investment and on international capital flows. The aim here is more modest—it is simply to examine the extent to which such forms of integration would be consistent with the achievement of production efficiency.

a. Integration credits applying to all direct investment by each company
Consider first the implications of introducing a form of integration that

applied to all income earned by the corporation, but that may not apply to all shareholders. Specifically, for $i=A,B$ and $j=A,B$, let

(5.10)
$$1-t_j^i = \frac{1-m^i}{1-c_j^i},$$

where m^i is the personal income tax rate of the investor in country i and c_j^i is the rate of integration credit offered to the investor in country i on income received from the corporation resident in j. This formulation therefore assumes that personal investment income is generally taxed on a residence basis at rate m^i, but that, in addition, some forms of investment receive an integration credit at rate $c_j^i > 0$ and others do not. In this case, the two no-arbitrage conditions for the investors—(eqn 5.1) and (eqn 5.2)—become

(5.1a)
$$s^A = \frac{(1-m^A)}{(1-c_A^A)} r^A = \frac{(1-m^A)}{(1-c_B^A)} r^B$$

and

(5.2a)
$$s^B = \frac{(1-m^B)}{(1-c_A^B)} r^A = \frac{(1-m^B)}{(1-c_B^B)} r^B.$$

Combining (eqn 5.1a) and (eqn 5.2a) with the no-arbitrage conditions at the corporate level—(eqn 5.3) and (eqn 5.4)—yields two conditions for production efficiency. The first is exactly the same as (eqn 5.6). The second is a slight modification of (eqn 5.7):

(5.7a)
$$\frac{1-c_B^A}{1-c_A^A} = \frac{1-c_B^B}{1-c_A^B} = \frac{1-T_B^B}{1-T_A^A}.$$

This formulation implies that a higher corporate tax rate must be offset by a higher integration credit. Thus if, for example, the corporate tax rate in country B is higher than that in country A, then all shareholders of the corporation in country B must be given a higher integration credit on income received from country B which offsets this effect. Of course, in the case of full integration, $c_B^A = c_B^B = T_B^B$ and $c_A^A = c_A^B = T_A^A$. In this case, (eqn 5.7a) holds—production efficiency is achieved since there is, in effect, no corporate-level tax but only residence-based personal income taxes.

More generally, (eqn 5.7a) implies that, for $T_A^A \neq T_B^B$, the rate of integration credit given to shareholders should be the same for all shareholders of each corporation, i.e. at the rate of the country of residence of the corporation.[18] However, it also implies a close link between the rates of integration credit applied in different countries. Without this link—i.e. the

---

[18] It should be noted that there is no implication here as to which of the two countries should bear the revenue costs of any relief; the discussion is confined to what the rate of relief should be.

ratios in (eqn 5.7a) being equal to each other—setting integration rates in this way either will not achieve production efficiency or will lead to the investor in one country investing only in one corporation.

Alternatively, one way of achieving (eqn 5.6) and (eqn 5.7a) is close to that described above: set all corporate tax rates equal, so that $T_A^A = T_B^B$ (as in (eqn 5.8)) and set integration credits at the rate of the residence country of the investor:

$$(5.9a) \qquad\qquad c_A^A = c_B^A \quad \text{and} \quad c_A^B = c_B^B.$$

This condition implies the existence of portfolio CEN, which, as noted above, combined with direct CEN and direct CIN, ensures production efficiency. It is interesting to note that the longer-term proposals of the Ruding Committee (Commission of the European Communities, 1992) are largely summarized by (eqn 5.8) and (eqn 5.9a). The committee proposed a common tax base together with tax rates within a narrow band, thus approximating direct CEN and direct CIN. It also proposed, on a reciprocal basis, relief for dividend taxation at the rate of the residence country. However, it is important to note here that portfolio CEN is only optimal in conjunction with direct CEN and direct CIN: if (eqn 5.8) does not hold, then portfolio CEN is not optimal—rather, integration credits should be the same for all shareholders of each corporation.

b. Different rates of integration credits for domestic and foreign direct investment By contrast, now consider the case in which the integration credit is available to all shareholders, but at different rates on domestic direct investment and FDI. Expressions (eqn 5.6) and (eqn 5.7) remain necessary conditions for production efficiency. Various possible combinations of corporate tax rates and integration credit rates could be permitted as long as these expressions continue to hold.

Two obvious examples can be looked at. First, consider the case in which, in the absence of the integration credit, the tax rates on domestic investment and outward FDI are the same—that is, as in (eqn 5.6). Clearly, introducing an integration credit that reduced the effective tax rate on one form of investment but not the other would be inconsistent with (eqn 5.6) and hence inconsistent with production efficiency.

However, suppose that there is a full integration credit for domestic investment $(c_A^A = T_A^A)$, which implies that the total effective tax rate for domestic direct investment financed by domestic portfolio investment is m^A. One way to achieve production efficiency in this case would be to exempt income from FDI from corporate tax, so that $T_B^A = 0$ (this would imply exemption in both country A and country B). In this case, the integration credit should apply only to income from domestic investment, so that $c_B^A = 0$, and the total effective tax rate for FDI financed by domestic portfolio investment is again m^A. It should be noted, however, that, in practice, if the integration credit is only available on distributed profits, then the effective corporate tax rate on domestic investment may be greater than zero.

3.2   Non-cooperative behaviour

The standard efficiency conditions for the behaviour of a country that does not co-operate were set out in Section 2. First, a capital-importing country should not tax the income from capital; introducing such a tax simply increases the required pre-tax rate of return, driving away capital. Since the immobile factors in the economy bear the incidence of the tax, it is more efficient to tax those factors directly. Second, a capital-exporting country should aim for production efficiency—applied to the pre-domestic-tax rates of return earned by domestic residents.

To analyse these conditions in the presence of FPI and FDI, it is necessary first to separate the overall corporate tax rate of the previous section, T_j^i, into two components. First, there is the corporate tax charged by the source country, j, (where the investment takes place) on income from capital accruing to the residence country, i; denote this S_j^i. Second, there is the corporate tax charged by the residence country of the corporation on the foreign-source income generated. The amount of tax charged by the residence country depends on the form of the tax system. As is well known, there are several ways that foreign-source income is dealt with in practice—exemption, partial credit,[19] and deduction. To maintain some generality, define the residence-country tax rate as $R_j^i(S_j^i)$, indicating that the residence-country tax rate depends on the source-country tax rate. The overall tax rate is defined by $1 - T_j^i = (1 - R_j^i(S_j^i))(1 - S_j^i)$. This formulation can incorporate a deduction system if $R_j^i(S_j^i) = S_j^i$, a partial credit system if $R_j^i(S_j^i) = \max\{S_i^i - S_j^i, 0\}$, and an exemption system if $R_j^i(S_j^i) = 0$, where S_i^i is the residence-country tax rate on domestic income.

Given these definitions, we can restate the relevant no-arbitrage conditions. Consider just the position of country A, acting to maximize its own welfare without co-operating with other countries. The individual investor in country A faces the same opportunities as before; the no-arbitrage condition is therefore as set out in (eqn 5.1). The two corporations also face the same opportunities, set out in (eqn 5.3) and (eqn 5.4),

[19] It is partial since if the tax already paid exceeds the domestic liability (before relief), no rebate is given.

but these can be written to identify the relevant tax rates imposed by each country:

(5.3b) $$r^A = (1 - S_A^A)p_A^A = (1 - R_B^A(S_B^A))(1 - S_B^A)p_B^A$$

and

(5.4b) $$r^B = (1 - R_A^B(S_A^B))(1 - S_A^B)p_A^B = (1 - S_B^B)p_B^B.$$

Production efficiency is achieved if the pre-residence-country-tax rates of return—i.e. the social rates of return to the residence country—on all investments undertaken are equal. Two of these rates of return are straight-forward: on purely domestic investment, the pre-tax rate of return is p_A^A; on outward FPI, it is r^B. However, there are two other relevant investments. The first is outward FDI by the corporation in country A. Define the social rate of return to country A of such investment as $q_B^A = (1 - S_B^A)p_B^A$—that is, the return net of taxes charged by country B. The second is outward FDI (from country B to country A) by the corporation in country B, which in turn is financed by outward FPI by residents of country A. The social return to country A of this form of investment is the pre-tax rate of return, p_A^B, less the tax levied by country B on the income, $R_A^B(S_A^B)(1 - S_A^B)p_A^B$.[20] Summarizing, and assuming that all such forms of investment are undertaken, production efficiency requires

(5.11) $$p_A^A = r^B = (1 - S_B^A)p_B^A = \{1 - R_A^B(S_A^B)(1 - S_A^B)\}p_A^B.$$

What combination of tax rates set by country A can achieve this condition? Combining (eqn 5.1), (eqn 5.3b), (eqn 5.4b), and (eqn 5.11) yields the following two conditions:

(5.12) $$(1 - t_A^A)(1 - S_A^A) = (1 - t_A^A)(1 - R_B^A(S_B^A)) = 1 - t_B^A$$

and

(5.13) $$S_A^B = 0.$$

The second of these conditions is simply a restatement in this context of the requirement that capital imports are not taxed. This applies even if they are ultimately funded by resident investors. That is, inward FDI should not be discouraged by taxing the returns to it, whatever the source of funding.

---

[20] This assumes that the FDI into country A has no effect on the prices of immobile factors within country A and hence on p_A^A. It is possible that higher inward FDI pushes up these prices and hence depresses p_A^A. In this case, the optimal tax structure would incorporate a tax on inward FDI to offset this effect; see Devereux (1998).

The first condition in effect simply restates the proposition that the domestic tax rate on all forms of income from capital should be the same. This implies, first, that the overall tax rates applied to income accruing to domestic investment and outward FDI are the same. One way of achieving this (although clearly not the only way—as we discuss further below in the context of integration) is that foreign taxes should be deducted in determining the corporate tax base, i.e. $S_A^A = R_B^A(S_B^A)$. Having made the deduction, all income accruing to the domestic corporation and hence to domestic investors should be treated in the same way. The first condition also makes clear, however, that this total tax rate should also be applied to outward foreign portfolio investment. That is, in the absence of any system of integration, the personal tax rate on such portfolio investment should equal the total of corporate and personal taxation on domestic investment.

It is useful to assess the role of integration systems in achieving condition (eqn 5.12). Suppose, for example, that $t_A^A = t_B^A$. Condition (eqn 5.12) could then hold only if integration systems in effect set the corporate tax levied on purely domestic corporations to zero, i.e. $S_A^A = 0$. However, an alternative possibility is simply a full integration system for domestic portfolio investment $(c_A^A = S_A^A)$, but only to the extent to which it finances domestic direct investment. Such a system would leave two possibilities for the treatment of foreign-source income from domestic investment. It could be exempt from corporation tax and paid direct to the shareholder without any integration credit, i.e. setting $R_B^A(S_B^A) = 0$ and $c_A^A = 0$ for this form of direct investment. Alternatively, the government could levy corporation tax on such foreign-source income at the full domestic rate, with a deduction for foreign taxes—i.e. setting $R_B^A(S_B^A) = S_A^A$—and then permit a full integration credit on all income paid by the domestic corporation to its shareholders.

Clearly, the exemption route has lower compliance costs and is simpler to administer.[21] This is the system that is currently in operation in Germany (see Harris (1996)). The alternative requires collecting tax on world-wide activities (in principle, without deferral, in order to treat them in the same way as domestic investment) and then rebating it to domestic shareholders in the form of an integration credit. Although no country achieves this in practice, New Zealand clearly has aims in this direction (it does not use a deduction system, but it does make an attempt to tax foreign-source income as it accrues, and it does have a full integration system) (New Zealand Treasury, 1994 and 1995). The compliance costs of these two routes are clearly very different.

---

[21] Although there would remain a need to combat avoidance opportunities by corporations reclassifying domestic-source income as foreign-source income.

4. FDI and imperfect competition

All of the models so far analysed are based on simple models of behaviour under perfect competition. It is assumed that a particular form of investment activity will take place, with a declining marginal product, up to the point at which the post-tax marginal product is equal on all types of activity. This makes it possible to analyse aggregate investment decisions by focusing on marginal investments and the tax rate on marginal investments.

The precise nature of the tax rates has not been discussed in detail. But all of the tax rates so far used have been *effective marginal tax rates (EMTRs)*. These describe the proportionate difference between the pre-tax and post-tax rates of return on a marginal investment project. For example, suppose that an investor required a post-tax rate of return of 6 per cent on an investment, which implied a pre-tax minimum rate of return of 10 per cent. Then the EMTR would be 40 per cent.

But, certainly at a microeconomic level, there may frequently be cases where the EMTR is not the most appropriate measure of taxation. Consider, for example, a multinational company that has some firm-specific advantage over its rivals—for example, a patent for a new product. Producing and selling the new product will earn an economic rent. The company can choose a location for production, but probably does so from a relatively small number of mutually exclusive options. The discrete nature of the choice of location implies that the effective marginal tax rate is unsuitable in measuring the impact of tax on the location choice—although it may remain relevant in determining the level of output conditional on the choice of location. Rather, the company will simply choose the location that provides the highest post-tax profit. But since this is not a marginal investment, it is more natural to consider the impact of taxation by measuring the reduction in the level of profit—or economic rent—available in each location.[22]

Consider the simple case of the profit-maximizing behaviour of a single representative firm that intends to supply a foreign market. There are increasing returns to scale at the plant level, at least over a range of output. There are also costs of exporting from home to serve the foreign market. There are two possible strategies open to the firm. Let strategy 1 be to produce at home and export to the foreign market, and strategy 2 be to produce and sell abroad. In the absence of taxation, the overall levels of profit from these two strategies are Π_1^* and Π_2^*, where the asterisk indicates the absence of tax. These levels of profit may differ from each

[22] See Devereux and Griffith (1998a and 1998b) for a fuller analysis of these issues.

other, depending on the level of transport costs and the degree of increasing returns to scale at plant level. However, the firm chooses the option that generates the higher post-tax level of profit, Π_1 or Π_2. That is, the decision rule is to choose, say, strategy 1 if

$$(5.14) \qquad\qquad \Pi_1^*(1 - T_1^*) > \Pi_2^*(1 - T_2^*).$$

Here, T_1^* and T_2^* are *effective average tax rates*—they are the proportionate reduction in the pre-tax level of profit.

An important distinction between portfolio and direct investment is therefore that location decisions associated with FDI are likely to be affected by effective average tax rates. By contrast, it is reasonable to assume that portfolio investment—which, by its nature, does not imply any controlling influence—expects to yield only the required rate of return and not a share of the economic rent (if a project was expected to earn an economic rent, its price to new investors would be higher). The impact of tax on portfolio investment can therefore be captured by the effective marginal tax rate.

There are relatively few models concerned with optimal taxation of capital income in the context of more realistic models of FDI. Exceptions are Janeba (1996), Haufler and Wooton (1999), and Devereux and Hubbard (1998), which are all based on a framework developed by, among others, Markusen (see, for example, Horstmann and Markusen (1992) and Markusen (1995)). Even these models, however, tend to be based on optimal tax setting when there is a specific form of FDI, typically by a single multinational firm with a set of well-defined options. Such models need to be developed to allow for the simultaneous existence of many multinationals making location choices, which are different from each other. Such an approach has not yet been developed; however, it seems unlikely that aggregating the investment flows of a number of multinationals will yield conditions under which the relevant tax rate becomes the effective marginal tax rate, as in the simple models.

5. Conclusions

This chapter has examined simple rules for the optimal taxation of income from international capital flows, when there exist two forms of such flows—foreign portfolio investment and foreign direct investment. Distinguishing between these two types of flows permits a richer analysis of optimal tax treatment, especially with regard to the appropriate specification of forms of integration of corporate and personal taxes.

The two types of flows are distinguished in two ways. First, the no-arbitrage conditions that govern the required post-tax rates of return are different, and reflect different levels of taxation. Second, the nature of the two flows is inherently different: it is reasonable to suppose that the expected rate of return on portfolio investment is the minimum required rate of return—since the price of the asset purchased will adjust until this is true. But this implies that the impact of the tax can be studied in a conventional way, using the effective marginal tax rate.

By contrast, direct investment is undertaken by corporations which frequently expect to earn an economic rent. To the extent that FDI flows reflect the location decisions of multinationals, it is reasonable to suppose that such flows are affected primarily by the effective average tax rate. This implies that the conventional result—that a tax with a zero effective *marginal* tax rate does not distort investment decisions—does not hold for the location decisions of multinationals. In turn, this implies that both the tax base and the tax rate are relevant to harmonization, even if the tax base is precisely targeted towards economic rent.

However, under more conventional assumptions, it is possible to examine the tax treatment of FPI and FDI consistent with achieving the goal of production efficiency. In the context of co-operative tax policy, for example, this distinction leads to two conditions: effective marginal tax rates on direct investment should be the same for any given company, and differences in such tax rates across countries should be offset by differences in personal tax rates. Overall, these conditions imply capital export neutrality, as in the existing literature.

One way of applying the conditions would be to set all effective marginal tax rates on direct investment equal—this implies a form of capital import neutrality as well as capital export neutrality—and to set effective marginal tax rates on portfolio investment on a residence basis. This combination is probably more feasible than others implied by the optimality conditions, although there are clearly practical difficulties in imposing a residence-based tax on portfolio investment. If the first condition holds, then integration credits should be given at the rate of the shareholder's country of residence. However, if it does not, then integration credits must be used to offset differences in the underlying corporate tax rates, implying that they should be the same for all shareholders of a given corporation.

A further issue in the role of the integration system appears for both co-operative and non-cooperative tax policy: the treatment of foreign-source income at the level of the corporation. If there is a full integration credit for domestic investment, then in both the co-operative and the non-cooperative cases, the choice for foreign-source income is either to exempt it entirely at the corporate level or to tax it with a deduction for foreign taxes but then give the integration credit in the same way as for domestic income. However, since the integration credit generally applies only when income is paid to the ultimate shareholder, deferral becomes important. Domestic corporate income is normally taxed on accrual, which implies that there is a residual tax on retained earnings. Unless foreign-source income is also taxed on accrual, there will be no equivalent level of (domestic) tax on foreign-source income.

References

Alworth, J. S. (1988), *The Finance, Investment and Taxation Decisions of Multinationals*, Oxford: Basil Blackwell.

——(1998), 'Taxation and integrated financial markets: the challenges of derivatives and other financial innovations', *International Tax and Public Finance*, 5: 507–34.

Auerbach, A. J., and Hassett, K. (1993), 'Taxation and foreign direct investment in the United States: a reconsideration of the evidence', in A. Giovannini, R. G. Hubbard and J. Slemrod (eds), *Studies in International Taxation*, Chicago: University of Chicago Press.

Boadway, R., and Bruce, N. (1992), 'Problems with integrating corporate and personal income taxes in an open economy', *Journal of Public Economics*, 48: 39–66.

Bond, E. W., and Samuelson, L. (1989), 'Strategic behaviour and the rules for international taxation of capital', *Economic Journal*, 99: 1099–111.

Cantwell, J. (1994), 'The relationship between international trade and international production', in D. Greenaway and L. Winters (eds), *Surveys in International Trade*, Oxford: Basil Blackwell.

Chennells, L., and Griffith, R. (1997), *Taxing Profits in a Changing World*, London: Institute for Fiscal Studies.

Commission of the European Communities (1975), 'Draft Directive concerning the harmonisation of systems of company taxation and of withholding tax on dividends', *Official Journal of the European Communities*, C253, COM(75) 392 final.

——(1992), *Report of the Committee of Independent Experts on Company Taxation*, Luxemburg (the Ruding Report).

Devereux, M. P. (1998), 'Some optimal tax rules for international portfolio and direct investment', Warwick University, mimeo.

——and Freeman, H. (1995), 'The impact of tax on foreign direct investment: empirical evidence and the implications for tax integration schemes', *International Tax and Public Finance*, 2: 85–106.

——and Griffith, R. (1998a), 'Taxes and the location of production: evidence from a panel of US multinationals', *Journal of Public Economics*, 68: 335–67.

——and——(1998b), 'The taxation of discrete investment choices', Institute for Fiscal Studies, Working Paper 98/16.

——and Hubbard, R. G. (1998), 'Taxing multinationals', Warwick University, mimeo.

——and Pearson, M. (1989), *Corporate Tax Harmonisation and Economic Efficiency*, London: Institute for Fiscal Studies.

——and——(1995), 'European tax harmonisation and production efficiency', *European Economic Review*, 39: 1657–81.

Diamond, P. A., and Mirrlees, J. (1971), 'Optimal taxation and public production, I: production efficiency; II: tax rules', *American Economic Review*, 61: 8–27; 261–78.

Dunning, J. H. (1977), 'Trade, location of economic activity and MNE: a search for an eclectic approach', in B. Ohlin, P. O. Hesselborn and P. M. Wijkman (eds), *The International Allocation of Economic Activity*, London: Macmillan.

——(1981), *International Production and the Multinational Enterprise*, London: George Allen and Unwin.

Feldstein, M. S., and Hartman, D. (1979), 'The optimal taxation of foreign source investment income', *Quarterly Journal of Economics*, 93: 613–29.

Frisch, D. J. (1990), 'The economics of international tax policy: some old and new approaches', *Tax Notes*, 30 April: 581–91.

Gordon, R. H., and Jun, J. (1993), 'Taxes and the form of ownership of foreign corporate equity', in A. Giovannini, R. G. Hubbard and J. Slemrod (eds), *Studies in International Taxation*, Chicago: University of Chicago Press.

Harris, P. (1996), *Corporate-Shareholder Income Taxation and Allocating Taxing Rights between Countries: A Comparison of Imputation Systems*, Amsterdam: International Bureau of Fiscal Documentation.

Haufler, A., and Wooton, I. (1999), 'Country size and tax competition for foreign direct investment', *Journal of Public Economics*, 71: 121–39.

Horst, T. (1980), 'A note on the optimal taxation of international investment income', *Quarterly Journal of Economics*, 94: 793–8.

Horstmann, I. J., and Markusen, J. R. (1992), 'Endogenous market structure and international trade', *Journal of International Economics*, 32: 109–29.

Hufbauer, G. C. (1992), *US Taxation of International Income: Blueprint for Reform*, Washington, DC: Institute for International Economics.

Huizinga, H., and Nielsen, S. B. (1996), 'The coordination of capital income and profit taxation with cross-ownership of firms', Economic Policy Research Unit, Copenhagen Business School, Copenhagen, mimeo.

——and——(1997), 'Capital income and profits taxation with foreign ownership of firms', *Journal of International Economics*, 42: 149–65.

Institute for Fiscal Studies (1978), *The Structure and Reform of Direct Taxation*, London: George Allen & Unwin (the Meade Report).

——, Capital Taxes Group (1991), *Equity for Companies: A Corporation Tax for the 1990s*, Commentary 26, London: Institute for Fiscal Studies.

Janeba, E. (1996), 'Foreign direct investment under oligopoly: profit shifting or profit capturing', *Journal of Public Economics*, 60: 423–45.

Keen, M. J., and Piekkola, H. (1997), 'Simple rules for the optimal taxation of international capital income', *Scandinavian Journal of Economics*, 99: 447–61.

King, M. A., and Fullerton, D. (1984), *The Taxation of Income from Capital*, Chicago: University of Chicago Press.

Krugman, P. R. (1991), *Geography and Trade*, Cambridge, MA: MIT Press.

McLure, C. E., Jr. (1992), 'Coordinating business taxation in the Single European Market: the Ruding Committee report', *EC Tax Review*, 1: 13–21.

Markusen, J. R. (1995), 'The boundaries of multinational enterprises and the theory of international trade', *Journal of Economic Perspectives*, 9: 169–89.

Mintz, J. (1996), 'The corporation tax', in M. P. Devereux (ed.), *The Economics of Tax Policy*, Oxford: Oxford University Press.

Neumark Committee (1963), 'Report of the Fiscal and Financial Committee', in *Tax Harmonisation in the Common Market*, Chicago: Commerce Clearing House.

New Zealand Treasury (1994), *The Economics of International Taxation*, Wellington.

——(1995), *The Current International Tax Regime*, Wellington.

OECD (1991), *Taxing Profits in a Global Economy*, Paris: Organization for Economic Co-operation and Development.

Razin, A., and Sadka, E. (1991), 'International tax competition and gains from tax harmonisation', *Economics Letters*, 37: 69–76.

Slemrod, J. B. (1995), 'Free trade taxation and protectionist taxation', *International Tax and Public Finance*, 2: 471–90.

——, Alworth, J., Devereux, M. P., Gordon, R. H., Huizinga, H., and Vann, R. (1996), *The Taxation of Income from International Investment*, Paris: Organization for Economic Co-operation and Development.

——, Hansen, C., and Procter, R. (1997), 'The seesaw principle in international tax policy', *Journal of Public Economics*, 65: 163–76.

Stiglitz, J. E., and Dasgupta, P. (1971), 'Differential taxation, public goods and economic efficiency', *Review of Economic Studies*, 38: 151–74.

US Department of the Treasury (1992a), *Integration of the Individual and Corporate Tax Systems: Taxing Business Income Once*, Washington, DC: US Government Printing Office.

——(1992b), *A Recommendation for Integration of the Individual and Corporate Tax Systems*, Washington, DC: US Government Printing Office.

van den Tempel, A. J. (1971), *Corporation Tax and Individual Income Tax in the European Communities*, Brussels: Commission of the European Communities (the van den Tempel Report).

6
The taxation of interest in Europe: a minimum withholding tax?

HARRY HUIZINGA AND SØREN BO NIELSEN

The increasing international mobility of production factors, especially capital, poses well-known problems for tax authorities in open economies. Of great importance to European Union (EU) countries is the challenge to national tax authorities posed by the liberalization of capital flows between EU countries, as evidenced by the European Council Directive of June 1988. According to the directive, member countries were to completely liberalize international movements of capital before 1 July 1990. To establish a genuine market for financial services, it was deemed important to lessen the obstacles arising from differences in taxation across member countries and across financial instruments, and from tax evasion. In this light, the European Commission proposed a directive in May 1989 concerning a common system of source tax on interest income in the European Community (EC).

The Commission specifically proposed the introduction of a minimum Community-wide withholding tax on interest payments made to all Community residents to counter the risks of distortion, evasion, and avoidance in the present system. The minimum tax rate should be 15 per cent, corresponding to about the average of existing withholding taxes on interest in EC countries. The minimum withholding tax proposal, however, failed to secure the necessary unanimous support from EC member countries, and so was rejected in late 1989.

Given that the main reason for considering a minimum withholding tax is interest tax evasion, it is somewhat frustrating that there is no definitive evidence as to the extent of such evasion in Europe. 'Episodic' evidence, related to the German tax experiments with *'Quellensteuer'* in 1991 and *'Zinsabschlagsteuer'* since 1993, is discussed in Janeba and Peters (1996) and Alworth (1996). Kazemier (1991) and Frank (1991) estimate figures for

Comments from Sijbren Cnossen, Bernd Huber, Eiji Tajika, and an external referee, as well as from participants in the ISPE conference and in the Economic Policy Research Unit (Copenhagen Business School) workshop on 'Taxation Issues' are gratefully acknowledged. The activities of EPRU are financed by a grant from the Danish National Research Foundation.

the evasion of interest taxation occurring in the Netherlands prior to that country's introduction of a general reporting system. Weichenrieder (1996) gives an account of Germany's fight against evasion and avoidance of various capital income taxes. The common message of these and other studies seems to be that evasion phenomena in the area of capital income taxation are sufficiently important to constitute a major problem for tax authorities in industrialized countries.

We therefore find it worth while to reconsider the EC proposal. Previous research has—mainly verbally—focused on issues such as the possible short-comings of the proposal in the incomplete coverage of withholding taxes, the expected aversion on the part of some countries against accepting the proposal, and the effects on financial markets and institutions (compare, for example, Frank (1991) and Huizinga (1994)). We instead concentrate on some of the analytics of the proposal. In line with some critics,[1] we stress the connection between minimum withholding taxes in the EU and the competition for financial business activity between tax havens inside and outside the EU.

This chapter presents a three-country model of withholding taxation and banking activity. One country is a typical, large, EU country; the second is a tax haven inside the EU; and the third country is a tax haven outside the EU. The large country's residents can place deposits in all three countries. Similarly, firms in the first country may borrow at home or abroad. The country of destination of deposits will generally be determined by the withholding tax policies of the two EU countries, interest rates, profit (cost) margins of banks, and any idiosyncratic costs associated with households undertaking financial transactions abroad rather than at home.

In a non-cooperative withholding tax equilibrium (in which the outside tax haven, for simplicity, is assumed to abstain from withholding taxes), both EU countries make use of the withholding tax although, for reasonable parameter values, that of the inside tax haven is much lower than that of the typical EU country. We then consider the effects of forcing the inside tax haven to levy a minimum withholding tax above the non-cooperative level. While welfare in that country is not affected by a slight

[1] Giovannini (1989, pp. 369–70) notes: 'Europe is not a closed economy, and taxing capital income at the same rate within the EEC, given the current structure of tax systems, will not avoid an outflow to tax havens. This outflow could occur through countries which are presently imposing few or no capital controls, giving rise to a boom of financial intermediaries in those countries, unless strict controls *vis-à-vis* the rest of the world are imposed.' And Tanzi (1995, p. 129) notes that, '... even if countries of the European Union would agree on some policy among themselves, the existence of tax havens and of countries outside the European Union that would not be party to the agreement would raise questions about the degree to which the agreed solution would solve the problem'.

increase in its withholding tax, the typical EU country experiences a first-order effect on its welfare. A higher withholding tax in the inside tax haven will induce some households in the typical EU country to invest at home instead of in the tax haven. Thereby, the typical EU country's withholding tax revenue and profits from domestic banking operations increase, improving welfare. On the other hand, those households that *a fortiori* place funds in the inside tax haven will end up paying higher taxes there, and this lowers welfare. In principle, therefore, a marginal increase in the withholding tax in the inside tax haven has ambiguous welfare consequences for the EU partner.

To get some feel for the possible magnitudes, we undertake some simulations. These show, as a general rule, that it is welfare-improving for the typical EU country to have the inside tax haven raise its tax. This is especially so if the typical EU country is allowed to adjust its own withholding tax in response to the rise in the tax in the partner country. The inside tax haven, on the contrary, generally loses from the requirement to raise its tax. The main reason for this is the loss of banking business to the outside tax haven and to the EU partner.

Our analysis suggests that previous attempts to analyse the withholding tax proposal, focusing exclusively on EU countries, are too narrow.[2] It seems vital to incorporate tax evasion opportunities arising outside the EU, even if it paints a bleaker picture of the overall proposal. Since the effects on inside tax havens are expected to be negative, some transfer of resources to these countries may be needed to persuade them to accept an increase in minimum withholding taxes on interest in the EU.

We structure the remainder of the chapter as follows. Section 1 briefly describes the motivation for the Commission's proposal for a minimum withholding tax in the EC as well as the main effects of the proposal itself, including envisaged exemptions. Section 2 then presents the three-country model and lays out the deposit (borrowing) pattern of households (firms) in the typical EU country. Next, Section 3 characterizes the non-cooperative withholding tax equilibrium and considers the effect of a marginal rise in the inside tax haven's tax rate. Subsequently, Section 4 presents the numerical simulations characterizing how a requirement for the inside tax haven to discretely raise its withholding tax affects welfare in that country and in its EU partner.

Section 5 offers a broader evaluation of the model and of the EC minimum withholding tax proposal. It also looks at other possible solutions to the interest tax evasion problem in Europe. Our overall conclusion is somewhat distressing. While the minimum withholding tax proposal may have some favourable features, there are also drawbacks associated with

---

[2] This holds, for instance, for Janeba and Peters (1996); see Section 5.

outside tax havens and with implementing the tax within an increasingly complex international financial system. So it may certainly not be an ideal response to the widespread evasion of residence-based taxation of interest in today's EU. But the prospects for alternatives, such as greatly strengthened multilateral assistance or a complete EU-wide reporting system for interest payments, are even more gloomy.

1. The proposal for a minimum withholding tax on interest

This proposal was shaped by the EC Commission during the first half of 1989. A thorough 'communication' from the Commission to the EC Council motivated and described the proposal, leading not only to the 'proposal for a Council directive on a common system of withholding tax on interest income'[3] itself, but also to an additional 'proposal for a directive concerning mutual assistance by the competent authorities of the Member States in the field of direct taxation and value-added tax'.[4]

The two proposals were generally designed to deal with the increased risks of avoidance or evasion of capital income tax which could result from the liberalization of capital movements. The liberalization entails that Community residents are free to transfer their savings into bank accounts in any other Member State. If residents then do not declare their foreign interest income to their national tax authorities and evade payment of tax, it can cause a substantial loss of tax revenue in Member States.

In considering what measures to propose in this context, the Commission took the following factors into account: '(a) the risk that savings will be shifted to banks and other financial institutions in third countries; (b) the possible loss of business for Community banks and financial institutions; (c) the risk of an appreciable increase in interest rates and hence of a rise in the cost of money for European firms and governments; (d) the risk of significant increase in administrative costs for both the public authorities and financial institutions resulting from the measures to be taken; (e) the need to maintain the internal balance of the

---

[3] The term 'interest' in the proposal is supposed to cover all income from claims of any kind, including capital gains etc.; see the Commission's comments to article 2 in the proposal.

[4] Compare COM(89) 60 final 3, 1989. The immediate reason for these initiatives was that article 6(5) of Council Directive 55/361/EEC of 24 June 1988 stated that 'the Commission shall submit to the Council, by December 1988, proposals aimed at eliminating or reducing risks of distortion, tax evasion and tax avoidance linked to the diversity of national systems for the taxation of savings and for controlling the application of these systems. The Council shall take a position on these proposals by 30 June 1989.'

systems for the taxation of income in the different Member States, while at the same time encouraging closer alignment of national tax systems'.[5] Previously, the Commission had indicated that three (not mutually exclusive) ways of reducing distortions and evasion in the field of portfolio investment would be: (1) the introduction of a central system with automatic information transfer to authorities; (2) the introduction of a general withholding tax; and (3) the strengthening of mutual assistance between national tax authorities. With the twin proposals of 1989, the Commission decided not to pursue the first route. Instead, the second route was considered the most appropriate response and led to the minimum withholding tax proposal. (The third route was represented by the—weak—additional proposal.)

The main feature of the proposals was a minimum rate of withholding tax on interest paid by debtors residing in the Community. Member States would be free to apply a higher rate of withholding tax either to their own domestic taxpayers only or to all recipients of interest. However, a series of exemptions were permitted: Member States would be free not to apply the withholding tax to tax-exempt savings income, to interest payments constituting industrial or commercial income, and to interest payments made to residents of third countries or to international loans (Eurobonds). The Commission finally suggested a minimum rate of withholding tax of 15 per cent.

The supplementary proposal amends a previous directive[6] to remove purely administrative restrictions on mutual assistance, and to facilitate the exchange of information in cases where the tax authorities of the Member State of the investor in question can show that there are clear grounds for a presumption of fraud.

As seen from point (a) above, the Commission was well aware of the risk of capital outflows to third countries as a means of escaping taxation; in particular, it suggested that the Community should open negotiations with the major third countries involved, either bilaterally or within a multilateral framework such as the OECD.

The 1988 directive stipulated that 'any tax provisions of a Community nature shall, in accordance with the Treaty, be adopted unanimously'.[7] As one would expect, this requirement determined the fate of the two proposals on minimum withholding tax and mutual assistance.[8] Delegations of

[5] COM(89) 60 final 3, communication p. 4.

[6] Directive 77/799/EEC.

[7] Article 6, para. 5 in the directive of 24 June 1988.

[8] Frank (1991, p. 42) even writes: 'the effect of this provision is to compromise and even to render impossible, the adoption by the Council of Ministers of truly effective measures against distortion, tax evasion, and tax avoidance'.

four of the then twelve Member States—the UK, Germany, Luxemburg, and the Netherlands—voted against the adoption of the minimum tax proposals. The first three opposed them because they regarded them as too much of a constraint, whereas the Dutch did so because they thought them inefficient. All that came out of the initiative was a completely toothless compromise proposed by the Presidency of the Council following the summit of EC Heads of State and Government in Strasburg in December 1989. Since then, the question of a minimum withholding tax has come up a few times (Belgium in 1993 reintroduced the idea of a minimum 15 per cent withholding tax on only international interest payments; see Huizinga (1994)) without this leading to any action.

2 A simple three-country model

2.1 Introduction

In this section, we consider a simple model outlining some of the issues associated with the minimum withholding tax proposal. The model is necessarily very stylized.[9]

The model has three countries: country A is a typical EU country; country B, another EU country, is an 'inside' tax haven; country C is an 'outside' tax haven. In the background, there is the rest of the world, determining the international rate of interest applicable to inter-bank operations, denoted i^*. This interest rate is the 'raw' cost of funds for financial institutions in all three countries.[10] Countries B and C are taken to be small relative to country A. We wish to concentrate on capital flight from country A into these countries and disregard households and firms in countries B and C in the following. Banks in all countries are included, though. We concentrate on two groups of non-bank private agents: households and firms in country A. All households wish to deposit one unit of the numeraire good each. All firms instead need a loan of one unit to carry out projects. The words 'households' and 'firms' should not be taken literally—households stand for all depositors and firms for all borrowers.

Households (firms) in country A can deposit with (borrow from) domestic banks. They can also transact abroad, although this will involve

[9] Tax competition models can become very complicated. The purpose of our model is the same as that of Kanbur and Keen (1993, p. 877), who, in their commodity tax competition article, wish to '... develop a model that is rich enough to capture some of the central features of the interaction between national tax systems in an integrated world but simple enough to yield sharp insights into some of the central questions ...'.

[10] For simplicity, we ignore intermediation charges on inter-bank operations.

costs that vary across households (firms). Applying an idea from Gros (1990), we index households (firms) from 0 to 1 reflecting these costs. Households (firms), for simplicity, are uniformly distributed on [0,1].

In general, all transactions between a bank and a private agent (household or firm) give rise to small amounts of profits accruing to the bank.[11] Inter-bank transactions, however, yield no such profits as they occur at the baseline international interest rate. In what follows, we look at households and firms in country A, banks in all three countries, and the governments in countries A and B.

2.2 Households (depositors)

When depositing at home, households earn a before-tax interest rate of $i^* - \delta_A$, where i^* is the bank cost of funds[12] and δ_A is the contribution to profits demanded by banks in country A on deposits from households. Households are subject to a withholding tax at rate t_A. (This tax may alternatively be a residence-based personal capital income tax, backed by a national reporting system.) For convenience, we take this tax to be a specific tax. This should not affect any qualitative results below.

Alternatively, households may place funds abroad. If they deposit in country B, they earn the going bank cost of funds, i^*, minus bank profits, $\delta_B = \delta^* \leqslant \delta_A$, and minus the withholding tax in country B, t_B. Depositing in country B, however, involves costs of βh for household h (h in [0,1]). These costs represent transportation and communication expenses and efforts to conceal the transaction to domestic tax authorities. Country A formally has a residence-based capital income tax system. In principle, then, interest earned by country A households abroad is subject to country A's tax, t_A. We assume, though, that households in country A do not report any interest income earned abroad to their domestic tax authorities, and that the latter cannot monitor the foreign investments undertaken by domestic residents. In particular, no agreement exists between the domestic and foreign tax authorities that would ensure an adequate transfer of information.

If the households deposit in country C, there is, for simplicity, no withholding tax levied. Households then earn the cost of funds, i^*, minus the

[11] More broadly, 'profits' may represent increased remuneration or utilization of local production factors. This way, profits are still counted as a net contribution to national income, as opposed to the case where they represent the cost of labour inputs that otherwise would be employed elsewhere in the economy.

[12] An appendix with a more general version of our model, featuring imperfect competition and interest rate setting in the banking sector in country A, is available from the authors upon request. The qualitative results using the more general model are comparable to those that follow here.

local contribution to bank profits, $\delta_C = \delta^*$.[13] Further, there is a transactions cost of γh. We shall assume that depositing funds in country C, the outside tax haven, is less convenient than doing so in country B, the inside tax haven. This may reflect a greater distance, a lower awareness of this opportunity, etc. To capture this, the transactions cost parameter, γ, for country C is assumed to exceed the corresponding parameter, β, for country B:[14]

$$(6.1) \qquad\qquad \gamma > \beta.$$

Next, we characterize which of country A's households prefer to invest at home rather than abroad. To start, investing in country A is preferred to investing in country B if

$$(6.2) \qquad\qquad i^* - \delta_A - t_A > i^* - \delta^* - t_B - \beta h.$$

Let the value of h at which households are indifferent be denoted h_2, so that

$$(6.3) \qquad\qquad h_2 = \frac{t_A - t_B + \delta_A - \delta^*}{\beta}.$$

For values of h greater than h_2, country A's households prefer to deposit at home, and vice versa.

Similarly, country A's households prefer investing at home rather than in country C if

$$(6.4) \qquad\qquad i^* - \delta_A - t_A > i^* - \delta^* - \gamma h.$$

Households are indifferent between the two investment opportunities at a borderline parameter h_0 with

$$(6.5) \qquad\qquad h_0 = \frac{t_A + \delta_A - \delta^*}{\gamma}.$$

For values of h in excess of h_0, it is more attractive to invest in country A, and vice versa.

Finally, investing in country B is preferred to investing in country C if

$$(6.6) \qquad\qquad i^* - \delta^* - t_B - \beta h > i^* - \delta^* - \gamma h,$$

---

[13] With altogether $\delta_B = \delta_C \leqslant \delta_A$, the model can account for the possibility that banks may be more effective or under greater competitive pressure in tax havens than in the typical EU country.

[14] In sum, the two tax havens in the model are asymmetric due to both differences in concealment costs and the absence of a withholding tax in country C. Some asymmetry is necessary in order to generate sensible results from the minimum withholding tax experiments in Sections 3 and 4.

with indifference occurring if $h=h_1$, where

(6.7) $$h_1 = \frac{t_B}{\gamma-\beta}.$$

With γ exceeding β and a positive tax rate t_B in country B,[15] country C is preferred at very low values of h, i.e. for $h < \min(h_0, h_1)$. Accordingly, households with very low transactions costs turn to the outside tax haven rather than to domestic banks or the inside tax haven. In the following, we further assume that, for intermediate values of h, country B is the preferred investment destination, while for very high values of h, households prefer to place their funds at home, in country A. For this to be the case, we should have

(6.8) $$h_1 < h_0 < h_2,$$

while the borderline h_0 between countries A and C becomes irrelevant, as, with $h=h_0$, country B is the preferred destination. Condition (eqn 6.8) is equivalent to

(6.8′) $$\frac{t_B}{\gamma-\beta} < \frac{t_A + \delta_A - \delta^*}{\gamma} < \frac{t_A - t_B + \delta_A - \delta^*}{\beta}.$$

Figure 6.1 illustrates how households with different h choose the country of destination for their deposits. On the horizontal axis is the excess return from investing in country B (rather than in country A), and on the vertical axis the similar excess return from investing in country C (rather than in country A). Point E in the figure represents the two excess returns for a household with negligible transactions costs, i.e. for $h=0$. Clearly, with $t_B > 0$, E lies above the 45-degree line, so that country C is the preferred destination.

Raising h above zero corresponds to moving down along the line EFGH. When reaching F, h has increased to h_1, and investment opportunities in countries B and C are equivalent in terms of net returns. Both opportunities are *a fortiori* preferred to country A. Raising h further, country B is the preferred destination until we reach point G, where the returns from investing in countries A and B are identical. Point G corresponds to $h=h_2$. For even greater h, tax havens lose their appeal and households deposit domestically. Finally, point H corresponds to maximum transactions costs, i.e. $h=1$.

---

[15] Naturally, we take the tax rate in country A to be greater than zero, too. The validity of the assumptions of positive tax rates will be checked later on.

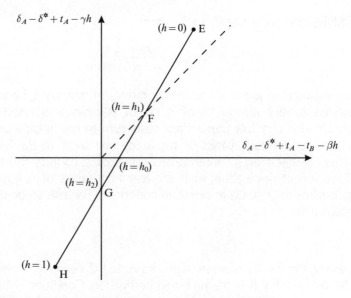

Fig. 6.1 The destination of deposits by country A households

2.3 Firms (borrowers)

Country A's firms can, in principle, borrow either at home or abroad. At home, the cost of borrowing equals the sum of the baseline interest rate, i^*, and the contribution to profits, δ_A. Borrowing abroad[16] results in a cost of borrowing of i^* plus bank profits of δ^* and transactions costs of ηf, where f is the index of domestic firms and η is a transactions cost parameter. If the profit parameter δ_A exceeds δ^*, then some of country A's firms indeed borrow internationally. Domestic borrowing is preferred to international borrowing if

$$(6.9) \qquad\qquad i^* + \delta_A \leqslant i^* + \delta^* + \eta f,$$

with indifference occurring at $f = f_I$, where

$$(6.10) \qquad\qquad f_I = \frac{\delta_A - \delta^*}{\eta}.$$

Obviously, for $f < f_I$, firms wish to borrow abroad, and vice versa.

---

[16] For simplicity, we assume that firms borrow from the rest of the world, not from the tax havens.

2.4 Banks in the three countries

Banks in all three countries can borrow and lend in the international inter-bank market at the rate i^*. As a result, they can always meet the demand for deposits and loans from households and firms in country A. Country C's banks receive deposits from households in country A in the amount h_1 to yield the following profits:

$$(6.11) \qquad P_C = h_1 \delta^*.$$

Country B's banks receive deposits of $h_2 - h_1$ from country A, yielding profits of

$$(6.12) \qquad P_B = (h_2 - h_1) \delta^*.$$

Finally, country A's banks receive $(1 - f_1)(i^* + \delta_A)$ in interest from firms and $i^*(f_1 - h_2)$ on net from inter-bank operations, while paying $(1 - h_2)(i^* - \delta_A)$ in interest to households in country A. Their total profits therefore amount to

$$(6.13) \qquad P_A = (2 - (h_2 + f_1)) \delta_A.$$

2.5 Governments

Next, we consider the optimal tax policies in countries A and B. In setting its withholding tax rate so as to maximize national surplus, each of the two governments takes the withholding tax of the other country as given. Further, it takes into account how a change in its own tax affects deposit decisions by country A's households. The two governments thus play a Nash non-cooperative tax game.[17]

Tax revenue is assumed to be scarce in both countries. As a result, the marginal costs of public funds (MCPFs) in the two countries, denoted by ρ_A and ρ_B, are assumed to exceed unity. The surplus to be maximized in the two countries comprises bank profits, tax revenues,[18] and (for country A) the difference between the total net interest earned by households (at home and abroad) and the total cost of borrowing for firms (at home and abroad). To see that this is the appropriate criterion, consider first the situation where the two profit parameters, δ_A and δ^*, are identical and no withholding tax is levied in country A. In this instance, there is no incentive for

---

[17] Alternatively, the authorities in country A could act as a Stackelberg leader and those in country B as a Stackelberg follower. A technical appendix available from the authors explores this alternative.

[18] Tax revenues represent the amount of public goods made possible by the revenues.

either households or firms to transact abroad, and the total national surplus becomes equal to zero. (Bank profits in country A exactly correspond to the difference between the total borrowing costs of firms and the net interest received by households and therefore are a simple transfer between agents in the private sector.) The introduction of a withholding tax in country A—motivated by a need for tax revenue—generally lowers the net earnings of households on their deposits while not affecting the borrowing costs on the part of firms.[19] The lower interest receipts by households are registered as part of the surplus in country A. In the surplus expressions, tax revenues are weighted by the respective MCPF (to generate the value of the public goods financed by the tax revenues).

To start with country B, tax revenue, denoted by T_B, equals $t_B(h_2 - h_1)$. The government thus maximizes the following surplus:

$$(6.14) \qquad S_B = \rho_B T_B + P_B = (\rho_B t_B + \delta^*)(h_2 - h_1).$$

Substituting for h_1 and h_2, we get

$$(6.14') \qquad S_B = \frac{(\rho_B t_B + \delta^*)}{\beta(\gamma - \beta)}[(\gamma - \beta)(t_A + \delta_A - \delta^*) - \gamma t_B].$$

The value of t_B that maximizes this surplus is given by

$$(6.15) \qquad t_B = \frac{(\gamma - \beta)(t_A + \delta_A - \delta^*) - \gamma \delta^*/\rho_B}{2\gamma}.$$

As expected, t_B goes up if t_A is increased. Similarly, t_B declines if the profit contribution, δ^*, rises. Thus, if banking services in country B become more profitable, then the withholding tax, t_B, will be lowered to attract more deposits from country A. Further, if public funds in country B become scarcer, as represented by a higher ρ_B, then more weight is put on tax revenues, leading to an increase in the tax rate t_B. Finally, if bank transactions in country A involve a higher profit margin, δ_A, there is room to increase the withholding tax for country B.

Next, we consider country A's surplus. As stated, it generally consists of (1) tax revenues weighted by the appropriate MCPF, (2) bank profits, and (3) the difference between the total earnings on deposits of households and the total cost of borrowing for firms. Tax revenue, T_A, equals $t_A(1 - h_2)$.

---

[19] In the more general model referred to in note 12, borrowing costs on the part of firms are affected via a change in the endogenous interest rate in country A.

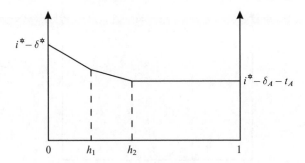

Fig. 6.2 Net interest earnings of households and the parameter *h*

Bank profits, P_A, are as in (eqn 6.13) above. The net interest receipts of domestic households from abroad can, with the aid of Fig. 6.2, be found as

$$(6.16) \qquad i^* - \delta_A - t_A + \tfrac{1}{2}[\beta h_2^2 + (\gamma - \beta)h_1^2].$$

Further, with the aid of Fig. 6.3, the gross borrowing costs to firms can be written as

$$(6.17) \qquad i^* + \delta_A - \tfrac{1}{2}\eta f_1^2.$$

In toto, country A's surplus is simply expressed as

$$(6.18) \qquad S_A = \rho_A t_A (1 - h_2) - t_A - \delta_A(h_2 + f_1) + \frac{\beta}{2}h_2^2 + \frac{\gamma - \beta}{2}h_1^2 + \frac{\eta}{2}f_1^2.$$

Again, we substitute for h_2, h_1, and f_1 from (eqn 6.3), (eqn 6.7), and (eqn 6.10). Next, we differentiate S_A with respect to t_A and solve for country A's optimal tax rate

$$(6.19) \qquad t_A = \frac{(\rho_A - 1)t_B + \beta(\rho_A - 1) - \rho_A(\delta_A - \delta^*) - \delta^*}{2\rho_A - 1}.$$

Note that the withholding tax in country A is higher, the higher is the withholding tax t_B in country B. Further, with the profit parameters δ_A and δ^* small enough and t_B non-negative, the optimum tax rate in country A is

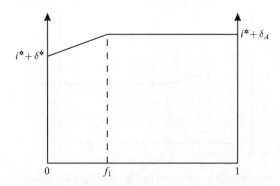

Fig. 6.3 Total borrowing costs of firms and the parameter f

positive. Also note that a higher profit margin abroad (at home) leads to a higher (lower) withholding tax in country A. Finally, the withholding tax in country A is seen to increase with the transactions cost parameter, β.

3. The non-cooperative withholding tax equilibrium

The two expressions for withholding tax rates in countries A and B, (eqn 6.15) and (eqn 6.19), in effect represent the reaction functions of the two governments. These Nash reaction functions are illustrated in Fig. 6.4 for moderate values of the profit parameters δ_A and δ^*. The reaction function for country A, denoted R_A, cuts the horizontal axis at a positive rate of t_A as long as $\delta^* + \rho_A(\delta_A - \delta^*) < \beta(\rho_A - 1)$. The reaction function for country B, denoted R_B, instead cuts the vertical axis for a negative value of t_B if $(\gamma - \beta)(\delta_A - \delta^*) - \gamma\delta^*/\rho_B < 0$. Hence we cannot be completely certain that the Nash equilibrium implies positive withholding tax rates in both countries. However, with profit parameters sufficiently small and the MCPFs sufficiently large, the Nash equilibrium tax rates will certainly be positive.

The Nash reaction functions yield the following explicit expressions for the optimal withholding tax rates in the two countries:

(6.20)
$$t_B = \frac{(\gamma - \beta)\beta(\rho_A - 1) + (\delta_A - \delta^*)(\gamma - \beta)(\rho_A - 1) - \delta^*(\gamma - \beta + \gamma(2\rho_A - 1)/\rho_B)}{2\gamma(2\rho_A - 1) - (\gamma - \beta)(\rho_A - 1)}$$

(6.21)
$$t_A = \frac{2\gamma\beta(\rho_A - 1) - (\delta_A - \delta^*)(2\gamma\rho_A - (\rho_A - 1)(\gamma - \beta)) - \delta^*\gamma(2 + (\rho_A - 1)/\rho_B)}{2\gamma(2\rho_A - 1) - (\gamma - \beta)(\rho_A - 1)}.$$

From these expressions, we confirm that both withholding tax rates are positive provided the national MCPF in country A, ρ_A, is sufficiently large

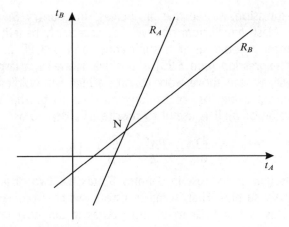

Fig. 6.4 The Nash withholding tax equilibrium

and the profit parameters, δ_A and δ^*, are sufficiently small. In other words, taxes are positive if tax revenue is badly needed and the profitability of banking business is limited. In the real world, this seems realistic enough.

It is interesting to consider the special case with profit parameters $\delta_A = \delta^* = 0$. This is the situation in which banking business adds nothing to local profits or the remuneration of local factors in general. With MCPFs greater than unity in the two countries, the ratio between the optimal withholding tax rates in countries B and A is simply given by $t_B/t_A = (\gamma - \beta)/(2\gamma)$. In other words, with only tax revenue and not the amount of bank business mattering, country B chooses a positive withholding tax rate that is less than half of country A's tax rate.

A marginal increase in the withholding tax in country B

The government in country B is assumed to maximize the social surplus with respect to the withholding tax, t_B, in the Nash equilibrium. A marginal increase in this tax then leaves the surplus in country B unchanged, as

(6.22)
$$\frac{dS_B}{dt_B} = 0.$$

However, a change in country B's withholding tax generally has a first-order effect on country A's surplus. To be precise, we find that the cross-effect, dS_A/dt_B, is given by the following surprisingly simple formula (using $dS_A/dt_A = 0$):

(6.23)
$$\frac{dS_A}{dt_B} = (1 - h_2)(\rho_A - 1) - (h_2 - h_1).$$

From this expression, we see that an increase in country B's withholding tax from the Nash equilibrium rate will not necessarily benefit country A. At first glance, it looks as if a sufficiently large MCPF in country A ensures that expression (eqn 6.23) is positive. However, a large MCPF in country A will, as seen above, work towards a high withholding tax in that country, implying a big loss of banking business to tax haven countries and a high value of h_2. It is useful to rewrite $dS_A/dt_B = 0$ as

$$(6.23') \qquad \frac{dS_A}{dt_B} = (\frac{\rho_A t_A}{\beta} + \frac{\delta_A}{\beta}) - (h_2 - h_1),$$

which reflects that an increase in country B's tax has two offsetting effects on country A's surplus. First, some investors switch from country B to country A. This is beneficial to country A, as it can now tax additional deposits, and bank profits increase. Second, depositors who remain in country B now face a higher tax, with negative implications for country A's surplus. As an aside, note that some marginal depositors switch from country B to country C without any implications for country A's surplus. To see how expression (eqn 6.23) depends on model fundamentals, we substitute for h_2 and h_1 using (eqn 6.3), (eqn 6.7), (eqn 6.20), and (eqn 6.21) to yield

$$(6.24) \qquad \frac{dS_A}{dt_B} = [N(\gamma - \beta)\beta]^{-1}[(\rho_A - 1)(2\rho_A - 1)(\gamma - \beta)\gamma\beta$$

$$- (\delta_A - \delta^*)(\rho_A - 1)(\gamma - \beta)(\gamma\rho_A + \beta(\rho_A - 1))$$

$$+ \frac{\delta^*}{\rho_B}\{\gamma^2\rho_A(\rho_B - \rho_A) + \gamma\beta(1 - \rho_B - 2\rho_A + \rho_A^2)$$

$$- \beta^2\rho_B(\rho_A - 1)\}]$$

in which

$$(6.25) \qquad N \equiv 2\gamma(2\rho_A - 1) - (\gamma - \beta)(\rho_A - 1) > 0.$$

It is in fact possible to sign this expression under certain circumstances. The first of the three major terms on the right-hand side is always positive (or zero for $\rho_A = 1$). The sign of the second term is negative under the maintained assumption of $\gamma > \beta$ (zero for $\delta_A = \delta^*$), whereas the sign of the third term depends on the relative size of the transactions cost parameters, γ and β, and of the two profit parameters, and on the size of the MCPFs in the two countries. With $\rho_A \geqslant \rho_B$ and $\delta_A \geqslant \delta^*$, the third term could well be negative. However, if the profit parameters are small enough and the MCPFs greater than unity, the right-hand side of (eqn 6.24) will be positive, so that in this instance the welfare effect in country A of forcing country B to raise its withholding tax marginally in fact is positive. More indirectly, using (eqn 6.23') and the definitions of h_1 and h_2, it is easy to see that $dS_A/dt_B > 0$, provided $t_A(\gamma - \beta)(\rho_A - 1) + t_B\gamma > 0$. As a corollary, if the Nash tax rates are both positive, then the welfare effect in country A of a higher tax in country B will be positive.

We sum up these theoretical insights in the following proposition:

> PROPOSITION. With γ exceeding β, with the marginal cost of public funds in either country above unity, and with low values of the profit parameters, the Nash equilibrium in withholding taxes features positive tax rates. In this case, a forced increase in the withholding tax rate on the part of country B will be beneficial to country A.

4. Some simulations with the model

In the end, we are interested in analysing not only a marginal increase in the withholding tax in country B, but also a discrete change up to some agreed minimum withholding tax rate for both countries A and B. To do this, we present some simple numerical simulations.

We proceed as follows: on the basis of reasonable model parameters, we first compute the Nash withholding tax rates in countries A and B, the amount of cross-border deposits (of households) and borrowing (of firms), and the two countries' surplus levels. We select a handful of alternative binding minimum tax rates for country B in the interval between the Nash rates of countries B and A. Country A is assumed either to keep its withholding tax rate unchanged at the Nash level or to respond in an optimal fashion (as given by its withholding tax reaction function) to the new value of the withholding tax in country B. We then compute the ensuing values of the surpluses in the two countries to see whether a minimum withholding tax in country B can in fact be Pareto-improving.

In the numerical calculations, the following parameter values are used: $\beta = 0.04$, $\gamma = 0.10$, $\delta_A = 0.002$, $\delta^* = 0.001$, $\rho_A = 1.5$, $\rho_B = 1.4$, and $\eta = 0.02$. The ensuing Nash withholding tax equilibrium, the extent of cross-border financial transactions, national surpluses, and bank profits are given in Table 6.1. We see that the withholding tax rates of countries A and B are 0.00944 and 0.00278, respectively. With an international interest rate of, say, $i^* = 0.06$, these specific tax rates correspond to *ad valorem* rates of 15.7 and 4.6 per cent, respectively.

The effect on country A's surplus of a marginal increase in country B's withholding tax is computed at 0.259 and hence is positive. Consequently, country A prefers the inside tax haven to raise its withholding tax.

Table 6.1 further illustrates the consequences of forcing country B to increase its withholding tax by 20, 40, 60, and 80 per cent, with the withholding tax rate in country A constant. While the experiments obviously

Table 6.1 The effects of forced increases in t_B from Nash equilibrium

	Initial Nash equilibrium	Increase in t_B with no response in t_A				Increase in t_B with reaction in t_A			
		20%	40%	60%	80%	20%	40%	60%	80%
t_A	0.009444	0.009444	0.009444	0.009444	0.009444	0.009583	0.009722	0.009860	0.009999
t_B	0.002776	0.003331	0.003886	0.004442	0.004997	0.003331	0.003886	0.004442	0.004997
h_1	0.046268	0.055521	0.064775	0.074028	0.083282	0.055521	0.064775	0.074028	0.083282
h_2	0.191699	0.177819	0.163938	0.150058	0.136178	0.181289	0.170878	0.160468	0.150058
h_0	0.104440	0.104440	0.104440	0.104440	0.104440	0.105828	0.107216	0.108604	0.109992
f_1	0.05	0.05	0.05	0.05	0.05	0.05	0.05	0.05	0.05
P_A	0.003517	0.003544	0.003572	0.003600	0.003628	0.003537	0.003558	0.003579	0.003600
P_B	0.000145	0.000122	0.000099	0.000076	0.000053	0.000126	0.000106	0.000086	0.000067
P_C	0.000046	0.000056	0.000065	0.000074	0.000083	0.000056	0.000065	0.000074	0.000083
S_A	0.002347	0.002497	0.002660	0.002836	0.003025	0.002498	0.002662	0.002840	0.003032
S_B	0.000711	0.000693	0.000639	0.000549	0.000423	0.000712	0.000683	0.000624	0.000534
dS_A/dt_B	0.258719	—	—	—	—	—	—	—	—

Note: $\beta=0.04$, $\gamma=0.10$, $\delta_A=0.002$, $\delta^*=0.001$, $\rho_A=1.5$, $\rho_B=1.4$, $\eta=0.02$.

are harmful to country B, they unambiguously benefit country A (with the values of parameters chosen). A careful weighting of the effects on national surpluses in the two countries is needed to determine whether the forced increase in the minimum withholding tax constitutes a potential Pareto improvement. A transfer of public funds from the authorities in country A to the authorities in country B has to be undertaken to ensure that the surplus in country B does not fall. With the parameter values selected, there is certainly scope for country A to compensate country B for its forced tax increase.

Alternatively, we assume that country A optimally adjusts its withholding tax rate following country B's tax increase, in accordance with (eqn 6.19). For the same higher values of the withholding tax in country B, the simulation results are reported in Table 6.1. In all cases, the authorities in country A are led to raise the domestic tax. This obviously raises the surplus in country A relative to the previous experiments. The surplus in country B also goes up (relative to the first set of experiments), as the increase in country A's withholding tax limits the loss of banking business and tax revenue in country B. In fact, due to the positive slope of country A's reaction function, a small increase in country B's tax with response in country A's tax actually improves both countries' welfare. For the parameters selected, this occurs for increases in t_B of between zero and some 22 per cent.[20]

Overall, the simulations suggest that for the typical EU country, an EU-wide minimum withholding tax could be rather beneficial. Conversely, any inside tax haven will be negatively affected, regardless of whether other EU countries take the opportunity to adjust their withholding tax to the higher minimum tax levels or not. As noted, the exception to this statement occurs for the case of a small forced increase in the tax haven's rate with a derived response in the typical EU country's tax. Anyhow, on the basis of our stylized model and the selected parameter values, it appears likely that the winner is able to compensate the loser.

The Nash equilibrium is depicted in Fig. 6.5 in the lower left corner of the figure (namely, point N; point S nearby is the Stackelberg equilibrium). We have also drawn the efficiency locus (contract curve) consisting of all Pareto-efficient withholding tax combinations for countries A and B. This locus is found by maximizing a weighted sum of the two countries' surpluses, $\mu S_A + (1-\mu)S_B$, with μ varying from 0 to 1. The locus is positioned somewhat further up and to the right of the Nash and Stackelberg equilibria, indicating that Pareto-efficient tax combinations generally have

---

[20] If country B is forced to raise t_B about 11 per cent or so, the gain in country B will be maximized, given that t_A is adjusted. In a way, this scenario replicates a Stackelberg equilibrium with country B as the leader and country A as the follower.

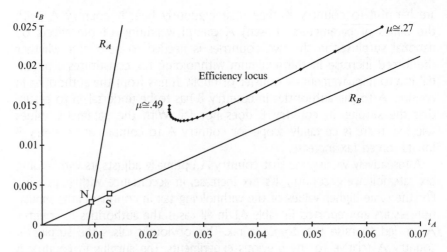

Fig. 6.5 Non-cooperative tax equilibrium and the contract curve

higher withholding tax rates for both countries than the two non-cooperative equilibria. Note that there is a tendency to opt for high tax rates when country B receives a high weight in the weighted objective function. For weights to country A lower than about 0.29, all deposits of households in that country are made in tax havens. Hence country B only has to worry about competition with the outside tax haven, and the only relevant tax instrument becomes t_B. On the other hand, for weights to country A exceeding about 0.49, it is efficient (for the two countries together) to eliminate the tax haven status of country B, with no deposits going from country A to country B. Then, *de facto*, the surplus in country A is maximized using only its own withholding tax rate, t_A.

5. Discussion

5.1 Remarks on the model

The model in Sections 2 to 4 has allowed us to come to grips with some of the key analytical aspects of the minimum withholding tax proposal. The different roles of typical EU countries, inside tax havens, and outside tax havens appear to be captured well by the model, as are the considerations governing withholding tax policy in the former two types of countries. The non-cooperative tax rates in the model are determined, in an intuitive way, by a trade-off between securing public funds, on the one hand, and bank profits, as a proxy for the benefits of banking business, on the other. Moreover, numerical simulations give an idea of the magnitudes of changes in tax rates and cross-border financial transactions, if the inside tax haven were to be forced to increase its withholding tax on account of a minimum withholding tax agreement.

Of course, the model is simplified to maintain tractability. First, we have focused on two particular aspects of tax competition: (1) competition between a typical EU country and tax havens, inside or outside the EU; and (2) competition between tax havens in the EU and outside it. In some sense, typical EU countries conceivably also compete with each other, but this aspect is of lesser importance and therefore excluded from the model. Second, we have ignored private agents in the inside tax haven. In principle, withholding tax policy in that country might also be governed by a desire to raise revenue from domestic savers or to prevent these savers from directing funds abroad. Other EU countries might attempt to attract savings from the inside tax haven country. Tax haven countries, however, tend to be rather small relative to typical large EU countries, so that these countries' savings are not a major concern for tax policy in any other country. The model's asymmetric treatment of the private sectors in the two EU countries therefore seems warranted.

Third, the model maintains a rather simple assumption as to the incidence of withholding taxes. Because of banks' unlimited access to the international inter-bank market with a fixed world rate of interest, depositors bear the full incidence of taxes in the model. In reality, the picture is more complicated, and there is evidence that a major part of the incidence may lie with debtors (see Huizinga (1994) and Eijffinger et al. (1996)).[21]

Fourth, the model contains some strong assumptions as to the tax treatment of savings. In the course of analysis, we have explicitly assumed that every saver in the typical EU country who places funds abroad is, in principle, liable to capital income taxes at home equal to the domestic withholding tax. Only the foreign withholding tax, however, is in fact paid when the investment is allocated abroad. Furthermore, we have taken the withholding taxes to apply to all financial returns. These assumptions can be qualified to take account of crediting arrangements as they actually exist among many countries. Also, a relatively large class of international investors—institutional investors—are subject to rather different tax treatments from those of individual investors. Often they are (close to) exempt from home-country taxation. At the same time, there is close surveillance by domestic authorities. For portfolio diversification reasons, institutional investors wish to allocate some funds abroad, but they are loath to pay

---

[21] In the more general model referred to in note 12, banks in country A (more correctly, their debtors) do bear part of the incidence of withholding taxes.

sizeable foreign withholding taxes. In addition, withholding taxes, as currently in force, are limited to simple financial transactions such as bank deposits, and they are very difficult to extend to derivative financial instruments (see below). Finally, political considerations might preclude the application of withholding taxes to certain financial instruments such as government bonds and Eurobonds.

There have been few analytical studies of a minimum withholding tax in Europe. Janeba and Peters (1996), however, investigate the proposal in their model of interest taxation in two (almost) symmetrical EU countries. The two countries have Leviathan governments, and they both tax an immobile base and compete for a mobile one. Focusing on the possible non-existence of non-cooperative tax equilibria in their paper, they also stress the desirability of tax discrimination between domestic and foreign depositors (such a distinction is irrelevant in our asymmetric model). Janeba and Peters ignore any outside tax havens, though.

5.2   Evaluating the minimum withholding tax proposal

The analysis in Sections 2 to 4 casts a mildly positive light on the proposal to install a minimum withholding tax in the EU. Typical EU countries seem to be able to gain from it, while inside tax haven countries in most cases stand to lose. However, the former should be able to compensate the latter.[22]

In order to advocate an EU-wide minimum withholding tax, it would, though, be necessary to overcome two lines of criticism. First, some argue that the minimum withholding tax, while seemingly beneficial, is not the most appropriate solution to interest tax evasion and distortions. Second, others argue that such a minimum withholding tax is very difficult to enforce properly in practice.

To deal with interest tax evasion, several experts propose a 'reporting system' similar to the one in use in five EU countries (Denmark, the Netherlands, Spain, France, and Sweden), to be extended to operate in the entire EU. The reporting system entails that domestic banks and other financial institutions automatically report to tax authorities (in Denmark, partially through a central register for securities) the amount of interest that has been paid out and to whom. If this system were to cover the entire EU, then information on all intra-EU interest payments could be recorded and exchanged between national tax authorities in the EU.

---

[22] This prediction, of course, raises the question as to why the withholding tax has yet found so little support, and, more specifically, why it has been so difficult to devise compensation arrangements that would work in practice.

As far as we know, the reporting systems function well in the above-mentioned five EU countries, ensuring a high degree of coverage in the tax system of interest earned domestically. It is an entirely different matter, though, to introduce such a system on an EU-wide basis, since this runs counter to the bank secrecy and blocking laws prevailing in many EU countries, not the least in tax havens. It requires considerable political will to remove these administrative and legal obstacles to the automatic exchange of information on interest payments in a comprehensive reporting system. In fact, at this stage, the requirement of unanimity in EU tax policy decisions suffices to prevent the reporting system from being adopted. The inside tax havens currently have very little incentive to remove any obstacles to information exchange; indeed, Bacchetta and Espinosa (1995) stress that, in circumstances of asymmetry between countries, there are strong disincentives to transmit information on capital income to other countries.

An EU-wide reporting system would allow member countries to continue to adhere to the residence principle in the taxation of interest. The reporting system is, therefore, strongly supported by many economists, including Frank (1991)—who, however, would like to see it coupled with a minimum withholding tax—Giovannini (1989), and others. Mayer (1989) goes one step further and suggests coupling the withholding of taxes on interest with a transfer of the associated tax revenue to the home country of the investor.[23] Such a system presupposes that the foreign tax authority not only collects taxes, but also is willing to transfer the revenue abroad in case of foreign investors; the incentives to undertake these functions would not be strong.[24]

As to the second line of criticism, the enforcement problems mainly have to do with significant exemptions from the withholding tax and with difficulties associated with applying the tax to new financial instruments. As seen in the presentation of the Commission proposal in Section 1, there would likely be a series of tax exemptions. In particular, the exemption of residents from third countries (giving an impetus to 'triangular arbitrage') and the non-application of the tax to interest from

[23] So that 'taxes are collected at source in the overseas country and a tax credit given for overseas taxes paid. The incentive to overtax is avoided by allowing the domestic country to claim tax credits from the overseas tax authority. The overseas tax authority is then merely acting as a tax collecting agent and deriving no tax revenue. This is exactly analogous to a local office of a national tax system.' (Mayer, 1989, p. 379.)

[24] This is also the reason we have ignored such transfers in our model of the minimum withholding tax above.

international loans (Eurobonds) can conceivably dilute the tax (see Frank (1991)).

Equally seriously, a host of new derivative financial instruments (DFIs) do not lend themselves well to withholding taxation. The tax presupposes an outgoing income payment but, for the DFIs, income may materialize in other ways, or there may be a series of ingoing as well as outgoing payments associated with the instrument. Often, a financial instrument can be imitated by a combination of other instruments. Only very carefully constructed capital gains and foreign exchange gains taxes can then ensure the necessary tax neutrality. See Alworth (1996) for an illuminating, if distressing, exposition of these problems. Alworth concludes by stating 'Simplistic approaches to international capital mobility such as those calling for a uniform gross basis withholding tax at source are doomed to failure under the inevitably complex and burdensome procedures which would need to be implemented in order to guarantee a minimally correct treatment of passive income flows' (p. 23).[25]

Other suggestions as to ways of alleviating the impacts of interest tax evasion are possible. A large part of the bank and enterprise gross capital income providing the basis for the payment of interest on deposits, company bonds, etc. in principle can be taxed more directly, namely at the level of production instead of the saver. This points in the direction of the comprehensive business income tax (CBIT) (see Cnossen (1996)). The CBIT includes the remuneration of firms' debt on the same basis as remuneration of equity in the tax on business income. Instead of deducting interest on debt, firms simply also pay a tax on interest on debt; conversely, such interest would no longer be subject to tax at the personal level, so that the personal income tax on capital income becomes superfluous.

The transition to a CBIT, if chosen, would not be an easy one. Firms might legitimately fear that the compulsory taxation of interest on debt at the level of the firm will lead to an increase in the cost of debt finance (in that the before-tax interest rate would not decline by enough). Further, opting for a CBIT is difficult in those countries where the marginal personal income tax rate applicable to interest is considerably higher than the corporate income tax rate (Cnossen, 1996). Finally, however, the potential evasion and circumvention problems associated with a CBIT would probably be mitigated if a CBIT were adopted in the entire EU.

Unfortunately, evasion of interest taxation is not the only difficulty in the area of capital income taxation these days; the predominant asymmetric treatment of debtors and creditors (often institutional investors) also

---

[25] At the same time, however, he acknowledges that movement toward a truly effective residence tax on individuals is not presently feasible in the EU.

reduces the revenue from such taxation. In view of these and other problems in taxing capital income, Gordon (1996) favours installing a comprehensive labour income tax in the form of a cash-flow tax on business, coupled with a personal tax on wages (and royalties etc.). This implies abolishing the taxation of the normal return to capital, while rents and entrepreneurial risk premiums would still be subject to tax.

The EU has not yet taken any significant action against the evasion of interest taxation in Member States. The Commission, though, remains worried about the erosion of the more mobile tax bases stemming from tax competition between members, and from the development of a parallel economy (through the relocation of tax bases towards the black economy). Therefore it is 'looking into the question of whether a minimum rate of effective taxation throughout the Union, which should be set at a level that would not be liable to drive businesses or wealth out of the EU, would help to achieve the necessary stabilization of revenue from the different types of taxation' (Commission of the European Communities, 1996, press release, pp. 1–2). Accordingly, the minimum withholding tax idea may be given a new lease of life.

References

Alworth, J. S. (1996), 'Taxation, financial innovation and integrated financial markets: some implications for tax coordination in the European Union', Università Luigi Bocconi, Milan, mimeo.

Bacchetta, P., and Espinosa, M. P. (1995), 'Information sharing and tax competition among governments', *Journal of International Economics*, 39: 102–21.

Cnossen, S. (1996), 'Company taxes in the European Union: criteria and options for reform', *Fiscal Studies*, 17(4): 67–97.

Commission of the European Communities (1996), 'Taxation in the European Union', Discussion Paper for the Informal Meeting of ECOFIN Ministers (including press release).

Eijffinger, S., Huizinga, H., and Lemmen, J. (1996), 'Short-term and long-term government debt and non-resident interest withholding taxes', CentER, Discussion Paper 9688.

Frank, M. (1991), 'Introduction of a common system of interest taxation in the EC Member States', *Public Finance*, 46: 42–65.

Giovannini, A. (1989), 'Capital taxation', *Economic Policy*, 9 (October).

Gordon, R. H. (1996), 'Tax evasion on international financial investments: what can be done?', University of Michigan, mimeo.

Gros, D. (1990), 'Tax evasion and offshore centres', in H. Siebert (ed.), *Reforming Capital Income Taxation*, Tübingen: J. Mohr.

Huizinga, H. (1994), 'International interest withholding taxation: prospects for a common European policy', *International Tax and Public Finance*, 1: 277–91.

Janeba, E., and Peters, W. (1996), 'Efficient tax competition and the gains from non-discrimination: the case of interest taxation in Europe', revised, Indiana University, Discussion Paper.

Kanbur, R., and Keen, M. (1993), 'Jeux sans frontières: tax competition and tax coordination when countries differ in size', *American Economic Review*, 83: 877–92.

Kazemier, B. (1991), 'Concealed interest income of households in Netherlands: 1977, 1979, and 1981', *Public Finance*, 3.

Mayer, C. (1989), 'Comment (on Giovannini)', *Economic Policy*, 9 (October).

Tanzi, V. (1995), *Taxation in an Integrating World*, Washington, DC: Brookings Institution.

Weichenrieder, A. (1996), 'Fighting international tax avoidance: the case of Germany', *Fiscal Studies*, 17(1): 37–58.

7

Levelling up or levelling down? Some reflections on the ACE and CBIT proposals, and the future of the corporate tax base

STEPHEN R. BOND

Corporate income taxes treat debt and equity differently. In all the OECD countries, interest payments on debt are deductible against income in the computation of taxable profits, but in none of the OECD countries is there any comparable deduction for the opportunity cost of using equity finance (see OECD (1991)).[1] The result is that investment financed by debt is treated more generously than investment financed by retained profits.[2] As a rough approximation, these corporate income taxes have no effect on the user cost of capital for investment financed by borrowing but increase the user cost of capital for investment financed by retained earnings.

The two principal proposals for reforming the corporate tax base over the last decade have shared the aim of equalizing the tax treatment of debt and equity finance, but have suggested that this should be achieved in diametrically opposed ways. The allowance for corporate equity (ACE)

This chapter has benefited from discussions with the author's colleagues Lucy Chennells, Michael P. Devereux, Malcolm Gammie, and Rachel Griffith, and from the comments of Sijbren Cnossen, Bernd Huber, Eiji Tanaki, two anonymous referees, and other participants at the ISPE conference. The research is financed by the Economic and Social Research Council (ESRC) Centre for Fiscal Policy at the Institute for Fiscal Studies. The views expressed here are solely those of the author and not those of the Institute for Fiscal Studies, which has no corporate views.

[1] Interestingly, Croatia has introduced an allowance for the opportunity cost of equity finance as part of its Interest-Adjusted Income Tax, implemented in 1994. See Rose and Wiswesser (1998) for a discussion.

[2] As discussed further in Section 1, new equity issues finance only a tiny proportion of company investment, so that the vast majority of equity-financed investment is in fact funded by retained company profits.

proposal advocates the introduction of a new tax allowance to reflect the opportunity cost of using equity finance,[3] whilst the comprehensive business income tax (CBIT) proposal advocates the elimination of interest deductibility.[4] The effect of the ACE proposal would be to reduce the user cost of capital for investment financed by retained profits, whilst the effect of the CBIT proposal would be to raise the user cost of capital for investment financed by debt.

In a closed economy, or in designing a co-ordinated world corporate income tax, the choice between these two proposals would seem to be quite straightforward. If we wished to encourage investment, we would tend to favour the ACE proposal, whilst if for some reason we wished to discourage investment, we would tend to favour the CBIT proposal. However, for small open economies in a world of increasingly mobile *physical* capital and uncoordinated tax setting, this chapter suggests that this distinction is not so clear-cut. At a given level of total corporate tax revenue, the ACE tax would require a higher statutory tax rate than the CBIT and would redistribute corporate tax payments towards relatively profitable companies. The effect may well be to discourage inward investment by geographically mobile multinational corporations.

Over the last fifteen years, most changes to corporate income taxes have either reduced the statutory corporate tax rate or broadened the corporate tax base, or both. We suggest that these trends may well be related to the increasing share of investment that is accounted for by multinational companies. Not only does the increasing importance of these mobile firms make company investment more sensitive to taxation than it was in the past, but the discrete location decisions of multinational companies may be influenced directly by the average tax rate or the statutory tax rate, and not just by the effect of company taxes on the user cost of capital. At a minimum, this implies that the ACE proposal will appear less attractive to a single government in a small open economy than it would in the context of co-ordinated international tax setting or in a world with much more limited international business integration. At the opposite extreme, we might suggest that the tide of history is flowing in the direction of the CBIT proposal rather than the ACE option.

The remainder of this chapter is structured as follows. Section 1 reviews the effects of existing corporate income taxes on the cost of capital, and

[3] See Institute for Fiscal Studies, Capital Taxes Group (1991) for a detailed presentation of the ACE proposal, or Bond et al. (1996) for a summary.

[4] See US Department of the Treasury (1992) for a detailed presentation of the CBIT proposal, or Cnossen (1996) for a summary.

how these would be changed under the ACE and CBIT proposals. Section 2 briefly describes the pattern of recent corporate tax changes in the developed countries. Section 3 considers the location decisions of multinational companies, and explains how these may be influenced by statutory tax rates and/or average tax rates and not just by the user cost of capital. Section 4 discusses the implications of this analysis for the ACE and CBIT proposals and, more generally, for the future of the corporate tax base.

Throughout this chapter, our focus is on taxes levied at the company level. This is not to deny that the treatment of dividends, capital gains, and interest under personal income taxes can have important effects on company behaviour, or that the integration of corporate and personal tax systems remains a pressing question. However, there are several reasons for our emphasis on the corporate tax base. First, the differential treatment of debt and equity is a feature of the corporate tax base, and both the ACE and CBIT proposals aim to tackle this distortion by reforms to the corporate tax base. Second, because most equity-financed investment takes the form of finance from retained profits and most interest payments by companies escape personal taxation (Cnossen, 1996), the effects of the tax system on the cost of capital depend almost exclusively on the nature of the corporate tax base. Third, both the CBIT and ACE proposals are designed to tax company profits principally at the company level, with company dividends being exempt from personal income tax, and capital gains on company shares being exempt or largely exempt from personal taxation.[5] Fourth, the tide of history is surely flowing in this direction. The degree to which corporate-source income is taxed under personal income taxes is retreating under a twin-pronged assault, from the growing importance of tax-exempt shareholders and from deliberate reductions in the taxation of investment income. For example, tax-exempt institutional investors now account for around half of aggregate share ownership in both the UK and the US. Examples of lower taxation include Individual Retirement Accounts (IRAs) in the US; Personal Equity Plans (PEPs) and Individual Savings Accounts (ISAs) in the UK; and the move to a schedular treatment of income, with investment income taxed at a low flat rate, in the dual income tax structures recently introduced in Sweden, Norway, and Finland. To what extent this trend is itself the result of increased international mobility of *portfolio* capital is an interesting question, but one that goes beyond the scope of the present chapter.

[5] Capital gains on company shares would continue to be taxed under the CBIT proposal, but only to the extent that the gain exceeds accumulated retained post-tax company profits since the shares were purchased.

1. Corporate taxes, and the ACE and CBIT proposals

It is well known that a corporate income tax that allows full deductions for true economic depreciation and the (opportunity) cost of finance leaves the user cost of capital unchanged (see King (1975), for example).[6] Under such a tax, an investment project that just earned the rate of return required to cover depreciation and financing costs would pay no tax. The tax base is effectively returns that exceed this minimum required rate of return, known variously as 'pure profits' or 'economic rents'. Notice that this tax base differs from conventional measures of accounting profits, even in the absence of inflation or uncertainty as to the appropriate rate of depreciation. Accounting profits generally deduct the explicit cost of interest payments associated with investment financed by debt, but make no adjustment for the opportunity cost of finance associated with invest-ment financed by equity (i.e. the interest that could have been earned if the shareholders' wealth had been invested elsewhere).

Conversely, it is well known that a corporate income tax that gives a deduction for true economic depreciation but not for the cost of finance, or that gives an inadequate deduction for depreciation, will raise the cost of capital.[7] In these cases, some investment projects that just earn the minimum required rate of return in the absence of the tax would become commercially unviable when such a tax is imposed.

Modern corporate income tax bases correspond very roughly to accounting measures of profit: taxable profits are net of allowances for depreciation and interest, but give no allowance for the opportunity cost of equity finance. Of course, there are many differences in the detail, depending on such factors as whether depreciation schedules are pre-scribed by the tax code or whether commercial depreciation deductions are allowed, whether any adjustments are made for inflation, what inven-tory valuation rules are adopted, and whether deliberate tax incentives are given for specific types of investment such as research and development or training. But, as a broad rule of thumb, we can conclude that corporate income taxes have rather limited effects on the cost of capital for invest-ment that is financed by borrowing, whilst there is a systematic tendency

---

[6] The marginal effective tax rate (METR), which measures the impact of the tax on the cost of capital, is zero for such a tax. See King and Fullerton (1984), for example. Throughout this chapter, we assume that the interest rate is not affected by the presence of the corporate tax—as would be appropriate, for example, in a small open economy.

[7] For these taxes, the METR is positive and measures the extent to which the cost of capital is increased by the tax.

for corporate income taxes to increase the cost of capital for investment that is financed by retained profits.

Despite this tax disadvantage, the vast majority of company investment in developed countries is, in fact, financed by retained profits. Funds raised by issuing new shares are typically lower than 10 per cent of investment spending, and this flow of finance is offset by share buy-backs and the use of retained profits to purchase shares from investors in cash-financed take-over activity. The net contribution of new share issues to financing capital formation is often estimated to be negative in the G7 countries.[8] Table 7.1 reports some recent estimates of the share of investment financed from different sources.

Given that little or no investment is financed by new share issues, and that retained earnings account for the overwhelming majority of equity-financed investment, it follows that dividend taxation is largely irrelevant for considering the impact of tax systems on the cost of capital. An investment financed by retained earnings involves substituting lower dividends today for an expectation of suitably higher dividends in the future. Unless the tax treatment of dividends is expected to change, a high or low personal tax rate on dividend income simply nets out of the calculation when considering the rate of return that shareholders will require

Table 7.1 Net sources of investment finance (%)

	US (1970–94)	UK (1970–94)	Germany (1970–92)	Japan (1970–94)
Internal	96.1	93.3	80.0	69.9
Debt	26.5	18.8	9.4	30.7
New equity	−7.6	−4.6	0.2	3.5

Note: Internal sources include retained profits and depreciation. The figures do not add up to 100 per cent because other sources of finance are not reported (such as trade credit and capital transfers).
Source: Corbett and Jenkinson, 1997.

[8] Until recently, Japan was an exception, but the pattern of investment finance in Japan has now converged towards the western model. Until the recent financial crises, a higher contribution from new equity issues had been found in the Asian 'tiger' countries with rapidly growing stock markets. These international patterns are consistent with a 'pecking order' view of investment finance, with the least-favoured new equity source being used only when investment demand is exceptionally high.

from investments financed by retained profits. Notice that this unimportance of dividend taxation for the cost of capital follows simply from the empirical fact that new share issues finance very little investment, and *not* from whether one subscribes to the 'new' theoretical view or the 'old' theoretical view of dividend taxation.[9]

At least so far as we are concerned with the impact of tax systems on the user cost of capital, it follows that the main distortion is that which results in a higher cost of capital for investment financed by equity (i.e. retained earnings) than for investment financed by debt. As discussed earlier, the source of this distortion lies in the corporate tax base, which allows a deduction for interest payments but no comparable deduction for the opportunity cost of using equity finance. Both the ACE and CBIT proposals advocate eliminating this distortion by reforming the corporate tax base. Given that personal taxation of corporate-source income is waning, these approaches are probably the only games in town if we are concerned with equalizing the tax treatment of debt and equity. However, there remains a fundamental difference between these two proposals.[10]

The ACE and CBIT proposals

The ACE proposal advocates extending the principle of interest deductibility to equity finance, so 'levelling down' the cost of capital for investment financed by retained earnings to that for investment financed by debt. Clearly, if tax depreciation schedules coincide with true economic depreciation, this has the effect of eliminating any effects of the corporate tax on the user cost of capital. In fact, other features of the ACE proposal ensure that this holds even if tax depreciation rules deviate from true economic depreciation. The essence is that, if the tax allowance for depreciation is

---

[9] Dividend taxation may matter more for new, small, fast-growing firms that are not generating sufficient profits to fund their desired investment and that are unable to borrow the difference. I am not suggesting that distortions in the tax treatment of retained profits and new equity are inconsequential. I am suggesting that they are not of first-order importance for considering the effects of the tax system on aggregate investment.

[10] It is of considerable interest that both the ACE and the CBIT proposals envisage further reduction in personal taxation of dividend income and capital gains on corporate shares. Taxing corporate-source income only at the corporate level elegantly avoids any 'double taxation' of dividends and eliminates the distinction between classical and imputation systems. The introduction of dual income tax structures in the Scandinavian countries can be viewed as a step in this direction, taxing investment income at a low flat rate.

'too low', this is exactly offset in present-value terms by calculating an allowance for the opportunity cost of equity finance that is 'too high'.[11] The result is that the ACE corporate tax leaves the cost of capital unchanged for all forms of investment finance. In present-value terms, the ACE tax is equivalent to a tax on 'pure profits' or 'economic rents'. Other advantages are that tax depreciation rules become irrelevant for anything other than the timing of tax payments, so that commercial depreciation charges could be allowed without needing complex anti-avoidance provisions to protect the corporate tax base, and that there is no need to index the ACE tax for inflation.[12]

The CBIT proposal advocates the abolition of interest deductibility, thus 'levelling up' the cost of capital for debt-financed investment to that for retentions-financed investment. Despite its name, the CBIT proposal is in some ways a less comprehensive reform than the ACE proposal. Detailed features of the tax schedule, such as the depreciation allowances, would continue to influence the cost of capital, and the effects of the CBIT system would continue to be sensitive to the rate of inflation. However, the main distinction between the two proposals is that the CBIT would increase the user cost of capital. The 'gain' from levelling the tax treatment of debt and equity appears to come only at the 'cost' of reducing the overall incentive to invest.

If we were discussing the reform of corporate taxation in a closed economy, or the design of a co-ordinated corporate tax for the whole world, the choice would indeed appear to be that simple. It may well be argued that company investment is not highly sensitive to the cost of capital, or that a lower level of investment would be beneficial, but it would be widely agreed that a higher cost of capital would tend to result in a lower level of investment.

However, for a small open economy in a world with an increasing mobility of *physical* capital between tax jurisdictions, the user cost of capital may no longer be the only route through which corporate taxes influence the level of domestic investment. If, as we suggest in Section 3, either the statutory tax rate or the average tax rate may influence the location

---

[11] The principle that true economic depreciation allowances are unnecessary for tax neutrality was established by Boadway and Bruce (1984). See Institute for Fiscal Studies, Capital Taxes Group (1991) for a detailed discussion of how the principle can be applied to a corporate income tax, and Bond and Devereux (1995) for the extension to uncertainty.

[12] The ACE tax could operate on an indexed or an unindexed basis; again, this affects only the timing of tax payments and not the present value of the tax liability.

decisions of multinational companies, then the effects of the ACE and CBIT proposals on these features must also be considered.[13]

It is straightforward to see that, in order to raise a given amount of tax revenue, the statutory tax rate must be higher under the ACE tax than under the CBIT: the ACE tax base is narrower than the CBIT base.[14] Whilst the ACE tax base permits deductions for the (opportunity) cost of all forms of finance, the CBIT base does not allow these deductions. Indeed, if the ACE and CBIT proposals were to be introduced on a revenue-neutral basis and with existing depreciation allowances, the CBIT reform would allow a reduction in the statutory tax rate compared with current systems, whilst the ACE reform would require an increase. Whilst the current corporate tax bases approximate to a tax on accounting profits after interest, the ACE system would tax only the proportion of such profits that constitute economic rents and exempt the 'normal' return on equity-financed investment, whilst the CBIT system would approximate to a tax on accounting profits before interest.[15]

Even if the statutory tax rate is not relevant, the two proposals also differ in their effects on the distribution of tax payments between companies. Whilst, if the proposals are considered on a revenue-neutral basis, it might appear that their effects on effective average tax rates should be the same, there is in fact a potentially important difference in the way a given total tax liability would be allocated across companies.[16] The essence of the ACE tax base is that it taxes only economic rents. Thus firms that only just earn the minimum required rate of return on their investments would pay no corporate tax under the ACE system; firms that only just exceed the minimum required rate of return would pay less tax than under the current systems; and the most profitable companies would have to pay more tax than under the current systems in order to preserve revenue neutrality. By

[13] There are also circumstances in which the average tax rate would affect investment in a closed economy: for example, for firms facing a binding financing constraint. See Hubbard (1998) and Devereux and Griffith (1998b) for further discussion.

[14] This is correct for any depreciation allowances under the CBIT that are less generous than 100 per cent first-year allowances (i.e. expensing). With 100 per cent first-year allowances, the CBIT proposal would be an R-based cash-flow corporation tax, which is a special case of the ACE tax.

[15] One counter-argument is that the lower cost of capital under the ACE tax results in higher investment than under the CBIT, and this additional investment generates additional taxable profits. However, this additional investment is, by definition, close to being marginal, and therefore generates very little extra tax revenue under the ACE tax.

[16] By the effective average tax rate, we mean the proportion of company profits or economic rents taken by the government in taxation.

contrast, the broader tax base and lower tax rate implied by the CBIT proposal would leave the most profitable companies with lower tax bills. If it is the case that geographically mobile multinational corporations tend to be among the most profitable companies, it may not be coincidental that the increase in the importance of foreign direct investment over the past fifteen years has been associated with a move to lower corporate tax rates and broader corporate tax bases in many countries.

2. Recent corporate tax reforms

Government revenues from corporate taxes have not collapsed in the last fifteen years. Indeed, corporate tax revenue as a share of GDP has risen modestly over the last decade in the US, and has been very stable in the OECD as a whole (Fig. 7.1). What has changed more systematically has been the structure of the corporate income taxes from which these revenues are collected.

Since 1980, the main statutory rate of corporate tax has fallen in Australia, Canada, France, Germany, Ireland, Japan, Sweden, the UK, and the US (Table 7.2), as well as in Denmark, Finland, and Norway (Cnossen, 1996).[17]

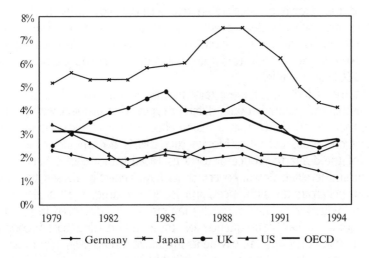

Fig. 7.1 Corporate tax as a share of GDP, 1979–94
Source: *OECD Revenue Statistics*, various years.

[17] The statutory tax rates reported in Table 7.2 do not include local taxes and surtaxes. For a more comprehensive analysis of recent trends in corporate taxation, see Chennells and Griffith (1997).

Table 7.2 Statutory corporate tax rates, 1980–96 (%)

	1980	1990	1996
Australia	50	39	36
Canada	46	38	38
France	50	37	33.3
Germany[a]	56	50	45
Ireland[b]	45	10	10
Italy	25	36	37
Japan	40	40	37.5
Sweden	57	30	28
UK	52	34	33
US	46	34	35

[a] Retained profits.
[b] Manufacturing.
Source: Price Waterhouse, various years.

In the UK (1984) and the US (1986), significant reductions in the statutory tax rate were accompanied by a significant broadening of the corporate tax base, with the elimination of 100 per cent first-year allowances in the UK in 1984, and the reform of accelerated depreciation allowances in the US in 1986. This approach has since been mirrored in several other countries. We can infer from Fig. 7.1 that the extent of base broadening has been sufficient to offset the impact of statutory rate reductions on corporate tax revenues in the OECD as a whole.

Whilst the stated aim of these reforms was typically to reduce the extent of differential treatments between different types of investment within a jurisdiction, there is no doubt that a major effect of them has been to reduce statutory corporate tax rates. Notice that this is not an inevitable consequence of the desire to reduce distortions. Faced with a choice between levelling up and levelling down, governments have generally chosen to remove the more generous tax allowances, and focus any largesse on achieving the maximum reduction in their statutory tax rate. As we discussed in the previous section, another consequence of these rate-cutting/base-broadening reforms is that corporate tax payments are redistributed away from relatively profitable companies and on to less profitable firms.[18]

---

[18] One intriguing exception to this general pattern concerns the tax treatment of research and development (R&D), where several countries have followed the US example and introduced new or more generous tax credits. Whilst there have been many reasons for governments wishing to promote R&D, it may not be entirely irrelevant that multinational companies tend to be among the most R&D-intensive.

3. Taxes and the investment decisions of multinational companies

Whilst all companies would prefer to pay less tax rather than more, are there any reasons to believe that the location of capital investment by multinational companies should be sensitive to either the statutory tax rate or to the average tax rate that they face? After all, the standard theory of company investment highlights the user cost of capital as the principal channel through which taxes are supposed to influence investment decisions. Why should multinational firms be any different?

One reason why the statutory tax rate may matter is that multinational companies have some scope for shifting profits between jurisdictions by the judicious use of transfer pricing and financial engineering. Shifting allowable costs into jurisdictions with a high tax rate and taxable revenues into jurisdictions with a low tax rate may well be no more than sensible tax planning from the company's viewpoint. Other things being equal, however, this will create an incentive to locate an operation in a country with a low statutory tax rate, so that some profits that have to be earned in a higher-tax location may be sheltered. Although hard evidence on the extent of profit shifting is difficult to come by, it has been suggested that the remarkable success of Ireland in attracting inward manufacturing investment may not be entirely unrelated to Ireland's 10 per cent corporate tax rate.

Even if we were convinced that the statutory tax rate itself was not important, there are still reasons to believe that the location of foreign direct investment will be sensitive to the effective average tax rate. In the appendix, we sketch a very stylized model of a multinational firm's location decision which illustrates this point.[19] The key features of the model are that the multinational firm has some market power in the domestic market, perhaps because it has unique access to a superior technology that is not available to its domestic rivals, and that the multinational firm has a choice between locating its production in the domestic market or locating abroad and competing in the domestic market as an exporter. The former feature implies that the multinational company earns economic rents; the latter feature implies that the multinational can avoid a rents tax imposed by the domestic government (on economic rents earned by producers operating within its jurisdiction) by choosing to locate elsewhere and export to the domestic market. Thus even a tax based on economic rents that has no impact on the user cost of capital may deter inward

---

[19] For rigorous analyses of less stylized models that have similar properties, see Markusen (1995) or Devereux and Griffith (1998a).

investment by multinational companies, if the rents tax is set so high that these firms can earn higher post-tax rents by locating elsewhere.[20]

This discussion suggests that, for a small open economy, one or both of the statutory tax rate and the effective average tax rate facing a potential inward investor may be important influences on the level of inward foreign direct investment. Some empirical evidence that the location choices of multinational companies and aggregate flows of foreign direct investment are influenced by effective average tax rates is presented in Devereux and Griffith (1998a) and Swenson (1994). Other implications of models of this type are that multinational firms are likely to be among the most profitable companies and that investment by domestic (non-multinational) producers is unlikely to be a perfect substitute for inward investment by multinational corporations.

4. Implications for reform of the corporate tax base

If it is accepted that one of the constraints that prevent governments from charging very high average or marginal tax rates on company profits is the impact of such tax systems on the level of company investment, this discussion of multinational company investment decisions has potentially important implications for the future of the corporate tax base.

In a closed economy, or in an economy open to trade but with very little cross-border investment activity, the main effect of corporate taxation on the level of investment would depend on the marginal effective tax rate or the impact of the tax system on the user cost of capital. Thus governments may be deterred from implementing corporate taxes that produce a substantial increase in the cost of capital but, given this, there is little reason (other than collection difficulties) for them to avoid taxes that result in high statutory or effective average tax rates. A government that wished to promote investment could easily choose a narrow corporate tax base such as the ACE tax, which taxes only economic rents, and achieve its desired level of revenue by setting a suitably high statutory tax rate.

However, with uncoordinated tax setting, the nature of the constraints facing a government in a small open economy with a high degree of mobility of physical capital may be very different. Suppose that inward investment by multinational companies is very sensitive to the statutory tax

---

[20] This distortion would not arise in the case of pure locational rents, which, by definition, cannot be earned elsewhere. However, it would be difficult to implement a tax that applied only to pure locational rents and not to more mobile sources of rents.

rate, whilst domestic investment by non-multinational firms is relatively insensitive to the cost of capital. A government in an open economy may then achieve a higher level of domestic investment by lowering the statutory tax rate and accepting a broader tax base, even though this results in a higher cost of capital.[21] More generally, the effect of a higher cost of capital on domestic investment will tend to be mitigated by the effect of a lower statutory tax rate on inward investment. A government in an open economy may therefore choose a lower rate and broader base than it would in a closed economy, or in a world with much lower mobility of physical capital.

Even if the statutory tax rate does not matter so directly, a similar argument can be formulated with reference to the effective average tax rate. We have seen that a lower tax rate and broader tax base will tend to lower the effective average tax rate facing the more profitable companies, and suggested that multinational firms are likely to be relatively profitable. Thus, even if multinational location decisions depend on the effective average tax rate rather than the statutory tax rate, a government in an open economy may still have an incentive to opt for a low statutory corporate tax rate and a broad corporate tax base.

These arguments suggest that the trend towards 'globalization' of business activities, without any corresponding globalization of company taxation, may have induced governments to adopt lower tax rates and broader tax bases than they chose hitherto. The increase in the importance of foreign direct investment flows over the last fifteen years or so has been accompanied by corporate tax reforms of this type.[22] This coincidence does not establish any causal link from globalization to tax changes, but other explanations for the general pattern of corporate tax reforms appear to be scarce.

If this hypothesis is correct, the implication for future corporate tax reforms clearly favours changes in the direction of the CBIT proposal rather than the ACE proposal. As we have emphasized, the CBIT proposal broadens the corporate tax base still further, by eliminating the deductibility of interest payments. Whilst current corporate tax bases still approximate to a tax on economic rents for investment that is financed by debt,

---

[21] Alternatively, a government may believe that this results in a better mix of investment, if it believes that there are significant positive spillovers from inward investment by 'leading-edge' foreign companies.

[22] Inward investment now accounts for around a quarter of UK manufacturing investment. Such figures probably underestimate the proportion of investment that is geographically mobile, since they exclude domestic investment by UK-based multinational firms that could also be located elsewhere.

the CBIT proposal would bring 'normal' returns on debt-financed investments into the tax base. By contrast, the ACE proposal narrows the tax base by excluding the 'normal' returns on equity-financed investments and taxing only economic rents. The corresponding increase in the statutory tax rate needed to achieve revenue neutrality, and the redistribution of corporate tax payments towards the more profitable companies, may be considered too prejudicial to inward investment for the ACE proposal to gain acceptance in a small open economy.[23]

It is tempting to ask why base broadening should stop with the elimination of interest deductibility. The process could clearly go further: eliminating allowances for depreciation would replace a net profits base by a gross profits base; and eliminating the deductibility of labour costs could see corporate income taxes eventually replaced by value added taxes.[24] Whether this route portends the eventual demise of corporate taxation may hinge on whether it is the statutory tax rate or the average tax rate that matters most for inward investment. If only the statutory tax rate is important, it is difficult to see what will prevent the corporate tax base from being broadened out of recognition. However, if the effective average tax rate facing inward investors is more important, and governments continue to feel constrained to raise some tax revenue from companies, the net-profit-before-interest tax base achieved under the CBIT may be a natural stopping-point. Whilst it is clear that moving from taxing economic rents to taxing net profits before interest is likely to favour highly profitable multinational firms, it is less clear that eliminating allowances for depreciation would favour these typically capital-intensive companies.

It should be emphasized that this outcome of uncoordinated tax setting may well be inefficient. Suppose it were generally agreed that, in a closed economy, a zero marginal effective tax rate would be optimal. In designing a corporate tax for the world as a whole, it would then be straightforward to co-ordinate on the ACE tax base or something equivalent. However, in the absence of co-ordination, individual governments may still feel compelled to choose a broader tax base and lower tax rate, with the result that the cost

---

[23] This analysis suggests an unfortunate trade-off between attracting inward investment (with a low statutory tax rate or effective average tax rate on profitable companies) and promoting investment by smaller domestic firms (with a low cost of capital). One way of alleviating this trade-off may be to target investment incentives at smaller companies, which are more likely to be domestic and relatively immobile.

[24] It is interesting to note that Italy has recently introduced a tax on corporate value added, albeit at a low rate.

of capital is higher and the level of investment lower than is optimal for the world as a whole.

If this inefficiency is perceived to be important, it may stimulate the search for greater international co-ordination of corporate taxation. However, progress to date does not give much cause for optimism. It is also worth stressing that the European Union should probably be regarded as a small open economy for this purpose. Even if co-ordination were achieved within Europe, the design of a harmonized European corporate tax would still be influenced by the desire to attract inward investment into Europe from America, Asia, and elsewhere.

Appendix: A simple model of taxes and multinational company investment

The model with no taxes

Consider the domestic market for some product, which, in the absence of trade or international investment, is supplied by a perfectly competitive domestic industry subject to decreasing returns to scale. In a closed economy, the equilibrium price is p_0 and domestic production is q_0 (Fig. 7.2a). This leaves residual demand RD (Fig. 7.2b).

Now suppose this market is opened up to trade, and the same product is produced by a foreign company that has unique access to a constant-returns-to-scale technology. If the foreign company enters the domestic market, it will act as a monopoly seller facing the residual demand curve RD. Let the unit cost of this foreign company producing abroad be c_A and let the unit cost of shipping the product to the domestic market be s. The foreign firm will export to the domestic market if $c_A + s < p_0$. If entry is profitable, the foreign firm maximizes its profits by charging a price p_1 and selling q_1 units of output. The foreign firm earns economic rents given by $q_1(p_1 - c_A - s)$ (Fig. 7.3).

Finally, suppose that foreign direct investment into the domestic economy is also permitted. Let the unit cost of the foreign (multinational) company producing the same product in the domestic economy be c_D. The foreign (multinational) firm will prefer to locate production in the domestic economy if $c_D < c_A + s$. If inward investment is profitable, the multinational company maximizes its profits by charging a price p_2 and selling q_2 units of output. The foreign firm then earns economic rents given by $q_2(p_2 - c_D)$ (Fig. 7.4).

The model with a rents tax

Now suppose that the domestic government allows both trade and foreign direct investment, but implements a company tax at rate t on economic rents earned by all producers within the domestic economy.

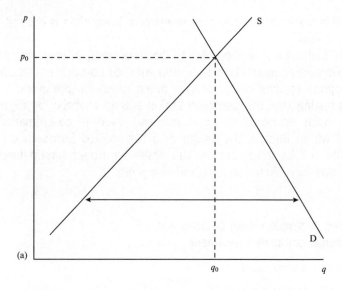

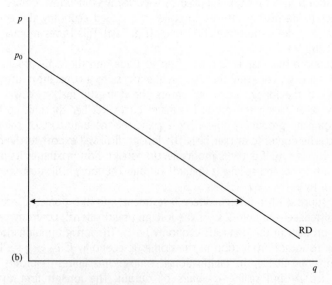

Fig. 7.2 Domestic market, no trade

If the foreign firm competes by producing abroad and exporting to the domestic market, it is not subject to this rents tax and continues to earn (post-tax) economic rents of $q_1(p_1 - c_A - s)$.

If the foreign firm locates production in the domestic economy, it now earns post-tax economic rents of $(1 - t)q_2(p_2 - c_D)$. Note that, because the tax falls only on

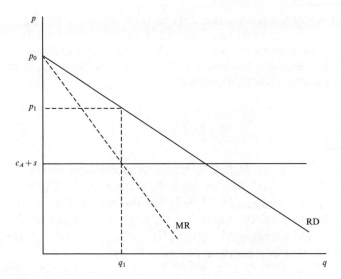

Fig. 7.3 Domestic market, with trade

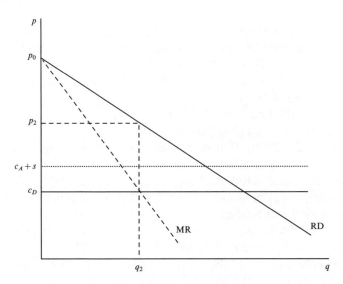

Fig. 7.4 Domestic market, with inward investment

economic rents, the cost of capital and the unit cost of production are not affected by the tax.

Clearly there exist tax rates t high enough that $(1-t)q_2(p_2-c_D) < q_1(p_1-c_A-s)$, even if $q_2(p_2-c_D) > q_1(p_1-c_A-s)$. Thus the existence of a company tax on economic rents may deter inward investment by a rent-earning multinational company.

The essence of this result is that if the rents tax imposed is too high, the multinational company can avoid paying this tax altogether by locating its production abroad and exporting to the domestic market. In the model outlined, it is also the case that if this inward investment is deterred by the rents tax, it will not be replaced by higher domestic investment.

References

Boadway, R., and Bruce, N. (1984), 'A general proposition on the design of a neutral business tax', *Journal of Public Economics*, 24: 231–9.

Bond, S. R., and Devereux, M. P. (1995), 'On the design of a neutral business tax under uncertainty', *Journal of Public Economics*, 58: 57–71.

——, ——, and Gammie, M. J. (1996), 'Tax reform to promote investment', *Oxford Review of Economic Policy*, 12: 109–17.

Chennells, L., and Griffith, R. (1997), *Taxing Profits in a Changing World*, London: Institute for Fiscal Studies.

Cnossen, S. (1996), 'Company taxes in the European Union: criteria and options for reform', *Fiscal Studies*, 17(4): 67–97.

Corbett, J., and Jenkinson, T. J. (1997), 'How is investment financed? A study of Germany, Japan, UK and US', *Manchester School*, 15: 69–93.

Devereux, M. P., and Griffith, R. (1998a), 'Taxes and the location of production: evidence from a panel of US multinationals', *Journal of Public Economics*, 68: 335–67.

—— and —— (1998b), 'The taxation of discrete investment choices', Institute for Fiscal Studies, Working Paper 98/16.

Hubbard, R. G. (1998), 'Capital-market imperfections and investment', *Journal of Economic Literature*, 36: 193–225.

Institute for Fiscal Studies, Capital Taxes Group (1991), *Equity for Companies: A Corporation Tax for the 1990s*, Commentary 26, London: Institute for Fiscal Studies.

King, M. A. (1975), 'Taxation, corporate financial policy and the cost of capital: a comment', *Journal of Public Economics*, 4: 271–9.

—— and Fullerton, D. (1984), *The Taxation of Income from Capital*, Chicago: University of Chicago Press.

Markusen, J. R. (1995), 'The boundaries of multinational enterprises and the theory of international trade', *Journal of Economic Perspectives*, 9: 169–89.

OECD (1991), *Taxing Profits in a Global Economy*, Paris: Organization for Economic Co-operation and Development.

Price Waterhouse (various years), *Corporate Taxes Worldwide Summaries*, various issues.

Rose, M., and Wiswesser, M. (1998), 'Tax reform in transition economies: experiences from participating in the Croatian tax reform process in the 1990s', in P. B. Sørensen (ed.), *Public Finance in a Changing World*, New York: Macmillan.

Swenson, D. (1994), 'The impact of US tax reform on foreign direct investment in the United States', *Journal of Public Economics*, 54: 243–66.

US Department of the Treasury (1992), *Integration of the Individual and Corporate Tax Systems: Taxing Business Income Once*, Washington, DC: US Government Printing Office.

8

Taxing capital income in the Nordic countries: a model for the European Union?

SIJBREN CNOSSEN

The body politic in the European Union (EU) can be classified, in a somewhat stylized fashion, into two camps when it comes to the taxation of capital income. One camp's answer to the question of whether or not capital income should be taxed is: 'Yes, but we don't have the nerve!'. This camp is afraid of the consequences for saving and investment, and hence employment, of taxing capital income positively. The other camp's answer is: 'No, but let's pretend!'. This camp appreciates the psychological effect of appearing to tax capital income positively, while at the same time being able to avoid the tax by employing an army of tax advisers. The two camps meet under the umbrella of hypocritical tax legislation that appears to tax capital income but in fact leaves it largely untouched by the taxman.

This chapter proceeds from the premiss that capital income should be taxed when maturing. Taxing current capital income positively contributes to a more progressive distribution of the annual tax burden. This seems important, to this author, in countries that favour a hands-off economic attitude whereby the income formation is left primarily to the free play of market forces. There seems to be no compelling reason, moreover, to abandon the current taxation of capital income on efficiency grounds.[1] Excess burdens are probably tolerable as long as capital income is taxed uniformly at a moderate rate. Also, it should not be forgotten that labour income taxes bring their own dead-weight losses in train. These might be higher,

The author is grateful to Krister Andersson, Lans Bovenberg, Flip de Kam, Jack Mintz, Leif Mutén, and Peter Sørensen for their perceptive comments on an earlier draft.

[1] For the efficiency argument as well as the tax burden distribution issue, see Gravelle (1994).

under an equal-yield assumption, if capital income were not taxed and labour income taxed correspondingly higher.

In the spirit of the ability-to-pay philosophy, capital income could be taxed together with and at the same marginal rate as labour income. If an open-economy country imposed a rate of tax (higher than in other countries) of, say, 50 per cent, then the effective taxation of current capital income, in the absence of world-wide co-operation, would indeed most likely reduce capital formation in that economy. Being the more mobile factor, capital would flee from its less mobile partner, labour, leaving labour less productively employed and hence earning a lower real wage. Alternatively, therefore, capital income and labour income might be taxed at marginal rates that would not exceed, say, 25 per cent. An effective top rate of 25 per cent on all income, however, might be too low to satisfy the revenue needs of countries that prefer to have a wide social safety net with high income transfers through the budget, and hence high taxes. In view of this dilemma, it would appear to be good tax policy to tax capital income at a lower marginal rate than labour income—in other words, to adopt a dual income tax (DIT) of the kind with which the Nordic countries have been experimenting since the early 1990s.[2]

This chapter reports on the design and rationale of, and experience with, the DIT. Section 1 describes the basic features of the DIT along with its practical application in the Nordic countries. Subsequently, Section 2 lists the main reasons why capital income should be taxed at a low, flat rate, while labour income should continue to be taxed at higher, progressive rates. Obviously, most issues bear on the appropriate tax treatment of capital income, which should be taxed once but not more than once. Section 3 explores the ways in which the Nordic countries avoid the double taxation of capital income, yet try to ensure single taxation. Special problems arise when labour income and capital income accrue jointly, as occurs in proprietorships and closely held companies. Section 4 reviews the solution that has been found to this important issue. Finally, Section 5 examines the conditions under which the DIT could serve as the model income tax for the Member States of the EU.

1. Basic features of the dual income tax

In the wake of the base-broadening, rate-flattening tax reform movements of the late 1980s, which affected nearly the entire industrial world,[3] the Nordic countries—Norway, Finland, Sweden, and Denmark—enacted sweeping changes of their personal and corporate income taxes (PTs and CTs). In

---

[2] For an excellent early analysis of the DIT reforms, see Sørensen (1994a).

[3] For a review, see Cnossen and Messere (1990).

the process, they transformed their nominally comprehensive, but factually concession-riddled, income taxes into effectively more comprehensive, if nominally less progressive, DITs. This section reports on these reforms, following a brief description of the most salient features of a pure DIT.

1.1 What is a dual income tax?

The pure DIT exhibits the following features:

1. All income is separated into either capital income or labour income, also called earned income or personal income. Capital income includes business profits (representing the return on equity), dividends, capital gains, interest, rents, and rental values. Labour income consists of wages and salaries (including the value of labour services performed by the owner in his or her business), fringe benefits, pension income, and social security benefits.
2. Basically, all capital income is taxed at the proportional CT rate, while labour income is subject to additional, progressive PT rates. To minimize tax arbitrage, the lower rate on labour income is set at the same level as the proportional CT rate.
3. Capital and labour income may be taxed entirely separately. Alternatively, the two forms of income may be taxed jointly at the CT rate, while gross labour income would subsequently be taxed at additional progressive PT rates. Joint taxation permits the offset of negative income from capital income sources against positive labour income, as well as the application of a joint basic allowance. Separate taxation enables the imposition of flat source taxes on various forms of capital income.
4. Double taxation of corporate profits at the company level and the shareholder level is avoided through a full imputation system under which dividends are grossed up by the CT attributable thereto and a credit for that CT is allowed against the personal capital income tax (=CT) on the grossed-up dividend. Alternatively but equivalently, double taxation can be avoided by exempting dividend income at the shareholder level.
5. Double taxation of retained profits at the company level in conjunction with the taxation of realized capital gains at the shareholder level is avoided by permitting shareholders to write up the basis of their shares by retained profits net of CT.
6. Single taxation of capital income is ensured through withholding or source taxes at the company level or at the level of other entities paying interest, royalties, or other capital income. In principle, withholding or source rates are set at the level of the CT rate. Consequently, these rates represent the final tax liability if capital income is taxed separately from labour income and no basic allowance applies.

7. Taxable profits of proprietorships and closely held companies, conventionally computed, are split into a capital-income component and a labour-income component. The capital-income component is calculated by applying a presumptive return to the value of the business's gross or net capital. Residual profits are considered as labour income.

1.2 Practice in the Nordic countries

Table 8.1 shows the basic features of the DITs in the Nordic countries in the order in which they come closest to satisfying the requirements of the pure DIT outlined above. A comparison of current tax rates with the rates

Table 8.1 Dual income taxes in the Nordic countries, 1999

	Norway	Finland	Sweden	Denmark
1. Year of introduction	1992	1993	1991	1987
2. Rates (%) in 1999[a]				
a. Capital income				
-corporate	28	28	28	32
-other	28	28	30	39.7–59
b. Labour income[b]	28–41.5	22.5–54.5	31–56	39.7–59
3. Costs only deductible at basic rate	Yes	Yes	Yes	No
4. Basic allowance for capital income	Yes	No	No	Yes
5. Elimination of double taxation of corporate profits				
a. Distributions	Yes	Yes	No	No
b. Retentions	Yes	No	No	No
6. Withholding taxes on non-residents[c]				
a. Dividends	Yes	Yes	Yes	Yes
b. Interest	No	No	No	No
c. Royalties	No	Yes	No	Yes
7. Income splitting				
a. Proprietorships	Yes	Yes	Yes	Yes
b. Closely held companies	Yes	Yes	Yes	No

[a] Including local taxes (national capital's tax if different).
[b] Not including employee (and employer) social security contributions, which raise average and marginal tax rates on labour income above the levels indicated in the table.
[c] Rates may be reduced by treaty; see Table 8.4.

Source: International Bureau of Fiscal Documentation.

prevailing prior to the reforms indicates that most income tax rates have been reduced, sometimes by as much as a half.[4] Since the rate reductions were accompanied by major tax-base-broadening moves, tax revenue, generally, did not suffer. The loss in revenue relating to the lowering of the tax rates on labour income was made up by the gain in revenue from the more effective taxation of capital income.[5] All countries retained a separate tax on corporate profits. Generally, the lowest rate on labour income equals or approximates the CT rate. Norway and Finland have adhered much more closely to the requirements of the pure DIT than have Sweden and Denmark.

In Norway, the basic (CT) rate of 28 per cent is levied on 'general income' from all sources (including capital income), while a two-step additional progressive rate schedule applies to 'gross personal income' (all income other than capital income). Noteworthy is that all costs of earning income and all allowances are deductible only from general income, i.e. at the rate of 28 per cent.[6] Double taxation of corporate profits, whether distributed or retained, is fully avoided. No withholding taxes apply to interest and royalty income payable to residents and exempt entities, or to non-residents. Profits of proprietorships and closely held companies are split into a capital-income component and a labour-income component, which are taxed on a current basis. Closely held companies are defined by reference to the size of the owners' shareholdings.

Finland has also implemented a fairly pure DIT. Unlike Norway, however, capital income and 'earned income' are not taxed jointly in the 'first bracket'. Instead, separate treatment prevails from the start, capital income being taxed, without basic allowance, at 28 per cent and earned income, over and above the basic allowance, at progressive rates of 22.5 to 54.5 per cent.[7] None the less, some link between the two forms of income is maintained,

---

[4] See table 1.1 in Sørensen (1998), who also provides a description of the various Danish reforms. For reviews of the reforms in the other Nordic countries, see Tikka (1993) for Finland, Skaar (1991) for Norway, and Mutén (1997) and Andersson and Mutén (1994) for Sweden.

[5] Sweden was an exception, as shown by Agell et al. (1996, p. 661), who argue that the reform was underfinanced by 2 or 3 per cent of GDP.

[6] As Peter Sørensen has pointed out to me, this limitation discriminates against wage-earners, since proprietorships can deduct their business costs against the top marginal tax rate on labour income. In other words, progressive surtaxes are levied on the gross income of wage-earners but only on the net income of proprietorships. This violates the equal treatment rule. Apparently, revenue was the reason for the limitation.

[7] Unfortunately, separate taxation also facilitated the introduction of diverging basic rates after 1995.

because negative income from capital can be offset against earned income in the form of a tax credit equal to 28 per cent of the negative amount. Double taxation of distributed profits is fully avoided, but the double tax on retained profits is not eliminated as it is in Norway. For profit-splitting purposes, closely held companies are defined as all companies that are not listed on the Stock Exchange, while the splitting takes place only when profits are distributed. No withholding taxes apply to interest and royalties payable to residents or non-residents in treaty countries.

Sweden introduced a fairly pure DIT in 1991 (with modification in 1994), but reintroduced double taxation of distributed profits in 1995. Income from all sources is split into capital income and earned income, which in turn consists of employment income and business income of the self-employed (not carrying on their business in the form of a closely held company). Capital income is taxed at 30 per cent (2 percentage points higher than the CT rate) and earned income at 31–56 per cent. As in Finland, the basic allowance cannot be deducted from capital income. Negative capital income can be offset against positive earned income through a 30 per cent tax credit (21 per cent for losses exceeding SEK 100,000). Dividend income is taxed twice, first at the corporate level at 28 per cent and subsequently at the personal level at 30 per cent.[8] Similarly, capital gains on shares are taxable at 30 per cent, even though CT has already been paid on retained profits.[9] Profits of proprietorships and closely held companies are taxed at the CT rate, until the profits are withdrawn or a capital gain is realized on the shares of an active shareholder—at which time the profits are split into a capital-income component and a labour-income component and taxed accordingly. There is no withholding tax on interest and royalties payable to residents or non-residents in treaty countries.

Although Denmark may be considered the cradle of the DIT, it honours its precepts mainly in the breach.[10] As early as 1985, the government made proposals for a pure type of DIT, but the subsequent 1987 income tax law imposed slightly progressive rates on other capital income in contrast to

---

[8] Relief from double taxation, however, is provided for dividends on shares in unquoted Swedish corporations. See 'Swedish Parliament passes new relief from double taxation provision', *Tax Notes International*, 6 January 1997, pp. 33–4.

[9] For one year, in 1994, dividend income was exempt in the hands of shareholders (a form of relief equivalent to imputation) and capital gains on shares were taxed at 15 per cent (half of the capital income tax rate) to reflect the fact that retained profits had already been taxed.

[10] Sørensen (1998) reports that Niels Christian Nielsen first advanced the idea of a dual income tax in the early 1980s. Nielsen was a member of two influential Danish committees on tax reform.

the proportional rate on corporate profits. In the early 1990s, further-more, the CT rate was reduced without a corresponding reduction in the capital income tax rate. Further modifications, away from a pure DIT, were made in 1994. As in Sweden, negative capital income can be offset against positive personal income (consisting of employment income, business income, and rental value income), but only against the first and second rate brackets of the three-bracket income tax schedule. Dividend income is taxed twice, i.e. at the corporate level and again at (reduced) PT rates. Capital gains are taxed according to a complicated separate schedule.

An assessment of the reforms against the requirements of a pure DIT reveals clearly that the most obvious shortcoming of all DITs is the absence of withholding taxes on interest and royalties payable to non-residents, which is not counteracted by rules on thin capitalization. This greatly diminishes the bite of the DITs on the profits of transnational com-panies and is an invitation to tax avoidance. In addition, Sweden has reintro-duced the double tax on distributed profits, while, along with Finland, it also taxes retained profits twice. The Danish PT/CT system can hardly pass for a DIT. As Sørensen (1998) concluded, 'Hence, the recent Danish tax reform marks a retreat from the principles underlying the 1987 reform and a move towards a rather incoherent type of schedular income taxation which bears little resemblance to neither a global income tax nor a pure dual income tax'.

In Norway and Finland, the introduction of the DIT caused few eco-nomic, political, or administrative problems. In Sweden, however, the adop-tion of the DIT coincided with a deep recession. Agell et al. (1996) conclude that the limitation of interest deductibility for homeowners—the after-tax interest rate for an average employee increased from *minus* 7 per cent in 1980 to *plus* 7 per cent in 1991—and especially the increase of at least 10 percentage points in value added tax on new housing and housing maintenance, squeezed short-term effective demand, causing a decline of gross national product by one percentage point. As these authors point out, however, in the longer run, the Swedish reform should improve the efficient allocation of resources (away from durable consumer goods towards investment goods) and strengthen incentives to invest in human capital. In addition, tax avoidance was made more difficult and the distribution of the tax burden became more progressive (through the more effective taxation of capital income). These general conclusions also seem to hold for the Norwegian and Finnish reforms.

2. Rationale of the dual income tax

In essence, the case for the DIT rests on two considerations. First, the mobility and fungibility of capital necessitate the application of low and proportional tax rates on capital income. Second, the immobility of labour and the unequal distribution of human capital make it possible and desirable to impose higher and progressive tax rates on labour income.

2.1 Why tax capital income at a low, uniform rate?

The literature on optimal taxation has argued persuasively that capital income should not be taxed at the same rate as labour income, since this does not take account of the greater elasticity of supply of capital compared with labour in terms of sensitivity to changes in the net real interest rate and the net real wage rate, both after tax, respectively (Atkinson and Sandmo, 1980). Extending this argument, it has been shown that a small, open economy that cannot enforce a residence-based tax in a world of full capital mobility acts optimally by placing the marginal tax burden exclusively on the immobile factor, labour (Razin and Sadka, 1991). In this limiting case of perfect capital mobility, any source-based tax on domestic investment raises the pre-tax return by the full amount of the tax so that the after-tax return continues to equate to the exogenously given world real rate of interest. Since the source-based capital tax cannot be shifted forward into product prices—consumers face world market prices without tax—it acts as an implicit tax on labour. If so, it is optimal to tax labour directly rather than indirectly, so as to avoid the welfare loss due to a lower level of investment.

In practice, capital is less mobile than assumed above. Physical capital, in the form of machinery and buildings, for instance, cannot readily be reallocated across countries in response to tax differentials. Furthermore, it should generally be possible to tax location-specific rents due to the high quality of the labour force and infrastructure, or the easy access to markets. Beyond that, the US and the UK, as residence countries, alleviate international double taxation by granting a credit for taxes paid abroad on repatriated foreign investment income, up to the level of the domestic tax. This enables source countries to tax investment income approximately up to the rate prevailing in residence countries. The CT, in turn, plays a role in protecting the integrity of the PT. Without a tax on corporate income, more capital would be placed in corporations, thereby eroding the base of the PT (see Gordon and MacKie-Mason (1994) for a recent view).

The foregoing analysis indicates that it should be possible to tax capital income positively, but that moderation is advisable, particularly by small, open-economy countries. In this connection, the CT rate emerges as an important linchpin in the taxation of capital income. In fact, there are good reasons for taxing all capital income, not just corporate profits, at the CT rate. These reasons concern the increasing substitutability of various forms of financial capital and various organizational forms for conducting business, which enable capital owners to obtain the lowest tax rate available for all their capital income.

To begin with, the self-employed can readily convert their proprietorships into closely held companies whose profits (including most of the labour income of the majority shareholders actively involved in running the company) are taxed at the CT rate. Complex legislation is required to counter this form of tax arbitrage (without actually achieving equal treatment). The most important vehicle, however, for avoiding the high PT rates on capital income is debt. Since interest is deductible from taxable income, debt can be used to finance assets that yield tax-exempt or hard-to-tax returns, or capital gains that are realized at a much later date than the date at which the interest is deductible. In fact, the symbiosis between interest deductibility at the business level and the existence of tax-exempt institutional investors, such as pension funds, implies that, as a rule, the normal return on capital may not be taxed at all. This effect is reinforced on the international scene by the substitution of hard-to-reach international debt for easier-to-tax equity.[11]

Sørensen (1994a) has pointed out that a lower tax rate should mitigate the lock-in effect of a capital gains tax that induces capital owners to postpone realization which frustrates the workings of the capital market. Similarly, a lower rate mitigates the effects of the tax on inflationary gains, which should not be taxed, but for which it is difficult to correct on practical grounds.[12] He has also argued that horizontal equity implies that capital income should be taxed at lower rates than labour income. On the assumption of equal income-earning capacities, a global income tax that taxes savings twice weighs more heavily on people who save or who enter the labour market early than on people who consume their income early or start working later in life. In this situation, a lower tax rate on capital

---

[11] Furthermore, the CT can be evaded by manipulating international intercompany transfer prices and by fictitious royalty payments for know-how placed in foreign subsidiaries. As a result, there is a gaping hole in the CT bucket through which much capital income seeps away. See Cnossen (1996) and the studies cited therein.

[12] To illustrate, if the nominal return on an asset is 10 per cent and the rate of inflation is 4 per cent, then a PT rate of 50 per cent must be reduced to 30 per cent $[0.5(0.1-0.04)/0.1]$ if only the real return is to be taxed. In fact, this example was also used in the Nordic debate. It should be noted, however, that the lower rate applies also when the inflation rate is zero.

income lessens the horizontal discrimination of taxpayers with different patterns of consumption or different earnings profiles.[13]

In sum, capital mobility and feasibility considerations lead to the conclusion that capital income should be taxed at a relatively low proportional rate. In practice, capital income can be taxed only if capital is kept in relatively immobile forms (buildings, machinery) or relatively immobile institutions (corporations). In these circumstances, capital income should be taxed as soon as it is separated from its base; in other words, source taxes are the appropriate instrument. This implies *in rem*, impersonal, taxing arrangements. This makes the proportional CT rate the obvious candidate for the rate at which other capital income should be taxed as well.[14] Moving toward lower uniform tax rates on capital income would enhance efficiency and might raise government revenue (Gordon and Slemrod, 1988).

2.2 Why tax labour income at higher, progressive rates?

Prima facie, much can be said for setting the top marginal tax rate on labour income at the same level as the low, proportional tax rate on capital income. This is the situation in New Zealand, as well as in, approximately, the US.[15] But in view of the relatively high preference for income redistribution through the budget in the Nordic countries, this equality of (top) rates is not possible, unless all progressivity is abolished by eliminating the basic exemption and deductions for pension and annuity contributions. The consequences of such a major reform for the after-tax income distribution of lower income groups and for savings are likely to be substantial and unacceptable.

The increasing mobility of capital, moreover, may make it necessary, in due course, to further lower the CT = PT rate on capital income. It would be unfortunate if an economically desirable reduction of the CT = PT rate

---

[13] Furthermore, Nielsen and Sørensen (1997) have postulated that the comprehensive PT tends to discriminate against investment in financial capital compared with investment in human capital. The reason is that the comprehensive PT offers immediate expensing of human capital investment (forgone wages), whereas financial investment is expensed over its useful life. It is argued that the higher tax on labour income under the DIT tends to correct for this distortion.

[14] For a plea to extend the reach of the source principle to strengthen the neutrality of the CT and the tax independence of the EU Member States, see Cnossen (1996).

[15] It should be noted, however, that New Zealand and the US do not effectively tax most interest.

on capital income were impeded by the link between that rate and the bottom rate on labour income which, in view of its revenue implications, could not be lowered. On the other hand, *ad hoc* adjustments of the effective capital income tax rate through base concessions would undo the administrative and neutrality advantages of the uniform statutory rate. The separate taxation of capital income, therefore, offers the Nordic countries an additional instrument to adjust to changes in international capital mobility without involving the rest of the income tax system. Conversely, the separate taxation of labour income makes it possible to increase the corresponding rate in order to finance, say, additional social expenditures.

Furthermore, a progressive rate on labour income provides the government with the opportunity to reduce the tax burden at the lower end of the labour income distribution through an earned income allowance (or, if desired, an earned income tax credit), as all the Nordic countries do. This enhances the progressive incidence of the labour income tax as well as the work incentives for low-skilled labour (if, as is likely, the income effect outweighs the substitution effect). The earned income allowance or tax credit can be financed by the differentially higher tax on high labour incomes. Because even high-skilled labour is relatively immobile, the risk of emigration is small.

An important argument in favour of a progressive tax on labour income is that human capital, and hence its rewards, may be distributed more unequally than private physical and financial wealth, especially in the Nordic countries. Wealth has increased enormously in the past century, but so has its more even distribution. Presently, most wealth is held collectively by the government (physical infrastructure, provision for education, and research and health facilities) or by institutional investors, such as pension funds or life assurance schemes. Free access to educational facilities has enabled people to develop their intellectual and physical skills more fully. To an important extent, however, the underlying talents are innate. Because differences in innate human capital lead to differences in earnings levels, it would not seem inequitable to tax higher incomes differentially more highly. Most significantly, perhaps, human capital is increasingly becoming a more important production factor than physical capital. Rank and status in modern societies are related less and less to differences in wealth and more and more to differences in human capital.

Finally, it may be pointed out that human capital is not taxed under the net wealth taxes in the Nordic countries, but privately held physical capital and financial capital are subject to net wealth tax (except in Denmark). Since asset values represent the capitalized value of the return on assets, the net wealth tax can be considered to be on a par with a tax on the income from capital. In other words, the effective DIT rate on capital is higher than indicated by the nominal rate if a net wealth tax is also levied. Pension contributions, moreover, are deductible from labour income (in contrast to deposits into conventional savings accounts) and the value of pension rights is exempted from net wealth tax (in contrast to the value of savings deposits). These arguments also seem to support a higher tax on labour income.

3. Taxation of corporate income

As discussed in the previous section, the DIT was largely inspired by the desire to tax capital income more effectively, but in a less distortionary manner. This meant that taxable profits should approximate economic income more closely and that double taxation of capital income should be avoided, but also that single taxation should be ensured. This section evaluates current practices in light of these objectives.

3.1 Computation of taxable profits

In line with the base-broadening, rate-flattening philosophy of the late 1980s, the Nordic countries used the DIT reforms to considerably tighten profit computation rules. Most concessions and incentives were abolished in an effort to establish a closer match between the private cost of business capital and the social cost of capital, which, in a small open economy, is given by the (risk-adjusted) international real rate of interest before tax. Norway, in particular, made a serious attempt to move closer to an economic concept of income. Table 8.2 shows current profit computation rules in the Nordic countries.

Most importantly, the Nordic countries abolished or severely restricted various generous tax deferment provisions.[16] As the hallmark of interventionist tax policies, substantial shares of profits could, in the past, be allocated to tax-free investment reserves administered by the central bank, to be used, upon permission, as a tool of the government's counter-cyclical economic policies. Furthermore, inventory reserves could be created by writing down inventories by as much as 40 per cent over and above proven obsolescence. Beyond that, profits could be placed in reserves that purported to dampen price, profit, and, to boot, tax fluctuations. As a result, corporations could place some 60–90 per cent of profits in tax-free reserves. After the reforms, Sweden was the only Nordic country that retained a profit

---

[16] For a useful review of the changes, see Lodin (1994).

Table 8.2 Profit computation rules in the Nordic countries, 1999

	Typical annual depreciation rates		Taxation of corporate capital gains	Valuation of inventories	Important special reserves	Loss offsets
	Machinery	Buildings				
Norway	*Declining balance* Pool basis: 20–30%	*Straight line* 2–5%	Taxed, rolled over, or booked in special gains and losses account, at the choice of the taxpayer	Historic cost; FIFO	None	Ten-year carry-forward; two-year carry-back at cessation
Finland	*Declining balance* Pool basis: 30%	*Declining balance* 4–7%	Taxed, rolled over, or booked in replacement reserve, at the choice of the taxpayer	Lowest of cost or market value; FIFO	None	Ten-year carry-forward
Sweden	*Declining balance* Pool basis: 30% with option of switch-over to straight line (20%)	*Straight line* 1.5–5%	Rolled over or taxed	Lowest of cost or market value; FIFO	Periodization fund: 20% of taxable profits may be allocated to a tax-free reserve for a period of five years	Indefinite carry-forward
Denmark	*Declining balance* Pool basis: 30%	*Straight line* 6%	Rolled over or taxed	Lowest of cost or market value; FIFO	None	Five-year carry-forward

Source: International Bureau of Fiscal Documentation.

periodization fund, presently permitting tax deferment on one-fifth of profits for five years. Purportedly, the fund serves to lower the effective tax on
equity compared with debt and to protect equity against inflation.

Currently, inventories have to be valued at cost or market value,
whichever is lower, and the cost of inventories is determined on a first-
in/first-out basis. This implies that nominal gains tend to be taxed. In all
Nordic countries, machinery and equipment can be written off on a pool
basis: purchases are added to the depreciable balance, sales are deducted,
and the balance is written down at a rate of 30 per cent. Generally, buildings and other long-lived assets are depreciated on a straight-line basis.
For all assets, capital gains can be written off from the cost of replacing
assets. Most countries have generous loss carry-forward provisions, but
the carry-back of ordinary losses is not allowed. Carry-back would serve a
similar goal to the previous profit equalization reserves, of course.

3.2 Avoidance of double taxation

Various measures have been taken to prevent the multiple taxation of capital income accruing to different legal or natural persons, domiciled in different taxing jurisdictions.

3.2.1 Current situation

As shown in Table 8.3, the double taxation of inter-company dividend payments is prevented through full imputation (Norway, Finland) or by
exempting dividend income at the level of the receiving company (Sweden,
Denmark). A straightforward exemption enables the subsidiary to pass its
tax preferences on to the parent company. The compensatory tax under
the imputation system does not permit this. A similar tax can, of course,
be levied at company level if an exemption applies, but Sweden and
Denmark do not have such a tax.[17] Income from foreign direct investment
is generally exempted, except in Norway which permits a gross-up and
credit by source.

Double taxation of subsidiary and parent company income would occur
with respect to retained profits if the parent company were to sell its
shares in the subsidiary. After all, the capital gain would (partly) reflect the
increase in the subsidiary's equity on account of the retained profits.
Norway is the only Nordic country that has introduced a consistent
scheme to avoid this form of double taxation. It permits a write-up of the

---

[17] These comments, and those in the following paragraph, do not apply, of
course, to companies that are eligible for group taxation, provision for which
exists in all Nordic countries.

Table 8.3 Methods of double-tax relief under the Nordic corporate and personal income taxes (CT and PT), 1999

	CT treatment of inter-company dividends and capital gains on shares			Method of CT–PT integration	
	Dividends received from domestic subsidiaries	Dividends received from foreign subsidiaries in treaty countries	Realized capital gains on shares in subsidiaries	Distributed profits	Retained profits
Norway	Full imputation	Gross-up and credit by source	Only gains in excess of the subsidiary's retained after-tax profits are taxable	Full imputation; excess credit not refundable, but carry-forward up to ten years possible	Only realized gains in excess of retained after-tax profits are subject to PT
Finland	Full imputation	Exemption	Gains subject to ordinary CT	Full imputation; excess credit not refundable	No integration; gains taxable at 28% PT
Sweden	Exemption	Exemption	Gains subject to ordinary CT	No integration; taxable at 30% PT	No integration; gains taxable at 30% PT
Denmark	Exemption	Exemption	Holding period <three years: gains taxable Holding period ≥three years: gains tax-exempt	Reduced PT: ≤DKR 36,000—25% >DKR 36,000—40%	Reduced PT: Holding period <three years—39–58% Holding period ≥three years—25/40%

Source: International Bureau of Fiscal Documentation.

basis of the shares held by the parent company (paid-in capital or acquisition costs) with the subsidiary's profits after CT. Therefore only realized gains reflecting untaxed gains of the subsidiary are taxed.[18] Denmark exempts realized gains on shares in subsidiaries held three years or longer, but Finland and Sweden tax realized gains on shares in full at the CT rate.

Of perhaps greater interest are the systems for relieving double taxation at the level of individual shareholders. Again, Norway and Finland permit full imputation, while unused tax credits, arising in the case of, say, exempt entities, are not refundable. After briefly exempting dividend income in shareholders' hands, Sweden introduced full double taxation following a change of government in 1994. Apparently, voters could not appreciate the equivalency between exemption and imputation, both with a compensatory tax at the corporate level to prevent the payment of dividends from untaxed profits. Denmark has a modified classical system under which dividend income is taxed at reduced PT rates. The double tax on retained profits through the capital gains tax on shares is fully eliminated under the Norwegian DIT system (see below), but the other Nordic countries tax retained profits twice.

3.2.2 Distributed profits

To relieve the double tax on distributed profits, Norway and Finland used the DIT reforms to convert their dividend deduction systems into imputation systems. In other words, they moved from double-tax relief at corporate level to double-tax relief at shareholder level.[19] Policymakers argued that the dividend deduction system benefited foreign shareholders more than it did domestic shareholders. While domestic shareholders had to pay PT on dividend income (and capital gains tax on realized share profits), the Nordic tax authorities could not ensure equivalent taxation of foreign shareholders. Presumably, this did not matter much as long as foreign investment was constrained to enter the Nordic countries through other

---

[18] Under the Norwegian arrangement, undertaxation might still occur due to the tax deferment effect.

[19] Until 1993, Sweden also had a dividend deduction system, but confined the relief to dividends paid out on newly issued shares (Annell deduction). This echoed the implications of the 'new view' on dividend taxation, which holds that only corporate investment financed by new shares is affected by the double tax on dividends under the classical system. Investment financed by retained profits is not affected, because dividends are effectively 'trapped' in the corporation. Hence, the tax on them, now or later, is capitalized in lower share prices restoring the original return-to-equity ratio. The new view contrasts with the 'traditional view', which holds that dividend pay-out and investment policies are affected by the double tax. For recent reviews and analyses, see Zodrow (1991) and Sørensen (1994b).

means, including the inducement to form investment reserves. When these constraints were abolished, however, the dividend deduction system would seem to confer an advantage on foreign shareholders relative to domestic shareholders. This could have been corrected by an increase in the level of withholding taxes on dividends paid abroad, but this would have required a renegotiation of double tax treaties—a time-consuming exercise at best.[20]

Under the DIT, imputation is equivalent to exemption of dividend income at the shareholder level, provided measures are taken at company level to ensure that dividends are not paid out of exempt profits (equivalent to the compensatory tax under imputation systems). As argued in Norway, and as shown by the experience in Sweden, however, outright exemption might be more difficult to sell politically than taxation with a full credit for the CT attributable to dividend income. As Tikka (1993), moreover, points out, exemption would have made it more difficult to maintain withholding taxes on dividends paid out to foreign shareholders (as a proxy for the domestic capital gains tax, which cannot be levied) who might invoke the non-discrimination clause included in most tax treaties. Furthermore, the elimination of dividend income from the personal income statement of shareholders might make them eligible for certain means-tested benefits, no doubt an unintended and undesirable side-effect. Hence imputation was chosen rather than exemption.

In evaluating the change from dividend deduction to imputation, Andersson et al. (1998) have pointed out that, in small open economies, the prices of shares (and other financial assets) are largely determined by foreign investors. Hence any increase in the CT on dividend income for foreign shareholders under imputation relative to dividend deduction will be reflected in lower share prices which tends to increase the corporate cost of capital. In this situation, double-tax relief for domestic shareholders merely increases the relative preference of domestic investors for shares over bonds. Investment in the corporate sector, however, is dampened rather than stimulated. Only double-tax relief at the corporate level, as granted before, (or, more directly, investment incentives at corporate level)

---

[20] In the 1970s, Germany made various not-quite-successful attempts to obtain an increase in its bilateral withholding taxes on dividend payments abroad under its split-rate system, which imposes a lower CT on distributed profits than on retained profits. Since foreign shareholders did not face the higher CT on dividends received, German subsidiaries of foreign parent companies would distribute profits at the lower CT rate and the parent would subsequently reinvest them in the German subsidiary.

would lower the cost of capital of domestic investment relative to foreign investment, because foreign shareholders would also benefit from the relief.

3.2.3 Retained profits

Under an imputation system that forms part of a DIT, there would be no place for a capital gains tax on shares if any gains realized by shareholders exactly corresponded to the increase in the after-tax profits retained by the corporation since the shares were acquired. In fact, a capital gains tax might even result in excessive profit distributions by corporations on account of the higher tax on retentions compared with the tax on distributions. This assumes that the corporation has no unrealized capital gains on its assets which, reflected in higher share values, could be realized free of tax by shareholders in the absence of a capital gains tax.

The Nordic countries have reacted differently to the problem posed by the double taxation of retained earnings in conjunction with the capital gains tax at the shareholder level. Finland and Sweden simply ignore it by taxing capital gains on shares at the capital income tax rate. Denmark has adopted various *ad hoc* measures, distinguishing between short-term and long-term gains, as well as 'small' and 'big' investors. Norway is the only country that has introduced a sophisticated and consistent system, called the RISK method,[21] to deal both with the danger of excessive distributions and with the unwarranted exemption of realized gains at shareholder level due to unrealized gains at corporate level.

Under the Norwegian RISK method, shareholders in Norwegian corporations are entitled to write up the acquisition costs of their shares by the profits net of CT retained by the corporation since the date of acquisition. The step-up of basis corresponds to the shareholder's share in the corporation's equity. Similarly, the basis is written down with negative RISK adjustments on account of losses or distributions out of previously accumulated earnings. Appropriate adjustments are also made if capital is paid in or paid out. The first-in / first-out principle applies if part of the same shareholding is sold.

However attractive from a theoretical perspective, the RISK method is difficult to implement properly (Andersson et al., 1998). Double taxation, for instance, would still occur if the profits of a subsidiary are reflected in a higher, stepped-up, basis of the parent company, but not in an adjusted basis of the parent's shareholders, because the gain has not yet been realized by the parent. Another set of problems arises from the fact that the

---

[21] RISK stands for Regulering av aksjenes Inngangsverdi med endring i Skattlagt Kapital: adjustment of basis by changes in capital subject to tax.

RISK adjustment date (i.e. 1 January) may induce controlling shareholders to compel the corporation to pay out dividends in the course of the year, then sell their shares and record a capital loss. Although the new shareholder would record a step-up of basis at the time of the next RISK adjustment date, the tax would still be forgone if the new shareholder did not realize his gain. Complex problems also arise in connection with corporate reorganizations. The Norwegian tax authorities have taken various measures to address these issues, but it cannot yet be said that the RISK method operates trouble free.

3.3 Ensuring single taxation

The DITs in Norway and Finland ensure that equity income is taxed once and only once. Compensatory taxes guarantee that no dividends are paid out of exempt profits without having borne CT, which subsequently is creditable against the shareholder's PT. Consequently, all recipients of company equity income (domestic individual shareholders, exempt entities, and foreign shareholders) pay the underlying CT. Furthermore, as shown in Table 8.4, foreign portfolio shareholders in treaty countries pay an additional 15 per cent withholding tax. This tax may be viewed as a substitute for the capital gains

Table 8.4 Nordic countries: common withholding tax rates on payments to residents and non-residents in major treaty countries, 1999 (%)

	Norway	Finland	Sweden	Denmark
Capital income tax rate	28	28	30	39.7–59
Dividends				
Domestic	—	—	—	25[a]
Foreign portfolio	15	15	15	15
Foreign parent	0; 5; 10	0; 5; 10	0; 5; 10	0; 5; 10
Interest				
Domestic	—	—	—	—
Foreign	—	—[b]	—	—
Royalties				
Domestic	—	—	—	—
Foreign	—	0	0	0

[a] Final tax liability if dividend income does not exceed DKR 36,000 (DKR 72,000 for married couples).
[b] In exceptional cases—i.e. permanent loans in lieu of contribution of capital—a final withholding tax is due (usually 10%).
Source: International Bureau of Fiscal Documentation.

tax levied from domestic shareholders on the excess of the selling price of shares over their stepped-up basis. Under the EU's Parent–Subsidiary Directive, no withholding tax is levied on dividends paid to qualifying companies in other Member States by Finland, Sweden, and Denmark.

The goal of ensuring single taxation is mostly honoured in the breach, however, with respect to interest and royalty payments to exempt entities, such as pension funds, and foreign debtholders or suppliers of know-how. This affects the portfolio choice of exempt investors in favour of bonds, and thereby the ownership structure of firms. The absence of a withholding tax on interest paid to foreign debtholders, moreover, leaves opportunities intact for evading or avoiding the CT or DIT on interest income by foreign as well as domestic debtholders. It increases the scope for international tax arbitrage through thin capitalization.[22] It is doubtful whether the legislation on controlled foreign corporations found in all Nordic countries is an adequate substitute for appropriate withholding taxes at the level of domestic companies.

3.4 Effects on financing and investment decisions

As noted above, one of the main objectives of the DIT reforms in the Nordic countries was to reduce the effect of the CT/PT system on financing and investment decisions. Generous tax deferment and write-off provisions were perceived to skew required pre-tax rates of return on investment across different types of assets and different modes of finance. Therefore one of the litmus tests of the reforms is whether or not this objective has been achieved.

Surprisingly, the answer could be that the reforms may have increased rather than decreased the impact of taxation on investment. This, at least, is the implication of a comprehensive, comparative study by Dufwenberg et al. (1994) on the influence of the Nordic CT/PT systems on real investment behaviour over the period 1966–90. The authors show that the estimated effect of the cost of capital on fixed investment differs very little when that cost is adjusted for the impact of taxes. Hence they conclude that the Nordic CT/PT systems, with the possible exception of the Danish system, have been effectively neutral towards investment in the period under review. The intuition is that companies have been able to use the generous range of tax allowances to shield their marginal investments from tax. By implication, the abolition of these allowances may have restored the impact of the CT/PT system on investment.

---

[22] For a treatment of these issues in the context of the EU, see Cnossen and Bovenberg (1997).

The study by Dufwenberg et al. (1994), however, concerns the impact of taxation on *aggregate* investment, not on the composition of investment. The DIT reforms in the early 1990s should affect the level of investment if, as intended, some measure of effective taxation of capital income has been restored. The accompanying increase in capital cost is the price that must inevitably be paid if it is considered desirable to tax the return on investment. At the same time, however, the reforms largely eliminated the differential taxation of capital income across sectors, assets, and modes of finance. By doing so, the reforms largely restored one of the market's most fundamental rules, which prescribes that economic considerations rather than tax motives should determine the behaviour of entrepreneurs.

This raises the question of whether the economic benefits from increased neutrality in the taxation of the composition of investment income outweigh the price that has to be paid in the form of a reduction of the overall incentive to invest because capital costs on average are higher. The answer requires further empirical research. It should be noted, however, that debt and interest deductibility, against the background of the growing innovation and internationalization of capital markets, may be expected partly to take over the role of the previous tax deferment and write-off provisions in dampening the effects of taxation on corporate real investment. Again, differential effects should occur, because transnational companies, in the absence of source taxes on interest and royalty payments abroad, are in a better position to shield their investments from taxation than are domestic companies. In addition, they can reduce taxable profits by manipulating their transfer prices.

The neutrality of the previous CT/PT systems has also been emphasized in the literature, initiated by Kanniainen and Södersten (1995), which explores the implications of uniform accounting conventions for the impact of taxation on investment. Until recently, dividend payments in any year by Norwegian, Finnish, and Swedish companies could not exceed taxable profits after tax. This protection of the equity base meant that corporate borrowing in any year could not exceed the increase in the company's net assets as recorded in the tax accounts. Hence, if it is assumed that companies would borrow all they could, depreciation for tax purposes in any year would equal gross investment minus borrowing, i.e. the amount of equity-financed investment. This in turn implied that all equity-financed investment would be written off immediately in the tax accounts. In conjunction with interest deductibility, it followed that the CTs could be characterized as neutral cash-flow taxes. This conclusion, however, does not hold under separate reporting which, following Denmark's lead, has recently been introduced in Norway and Finland. Under separate reporting, commercial profits are permitted to diverge from tax profits. Hence investments will be influenced by the parameters of the CT/PT system.

In conclusion, the most obvious implication for equity is to impose withholding taxes on interest and royalty payments made abroad and to strengthen the verification of transfer pricing practices. Most likely, however, efficiency would suffer because foreign investment would be deterred. If the returns on foreign investments are to be taxed without inducing capital flight, international agreement is required to co-ordinate the imposition of source taxes on interest and royalties. As long as such co-operation is not forthcoming, the emphasis should probably be on tax concessions at the company level, rather than at the shareholder level, to treat domestic investment on a par with foreign investment.

4. Treatment of proprietorships and closely held companies

Capital income and labour income must be split when both income components accrue jointly. This occurs with the earnings of the self-employed as well as for active shareholders in closely held companies who are able to determine their own salaries and dividend pay-outs and hence their total tax liabilities. While all Nordic countries have income-splitting rules for these two groups of taxpayers, the specific details differ between countries. Table 8.5 provides an overview of the various rules, which are reviewed and evaluated below.[23]

4.1 Main features

4.1.1 Source or fence model?

The position of the self-employed and active shareholders in closely held companies can be looked at from two angles. On the one hand, the focus may be on the (imputed) income from the labour that these persons perform in the business. Equal treatment of this income *vis-à-vis* the labour income of wage-earners requires current taxation at progressive PT rates, whether or not the income is withdrawn from the business. This is called the 'source model' in the Nordic countries, because all income is attributed to one of two sources, i.e. labour or capital. On the other hand, if the focus is on the treatment of the imputed return on business capital, then a comparison with the treatment of the retained profits of publicly held corporations seems appropriate. Accordingly, under the 'fence model', profits are not split, but a 'fence' is erected between the 'business sphere' and the 'private sphere' of the proprietor or shareholder, and the labour-income component, like the capital-income component, is taxed at the

---

[23] This section draws on Hagen and Sørensen (1996).

Table 8.5 Profit-splitting rules in the Nordic countries, 1999

Rules	Norway	Finland	Sweden	Denmark
1. Source or fence model?	Source model. Profits are split and allocated on current basis.	Source model for self-employed, but fence model for unlisted companies.	Fence model. Retained labour income taxable at CT rate. Profits are split only upon withdrawal.	Fence model. Retained labour income taxed at CT rate. Profits are split only upon withdrawal. Source model is optional.
2. To whom applicable?	1. Self-employed 2. Active shareholders in closely held companies jointly owning two-thirds or more of all shares entitled to two-thirds or more of profits[a]	1. Self-employed 2. All companies not listed on the Stock Exchange	1. Self-employed 2. Active shareholders in closely held companies	Self-employed only
3. Labour or capital income first?	Capital income	Capital income	Capital income	Capital income
4. Which capital value?	Historic cost	Historic cost	Historic cost	Historic cost

	Gross method	Net method	Net method	Net method
5. Gross or net method?	Gross method	Net method	Net method	Net method Gross method if source model is opted for
6. How is the presumptive return set?	Interest on five-year government bonds plus 6% points	Self-employed: 18% Unlisted companies: 15%	Interest on ten-year government bonds plus 1% point	Average interest rate on bonds during first six months of the year
7. How are current losses treated?	1. Offset against current income from other sources at basic rate 2. Ten-year carry-forward	1. Offset against current income from other sources through tax credit at CT rate 2. Ten-year carry-forward	1. Offset against retained profits of earlier years and current earned income 2. Indefinite carry-forward	1. Offset against retained profits of earlier years, current capital income, and current earned income 2. Five-year carry-forward

proportional capital income tax rate as long as the income is retained in the business.

As indicated in Table 8.5, Norway and Finland (for the self-employed) have introduced the source model, under which profits are split exhaustively and taxed currently. Sweden, Denmark, and Finland (for unlisted companies) however, have adopted the fence model: retained labour income is taxed at the capital income tax rate; subsequent withdrawals of profits, however, are split into a labour-income and a capital-income component, and taxed at the appropriate PT or CT rate.

Obviously, given the precepts of the DIT, the source model treats capital income and labour income accruing to the self-employed and active share-holders on a par with other capital or labour income. The fence model, on the other hand, favours labour income retained by these persons in their business. Wage-earners, after all, do not have the opportunity to save at the low capital income tax rate until the savings are withdrawn. Although the labour income retained by the self-employed or active shareholders is even-tually taxed, they benefit from being able to defer the tax payment. This deferment is equivalent to an interest-free loan from the government for the amount of tax deferred. Care must be taken, moreover, that the tax on retained labour income is not avoided. In contrast, no additional tax is payable under the source model if profits are distributed out of fully taxed labour or capital income. Beyond that, the fence model produces the famil-iar 'lock-in' effect: retained income is not made available on the capital mar-ket where it can compete with other resources for the best alternative use.

In favour of the fence model, it might be argued that small businesses possibly face equity costs exceeding the social cost of capital, because they do not have the opportunity to diversify all their socially diversifiable risks. In addition, it has been pointed out that small businesses are con-fronted with asymmetric information which gives rise to credit rationing (see, for example, Stiglitz and Weiss (1981)). However, these arguments, as Hagen and Sørensen (1996) point out, are rather speculative. Firm size, moreover, is not systematically related to the form in which business is carried on. Also, there are better ways to stimulate the development of small businesses under the source model (see below). In any case, it is obvious that the fence model fails to ensure equal treatment between the self-employed and active shareholders, on the one hand, and wage-earners, on the other hand. For these reasons, the following discussion focuses mainly on the implications of the source model.

4.1.2   To whom applicable?

The profit-splitting rules, regardless of the model being used, are obviously applicable to the self-employed, but in Norway, Finland, and Sweden the same rules are also used to split the income of 'active' shareholders in closely held companies. Accordingly, some definition of active shareholder-ship must be provided. Finland does this simply by deeming all companies not listed on the Stock Exchange to be closely held companies, even though some or all shareholders may not be actively involved in running the company. Consequently, these passive shareholders may be discriminated against, because their total tax bill may be higher on account of the deemed attribution of labour income, even though no work has been performed for the company.

Norway provides a definition of active shareholders which assumes that the effective control of the company is related to the size of the share-holding by an individual, jointly with his or her spouse and kin. In other words, the size of the holding is irrefutable proof that the majority share-holder(s) can influence the level of their salaries and/or dividend incomes and hence their total tax bills. By implication, shareholders whose holdings fall below the ownership criterion enjoy only capital income taxable at the proportional rate. Under its fence model, Sweden confines the profit-splitting rules to active shareholders in closely held companies. Denmark applies them only to the self-employed.

4.1.3 Labour or capital income first?

In splitting the profits of the self-employed and/or active shareholders, in all Nordic countries, the taxable return on capital is estimated first. Accordingly, labour income is a residual item. There are two reasons for this choice. First, the appropriate return on labour is extremely difficult to estimate, because diligence, effort, and ingenuity may diverge widely, as may the hourly wage rate relating to various kinds of labour and the number of hours worked. Even if the information were available, it would be exceedingly difficult to check its accuracy. Second, if labour income were determined first, the marginal PT rate on the profits of the self-employed and active shareholders would exhibit a regressive incidence. After all, additional earnings would then be taxed at the proportional capital income tax rate instead of at the progressive labour income tax rate.

4.1.4 Which capital value?

On the basis of these arguments, all the Nordic DITs prescribe that taxable capital income should be calculated first by multiplying the value of the business's assets by a presumptive return, and that residual profits should be considered as labour income. In all countries, also, the value of business assets is based on their historic cost reduced by depreciation allowances for tax purposes. Hence the replacement value of the business assets is not used as the basis to which the presumptive return is applied.

Administrative reasons favour this choice.[24] In contrast to replacement values, historic or acquisition costs can easily be ascertained from business accounts. Generally, historic costs would not be subject to dispute.

It should be noted that intangible assets, such as goodwill and research and development costs, generally are not included in the capital base, unless these assets have been paid for or their costs have been capitalized by the business. Also, the value of financial assets, which yield an identifiable return accruing independently from normal business profits, is not included in the base, because the return can be directly earmarked as income from capital.

4.1.5   Gross or net method?

Another decision point concerns the question of whether the presumptive return on capital should be calculated over the value of all business assets (gross method) or whether equity for tax purposes (the value of all assets less debts) should be taken as the basis for computing taxable capital income (net method). Under the gross method, the presumptively determined gross return on equity and debt is reduced by the interest actually paid to calculate taxable net capital income. The gross return, furthermore, is subtracted from total profits (increased by the interest actually paid) to calculate taxable labour income. Under the net method, in contrast, presumptively determined capital income is subtracted directly from net profits (i.e. net of interest paid) to ascertain taxable labour income. The effective tax rate on total undivided profits would be the same under both methods if the presumptive rate of return equals the interest rate payable on debt. That should rarely occur.

When the presumptive rate of return differs from the interest actually paid, the net method offers the opportunity to influence the effective tax rate on total undivided net profits (on the assumption that the balance-sheet total remains unchanged). It would be advantageous, for example, to convert business debt into private debt and to replace it by equity if the presumptive rate of return were higher than the actual interest rate. In this manner, progressively taxed returns on labour performed in the business can be converted into proportionally taxed returns on capital. If, on the other hand, the presumptive rate of return were lower than the interest rate actually paid, then businessmen would be able to reduce their total

---

[24] In addition, as Hagen and Sørensen (1996) point out, valuation at historic cost could serve to counteract the distortionary reduction of the cost of capital if actual depreciation exceeds economic depreciation. This argument, however, assumes that there is no inflation.

tax bills by listing private debt as business debt. Even if both rates of return were the same, it would still be possible to influence the total effect-ive tax rate by withdrawing capital from the business after the reference date (usually the balance-sheet date) and paying it into the business again before the next reference date.

This form of tax arbitrage is not possible under the gross method, because the presumptive rate of return is applied to a base—i.e. the value of the business's total assets—that is not influenced by the financing structure of the business. The gross method, however, is not neutral with respect to investment decisions if the presumptive rate of return is higher than the interest rate. Debt-financed investments would then be stimu-lated. In the opposite, presumably less prevalent, case, investments would be discouraged. These distortions of investment decisions would not occur under the net method.

To some extent, therefore, the choice between the net method and the gross method is a choice between investment neutrality, on the one hand, and minimizing arbitrage opportunities, and hence complexity, on the other hand. In considering the pros and cons, it should be noted that the gross method encourages investments by proprietorships and closely held companies if the government sets the presumptive rate of return above the going interest rate. Simplicity, moreover, is an important concern. For these reasons, the gross method seems to have the edge. Even then, how-ever, it makes sense to maintain existing distinctions between inherently private, inherently business, and mixed private/business assets or liabilities, because the gross method offers the same opportunities for tax arbitrage as the net method if the balance sheet is lengthened.

4.1.6 How is the presumptive return set?

It would seem obvious to take a nominal rate of interest (the real interest rate plus the inflation rate) as the starting-point for setting the presump-tive return, because historic cost is chosen as the basis for valuing busi-ness assets. The level of the interest rate is, to some extent, arbitrary, because different businesses are confronted with different rates of interest depending on their risk profile. Norway has simply chosen the rate of interest on five-year government bonds. This rate is increased by a pre-mium for entrepreneurial risk in order not to discourage risk-bearing investments.[25] In practice, the level of the risk premium is largely a political

[25] In a revised version of Hagen and Sørensen (1996), included in Sørensen (1998), it is pointed out that the risk premium seems unwarranted under a pro-portional labour income tax with full loss offsets. It is conceded, however, that, in practice, loss offsets are imperfect.

choice. Presumably for this reason, Finland annually determines the total rate of return without making a distinction between the interest element and the risk premium. Denmark does not take account of a risk premium; neither does Sweden, except in the case of closely held companies.

4.1.7 How are current losses treated?

Generally, the foregoing rules for determining the presumptive income from capital of the self-employed and active shareholders are also applicable to current losses. The question arises, however, of whether these losses should be offset only against future positive capital income or also against current income from labour.

Norway has solved the issue by merging capital income and labour (personal) income in the first income bracket to which the capital income tax rate applies. Finland, which treats capital and labour income as separate sources from the start, obtains the same result by allowing capital income losses to be offset against labour income through a tax credit calculated at the capital income tax rate. Since labour income can be retained in the business at the capital income tax rate, Sweden and Denmark provide for loss-offset ordering rules. Thus losses can be offset against retained (labour) income of earlier years before they are offset against current capital income or earned income. In all countries, losses that cannot be offset against current income can be carried forward—for five years (Denmark), ten years (Norway, Finland), or indefinitely (Sweden).

4.2 Concluding comments

Under the DIT, the labour income of the self-employed and active shareholders in closely held companies should be taxed on a par with the labour income of wage-earners, while capital income accruing in proprietorships and closely held companies should be taxed on a par with the capital income of other wealth-holders. Clearly, the source model, under which the total profit of these entities is allocated on a current basis to the parties entitled thereto, best meets this equal treatment rule.

Sørensen (1994a) has labelled the compulsory profit-splitting rules the Achilles' heel of the DIT, because they involve considerable administrative complexity. It should be noted, however, that such rules are needed in any income tax system under which the top marginal PT rate is higher than the proportional CT rate. Such systems, after all, permit the self-employed to convert labour income, subject to high progressive rates, into proportionately taxed capital income by incorporating their businesses. To this observer, the profit-splitting rules of the source model are more equitable and seem easier to administer than some of the tortuous and arbitrary provisions for the prevention of undertaxation of the self-employed currently on the statute books in countries without a DIT. Under these provisions, the profits of proprietorships are generally taxed at the progressive PT rates, while the profits of closely held companies are taxed at the proportional CT rate. As under the Swedish and Danish fence model, profits of closely held companies are taxed again upon withdrawal at either progressive PT rates or at a flat capital gains tax rate if the whole or part of the substantial interest in a closely held company is sold. The tax deferment opportunities for closely held companies are obviously ways to shelter small and medium-sized businesses from the full impact of the high marginal PT rates. This goal, however, is achieved at considerable costs in terms of economic distortion (lock-in effects) and administrative complexity.

Under DITs, small and medium-sized businesses are stimulated more directly, and perhaps at lesser economic and administrative cost, through the level of the risk premium, which offers relief to capital-intensive businesses. But the tax burden on labour-intensive firms can also be mitigated. In Norway, for example, 11 per cent of the payroll (excluding the salaries of active shareholders) can be deducted from the total proceeds from labour of the active shareholders (which increases the proportionately taxed proceeds from capital), provided the return on labour of individual active shareholders does not fall below 145 per cent of the salary of the best-paid ordinary employee. Furthermore, the return on labour per active shareholder cannot exceed NOK 1,445,000. In Finland, 10 per cent of the payroll is taxable as capital income.

5. Towards a European dual income tax?

Tax co-ordination in the EU rests on neutrality and subsidiarity considerations. Neutrality in the field of capital income taxation within, as well as between, Member States implies approximate uniformity of the overall effective tax rates (CT + PT) on the return to equity, whether retained or distributed, and the return to debt, as well as greater uniformity of effective tax rates, regardless of whether the return of an investment accrues to domestic or foreign investors. Subsidiarity, still evolving, seems to imply that Member States should co-operate in allocating the capital income tax base in the EU to individual Member States in such a way that overtaxation or undertaxation across Member States is avoided. In addition, and no less important, it seems to mean that Member States should be able to tax the capital income arising within their borders without the need for day-to-day co-operation with other Member States (Cnossen, 1996). Does the DIT have the potential to meet these requirements?

To begin with, currently, domestic and cross-border investment decisions in the EU are distorted by a crazy quilt of widely diverging tax rates on capital income: retained profits, distributions, and interest, as well as capital gains, royalties, and other forms of capital income. Current dividend relief systems repair only a minor defect of classical CT/PT systems and greatly complicate the treatment of outward and inward dividend income. More importantly, the deductibility of interest at the corporate level, in conjunction with the existence of exempt domestic and foreign sectors, creates an enormous loophole in the CT and greatly distorts the debt–equity choice. Beyond that, the application of the source principle to equity income and the residence principle to debt income (although debt and equity have become nearly complete substitutes) has resulted in an arbitrary division of the capital income tax base between the Member States. Indeed, the present systems can be rationalized only if they serve to alleviate the distortions of the nominal tax rates on real investment decisions. They probably do—but at the high price of an extremely complicated set of tax rules and little, if any, revenue.

The DIT has the potential to treat capital income arising within Member States more neutrally than current CTs and PTs do. Basically, all capital income originating in any particular country would be taxed at the same rate. Double taxation of corporate profits would be avoided through imputation or, preferably, exemption of dividend income, and by taxing capital gains only if and to the extent that they exceed the written-up basis of shares. Other capital income would be taxed at the personal level, although source taxes could obviate the need for doing so with respect to interest and royalties.

If the DIT is to serve as the model for taxing capital income in the Member States of the EU, then agreement should be reached on the comprehensive application of the source entitlement principle with respect to all forms of capital income.[26] All inward dividend income should be exempted from CT and PT, and all outward dividend income from withholding tax, whether from direct investment or portfolio shareholding. Likewise, imputation tax credits should not be extended to non-resident

---

[26] The advocacy of the pure source principle for capital income taxation raises the question of whether labour income should not also be taxed on a source basis. The answer is that the proposed flat capital income tax, like the CT, is an *in rem* tax that lends itself naturally to the source principle, whereas the application of a progressive labour income tax schedule does not seem to make much sense on ability-to-pay grounds unless the schedule is applied to world-wide labour income. In view of the immobility of labour, in practice, the labour income tax is inherently residence-based.

shareholders. Perhaps more importantly, a source tax equal to the CT rate should be imposed on interest and royalties. In no case would this tax be refundable to non-residents (or domestic exempt entities). This would move the DIT in the direction of the comprehensive business income tax (CBIT), proposed by the US Department of the Treasury (1992), which taxes all earnings on equity as well as debt at the company level and exempts these earnings at the level of the recipients.

The proportional, *in rem* taxation of all corporate earnings would obviate the need for thin-capitalization rules. Also, the lack of external neutrality of current imputation systems would be a matter of the past. Tax credits would not be extended to out-of-state shareholders, because the proportional rate in source states and the exemption of capital income in domicile states would approximately ensure non-discriminatory treatment. Manipulation of transfer prices (prices charged to foreign affiliated companies) would still be possible to influence the allocation of profits (and thus CT revenues) between the Member States, but a minimum CT rate, as proposed by the Ruding Committee (Commission of the European Communities, 1992), should reduce the incentive for this form of tax arbitrage. In this connection, it should be emphasized that approximation of statutory tax rates seems more important than approximation of effective tax rates. Differences in statutory rates are important for exploiting opportunities for tax avoidance (transfer pricing, thin capitalization). Effective tax rates, on the other hand, affect the ascertainment of taxable profits (depreciation, inventory valuation) with respect to less mobile physical capital. Tolerable differences in effective tax rates would increase the operational independence of the Member States.

The DIT would reduce the cost of equity-financed investment and increase the cost of debt-financed investment. This should benefit new, starting enterprises, which face difficulties in attracting debt because they do not yet enjoy a high credit rating, own mainly non-liquid assets (such as firm-specific machinery) against which it is difficult to borrow, or generate insufficient taxable profits to be able to deduct interest. Furthermore, the lower cost (and therefore the higher relative return) of equity should promote shareholding, make mergers (to avoid the double tax on dividends) less attractive, induce pension funds to change the composition of their portfolios in favour of shares, and form a natural barrier against easy foreign acquisition of domestic firms. In short, the dynamics of the market would be strengthened and ownership patterns would more closely reflect underlying market forces.

Phase-in issues should be given due attention. Although the more effective taxation of interest income is clearly a goal worth pursuing, gradual and concerted action is called for. Caution is advisable because the current tax-induced changes in corporate financing patterns may, to a large extent, serve to reduce the distortions of real investment and saving decisions. Higher before-tax rates, moreover, would dampen (debt-financed) investment demand. Co-ordination with the US and Japan would be essential in order to prevent tax-induced capital outflows due to a higher cost of capital in the EU, and to jointly constrain tax haven practices. A start could be made with a common minimum EU withholding rate. Interest paid to out-of-state residents should be included in the base.

References

Agell, J., Englund, P., and Södersten, J. (1996), 'Tax reform of the century: the Swedish experiment', *National Tax Journal*, 49: 643–64.

Andersson, K., Kanniainen, V., Södersten, J., and Sørensen, P. B. (1998), 'Corporate tax policy in the Nordic countries', in P. B. Sørensen (ed.), *Tax Policy in the Nordic Countries*, New York: MacMillan.

——and Mutén, L. (1994), 'The tax system of Sweden', *Tax Notes International*, 9 (10 October): 1147–63.

Atkinson, A. B., and Sandmo, A. (1980), 'Welfare implications of the taxation of savings', *Economic Journal*, 90: 529–49.

Cnossen, S. (1996), 'Company taxes in the European Union: criteria and options for reform', *Fiscal Studies*, 17(4): 67–97.

——and Bovenberg, L. (1997), 'Company tax coordination in the European Union: some further thoughts on the Ruding Committee Report', in M. I. Blejer and T. Ter-Minassian (eds), *Macroeconomic Dimensions of Public Finance: Essays in Honour of Vito Tanzi*, London: Routledge.

——and Messere, K. (1990), 'Personal income tax reforms in OECD member countries', in S. Cnossen and R. M. Bird (eds), *The Personal Income Tax: Phoenix from the Ashes?*, Amsterdam: North-Holland.

Commission of the European Communities (1992), *Report of the Committee of Independent Experts on Company Taxation*, Luxemburg (the Ruding Report).

Dufwenberg, M., Koskenkylä, H., and Södersten, J. (1994), 'Manufacturing investment and taxation in the Nordic countries', *Scandinavian Journal of Economics*, 96: 443–61.

Gordon, R. H., and MacKie-Mason, J. K. (1994), 'Tax distortions to the choice of organizational form', *Journal of Public Economics*, 55: 279–306.

——and Slemrod, J. (1988), 'Do we collect any revenue from taxing capital income?', in L. H. Summers (ed.), *Tax Policy and the Economy*, 2, Cambridge, MA: MIT Press.

Gravelle, J. (1994), *The Economic Effects of Taxing Capital Income*, Cambridge, MA: MIT Press.

Hagen, K. P., and Sørensen, P. B. (1996), 'Taxation of the self-employed: taxation principles and tax reforms in the Nordic countries', in S. Cnossen (ed.), *Towards a Dual Income Tax? Scandinavian and Austrian Experiences*, Rotterdam: Foundation for European Fiscal Studies; a revised version is included in P. B. Sørensen (ed.), *Tax Policy in the Nordic Countries*, MacMillan, New York, 1998.

International Bureau of Fiscal Documentation, *European Taxation*, looseleaf, Amsterdam.

Kanniainen, V., and Södersten, J. (1995), 'The importance of reporting conventions for the theory of corporate taxation', *Journal of Public Economics*, 57: 417–30.

Lodin, S-O. (1994), *The Nordic Reforms of Company and Shareholder Taxation: A Comparison*, Stockholm: Federation of Swedish Industries.

Mutén, L. (1997), 'Dual income tax: the Scandinavian experience', in J. G. Head and R. Krever (eds), *Company Tax Systems*, Burwood, Australia: Australian Tax Research Foundation.

Nielsen, S. B., and Sørensen, P. B. (1997), 'On the optimality of the Nordic system of dual income taxation', *Journal of Public Economics*, 63: 311–29.

Razin, A., and Sadka, E. (1991), 'International tax competition and gains from tax harmonization', *Economics Letters*, 37: 69–76.

Skaar, A. A. (1991), 'Norway enacts tax reform of the century', *Tax Notes International*, 3 (November): 1169–72.

Sørensen, P. B. (1994a), 'From the global income tax to the dual income tax: recent tax reforms in the Nordic countries', *International Tax and Public Finance*, 1: 57–79.

—— (1994b), 'Some old and new issues in the theory of corporate income taxation', *Finanzarchiv*, 51: 425–56.

—— (ed.) (1998), *Tax Policy in the Nordic Countries*, New York: MacMillan.

Stiglitz, J. E., and Weiss, A. (1981), 'Credit rationing in markets with imperfect information', *American Economic Review*, 71: 393–410.

Tikka, K. S. (1993), 'A flat rate tax on capital income: the Finnish reaction to international tax competition', in *Tax Reform in the Nordic Countries 1973–1993*, Nordic Council for Tax Research, Jubilee Publication.

US Department of the Treasury (1992), *Integration of the Individual and Corporate Tax Systems: Taxing Business Income Once*, Washington, DC: US Government Printing Office.

Zodrow, G. R. (1991), 'On the "traditional" and "new" views of dividend taxation', *National Tax Journal*, 44: 497–509.

9

Transfer pricing and income shifting in integrating economies

T. Scott Newlon

As barriers to cross-border trade and investment have fallen and business has become more globally integrated in recent years, many countries have become increasingly concerned about multinational enterprises (MNEs) shifting taxable income out of their jurisdictions into low-tax foreign jurisdictions. MNEs may do this by manipulating their transfer prices, which are the prices established for transfers of goods and services and the lending of funds between entities within the MNE. MNEs may also shift income by tinkering with the financial structure of MNE group members so that debt, and the associated interest expense, are shifted across borders. Income shifting can erode national tax bases and distort the financial and real investment decisions of MNEs. And countries may respond to these pressures by competing for tax base and capital in ways that exacerbate the distortions and further erode the taxation of company income.[1]

This chapter reviews the pressures and distortions created by income shifting within MNEs and examines how various policies may ameliorate or exacerbate these problems. Since income shifting inherently involves more than one country, policies of one country may create positive or negative spillovers for other countries, and international policy co-ordination may be necessary if such spillovers are to be properly accounted for. In reviewing policy responses to income shifting, particular notice will be given to the possibility and desirability of such co-ordination.

The author gratefully acknowledges helpful comments from Sijbren Cnossen, Harry Grubert, Sheena McConnell, Jack Mintz, Don Rousslang, Emil Sunley, two anonymous referees, and the participants at the ISPE conference. The views expressed in this chapter are those of the author alone and should not be construed as reflecting the views or policies of the US Treasury Department.

[1] Although tax bases clearly are also affected by MNE investment location decisions, and these decisions are also influenced by differences in company taxation across countries, the focus here is on income shifting through transfer pricing and financing decisions within MNEs.

The chapter is organized as follows. Section 1 describes the nature of the cross-border income-shifting problem under standard company income taxes when tax rates differ among countries. It also discusses the potential effects of income shifting on MNE and country decisions. Section 2 reviews the empirical evidence on the magnitude of income shifting by MNEs. Section 3 examines potential policy responses while maintaining company income taxes. Section 4 analyses the effects of alternative company tax systems on income-shifting incentives. Finally, Section 5 presents some concluding remarks.

1. The problem

Under the tax rules of most countries, primary taxing rights on income are generally accorded to the country that is deemed to be the source of the income. This creates an issue of how to determine how much of an MNE's income has its source in each of the countries in which it operates.

Currently, the international norm for dealing with this issue is the separate-entity approach applied in accordance with the arm's-length principle. The separate-entity approach entails respecting the separate legal status of affiliates within the MNE. The arm's-length principle requires that the dealings—for example, transfers of goods, intangibles, services, or funds—between these affiliates be structured in a way that independent enterprises could have agreed to. This implies that transfer prices established for transactions between different parts of an MNE should be set at the level that would have prevailed had the transactions taken place between unrelated parties. It also implies that the financial structure of affiliates within an MNE group (in particular, the extent to which debt finance is used) should be consistent with the financial structure that an independent enterprise would have. The separate-entity approach and the arm's-length principle are enshrined in the OECD Model Tax Convention, the OECD Transfer Pricing Guidelines, and hundreds of bilateral income tax treaties.

There are several practical and conceptual obstacles to the application of the arm's-length principle. Perhaps the most difficult issues arise with respect to the transfer of intangibles, such as know-how, proprietary technology, and trade marks. A substantial body of literature suggests that such intangibles are often transferred across borders within an MNE precisely to avoid failures in arm's-length markets for information.[2] In these

---

[2] For surveys of this literature, see Ragazzi (1973), Rugman (1980), and Caves (1982). This literature effectively extends the literature suggesting that a principal reason for the existence of modern corporations is to exploit valuable intangibles while avoiding failures in the market for information. See, for example, Williamson (1971).

situations, there will be no comparable arm's-length transactions to use in valuing the transfer of intangibles within an MNE.

Another obstacle is that all firms in an industry may have integrated production to exploit economies of scope and scale, resulting in the absence of arm's-length markets for the intermediate goods that are transferred across borders within the firm. Moreover, even if there were market transactions to use one of the standard methods for estimating an arm's-length price, those methods do not take into account the existence of integration economies because they use as bench-marks transactions between firms that have not integrated their production.[3]

On a practical level, tax authorities sometimes find themselves at a disadvantage in identifying arm's-length prices because they have less information about an MNE's business than does the MNE. The MNE may have little incentive to correct this information asymmetry.

As the integration of cross-border production expands, the growing number of related-party transactions within MNEs represents a problem in itself. Tax authorities can incur substantial enforcement costs, and MNEs substantial compliance costs, in attempting to determine appropriate prices for a significant number of those transactions.

Finally, the arm's-length principle is of limited usefulness as a guide for determining the appropriate financial structure, and therefore interest expense, for affiliates within an MNE. Otherwise similar independent companies may often be observed operating under a wide range of financial structures.

1.1   Incentives for income shifting

The difficulties in applying the arm's-length principle leave MNEs scope to manipulate transfer prices and financial structures to shift income across borders. The tax benefits to an MNE of shifting income from one jurisdiction to another are determined in the first instance by the difference between the statutory tax rates of the jurisdictions, because the statutory tax rate generally applies at the margin to the respective changes in revenues and deductions.

Where the host-country tax rate on the income of an affiliate is higher than the home-country tax rate faced by the parent company, the tax benefit of shifting income to the parent through transfer pricing or interest deductions is determined simply by the difference in tax rates. But where the parent faces a higher tax rate than a foreign affiliate, the tax benefit of

---

[3] There may be no single theoretically correct way to divide such benefits across locations, and different transfer pricing methods would lead to different allocations of the benefits of scope economies within the MNE (Berry et al., 1992).

shifting income to the affiliate depends, in part, on how the home country taxes the foreign income of resident companies. In general, either the income of the foreign affiliate will be exempt from home-country tax or the home country will tax that income but the tax is deferred until the income is repatriated to the home country and a foreign tax credit against home-country tax is provided for foreign income and withholding taxes.[4]

If income of a low-tax foreign affiliate is exempt from home-country tax, there is always an incentive for an MNE to shift income from the parent to that affiliate. If the income of the low-tax affiliate is subject to home-country tax, then the benefit of shifting income rests entirely on the benefit of deferring home-country tax. If there is no deferral of home-country tax, then the income shifted to the foreign affiliate immediately bears the home-country tax anyway, so there is no benefit from shifting income.[5] Where there is deferral, the benefit of shifting will depend on the after-tax rate of return available in the country to which the income is shifted relative to the after-tax return available in the home country. As shown by Scholes and Wolfson (1992) and Hines and Rice (1994), if repatriation can be deferred indefinitely, deferral is beneficial if and only if the after-tax rate of return in the foreign country, $r_f(1-\tau_f)$, exceeds the after-tax rate of return if the income were repatriated, $r_h(1-\tau_h)$.

Income shifting to low-tax affiliates is clearly advantageous in a broader class of cases when the affiliate income is exempt from home-country tax than when the income is subject to home-country tax. However, in practice, the difference in shifting incentives between exemption and taxation with a foreign tax credit and deferral is often less than it appears to be. Where there is a foreign tax credit and deferral, there are often ways to avoid repatriation tax on shifted income even if the shifted income is immediately repatriated. One way arises because foreign tax credits are generally limited to the amount of the domestic tax liability on the foreign income, so that high-tax foreign income generates excess foreign tax credits. To the extent that high- and low-tax foreign income can be mixed together, the residual home-country tax on repatriated low-tax foreign income can be offset by excess foreign tax credits from the high-tax income.[6] In addition, as

---

[4] Japan, the UK, and the US are among the few countries that tax all worldwide income of resident companies while providing a foreign tax credit and, generally, deferral for income of foreign subsidiaries. Most other countries exempt at least some important classes of foreign affiliate income from tax.

[5] This ignores the possibilities sometimes available for shielding repatriated income from home-country tax under a foreign tax credit system. Those are discussed below.

[6] It would probably be impractical for foreign tax credit rules completely to prevent such mixing because of the detailed tracing that would be required for income passing between foreign affiliates.

Altshuler and Grubert (1996) point out, income from a low-tax foreign subsidiary can be effectively repatriated without triggering the repatriation tax if the parent can borrow against the low-tax subsidiary's passive assets or if the low-tax subsidiary uses the income to purchase equity in a high-tax subsidiary, which then uses the funds to make distributions to the parent.

There may also be non-tax reasons for an MNE to shift income across borders—for example, to avoid import duties and capital or exchange controls. In some cases, these may offset the tax incentives to shift income out of a country.

1.2 Efficiency effects

The presence of income-shifting possibilities potentially results in real resource costs through distortions to MNEs' investment and financing decisions.[7] Perhaps the most obvious distortions are those to investment location decisions. The incentive to locate some operations in low-tax jurisdictions is increased because of the opportunity such operations provide to shield high-tax income from tax through income shifting. For example, a low-tax subsidiary may be interposed as an intermediary in sales between two high-tax countries in order to park some income in the low-tax jurisdiction. Domestic sales may also be routed through a low-tax foreign affiliate. Proprietary technology or processes developed through research and development in a high-tax country may be used for production in a low-tax country because that provides an opportunity to shift some of the returns attributable to those intangibles to the low-tax country—for example, if the high-tax affiliate is paid less than full value for the right to use those intangibles.

In some cases, however, income shifting may offset some of the distorting influence tax rate differentials have on investment location decisions. To the extent that income can be shifted out of a high-tax jurisdiction, its high tax rate presents less of a disincentive to locate investment there. If at the margin all income were shifted out of the high-tax location, then its tax rate would have no effect on the amount of investment there.[8]

---

[7] Distortions to the form of organization of economic activity may also result. For example, to take advantage of cross-border income-shifting possibilities, a firm may choose to use a subsidiary to exploit an intangible asset in a foreign country when it could be more efficient simply to license an unrelated firm (Grubert, 1989).

[8] Of course, the revenue lost from income shifting may result in higher levels of other distorting taxes or suboptimal levels of public services.

In general, manipulation of the financial structure and location of debt within an MNE seems less likely to impose real efficiency costs on the MNE. For example, since there is no real distinction between debt and equity for financing transactions within the MNE group, shifting debt and the associated interest expenses among entities within an MNE probably does not result in any efficiency losses as long as it involves lending within the MNE. However, if it involves distortions to which part of the MNE borrows from external sources, there may be real costs. The degree to which costs are imposed depends upon the extent to which capital markets view all entities within the MNE as simply being parts of a whole, so that they examine the capitalization of the MNE group rather than its separate parts when evaluating financial risk.[9]

Income-shifting possibilities may also cause tax burdens to vary across industries and firms. Those firms that can most easily shift income across borders—for example, those that engage in substantial cross-border activity and have difficult-to-value intangibles—may face lower tax burdens than other firms.

The realities of transfer pricing practice may also lead to variations in tax burdens and in the nature of the company tax across firms and industries. Firms and tax authorities are increasingly using methods for establishing and evaluating transfer prices that are not based directly on market prices, but instead use profit splits or the sales margins, input cost margins, or rates of return on capital for representative independent firms. These methods can change the corporate income tax from a tax on equity income to a tax on sales, input costs, capital, or other factors.[10] And the effective rate of the tax may vary across industries depending upon what margins or rates of return are representative for each industry.

Up to this point, I have ignored the costs to MNEs of income shifting. Two kinds of costs MNEs may incur are (1) distortions to resource allocation within the MNE and (2) penalties if income shifting is detected by the tax authorities. Distortions to resource allocation within an MNE can arise to the extent that managers of the MNE's affiliates view tax transfer

---

[9] Any additional risk that providers of debt capital might otherwise be exposed to from lending to a subsidiary rather than the parent may be removed if the parent explicitly or implicitly guarantees the subsidiary's debt.

[10] This is more likely to occur if the firm uses such methods to set its transfer prices than if the tax authority uses them. In the latter case, tax authorities generally consider a range of results corresponding to a statistical confidence interval to be acceptable.

prices as shadow prices.[11] As Caves (1982) puts it, '...the MNE hoping to confuse the tax collector runs some danger of confusing itself...'. This could occur to the extent that management of the entities within the MNE is decentralized and there are limitations on the ability to keep two sets of books.[12]

In addition to explicit fines, penalties for income shifting include the possibility of double taxation. Double taxation occurs if the tax authorities in the jurisdiction to which income was shifted do not permit an adjustment downward in the MNE's taxable income corresponding to an upward adjustment to taxable income made by the tax authorities in the jurisdiction from which income was shifted.[13] These costs represent transfers between MNEs and country fiscs, but real resource costs may also be expended to resolve a case, particularly if litigation results.

1.3   Effects on competition for tax base

If cross-border income shifting is quantitatively important, one would expect countries, acting independently and competing for tax revenue and capital, to take it into account in their tax policies. Since income-shifting incentives are determined primarily by statutory tax rates, one would expect income-shifting activity to exert downward pressure on the setting of company tax rates. Higher rates induce more revenue loss from shifting out of a country, while lower rates induce a gain, at the expense of other countries, from shifting into the country. Gordon and MacKie-Mason (1995) construct a model in which the presence of cross-border income shifting leads to this result.

Tax competition related to income shifting may also reveal itself in the enforcement of transfer pricing rules. But there are opposing forces at work. On one hand, countries with high tax rates may compete for MNE investment by lowering their actual effective tax rate through lax enforcement of transfer pricing rules. On the other hand, countries may compete for tax base through aggressive enforcement of transfer pricing

[11] It should be noted that arm's-length prices are not necessarily the same as efficient shadow prices for resource allocation within the MNE. For example, intangibles often have the characteristics of a public good within a firm, in which case the efficient internal price might be zero.

[12] However, Wilson (1993) presents survey evidence that MNEs attempt to construct incentive mechanisms for their managers that are unaffected by tax transfer prices.

[13] Bilateral tax treaties generally provide a mutual agreement mechanism for these so-called corresponding adjustments, but that mechanism has limitations which are discussed below.

rules, since in such a case MNEs may choose to err on the side of over-reporting income to avoid becoming entangled in a dispute with the tax authorities. If MNE investment in a country is highly elastic with respect to the tax burden it faces, then the first effect is likely to dominate the second.

If over-aggressive enforcement results, double taxation of MNEs may occur as more than one tax authority lays claim to taxing rights over the same income. Bilateral tax treaties provide a mechanism for resolving conflicts in such cases through mutual agreement between the 'competent authorities' of each country. For the mechanism to work, both countries must agree on the appropriate result. In many cases, the tax rates of the countries involved may differ little, and the MNE may find itself effectively a third party to the competent-authority discussions with little stake in what agreement is reached, only caring that an agreement ultimately *is* reached. Since the issues involved are often complex, and the interests of the tax authorities involved are opposed, agreement is not assured.

2. Empirical evidence on the importance of income shifting

The appropriate policy responses to transfer-pricing and income-shifting pressures depend on the quantitative importance of income shifting by MNEs. If income shifting were quite limited in scope, then there would be little cause for radical policy measures to counter it.

Much of the empirical evidence on income shifting comes from analyses of US data and experience. The evidence can be divided into three types: (1) simple comparisons of aggregate data on the reported profitability and tax payments of MNEs; (2) evidence from tax audits of MNEs; and (3) econometric studies of transfer pricing and income reporting.

2.1 Simple comparisons of aggregate data

Patterns in the aggregate reported income of US MNEs and foreign-controlled US companies may be consistent with substantial cross-border income shifting. Table 9.1 compares reported taxable income of US-controlled and foreign-controlled US companies from 1987 to 1993. In each year, on average, foreign-controlled companies reported lower taxable income as a percentage of their assets or sales than their US-controlled counterparts. Table 9.2 presents information on the reported profitability of foreign subsidiaries of US MNEs. It shows a negative correlation between the effective tax rate faced by subsidiaries and their reported income as a percentage of assets, sales, or equity.

Table 9.1 Profitability of foreign-controlled and domestic companies in the US, 1987–93

	1987	1988	1989	1990	1991	1992	1993
Ratio of taxable income to assets							
Foreign-controlled company	0.58	1.15	0.57	0.24	−0.22	0.30	0.54
Domestic company	2.14	2.51	2.26	2.14	1.95	2.03	2.32
Ratio of taxable income to gross receipts							
Foreign-controlled company	0.88	1.81	0.94	0.42	−0.40	0.52	1.04
Domestic company	4.34	5.31	4.91	4.65	4.42	4.71	5.64

Source: Calculations from US Treasury corporate tax return data.

Table 9.2 Effective tax rates and reported income of foreign subsidiaries of US multinational enterprises, 1992

	Income/assets	Income/sales	Income/equity
All industries			
Effective tax rate:			
less than 10%	0.102	0.098	0.196
10–20%	0.071	0.058	0.165
more than 20%	0.054	0.042	0.155
Manufacturing			
Effective tax rate:			
less than 10%	0.133	0.124	0.208
10–20%	0.051	0.040	0.124
more than 20%	0.056	0.043	0.146
Trade			
Effective tax rate:			
less than 10%	0.114	0.092	0.325
10–20%	0.088	0.036	0.207
more than 20%	0.056	0.026	0.186

Source: Calculations from US Treasury corporate tax return data.

While the figures in Tables 9.1 and 9.2 are suggestive of income shifting, other explanations cannot be ruled out. These patterns may be at least partially the result of heterogeneity in the companies being compared. Companies may differ in non-tax characteristics in ways that are correlated with tax rates or foreign ownership.

2.2 Tax audits

Results of tax audits provide some direct evidence that MNEs do respond to incentives to shift income through transfer pricing. Early evidence of this kind is provided by Lall (1973) and Vaitsos (1974), who present results from Colombian audits of MNEs in the pharmaceutical, rubber, and electrical industries. The audits produced estimates of a substantial degree of overpricing of intra-firm imports into Colombia. For example, Lall (1973) reports that the 11 pharmaceutical firms examined by the tax authorities overpriced imports by up to 155 per cent.[14]

Table 9.3 Selected US transfer pricing cases

Company (product)	Income adjustment (million dollars)		Income shifted to:
	Proposed	Sustained	
Du Pont (chemicals)	18	18	Switzerland
Bausch and Lomb (contact lenses)	9	2	Ireland
Eli Lilly (pharmaceuticals)	71	36	Puerto Rico
G. D. Searle (pharmaceuticals)	117	63[a]	Puerto Rico
Perkin-Elmer (scientific instruments)	29	12	Puerto Rico
National Semiconductor (semiconductors)	122	41	Various Asian affiliates
Seagate Technology (disk drives)	171	53	Singapore

[a] Income adjustments for tax years not before the Tax Court were reportedly settled by a payment of $160 million (Wheeler, 1988).

[14] Plasschaert (1994, ch. 13) also reports on transfer pricing adjustments from a few tax audits in other countries.

Table 9.3 summarizes the results of some important US transfer pricing cases. As might be anticipated, many of these cases involve firms for which intangibles play an important role and the alleged income shifting was often to low-tax foreign locations. But, while these cases provide evidence that MNEs do respond to incentives to shift income across borders, they give little indication of the extent of the problem, for three reasons. First, Table 9.3 does not show how much income shifting is detected by tax authorities, since it presents only cases that resulted in litigation. Many transfer pricing cases are quietly settled without reaching that stage. Second, it does not provide any indication of how much income shifting goes *undetected* by the authorities. Third, caution should be exercised in inferring the actual amount of income shifting from the decisions of the courts.[15]

2.3 Econometric studies

Econometric studies could provide more insight into the scope of the income-shifting problem because they can control for observable heterogeneity among firms and estimate undetected income shifting. Table 9.4 summarizes econometric studies that provide some evidence on income shifting by MNEs.

Two studies examine the activities of US oil companies for evidence of income shifting using different data and methods, and arrive at different results. Jenkins and Wright (1975) analyse the pattern of reported profit rates for the foreign affiliates of US oil companies and find that affiliates located in low-tax countries report significantly higher profit rates than those in other countries. Bernard and Weiner (1990) compare arm's-length market prices to transfer prices for transactions between US oil companies and their affiliates and find no evidence that differences between transfer prices and market prices are related to the tax rates faced by the affiliates in a manner consistent with income-shifting incentives. It is unclear whether differences in method or the time period covered account for the two studies' different results.

Kopits (1976) examines data aggregated by country and industry on royalty payments from foreign subsidiaries of US MNEs. Kopits finds that the relative tax price of returning income via royalty payments versus dividends is negatively correlated with the level of royalty payments by

---

[15] See Frisch and Horst (1989) for examples of questionable aspects of the analysis contained in the US Tax Court decision in the Bausch & Lomb case.

foreign subsidiaries, and interprets this as evidence that US MNEs manipulate royalty pay-outs for tax reasons. While transfer price manipulation may explain these results, as Hines (1996) points out, firms are also more likely to choose to use US intangibles in a foreign location, and thus create a stream of returning royalty payments from that location, if the tax costs associated with the returning royalties are low.

Two studies examine the relationship between the reported profitability of foreign affiliates of US companies and host-country tax rates using aggregate data. Grubert and Mutti (1991) find that reported profitability is strongly negatively related to host-country tax rates. This relationship holds for two measures of foreign tax rates—statutory and average rates—and two measures of profitability—the ratio of after-tax profits to equity or sales. Hines and Rice (1994) find a substantial negative relationship between host-country tax rates and pre-tax financial and non-financial profits, controlling for capital and labour inputs. Their results from one specification imply that a 1-percentage-point reduction in the statutory tax rate increases reported pre-tax non-financial income by 3 per cent.

One problem with the use of aggregate data in Grubert and Mutti (1991) and Hines and Rice (1994) is that the estimates of income shifting could simply reflect systematic differences in the characteristics of firms that invest in low-tax countries. Firm-level data provide a greater opportunity to control for heterogeneity among firms.

Harris et al. (1993) use firm-level data to investigate the relationship between US tax liabilities and whether there are foreign affiliates in high- or low-tax locations. They reason that the presence of low-tax affiliates should give US firms the opportunity to reduce US tax liabilities by shifting income out of the US, while high-tax affiliates provide firms with the opportunity to save taxes by shifting income to the US and thereby increasing US tax liabilities. They find that the presence of affiliates in low-tax (high-tax) locations is associated with significantly lower (higher) US tax liabilities as a percentage of US assets or US sales. There are some difficulties in interpreting these results. For example, as Mutti (1993) points out, the magnitude of the estimated coefficient on the dummy variable for Ireland implies an amount of income shifted to Ireland that is greater than all of the income declared in Ireland. It is likely that something in addition to, or other than, income shifting to Ireland is driving the magnitude of this result.

Using detailed firm-level data taken from US corporate tax returns, Rousslang (1997) estimates a considerably smaller amount of income shifting by US MNEs. Rousslang takes the difference between the reported after-tax profitability of an MNE affiliate and the average after-tax profitability of

Table 9.4 Econometric studies of MNE income shifting

Study	Approach	Data	Results
Jenkins and Wright, 1975	Relate tax and profit rates for foreign affiliates of of US oil companies.	US Commerce Department, Bureau of Economic Analysis. Aggregate by country. 1966 and 1970.	Profit rates negatively related to tax rates.
Bernard and Weiner, 1990	Compare oil company transfer prices to arm's-length market prices.	US Energy Information Administration. 144 country–year observations. 1973 to 1984.	Differences in the ratios of transfer price to market price not significantly related to tax rates.
Kopits, 1976	Relates royalty payments and tax prices for foreign subsidiaries of US firms.	Internal Revenue Service, Statistics of Income. Aggregate by country and manufacturing industry. 1968.	Royalty payments negatively related to their tax price.
Grubert and Mutti, 1991	Relate tax and profit rates for foreign manufacturing affiliates of US firms.	US Commerce Department, Bureau of Economic Analysis. Aggregate by country. 1982.	Profit rates negatively related to tax rates.
Hines and Rice, 1994	Relate tax rates and profit for non-bank foreign affiliates of US firms.	US Commerce Department, Bureau of Economic Analysis. Aggregate by country. 1982.	Profit negatively related to tax rates, controlling for capital and labour inputs.
Harris et al., 1993	Relate US tax liabilities of US firms and their ownership of low-tax [high-tax] foreign affiliates.	Compustat. 200 manufacturing firms. 1984 to 1988.	Having a subsidiary in a low-tax [high-tax] region associated with lower [higher] US tax liability.
Rousslang, 1997	Compares after-tax profitability of a US manufacturing MNE's operations in each country to the average after-tax profitability of the MNE group.	US Treasury corporate tax return data. Cross-section of 370 US parent companies and their 4,906 foreign subsidiaries. 1988.	Firms estimated to shift between $5.9 billion and $8.0 billion across borders. Estimates that 60% of the income shifting may be explained by income tax avoidance.

Study	Description	Data	Findings
Harris, 1993	Compares impact of 1986 tax rate reductions on US income and taxes of US MNEs and other firms.	Compustat. 866 to 2,072 firms. 1984 to 1990.	Relative to other firms, US MNEs with high interest, research and development, rent, and advertising expenses had higher US income and taxes after 1986.
Klassen et al., 1993	Compare impact of 1986 tax rate reductions on US and foreign income–equity ratios of US MNEs and other firms.	Compustat. 191 firms. 1984 to 1990.	From 1986 to 1987, increase (decrease) in profitability of US (foreign) operations of US MNEs relative to profitability of other firms. The result was reversed from 1987 to 1988.
Collins et al., 1996	Relate foreign effective tax rates on foreign operations of US MNEs and their reported foreign profit margins.	Compustat. 577 manufacturing firms. 1984 to 1992.	US MNEs with foreign effective tax rates above US rate report lower foreign profitability.
Grubert et al., 1993	Compare profitability of foreign- and US-controlled US firms.	US Treasury corporate tax return data. Cross-section of 600 foreign-controlled and 4,000 US-controlled firms. 1987. Panel of 110 foreign-controlled and 1,300 US-controlled firms. 1980 to 1987.	Non-tax factors explain about one-half of profitability differences. Foreign-controlled firms' profitability concentrated near zero.
Grubert, 1997	Compares profitability of foreign- and US-controlled US firms.	US Treasury corporate tax return data. Cross-section of 1,208 foreign-controlled and 4,610 US-controlled firms. 1993. Panel of 344 foreign-controlled and 1,588 US-controlled firms. 1987 to 1993.	Non-tax factors explain about three-quarters of profitability differences. No differences in profitability between firms with majority foreign ownership and those with 25–50% foreign ownership. Foreign-controlled and firms' profitability concentrated near zero.

the MNE group as a whole as a measure of the extent of income shifting between that affiliate and other group members. Based on this assumption, he calculates that US manufacturing MNEs shifted up to $8.0 billion across national borders. This represented less than 4 per cent of the world-wide income of these firms. Regression results indicate that income tax avoidance may explain about three-fifths of this quantity.

Harris (1993) examines the income-shifting responses of US companies to the tax rate reductions of the 1986 Tax Reform Act. He hypothesizes that US MNEs would respond by shifting income into the US. He finds that, relative to other corporations, US MNEs with relatively high amounts of interest, research and development, rent, or advertising expenses increased their US taxes and income after 1986. This result is consistent with income shifting, but, as Shackelford (1993) notes, other explanations are possible. For example, it may be that firms with these characteristics simply performed better than other firms in the period after 1986 or were more likely to be affected by changes in the tax law— such as introduction of the Alternative Minimum Tax—that increased US tax liabilities. In addition, because the years examined are those immediately preceding and following the 1986 Tax Reform Act, firms may have shifted income between years to benefit from the lower future tax rates. Systematic differences between the US multinationals and domestic US companies and the foreign MNEs could affect the amount of this intertemporal shifting and might bias the results.

Klassen et al. (1993) compare changes in the ratio of income to equity of the US and foreign operations of US MNEs to changes in the same ratio for US domestic companies and foreign MNEs. They find results consistent with income shifting for 1986–87, i.e. the ratios of income to equity for the US (foreign) operations of US MNEs increase (decrease) relative to those ratios for domestic or foreign firms. However, the results are reversed for the 1987–88 period, even though the US corporate tax rate fell substantially in 1988. This puzzling result casts some doubt on the interpretation of the results for 1986–87.

Collins et al. (1996) exploit cross-sectional differences in effective tax rates as well as changes in effective tax rates over time to estimate income shifting. They find that US MNEs facing effective foreign tax rates, averaged over all their foreign income, in excess of the US statutory rate report lower foreign profit margins controlling for other characteristics of the firms. Based on their estimates, they calculate that these US MNEs, on average, shifted income of about $4.5 billion per year back to the US. On the other hand, they find no relationship between the foreign effective tax rate and foreign profit margins for MNEs facing effective foreign tax rates lower than the US rate.

Using firm-level data from US tax returns to examine the effects of taxes on the composition of the income and payments of foreign subsidiaries of US MNEs, Grubert (1996) finds a significant negative relationship between reported subsidiary income and the statutory tax rate of the host country. He also finds a positive relationship between interest payments and statutory tax rates. Both of these results are consistent with income shifting. In a counter-intuitive result, he finds a negative relationship between royalty payments to US parents and host-country tax rates. His explanation for this result is that lower host-country tax rates lead to incentives to increase subsidiary income, perhaps through the transfer of intangibles, and that this indirectly increases royalty payments back to the parent.

Using cross-section and panel data, Grubert et al. (1993) and Grubert (1997) investigate non-tax reasons for the differences in reported profitability between foreign- and US-controlled US companies illustrated in Table 9.2. Grubert et al. (1993) find that approximately one-half of the initial differential in reported profitability can be explained by the effects of company age, industry, debt,[16] exchange rates, growth, and other factors. It is unclear to what extent the remaining differential is attributable to the effects of income shifting or some other characteristic of foreign-controlled companies that is not observable from the data.[17]

Using more recent data, Grubert (1997) finds that up to three-quarters of the differential in reported profitability can be explained by observable non-tax factors. Interestingly, he also finds no significant difference in reported profitability between US companies that are majority-owned by foreign entities and those that are 25 to 50 per cent owned. One would expect the scope for income shifting to be diminished in the latter group because it might conflict with the interests of the other owners. This suggests that much of the remaining unexplained differential may be due to non-tax factors.

2.4 Summary

A number of studies provide evidence consistent with income shifting by MNEs. There are, however, several reasons to be cautious about the

---

[16] Grubert et al. (1993) find no evidence that thin capitalization accounts for a significant proportion of the differential between foreign- and US-controlled companies; there is little difference between the debt–asset ratios of the two groups.

[17] In principle, the amount of income shifting is not bounded by the remaining unexplained differential, since there may be other unobservable characteristics that *increase* the taxable income of foreign-controlled companies relative to US-controlled companies.

interpretation of this evidence. First, some studies find evidence consistent with little or no income shifting. Second, firms and MNEs are heterogeneous in numerous ways that cannot be observed from the data and may confound the results of these studies. We cannot rule out the possibility that tax rates may be correlated with unobserved factors that affect the profitability of MNE affiliates. And comparisons of MNE affiliates and other firms may also be confounded by unobserved heterogeneity. Finally, while the evidence suggests that income shifting should continue to be a serious policy concern, the absolute magnitude of the estimates does not indicate that countries imposing significant company income taxes are in immediate danger of having their tax bases disappear.

3.   Policies to reduce income-shifting problems under company income taxes

This section explores various policies that can be implemented within the framework of a company income tax to reduce income-shifting pressures. These range from policies that are already being implemented to some degree to more radical policies. Some of these policies can be implemented with little international co-ordination, while others may require substantial co-ordination among countries.

3.1   Enforcement

One approach to transfer pricing problems is to increase enforcement efforts. However, given the fundamental difficulties in applying the arm's-length principle, this approach on its own could entail large monitoring costs. As discussed earlier, more aggressive enforcement may also heighten the potential for disputes with other tax authorities and double taxation. Several policies may help reduce these costs.

3.1.1   Penalties

Penalties for cross-border income shifting may deter such behaviour and reduce the resources that need to be devoted to monitoring MNEs. As Becker (1968) showed, to the extent that penalties entail only a transfer of resources from the penalized firm to the government, it is efficient to substitute higher penalties for monitoring of undesired behaviour.

Sizeable penalties for transfer pricing abuse may, however, impose real distortions and costs. Given the difficulties in many cases in establishing the arm's-length price for a transaction between related parties, even an MNE acting in good faith may be uncertain that the price it determines to be 'arm's length' will be accepted by the tax authority as such. Even if the tax authority is unbiased, the potential penalty may still represent an expected tax on the MNE because the consequences of the tax authority determining that an MNE has under-reported income are not symmetric to the consequences of the tax authority determining that the MNE has over-reported income. In the former case, taxable income will be increased, additional tax assessed, and, potentially, a penalty imposed. In the latter case, the tax authority usually will not change the MNE's transfer prices and taxable income. The expected tax will make a jurisdiction imposing large penalties a less attractive location for investment by MNEs, and this cost must be weighed against the benefits from improved compliance and reduced monitoring costs.

Variation in penalty levels across jurisdictions also may create incentives for MNEs to shift income so that income is over-reported in jurisdictions with relatively high penalties. Countries may therefore be induced to compete for tax base by raising the level of their transfer pricing penalties. The extent to which international co-ordination would be required to check this kind of competition is unclear, since the incentive to increase penalties would be tempered by the disincentive high penalties would present to foreign investment.

3.1.2 Information reporting and exchange

As discussed earlier, a principal challenge to tax authorities evaluating the transfer prices of an MNE is obtaining information on the MNE's activities and transactions. The MNE can have an incentive to keep the tax authorities in the dark, since that weakens the tax authorities' ability to challenge the MNE's transfer prices.

Some countries have sought to address this problem by imposing specific information reporting requirements for MNEs operating in their jurisdiction.[18] MNEs may be required to report their ownership structure, cross-border transactions and payments, and the accounts of foreign affiliates. Specific sanctions may be imposed for failure to report information.

While information reporting requirements may be helpful, it would be impractical to require firms to collect and report all information that might be relevant to a transfer pricing investigation. Moreover, tax authorities often lack the legal authority and means to obtain and verify information relevant to an MNE's operations in a foreign jurisdiction. Some countries, including some OECD countries, restrict the access of foreign countries to information

[18] The US instituted broad information-collection and information-reporting requirements under section 6038A and the transfer pricing penalty provisions. Other countries recently have moved to institute or expand such requirements, including Australia, Canada, Korea, Mexico, New Zealand, and the UK.

needed to administer their taxes.[19] In at least some cases, laws that limit the ability to share information with foreign tax authorities may provide a competitive advantage in attracting foreign capital. Broad international co-ordination of policies may be helpful, if not essential, in this area because individual countries may be unwilling to give access to tax information unless they can be assured that their competitors will also give such access.

3.1.3   Co-ordinating application of transfer pricing rules

As noted above, the scope for disagreement about the proper application of the arm's-length principle, and the opposing interests of the tax authorities involved, create the potential for costly disputes and double taxation. The competent-authority procedure under bilateral tax treaties provides a mechanism to resolve these disputes, but it does not force their resolution. The OECD Committee on Fiscal Affairs also provides a forum for OECD countries to come to common understandings about how the arm's-length principle should be applied. These understandings are reflected in the OECD Transfer Pricing Guidelines, which member countries have agreed to follow in resolving double taxation disputes. However, the OECD guidelines deal largely with issues of general principle, which leaves wide scope for disputes in particular transfer pricing cases.

These mechanisms for international co-ordination have succeeded so far in avoiding widespread double taxation. Given the growing importance of cross-border business and the increased focus by many countries on transfer pricing enforcement, their continued success is not assured. In the future, some mechanism to ensure resolution of transfer pricing issues may be required. The EC Tax Arbitration Convention provides one model for such a mechanism.

3.2   Current taxation of foreign income

One way to substantially reduce income-shifting incentives is to provide for the current taxation of income earned by foreign affiliates of domestic companies. If a limited foreign tax credit is provided, the income-shifting incentives would be the same as under deferral when foreign income is repatriated at the margin. In particular, for a parent with a foreign-tax-credit deficit, there would be no incentive to shift income to low-tax foreign affiliates, since ultimately parent and affiliate face the same combined rate of tax, the home-country rate. But a parent with excess foreign tax credits

---

[19] For example, Ireland and the UK will not collect information on behalf of a tax treaty partner unless their own tax is at stake, and Austria, Luxemburg, and Switzerland maintain bank secrecy.

faces no residual home-country tax, so the incentive to shift income to a low-tax foreign subsidiary would still be determined by the difference between parent and subsidiary tax rates. Limiting the scope for cross-crediting from high- to low-tax sources of foreign income would limit the cases in which such incentives would remain. However, unless an unlimited foreign tax credit was provided, an incentive would remain to shift income from high-tax foreign affiliates to the parent or low-tax foreign affiliates.

About one-half of OECD countries already provide for current taxation of the income of foreign subsidiaries of domestic companies in limited circumstances under what are commonly known as controlled foreign corporation (CFC) rules. CFC rules can be directed toward income from particular activities and investments or income that is lightly taxed in the foreign jurisdiction. CFC rules of the former type are generally directed at activities and investments that are especially mobile.[20] Application of CFC rules of the latter type may be governed by a list of specific countries (or tax regimes within countries), or by an effective tax rate criterion.

Controlled foreign corporation rules limit, to some extent, the benefits from income shifting. Current taxation of passive foreign income limits the benefits deferral confers on shifted income, and current taxation of activities in low-tax jurisdictions also limits the benefits from income shifting. In general, the broader the current taxation of foreign income, the better it is at reducing income-shifting incentives. Limiting current taxation to particular categories of income or to income subject to preferential tax regimes can give rise to substantial complexity and difficulty in enforcement. To prevent firms avoiding tax by mixing income from different sources, detailed tracing requirements are necessary. These can be difficult to apply because they may require tracing income through tiers of foreign affiliates. And the process of differentiating between 'good' and 'bad' tax regimes that is required under some CFC rules can be distorted by political pressures.

To limit income-shifting incentives, ideally all income of foreign affiliates would be taxed as it accrues. At this point, the world is far from this ideal. CFC rules exist in only a limited number of countries and, in many cases, the rules are quite limited in scope. This may be largely due to competitiveness concerns. A firm that has the benefit of exemption or deferral for the income it earns in or shifts to a low-tax jurisdiction has an advantage over a firm that faces current home-country tax on those earnings. For this reason, some form of international co-ordination may be necessary to promote broader application of such rules.

---

[20] For example, the US subpart F rules cover income from passive investments and certain sales, services, and transportation operations located in low-tax foreign jurisdictions.

3.3   Approximation of company tax rates

The most obvious means of reducing income-shifting incentives is to limit differences in company tax rates among countries. Approximation of company tax rates may be effected through explicit co-ordination—for example, by agreement to a relatively narrow band of acceptable rates, as was done in the European Union VAT Directive, or a minimum tax rate. Although this involves the abandonment of autonomy in respect of one of the most important tax policy instruments, in the absence of other measures to counteract income-shifting and tax-competition pressures, convergence of company tax rates may eventually occur even in the absence of explicit co-ordination, but at lower rates than might otherwise be deemed desirable.

3.4   Thin-capitalization measures

Current taxation of foreign income would alleviate the problem of the cross-border shifting of debt and interest expense to some extent. There would no longer be an incentive for a high-tax parent to bear relatively more of the MNE's interest expense. There would, however, remain an incentive to shift interest expense to high-tax foreign affiliates.

Some countries have thin-capitalization rules to address this problem for affiliates of foreign MNEs operating within their borders. These rules typically place a ceiling on interest deductions based on a maximum debt–asset ratio or a maximum ratio of interest payments to income. In many cases, these rules are of limited effectiveness because they apply only to borrowing from related parties[21] and the debt–asset thresholds are sufficiently loose that they may allow significant debt shifting. The difficulty with tightening these rules is that seemingly reasonable thresholds can quite easily be breached by MNEs that are highly leveraged on a group-wide basis. Applying such rules on a piecemeal basis to the various affiliates of an MNE may lead to taxation of more than 100 per cent of the MNE's income and to distortions to the MNE's financing decisions.

Interest allocation rules are, in principle, probably more effective in addressing this problem. One approach is to allocate an MNE's group-wide interest expense among its affiliates based, for example, on their assets.[22] If there were uniformity in the allocation approach adopted

---

[21] US rules apply also to borrowing that is guaranteed by a related party.

[22] US tax rules currently provide for allocation of interest expense to foreign income, but the US rules adopt a 'water's-edge' approach, which does not take into account the interest expense of foreign subsidiaries. This can distort US MNEs' financing decisions. See Hufbauer (1992) for an alternative proposal.

within a group of countries, debt shifting would be eliminated without overtaxation (or undertaxation) of MNE income. Unless, however, there is information exchange between home- and host-country tax authorities, it could be difficult for a tax authority to obtain adequate information to apply such an approach to foreign-based MNEs.

Any tax system that did away with the deductibility of interest at the business level would also eliminate the debt-shifting problem. This would be true, for example, of the US Treasury's comprehensive business income tax proposal (US Department of the Treasury, 1992).

3.5 Formula apportionment

Although it is beyond the scope of this chapter to include a complete discussion of formula apportionment, it would be remiss not to mention this alternative to the taxation of MNEs based on the separate-entity approach and the arm's-length principle. To the extent that formula apportionment eliminates the need to determine transfer prices within an MNE, it could reduce opportunities for income shifting and, potentially, lower administrative and compliance costs.

The merits and drawbacks of formula apportionment on an international level have been analysed more completely elsewhere.[23] Given the fundamental obstacles to the adoption of formula apportionment at the international level, it seems unlikely that it will become a viable alternative to the separate-entity approach and the arm's-length principle in the near future.

4. Income-shifting incentives under alternative tax systems

Considerable interest has been expressed in recent years in replacing taxes on company equity income with a tax on company cash flow, either by itself or, as in the Hall and Rabushka (1995) Flat Tax, as part of a consumption tax system. Although transfer-pricing and income-shifting issues are only one consideration in the choice of a company tax system, it is important to understand what those issues are under the alternative tax systems.

There are many possible variations on company cash-flow taxes. To limit the scope of the analysis, I focus on the three types of such taxes identified in the Meade Report (Institute for Fiscal Studies, 1978): R-base, R+F-base, and S-base taxes.

---

[23] See, for example, Chapter 10 by McLure and Weiner, McLure (1997), and Weiner (1999).

4.1 R-base cash-flow tax[24]

In the terminology of the Meade Report, an R-base cash-flow tax applies to real (as opposed to financial) transactions. The base can be defined as

$$[9.1] \qquad\qquad R - C - I,$$

where R is current revenues, C is current costs, and I is current investment expenditure.

Debt shifting is clearly no longer an issue under this tax, since interest is not deductible. MNEs would wish to shift debt to their affiliates in countries that maintained company taxes in which interest remained deductible, but that debt shifting would not affect tax liabilities of countries adopting the cash-flow tax.[25]

Transfer pricing incentives are determined largely by how foreign investment, exports, and imports come into the base. One possibility is that foreign investment is simply ignored and R represents revenues from domestic and export sales of the domestic operation, C represents costs from domestic purchases and imports of the domestic operation, and I is investment in domestic and imported capital goods by the domestic operation. This is an origin-principle tax along the lines of the business component of the Hall and Rabushka (1995) Flat Tax. In this case, transfer pricing remains an issue, because the domestic tax base is affected by the valuation of export sales and import costs.

The transfer pricing problem may be worse under this system than it is under current company income taxes for two reasons. First, some of the existing backstops to the transfer pricing rules based on the taxation of foreign income—in particular, CFC rules—would be gone. Second, with interest no longer deductible, companies would have opportunities to shift revenue from taxable sales to untaxed interest in sales made on credit to unrelated parties located in countries that still provide interest deductions. For example, a company selling merchandise on credit to a buyer in an income tax country could trade off a decrease in the sales price for an increase in the interest charged, thereby decreasing the selling company's tax liability without increasing the buyer's total tax liability in its country.

A second possibility is that foreign investment is accorded full cash-flow treatment, so that net contributions of capital to a foreign affiliate, whether debt or equity, are deductible from the tax base, and receipts of dividends and interest from the foreign affiliate are included in the base. In

[24] This discussion draws in part on Grubert and Newlon (1995).

[25] Another issue is that countries maintaining a tax on the world-wide income of resident companies might not provide a foreign tax credit for this type of cash-flow tax. See McLure and Zodrow (1997) for an argument that a foreign tax credit should be provided in this case.

this case, shifting revenue to a foreign affiliate through transfer pricing would be equivalent to making a capital contribution, since both are deductible, but when that revenue (and any earnings from its investment abroad) is eventually returned, it would incur the home-country tax. Therefore domestic companies could not avoid domestic tax through transfer price manipulation. MNEs would, however, have an incentive to avoid foreign tax by shifting revenue to the home country unless a full credit was allowed for foreign taxes. In addition, foreign-based MNEs would have an incentive to shift income out to lower-tax jurisdictions.

A third possibility is to apply the tax on the destination principle, so that export revenue would be exempt from tax and imports would be taxed (or, equivalently, the cost of imports would be non-deductible).[26] In that case, the pricing of exports and imports would have no impact on the tax base. Thus transfer pricing would become irrelevant as a tax issue.[27]

There might, however, be an issue of whether such a tax could be imposed on a destination basis without being considered to violate the GATT. If, however, it was explicitly linked to a tax on wages at the same rate, as in the Hall and Rabushka (1995) proposal, it is clearly equivalent to a consumption tax and there should be no objection, in principle, to imposing it on the destination principle.[28]

4.2   R + F-base cash-flow tax

Under an R + F-base (for real plus financial transactions) cash-flow tax, the base can be defined as

$$(9.2) \qquad\qquad R - C - I + B - i,$$

where B denotes net new borrowing and i denotes net payments of interest. The incentives for transfer pricing under this tax are basically the same as under the R-base tax. If foreign investment is exempt, there is an incentive to shift revenue to low-tax jurisdictions. If there is cash-flow

---

[26] Where wages are taxed separately and on an individualized basis, as in the Hall and Rabushka (1995) Flat Tax, it would be impractical to calculate precisely correct border tax adjustments.

[27] Export revenue could be made exempt and imports taxed under a company income tax as well. This would also eliminate transfer pricing incentives, except perhaps in the case of imports of capital goods, where the difference between the current tax on the import and the present value of future depreciation deductions associated with it would create incentives to misstate its price.

[28] See Hufbauer (1996) for an extended analysis of this issue. There could be some objections if exemptions and graduated rates applied to wages. However, these might be overcome if the exemptions and graduated rates were recast in the form of wage subsidies.

treatment of foreign investment, incentives to shift income to low-tax foreign subsidiaries are eliminated. But incentives to shift income back to the parent to reduce foreign taxes remain unless a full credit is provided for foreign taxes. And foreign-based MNEs have an incentive to shift income out of the country to lower-tax jurisdictions. Transfer pricing incentives disappear if the tax is applied on the destination principle.

The new income-shifting wrinkle in this case relates to incentives to shift income through debt transactions. Unless there is cash-flow treatment of foreign investment and full crediting of foreign taxes, there is an incentive to misstate interest expense on inter-affiliate lending to shift revenue to low-tax affiliates. Note that there is no thin-capitalization incentive relative to borrowing from unrelated parties because, at market interest rates, the value of the tax on new borrowing is equal to the present value of the future deductions for payments of interest and principal. It is only in cases of transactions with affiliates, where non-market rates of interest can be charged, that income shifting becomes possible.

4.3   S-base cash-flow tax

Under an S-base cash-flow tax, only net distributions to shareholders are taxed. For a domestically-based MNE, this tax cannot be avoided by transfer pricing or debt shifting.[29] Unless, however, foreign taxes are fully creditable against the home-country S-base tax, there will be an incentive to minimize foreign tax by shifting income out of affiliates in other countries. MNEs based outside a country imposing such a tax may also have an incentive to shift income out of operations in that country to low-tax jurisdictions elsewhere.

5. Conclusions

A substantial body of empirical evidence indicates that cross-border income shifting by MNEs is of some significance. Just how significant is still unclear, given the possible flaws and sometimes mixed results of the empirical estimates of income shifting. It is also unknown how recent measures by many tax authorities to heighten enforcement efforts may affect the magnitude of the problem. Given the potential extent of the problem, however, and the clear difficulties and costs faced by tax authorities in monitoring transfer prices and income shifting, it is easy to make a

---

[29] The present value of tax liabilities can only be reduced by lowering the present value of distributions to shareholders, which presumably is not in the firm's interest.

case for a limited set of policies to reduce income-shifting incentives and enforcement costs. These policies could include the following:

1. Co-operation among countries in enforcement efforts, including particularly the acquisition and exchange of information on behalf of other countries' tax authorities. This could substantially lower the costs and increase the effectiveness of each country's enforcement activities.
2. Co-ordination among countries to resolve transfer pricing issues and cases, including mechanisms to force resolution of disputes.
3. Giving MNEs incentives to assemble and provide information relevant to the assessment of their transfer prices. This may help redress the information asymmetry between MNEs and tax authorities.
4. Scaling back, or even eliminating, deferral to reduce or eliminate the incentive to shift income to low-tax foreign affiliates. This policy also reduces tax distortions to MNEs' investment location decisions.
5. Implementing interest allocation rules for MNEs.

The effectiveness of these policies is enhanced by, or requires, some degree of international co-ordination. Some co-ordination along these lines already takes place—for example, through bilateral tax treaties, the OECD Transfer Pricing Guidelines, and the EC Tax Arbitration Convention. Broader and more consistent application of such measures may require binding multilateral agreements. Individual countries may otherwise be reluctant to implement policies that might cause them to lose tax base and capital to those countries that did not implement the policies. And, along with the 'carrot' of tax base protection that such an agreement might offer, there might need to be some form of 'stick' to discourage countries from free-riding by not entering into the agreement.[30] In the near term, the European Union (EU) may provide the greatest opportunity for such an agreement, since the mechanisms for policy co-ordination exist there and, given the geographic proximity and economic integration of the Member States, the gains from co-ordination are likely to be the greatest. Until now, the EU has made little progress toward approximation of company taxes, but agreement on the relatively modest measures outlined above may be a more realistic possibility.

At this stage, the need for more radical measures—such as formula apportionment, approximation of company tax rates, or substitution of income taxes with destination-principle consumption taxes—solely

---

[30] Slemrod (1990) proposes a multilateral treaty of this sort in which the sticks to be used against non-signers are withholding taxes imposed on payments to those countries and home-country accrual taxation of income from foreign subsidiaries located in those countries.

to address income-shifting problems remains to be proven. If, however, fundamental tax reform is considered for other reasons, income-shifting issues should be a factor in the analysis.

References

Altshuler, R., and Grubert, H. (1996), 'Balance sheets, multinational financial policy, and the cost of capital at home and abroad', National Bureau of Economic Research, Working Paper 5810.

Becker, G. S. (1968), 'Crime and punishment: an economic approach', *Journal of Political Economy*, 76: 169–217.

Bernard, J-T., and Weiner, R. J. (1990), 'Multinational corporations, transfer prices, and taxes: evidence from the US petroleum industry', in A. Razin and J. Slemrod (eds), *Taxation in the Global Economy*, Chicago: University of Chicago Press.

Berry, C. H., Bradford, D. F., and Hines, J. R., Jr. (1992), 'Arm's-length pricing: some economic perspectives', *Tax Notes*, 10 (10 February): 731–40.

Caves, R. E. (1982), *Multinational Enterprise and Economic Analysis*, Cambridge: Cambridge University Press.

Collins, J. H., Kemsley, D., and Lang, M. (1996), 'Cross-jurisdictional income shifting and earnings valuation', University of North Carolina, unpublished paper.

Frisch, D. J., and Horst, T. (1989), 'Bausch & Lomb and the White Paper', *Tax Notes*, 8 (8 May): 725–34.

Gordon, R. H., and MacKie-Mason, J. K. (1995), 'Why is there corporate taxation in a small open economy? The role of transfer pricing and income shifting', in M. S. Feldstein, J. R. Hines, Jr., and R. G. Hubbard (eds), *The Effects of Taxation on Multinational Corporations*, Chicago: University of Chicago Press.

Grubert, H. (1989), 'A proposed reinterpretation of the arm's length principle in transfer pricing', US Department of the Treasury, unpublished paper, April.

——(1996), 'Taxes and the division of foreign operating income among royalties, interest, dividends and retained earnings', US Department of the Treasury, unpublished paper, November.

——(1997), 'Another look at the low taxable income of foreign-controlled companies in the United States', US Department of the Treasury, unpublished paper, January.

——, Goodspeed, T., and Swenson, D. (1993), 'Explaining the low taxable income of foreign-controlled companies in the United States', in A. Giovannini, R. G. Hubbard, and J. Slemrod (eds), *Studies in International Taxation*, Chicago: University of Chicago Press.

—— and Mutti, J. (1991), 'Taxes, tariffs and transfer pricing in multinational corporate decision making', *Review of Economics and Statistics*, 73: 285–93.

—— and Newlon, T. S. (1995), 'The international implications of consumption tax proposals', *National Tax Journal*, 48: 619–47.

Hall, R. E., and Rabushka, A. (1995), *The Flat Tax*, Stanford, CA: Hoover Institution Press.

Harris, D. G. (1993), 'The impact of US tax law revision on multinational corporations' capital location and income-shifting decisions', *Journal of Accounting Research*, Supplement, 31: 111–40.

——, Morck, R., Slemrod, J., and Yeung, B. (1993), 'Income shifting in US multinational corporations', in A. Giovannini, R. G. Hubbard, and J. Slemrod (eds), *Studies in International Taxation*, Chicago: University of Chicago Press.

Hines, J. R., Jr. (1996), 'Tax policy and the activities of multinational corporations', National Bureau of Economic Research, Working Paper 5589.

—— and Rice, E. M. (1994), 'Fiscal paradise: foreign tax havens and American business', *Quarterly Journal of Economics*, 109: 149–82.

Hufbauer, G. C. (1992), *US Taxation of International Income: Blueprint for Reform*, Washington, DC: Institute for International Economics.

—— (1996), *Fundamental Tax Reform and Border Tax Adjustments*, Washington, DC: Institute for International Economics.

Institute for Fiscal Studies (1978), *The Structure and Reform of Direct Taxation*, London: George Allen & Unwin (the Meade Report).

Jenkins, G. P., and Wright, B. D. (1975), 'Taxation of multinational corporations: the case of the United States petroleum industry', *Review of Economics and Statistics*, 57: 1–11.

Klassen, K., Lang, M., and Wolfson, M. (1993), 'Geographic income shifting by multinational corporations in response to tax rate changes', *Journal of Accounting Research*, Supplement, 31: 141–73.

Kopits, G. F. (1976), 'Intra-firm royalties crossing frontiers and transfer pricing behaviour', *Economic Journal*, 86: 791–805.

Lall, S. (1973), 'Transfer pricing by multinational manufacturing firms', *Oxford Bulletin of Economics and Statistics*, 35: 173–95.

McLure, C. E., Jr. (1997), 'US federal use of formula apportionment in the taxation of income from intangibles', *Tax Notes International*, 14 (10 March): 859–71; also in US Department of the Treasury, *Conference on Formula Apportionment*, 12 December 1996, Washington, DC.

—— and Zodrow, G. (1997), 'The economic case for foreign tax credits for cash flow taxes', Stanford University, Hoover Institution, unpublished paper.

Mutti, J. (1993), 'Comment', in A. Giovannini, R. G. Hubbard, and J. Slemrod (eds), *Studies in International Taxation*, Chicago: University of Chicago Press.

Plasschaert, S. (ed.) (1994), *Transnational Corporations: Transfer Pricing and Taxation*, New York: Routledge for the United Nations Library on Transnational Corporations, 14.

Ragazzi, G. (1973), 'Theories of the determinants of direct foreign investment', *IMF Staff Papers*, 20: 471–98.

Rousslang, D. J. (1997), 'International income shifting by US multinational corporations', *Applied Economics*, 29: 925–34.

Rugman, A. M. (1980), 'Internalization as a general theory of foreign direct investment: a re-appraisal of the literature', *Weltwirtschaftliches Archiv*, 116: 365–79.

Scholes, M. S., and Wolfson, M. A. (1992), *Taxes and Business Strategy: A Planning Approach*, Englewood Cliffs, NJ: Prentice Hall.

Shackelford, D. A. (1993), 'Discussion of "The impact of US tax law revision on multinational corporations' capital location and income-shifting decisions" and "Geographic income shifting by multinational corporations in response to tax rate changes"', *Journal of Accounting Research*, Supplement, 31: 174–82.

Slemrod, J. B. (1990), 'Tax principles in an international economy', in M. J. Boskin and C. E. McLure, Jr. (eds), *World Tax Reform: Case Studies of Developed and Developing Countries*, San Francisco: International Center for Economic Growth.

US Department of the Treasury (1992), *Integration of the Individual and Corporate Tax Systems: Taxing Business Income Once*, Washington, DC: US Government Printing Office.

Vaitsos, C. V. (1974), *Intercountry Income Distribution and Transnational Enterprises*, Oxford: Clarendon Press.

Weiner, J. M. (1999), 'Using the experience in the US states to evaluate issues in implementing formula apportionment at the international level', Office of Tax Analysis, Paper 83, Washington, DC: US Department of the Treasury; also *Tax Notes International*, 13 (23 December 1996): 2113–44; also in US Department of the Treasury, *Conference on Formula Apportionment*, 12 December 1996, Washington, DC. Available in the working paper series of the Office of Tax Analysis at 'www.ustreas.gov / OTA / ota83.pdf'.

Wheeler, J. (1988), 'An academic looks at transfer pricing in a global economy', *Tax Notes*, 40 (4 July): 87–96.

Williamson, O. E. (1971), 'The vertical integration of production: market failure considerations', *American Economic Review*, 61: 112–23.

Wilson, G. P. (1993), 'The role of taxes in location and sourcing decisions', in A. Giovannini, R. G. Hubbard, and J. Slemrod (eds), *Studies in International Taxation*, Chicago: University of Chicago Press.

10

Deciding whether the European Union should adopt formula apportionment of company income

CHARLES E. MCLURE, JR. AND JOANN M. WEINER

This chapter raises issues that the European Union (EU) should consider in deciding whether formula apportionment (FA) should replace separate accounting (SA) based on the arm's-length system (ALS) as the primary method of determining the geographic source of income of companies operating in more than one Member State of the EU.[1] It begins (in Section 1) with a brief description of the two methods of income attribution, the problems that will increasingly plague reliance on SA as the

The views expressed here are those of the authors and should not be construed as reflecting the views or policies of the US Department of the Treasury. The authors wish to thank Sijbren Cnossen, their discussants at the ISPE conference— W. Steven Clark and Paul Bernd Spahn—other participants in the ISPE conference, Jack Mintz, Walter Hellerstein, and Paul McDaniel for comments that have been useful in revising the chapter following the conference.

[1] On 12 December 1996, the US Department of the Treasury held a conference on formula apportionment, which addressed many of the issues surrounding adoption of the formula apportionment system at the international level. Both of the authors of this chapter presented papers at that conference; they are available in US Department of the Treasury (1996). Joann Weiner's conference paper (also available as Weiner (1999)) evaluated many of the implementation issues involved in considering adopting formula apportionment at the international level. As most of these issues are also relevant for the EU, this chapter draws heavily from that document. (For an early analysis of the issue for the Europeans, see Weiner (1991).) Charles McLure's conference paper (also available as McLure (1997a)) provided preliminary thoughts on using formula apportionment to tax income from intangibles. Other participants discussed issues concerning enforcement and administration, defining a unitary business, and international considerations.

economic integration of Europe proceeds, and the advantages of FA in addressing those problems. Section 2 describes some conceptual weaknesses of FA and various transitory, technical, and political issues that the EU would face in shifting to FA. Section 3 examines previous company tax reform efforts by the European Commission and the impact of European integration on possible reform. Section 4 appraises FA in the light of some important tax policy objectives and constraints of the EU.

Section 5 returns to the issues raised in the title, 'Deciding whether the European Union should adopt formula apportionment of company income'. Rather than attempting to reach a definitive decision, the section provides a brief list of things the EU should not do, if it were to adopt formula apportionment.

1. The two alternatives

Both SA and FA are methods of determining the geographic source of income. Either could underlie a primarily source-based system, such as that used in France, which exempts certain income from foreign sources, or a system that combines source- and residence-based taxation, such as that used in the UK, which uses foreign tax credits (FTCs) to avoid double taxation (and, in the process, accords primacy in the taxation of business income to source nations). In the latter case, FA would presumably be used to calculate limitations on the availability of FTCs, as well as to determine the source of income for source-based taxation.[2] For ease of exposition, we address this second use of source attribution primarily in footnotes.

The contrast between SA and FA can be seen in either a narrow or a broad context. Viewed narrowly, FA is an alternative to the use of arm's-length pricing to determine the geographic source of income within the present system based on SA. Seen more broadly, adoption of FA, together with unitary combination (to be defined below), would represent a more fundamental shift in policy—essentially, an abandonment of SA.

1.1 The existing company income tax systems in EU Member States[3]

For the most part, the existing systems of company taxation in Member States of the EU respect the legal boundaries between affiliated companies chartered in different countries; parents and each foreign subsidiary are

---

[2] Countries that employ world-wide tax systems limit FTCs to the domestic tax liability on the foreign income; that is, they do not make refunds when foreign taxes exceed the home-country tax liability. It is thus necessary to determine the geographic source of income to apply such limitations.

[3] This section discusses policies existing in 1997, the time at which the ISPE conference was held. The chapter also generally refers to the European Union, which formally came into existence on 1 November 1993, in accordance with the

treated as separate entities for tax purposes. Profits attributable to a permanent establishment (i.e. a branch) of a foreign company are also determined as if the establishment were a separate enterprise dealing independently with the parent enterprise. For this reason, the system is said to be based on *separate accounting*.

1.1.1 Territorial scope

Countries may tax their resident companies on all of their income, wherever earned, or they may tax their resident companies only on the income earned in the home country. The former approach is known as world-wide, or residence-based, taxation; the latter approach is known as territorial, or source-based, taxation. Countries employing residence-based taxation generally include the active income of foreign subsidiaries in the taxable income of domestic parents only when it is actually (or deemed to be) repatriated as dividends. That is, they allow the home country's tax on the active income of foreign subsidiaries to be deferred until the parent receives the income. By comparison, countries commonly tax currently the income of foreign branches, which are not legally-separate entities, whether the income is distributed or not. Countries employing source-based taxation generally exempt foreign-source income from home-country taxation. However, to prevent tax avoidance, these countries often provide exceptions to the general rule of exemption.

Under residence-based systems, the treatment of income and losses of foreign operations varies with the legal form of the foreign operation. Because foreign subsidiaries are treated as separate taxpayers, rather than as part of the parent company, losses of foreign subsidiaries ordinarily cannot be used to offset profits of the parent.[4] By comparison, since a permanent establishment (branch) is considered to be part of the parent, and not a separate taxpayer, losses of a permanent establishment may be used to offset profits of the parent.

The EU has considered allowing broader profit and loss offset for operations located within the EU in the 1989 proposal by the European Commission for a council regulation to create a Statute for a 'European Company' (*Societé Européenne*, or SE).[5] This new legal entity would be

Treaty on European Union, signed in Maastricht on 7 February 1992. The Union Treaty added to the existing European Communities' agreement, common foreign and security policy and close co-operation on justice and home affairs.

[4] Some EU Member States have provisions for consolidating foreign subsidiaries with domestic operations.

[5] The European Commission submitted a proposal in 1989 (see Commission of the European Communities (1989)) and amended it in May 1991 (see Commission (1991a)). The Council has not yet approved the regulation.

subject to the tax law of the Member State where its registered office is located. The Statute is intended to facilitate the restructuring of companies across the borders of Member States. Since an SE would be a European entity, rather than an entity of a single country, it could offset losses of an SE's foreign permanent establishment against the SE's aggregate EU profits.

1.1.2 Transfer pricing

Under the separate-accounting method, the parent company divides income among affiliated companies, each of which keeps its own accounts, through application of the arm's-length pricing system. Under the traditional application of this system, transfer prices (including terms of financial transactions) are to be arm's-length prices—the prices that would prevail in transactions between unrelated enterprises operating independently at arm's length. All Member States of the EU generally use the arm's-length system to implement the separate-accounting method.

The member countries of the OECD have adopted the arm's-length *principle* as the international transfer pricing approach that should be used for tax purposes by multinational enterprises and tax administrations.[6] The OECD's first transfer pricing guidelines, issued in 1979, placed primary reliance on three pricing methods (now called transaction methods): comparable uncontrolled price, resale price, and cost plus.

The OECD updated these guidelines in 1995 to endorse additional methods that reflect the increased integration of national economies and technological progress. The revised guidelines include new 'transactional profit methods' that may be used to approximate arm's-length conditions.[7] Known as the 'profit split' and the 'transactional net margin' methods, they are to be used when traditional transaction methods cannot be applied reliably or cannot be applied at all. The profit-based methods examine the profits that arise from particular transactions among associated enterprises and are designed to reach an outcome that is consistent with the arm's-length principle.

[6] See OECD (1995a, ch. 1). The US has a set of regulations in section 482 of the Internal Revenue Code governing the arm's-length *standard*. These regulations, which were updated in 1994, provide general guidelines for applying the arm's-length standard and discuss factors that must be considered in determining the comparability of transactions. The three traditional methods—comparable uncontrolled price, resale price, and cost plus—are transaction-based, while two new methodologies—profit split and comparable profits—are profit-based. For a history of the development of the arm's-length standard, see US Department of the Treasury and Internal Revenue Service (1988). Given the difference in terminology used by the OECD and the US, we have chosen to employ the neutral term 'arm's-length system' (ALS).

[7] See OECD (1995a, ch. 3).

The latter two methodologies sometimes use formulas to determine the arm's-length results for certain transactions. These formulaic approaches differ from FA, as applied by the US states, in one significant way: using the OECD's terminology, the formulas are not 'predetermined', as they would be under 'global formulary apportionment'. Instead, the OECD methodologies focus on *transactions* and are based on a detailed economic analysis of the functions performed, risks borne, and resources employed by each controlled taxpayer. Finally, it is worth noting that the OECD envisages methodologies based on formulas being used within the context of the existing system of separate accounting.

1.1.3 Other issues

The method of taxing company income now employed in the EU contains several other salient features. Many European systems distinguish between sources and categories of income. Thus income is generally classified as income from sales of goods, as royalties from the licensing of intangible assets, or as income from the provision of services. Each of these types of income is taxed differently. Income from the sale of property is subject to income tax, provided it is earned by a permanent establishment; it is subject to withholding taxes only when distributed to a foreign parent. Royalties are subject to withholding taxes but not to income taxes. Income from services is subject to income tax if provided by a person who has a permanent establishment or who is physically present in the country, commonly over an extended period of time. Withholding taxes deserve special note because they are imposed on a gross basis (that is, without deductions for expenses) and they are imposed on payments for the use of intangible assets but not on the sale of goods or services.

1.2 Problems with SA/ALS

Seen from the narrow point of view of determining income within the context of separate accounting, two broad types of problems exist with SA/ALS.[8] The first concerns the *existence* of comparable arm's-length prices, while the second concerns difficulties in *monitoring* transfer prices. Although the second may attract more attention than the first, it is probably less important when considering whether the EU should adopt FA. In addition, other issues arise under a broader view of separate accounting.

---

[8] A detailed analysis of the drawbacks of SA/ALS is beyond the scope of this chapter. See, however, US General Accounting Office (1992). For additional statements, see Miller (1993 and 1995), Avi-Yonah (1995), and Hellerstein (1993).

1.2.1   The existence of an arm's-length price

A general problem with SA/ALS arises where there is substantial economic interdependence between affiliated companies. In this case, it may be theoretically impossible to find an arm's-length price and, thus, to determine the source of the joint income of the group of companies. Economic interdependence can result, *inter alia*, from joint production, shared expenses (for example, overheads), and other economies of scale or scope. While economic interdependence is especially likely where vertical integration exists, it can also be found in horizontal relations between related firms engaged in similar activities—and, indeed, between firms engaged in seemingly dissimilar activities. (See also McLure (1983a, 1983b, and 1984a).) When these affiliated companies are located in different countries, as will increasingly be true as the barriers to cross-border mergers continue to fall in the EU, the difficulties in finding appropriate transfer prices may multiply.

Even without substantial economic integration, it can also be difficult to find arm's-length prices for the internal transfer of certain types of goods or services. Where the products involved are standardized and are traded between unrelated parties (for example, oil or commodities of a particular type), it is relatively easy to employ market tests to determine whether transfer prices are market-based. But, where products are unique and not commonly traded between unrelated parties, it is inherently difficult to know their value, much less to find a comparable market price. This description characterizes many intangible assets (patents, copyrights, trade marks, and other intellectual property) that constitute much of the value of modern corporations. (On this, see Dexter (1976) and McLure (1997a) and literature cited therein.)

1.2.2   Monitoring transfer prices

Monitoring transfer prices is another problem that arises under SA/ALS. Under SA/ALS, when tax rates differ across jurisdictions, taxpayers have an incentive to adjust the transfer prices used to value goods and services, including the terms of financial transactions (hereafter 'products') flowing between affiliated companies, to attribute taxable profits to jurisdictions where tax rates are lowest. Profits may be shifted to tax havens (countries that levy low taxes and shelter financial accounts from scrutiny by tax authorities in a deliberate effort to provide vehicles for avoiding taxes of residence countries). In the absence of close scrutiny by the tax authorities, such tax haven profits can be sheltered from residence-based taxation. Even if the residence country did not allow deferral, the failure of the tax haven to share information with tax authorities can result in this tax haven income being subject to little or no residence taxation. When combined with deferral of residence-based taxes, the existence of tax havens aggravates the income-shifting problem for all countries taxing the world-wide income of their residents.

Many countries that tax on a residence basis with deferral attempt to curb this tax avoidance incentive with provisions that restrict or eliminate deferral for certain types of income.[9] For example, under the 'subpart F' rules of the US Internal Revenue Code, the US requires current taxation of various types of easily movable and low-taxed income of certain controlled foreign corporations (CFCs).[10] In the US and more generally in other countries, the type of potentially abusive transactions that CFC legislation is designed to address involves minimizing current home-country tax by (1) shifting active income from a high-tax area to a related company in a low-tax area and (2) accumulating passive income in a related company in a low-tax area, combined with deferral of home-country taxation of both types of income. In the first case, the parent company may sell products or services to what is known as a foreign base company, which then makes the sale to the ultimate customer. Prices on these sales can be artificially set to attribute the profit to the subsidiary located in the low-tax area. In the second case, the parent may accumulate passive income, such as interest, dividends, rents, royalties, etc., in a related company in a low-tax area. The subpart F rules subject these types of income to current taxation. Although the details of the legislation vary across countries, as of 1996 nine EU countries (and sixteen OECD countries) have adopted roughly similar CFC legislation (OECD, 1996).

Countries that employ only territorial taxation have a limited need for CFC-type legislation, since they generally exempt foreign-source profits from home-country taxation, but they must carefully craft the source-of-income rules. However, even countries that tax on a territorial basis need to deal with potential abuse, especially that related to tax havens. Thus countries that tax on a territorial basis generally limit the exemption from home-country tax to active business income and deny the exemption for passive income and income earned in certain jurisdictions.

---

[9] Deferral has a tax benefit only when foreign rates are lower than home-country rates. By manipulating transfer prices to shift income to foreign sources, a taxpayer can also increase the FTC limitation (and thus the amount of potentially creditable taxes), thereby avoiding the simultaneous existence of both excess FTCs and domestic tax liabilities.

[10] The US generally defines a CFC as any foreign corporation in which more than 50 per cent of all classes of stock, by combined voting power or total value, is owned directly or indirectly by US shareholders each with 10 per cent or more of all voting stock on any day during the CFC's taxable year. A US shareholder is taxed currently on its pro rata share of the CFC's undistributed subpart F income.

1.2.3 Other issues

The existing SA/ALS draws a number of distinctions that will become increasingly untenable. For example, in a world of electronic commerce, it will become more and more difficult to distinguish among income from the sale of goods, the use of intangible assets, and the provision of services. (On this, see McLure (1997b).) Moreover, with the advent of various forms of new financial products, it is often difficult to distinguish between payments labelled as interest on indebtedness, which are tax-deductible expenses, and payments labelled as dividends from profits, which are not tax-deductible.

1.2.4 How well is SA/ALS performing?

Although the Europeans have used the SA/ALS approach for decades, it is difficult to find empirical evidence on how well separate accounting is performing in Europe.[11] The Europeans seem satisfied, at present, with the separate-accounting method as a means of preventing profit shifting. However, as mentioned earlier, many of the EU countries are recognizing a greater need for anti-abuse legislation to prevent income shifting. They also are increasingly aware that some companies may engage in profit shifting to take advantage of special tax incentives offered in other countries. Finally, increased economic interdependence will strain the SA/ALS approach as it becomes increasingly difficult to untangle the transactions and activities of highly-integrated companies doing business throughout the EU.

This concern is not new. In its 1992 study of company tax systems in the European Community, the Ruding Committee evaluated this issue, noting (Commission of the European Communities, 1992, p. 40):[12]

> While transfer-pricing is a necessary business practice in integrated groups of firms, it can sometimes be very difficult to ascertain the correct range of 'arm's length' prices, because there may be no comparable market prices for the transaction in question. ... the use of separate accounting methods of determining taxable profits may present firms with the opportunity to shift profits from high- to

---

[11] All of the econometric evidence cited by Newlon in this volume comes from studies of US data. Some of these studies provide evidence consistent with income shifting by multinational enterprises, while others give evidence that is also consistent with little or no income shifting.

[12] The Ruding Report is the name commonly given to the Report of the Committee of Independent Experts on Company Taxation (the Ruding Committee). Mr Onno Ruding, a former Dutch Finance Minister, was the chairman of the committee, which also included eight independent European tax experts. For the mandate given to the committee, see Commission of the European Communities (1990). Mr Ruding discussed the European experience with company tax reform as part of the US Treasury's 1996 conference on formula apportionment.

relatively low-tax countries by adjusting transfer prices ... [This] problem ... will be compounded by the increased cross-border integration of business activities within the Community. In the longer term, this will tend to make it increasingly difficult to determine taxable profits separately for each part of a multinational enterprise in every Member State on the basis of separate accounting methods.

1.3 The formula apportionment alternative

Having faced the cross-border integration problems for many years, the subnational governments in some countries, such as the US states and the Canadian provinces, have long employed formulas instead of arm's-length prices to divide the income of companies operating in more than one state or province.[13] Such formulas attribute to the taxing jurisdiction a fraction of the total income of a company equal to the weighted average of the jurisdiction's share in various economic activities of the company (commonly called 'apportionment factors' in the US literature). Although the approach is the same in the states and in the provinces, the formulas used to apportion income vary. For example, the apportionment formulas used by the US states commonly include payroll, property, and sales (gross receipts). All of the Canadian provinces use the same two-factor formula that includes only payroll and sales. The formulas used initially by the US states and some discussions of FA refer to a formula that would consider costs, assets, payroll, and sales.[14] The basic approach is the same, however: take the company's total income and apportion it to each location where the company does business using a predetermined formula whose elements represent the factors that generate income. The next section describes and discusses problems encountered in the implementation of FA. At this point, we highlight a different issue—the fundamental change that occurs when FA occurs in the context of unitary combination.

1.3.1 Unitary combination

If formula apportionment is applied only to the income of individual firms, rather than to the income of the firm and some or all of its affiliates, and taxing jurisdictions do not have comparable systems of company taxation, the transfer pricing problem inherent in SA/ALS described above is not completely overcome. That is, if not all jurisdictions impose company income taxes, or if some impose very low rates or provide important tax exemptions, firms have an incentive to set up a legally

[13] See Weiner (1994) for a detailed history of the shift from SA to FA in the US. Smith (1976) and Daly (1992) provide historical summaries for Canada.

[14] See OECD (1995a, p. III-22).

separate subsidiary in a low-tax state and shift income to it. Since corporate tax rates imposed by the US states vary widely (ranging from 0 to over 10 per cent), the opportunities for abuse through income shifting to related firms operating in low-tax states are obvious.

To prevent this, many states 'combine' the income and factors of related companies deemed to be engaged in a 'unitary business' to calculate the part of the income of the group they will tax. (Thus the term 'unitary combination', or UC.) Under UC, members of an affiliated group of corporations that are found to be part of a unitary group are combined and effectively treated as a single entity for tax purposes.[15] The individual members of the combined group need not all be subject to the taxing jurisdiction of the state, i.e. the individual members need not have nexus themselves. They merely need to be part of a unitary group that has some connection with the state.[16]

Although Canada does use formula apportionment, it has not adopted the unitary approach. In Canada, provincial income taxes are applied on a separate-entity basis (i.e. each legally-separate entity doing business in more than one province must file a return in each and apportion taxable income among the provinces based only on its own activities in each). This approach arises because the federal government does not allow consolidation and the provinces utilize the federal tax base. However, even though the tax base and methodology of apportionment used in Canada are essentially uniform, provincial tax rates differ; at times, they have differed by as much as 10 percentage points. The lack of consolidation allows related companies to reallocate their tax bases to low-tax provinces and reduce their overall tax liability.[17] Although differences in labour and other costs may offset some of the variation in profits taxes, there is some

---

[15] See Duncan (1996) for additional helpful definitions.

[16] All of the states that tax corporate income use formula apportionment (but one does so only if separate accounting fails fairly to reflect income earned in the state). About half of the states either require combined reporting or make it available on an optional basis. Some states do not allow taxpayers to file on a unitary basis, but courts in at least two states have ruled that corporations operating a unitary business have a right to file a combined report. Courts in one state have ruled that the state must demonstrate that transactions among members of a unitary group are not at 'arm's length' before it may require combination. See Duncan (1996).

[17] Daly (1992) asserts that the federal and provincial governments have maintained separate-entity taxation to prevent companies from transferring losses to profitable companies within a group and thus reducing tax revenue. By comparison, at the ISPE conference, Jack Mintz claimed that Canada eschews consolidation because of its complexity.

evidence that companies artificially shift income between provinces to take account of differences in corporate tax rates.[18]

If tax rates continue to differ widely within the EU so that profit shifting across separate entities remains attractive, and as economic interdependence between affiliated companies increases, a system of formula apportionment that requires unitary combination (FA/UC) seems to be the only alternative apportionment-based income tax system worthy of consideration; the analysis that follows assumes such a system. On the other hand, if the Member States adopt similar definitions of income and comparable tax rates, perhaps imposed by a relatively narrow band of acceptable rates,[19] unitary combination may not be needed. (The common tax base and fairly narrow rate spread may help explain Canada's ability to avoid unitary taxation.) For that matter, if such harmony in rates and bases could be reached, many of the transfer-pricing problems of SA/ALS would also be alleviated. Even with this much uniformity, however, it is worth while to consider the FA/UC alternative, because of the first problem identified above—that of finding arm's-length prices for groups of related companies that are highly integrated or that rely heavily on transfers of intangibles.

As noted earlier, while formula apportionment can be seen as an alternative to separate accounting as a means of determining the source of income within the current system, when joined with unitary combination it can change the system in more fundamental ways. In a system of FA/UC, transactions between members of a unitary group, such as purchases of products, payments for the use of assets (including intangible assets), and financial transactions (including the payment of interest and dividends) are ignored. Moreover, within a unitary group, distinctions between interest and dividends and distinctions between the sale of goods, the use of intangible assets, and the provision of services become meaningless for tax purposes; all are ignored. Furthermore, it makes no sense to impose withholding taxes on royalties or on dividends. In short, unitary combination and separate accounting are two quite different ways of treating related companies. This key fact is often not adequately appreciated.[20]

---

[18] Daly and Weiner, 1993. See also Daly (1992) and literature cited therein.

[19] The Commission of the European Communities has frequently discussed the need for a maximum tax rate spread. For example, the Ruding Committee (Commission of the European Communities, 1992, pp. 209–10) proposed requiring a minimum rate of 30 per cent and limiting the spread to an amount that resulted in a ten-point difference in maximum rates.

[20] Indeed, the version of this chapter distributed before the ISPE conference did not pay enough attention to this distinction. We wish to thank Paul McDaniel for noting this.

1.3.2　Water's-edge limitation

A few US states have applied unitary combination on a world-wide basis. That is, to calculate profits subject to taxation by the state, they have combined the income and factors of foreign entities (parents, subsidiaries, and sister corporations) with those of domestic entities with which they were deemed to be unitary. They argued that, even if the foreign affiliates had no activities in the US, since they were a part of the unitary business, they should be included in the combined report of the entity operating in the state in order to measure the income of the in-state entity accurately.[21]

Being at odds with the SA/ALS employed by most countries, world-wide unitary combination evoked strong protest during the early 1980s from many of the trading partners of the US—including several members of the European Community—even though only a handful of states (most notably California) then used world-wide combination.[22] Although the US Supreme Court found world-wide combination constitutional (in *Container* in 1983, for groups with US parents, and in *Barclays Bank* in 1994, for groups with foreign parents), the states, acting independently, but under the threat of federal legislation and pressure from multinational corporations and foreign trading partners of the US, have abolished

---

[21] California instituted unitary combination in the 1930s as a means of preventing taxpayers from shifting income to affiliates located outside the state. It accepted world-wide combination for US-based companies in the 1940s. In the early 1960s, it accepted a taxpayer's request to file a unitary return whenever a unitary business existed. The state subsequently extended the required use of world-wide unitary reporting to foreign-based businesses. See Miller and Campion (1996).

[22] In 1985, the UK even went so far as to introduce retaliatory legislation against companies from states employing world-wide unitary combination that were doing business in the UK. A similar effort occurred in 1993, although in neither case was the legislation enacted. (Germany and the European Commission also threatened retaliation in 1993, but neither indicated what form the retaliation would take.) The world-wide unitary tax controversy arose in the late 1970s partly from a provision, which the US Senate rejected, to include a prohibition on state use of the technique in a bilateral income tax treaty between the UK and the US, and partly from the cases filed against California, most notably by Barclays Bank, a UK company. A number of European countries filed briefs supporting Barclays's challenge to California's law. The Supreme Court ruled in favour of California, and thus in favour of world-wide unitary combination, when it heard the Barclays case in 1994. (On this experience, see US Department of the Treasury (1984), McLure (1984b and 1985), and Devgun (1996).)

mandatory world-wide combination. (See Table 10.1.)[23] As of 1996, water's-edge taxation is available in all of the states.[24]

Because world-wide unitary combination would raise many of the questions and controversies to be described in Section 2, a water's-edge limitation seems the appropriate recommendation for the EU at this time. In particular, it is difficult to believe that those who so recently were vehemently opposed to application of world-wide combination by the US states would soon favour its adoption by the EU. Moreover, it may be easier to gain agreement within a group of countries that already have substantial economic integration than within a more diverse group of countries. Thus the analysis that follows is based on such a 'water's-edge' limitation, in which the income to be apportioned by formula would be that of a unitary group determined, through the application of SA/ALS, to be earned within the EU.[25]

A system based on FA/UC would overcome some of the problems of SA/ALS identified above, at least as far as the EU water's-edge group is concerned. First, FA/UC recognizes the conceptual impossibility of employing the ALS where economic interdependence exists or where goods or services are not transferred in market transactions. Second, transfer prices for transactions between members of the water's-edge group cannot be manipulated to shift income to low-tax jurisdictions within the EU. (While there may be some opportunity to manipulate factors in the apportionment formula, these seem to be quite limited, as the factors involve transactions with third parties, such as payment of wages and salaries, investment in capital goods, and sales.[26])

[23] For the arguments in favour of and against world-wide unitary combination, as well as the Supreme Court's analysis of the issue, see the briefs filed in *Container* (1983) and *Barclays Bank/Colgate Palmolive* (1994).

[24] Alaska is the only exception to this pattern. It requires oil companies to file a world-wide combined report. (See Duncan (1996).) Many multinational companies prefer to file on a world-wide basis since doing so can reduce their state tax liability, and some states give companies the option to choose either water's-edge (defined in the next paragraph of the text) or world-wide combination. In fact, California's initial proposal in 1993 to make water's-edge combination mandatory was blocked in favour of continuing to allow companies the option to choose the scope of taxation. (See Coffill and Willson (1993) and Miller and Campion (1996).)

[25] The 'water's edge' can be defined in many ways, and might include all affiliates of a unitary business that are resident in the EU or that are doing business in the EU. The water's-edge group would generally exclude the income and operations of all affiliates that did not do business in the EU. (These would be included in a world-wide unitary group.)

[26] In comments made on the paper at the ISPE conference, Steven Clark noted that buyers of a bundle of tangible and intangible products might agree to

Table 10.1 State legislation relating to world-wide combined reporting

State	Year effective	Legislation
Alaska	1992	In 1991, adopted mandatory water's-edge legislation for taxpayers who are not subject to the provisions for oil and gas producers and pipelines, effective 1 January 1992 (HB 12). Alaska Stat. § 43.20.073.
California	1988	Granted taxpayers the option to limit combination to the US water's edge. Law adopted September 1986 (SB 85). Cal. Rev. & Tax. Code, Art. 1.5 § 25110.
	1994	Revised water's-edge-election provisions. Law adopted October 1993 (SB 671). Cal. Rev. & Tax. Code, § 25111, 25115.
Colorado	1986	Limited combined reporting to income bound by the US water's edge. 1985 Colo. Sess. Laws, ch. 309, codified at Colo. Rev. Stat. § 39-22-303(11)(a).
Florida	1982	Adopted elective world-wide combined reporting in 1983, retroactive to 9 January 1982. Fla. Income Tax Code, Fla. Stat. Sec. 220.135, as amended by Laws of 1983, ch. 83-349.
	1984	Passed SB 1A to repeal world-wide combined reporting, effective 9 January 1984. SB 1A. Fla. Laws of 1984, ch. 84-549.
Idaho	1986	Adopted legislation allowing binding water's-edge election or world-wide combination. 1986 Idaho Sess. Laws ch. 342, codified at Idaho Code § 63-3027B.
	1993	Unless the taxpayer makes a water's-edge election, Idaho taxable income of a unitary group of corporations with foreign subsidiaries includes the foreign and domestic income of all member corporations, effective retroactively to 1 January 1993. CH. 284, Laws 1993 (HB 404).
Indiana	1985	Enacted legislation prohibiting the Department of Revenue from requiring combined reports of an Indiana taxpayer with another entity if that other entity is a foreign corporation or a foreign-operating corporation. SB 75, signed April 1985 to take effect retroactively to 1 January 1985. 1985 Ind. Acts, P.L. 75 codified at Ind. Code Sec. 6-3-2-1 *et seq.*, CCH Par 95-132 *et seq.*, P-H par 12,200 *et seq.* A taxpayer may not be required to use domestic combined reporting unless it cannot fairly reflect its adjusted gross income under existing law. Ind. Code § 6-3-2-2(p), CCH ¶ 95-149b, P-H ¶ 12,216.5.

Table 10.1 *continued*

State	Year effective	Legislation
Massachusetts	1981	With no change in Massachusetts state law, Department of Revenue instructed auditors to assess corporations on a world-wide unitary approach instead of on a separate-entity theory.
	1984	On 11 December 1984, the Massachusetts Supreme Court ruled that the Tax Commission did not have the authority to use the unitary-business approach. *Polaroid Corporation & Others v. Commissioner of Revenue*, 393 Mass 490 (1984).
Montana	1988	In 1987, adopted water's-edge-election legislation, effective 1 January 1988. Mont. Code Ann. §§ 15-31-321, 15-31-322 (1987) § 290.17 (subdiv. 4)(f).
New Hampshire	1986	Adopted water's-edge limitation on combined reporting for its business profits tax. 1986 N.H. Laws ch. 153, codified at N.H. Rev. Stat. Ann. ch. 77-A:1 *et seq.*
North Dakota	1989	In 1987, adopted water's-edge election, effective 1 January 1989. N.D. Cent. Code § 57-38.4-01 *et seq.* (1987), as amended by N.D. Laws (H.B. 1164).
Oregon	1986	In 1984, amended corporate income tax law (HB 3029) to provide that if an Oregon corporate taxpayer's income is included in a federal consolidated return, 'the corporation's Oregon taxable income shall be determined beginning with federal consolidated taxable income of the affiliated group', effective 1 January 1986. Laws of 1984, Chap. 1, 2d Spec. Sess. OR. VAB. 3029, 1984 Or. Spec. Sess. 1, ORS § 317.715.
Utah	1986	In 1987, adopted water's-edge legislation, effective 1 January 1986. 1986 Utah Laws H178, codified at Utah Code Ann. § 59-13-65 *et seq.*

Note: The only case where world-wide combination is mandatory is for oil and gas producers and pipelines in Alaska.

Sources: Hellerstein and Hellerstein, 1993, pp. 8–185, 8–196; Hellerstein and Hellerstein, 1989, pp. S261–S278; Ferguson, 1986; Harper and Lewis, 1988; Commerce Clearing House, various years.

However, many of the problems of SA/ALS are not overcome. For example, a water's-edge limitation would not deal with interdependence between related firms within and outside the EU or affect the possibility of shifting income to affiliates outside the EU (including those chartered in tax havens). Moreover, it would not affect the need to distinguish between interest and dividends or between types of income paid to (or by) members of a corporate group within the water's edge by (to) those outside, or the need for withholding taxes on royalties and dividends moving from the water's-edge group to affiliates outside. To avoid some of these complications with a water's-edge limitation to FA/UC, world-wide unitary combination may need to be considered as an option for the future (see Weiner (1996 and 1999) for issues to consider in connection with this suggestion).

2. Problems with FA/UC

While FA/UC would solve some problems that characterize SA/ALS, it suffers from problems of its own. At the very least, it faces transitory problems, and thus may not be appropriate to the present situation in the EU, which is facing other issues relating to economic and monetary union. Some conceptual, transitory, technical, and political problems are discussed below. Whether they can be resolved remains to be seen.

2.1 Conceptual problems

Formula apportionment is conceptually inferior to separate accounting *if* separate accounting can be applied. First, FA does not attempt to determine the true source of income; it is based on an implicit assumption that profitability, compared with whatever factors appear in the apportionment formula, is uniform across related companies operating in different jurisdictions. This assumption underlay objections to use of world-wide combination by the US states; it seems particularly unlikely, for example, that profits, as a percentage of payrolls, are comparable in the US and in less-developed countries. Even if comparable profitability is a politically acceptable assumption within the US, it may not be acceptable within the EU. This objection may be transitory, to be eliminated as the creation of a Single European Market leads the economies of members to converge. (Evidence from the US states suggests that greater integration does bring about economic convergence.)

manipulate the values assigned to the two components in order to facilitate shifting of the buyer's tangible property factor between jurisdictions.

Second, it is clear that FA can sometimes greatly distort the geographic attribution of income. This situation arises when income can clearly be identified with a particular location—for example, a well-head. This was most obviously the case in the oil industry during the height of the energy crisis.[27]

Third, application of the same formula to all industries, while simple, can create inequities and distortions. (Consider, for example, the insignificant roles played by payrolls in banking, by physical capital in professional sports, etc.) Thus certain industries will require special formulas. (Some US states use special formulas for transportation, communications, financial intermediaries, pipelines, professional sports, etc.[28]) If components of a conglomerate company operate in industries using different formulas, it would be necessary to determine the boundaries of the industries and to apply the ALS (or a hybrid formula) to split income between industries.

Fourth, EU adoption of FA/UC may complicate relations with non-EU countries. This would be a bitter pill, given the role some European countries played in soundly rejecting global formulary apportionment during the revisions to the OECD's transfer pricing guidelines. If, as would seem likely, application of FA/UC in the EU were limited to the water's edge, relations with non-EU countries might not become more complicated, but multinational enterprises and tax administrators would need to apply two sets of source attribution rules—one (SA/ALS) to determine the division of income between the EU and the rest of the world and another (FA/UC) to apportion EU-source income among the individual Member States.[29] Thus this option indicates a need to preserve detailed rules for both approaches for some period.

[27] One of the authors (McLure) knows of a particularly egregious example in which one state implicitly attributed less income to a foreign oil-producing country than that country collected from the taxpayer in income and related taxes! Oil-rich members of the EU may not accept a system that can give such outrageous results. Of course, they may take unilateral actions to protect their revenues by levying separate deductible taxes intended to capture a large portion of economic rents.

[28] See, for example, the recommendations made in Multistate Tax Commission (1996).

[29] If the EU were to adopt world-wide combination, the reaction would probably be milder than the opposition in the 1980s to use of world-wide combination by some US states. Such a development would tend to diminish use of SA/ALS by other countries and might well lead to a world-wide shift to FA/UC with world-wide combination. This chapter presumes that all EU Member States agree to adopt FA/UC at the same time. Weiner (1999) evaluates whether countries should unilaterally or multilaterally move to FA/UC.

2.2 Transitory problems

In addition to the inherent problems of FA/UC discussed above, there are problems that are important, but perhaps transitory in the EU context. One problem concerns the accounting conventions and institutional structure of the EU. In both the US and Canada, one financial accounting system applies throughout the country. Thus companies doing business in more than one jurisdiction do not need to recast their financial accounts to meet various accounting standards.

The umbrella of a federal system leads to a high degree of conformity between the tax laws of the federal governments of those two countries and those of their states or provinces. Thus subnational tax bases are much more similar within these federal economies than are those of the EU Member States. Much of this similarity derives from the explicit federal structure of the US and of Canada, a structure that does not (and may never) exist within the EU. The lack of barriers to cross-border investment, however, may also explain a great deal of the similarity, suggesting that elimination of barriers may lead to convergence of tax bases.

Finally, in the US, with few exceptions, taxpayers do not attempt to determine profit on a state-by-state or province-by-province basis. (In Canada, as the provinces have not adopted unitary taxation, this statement only applies within the same company.) Indeed, one reason given for the development of FA in the US was that the lack of tax and other barriers to cross-border expansion (for example, no state can impose a withholding tax or treat a cross-state merger any differently from a within-state merger) made it unnecessary for multi-state companies to maintain separate accounts on a state-by-state basis.

State corporate taxation in the US did not begin with apportionment.[30] In the initial period of state corporate income taxation, most firms operated within a single state, and neither firms nor states required an alternative to

---

[30] Hawaii, then a territory, had introduced a tax on corporate income in 1901 that was modelled after the US federal tax of 1894. Wisconsin became the first state to adopt the corporate income tax, in 1911. Shortly after the adoption of the 16th Amendment in 1913, which provided for a federal income tax, the states realized that a federal corporate income tax made it feasible for them also to adopt a corporate income tax, and by the end of the 1920s, seventeen states had adopted the corporate income tax. As of 1996, all of the states except two began the computation of the state income tax base (whether for a single corporation or a member of a group) with federal taxable income. The seven Canadian provinces that have entered into tax collection agreements with the federal government use the federal base, and the remaining three use a base that is very similar to the federal base. This history is detailed in Weiner (1994).

separate accounting for income tax purposes. Formula apportionment was available, but separate accounting was more commonly used. However, business expansion across state lines was pushing the states toward an apportionment system and, by 1920, the eight taxing states used a range of formulas for corporate income tax purposes. This uncoordinated development led the National Tax Association (NTA) to attempt to provide a uniform solution to the problem of multi-state business taxation. In 1922, the NTA called for uniform adoption of a two-factor property and business formula.[31] Although the states did not adopt this recommendation, formula apportionment was becoming more widely used and, by 1938, a survey by the NTA revealed that the states and companies preferred FA to SA/ALS. For example, one business leader noted that apportionment has 'distinct advantages and conveniences' in state taxation since 'American business has grown freely across state lines without the necessity heretofore of keeping complete accounts for each branch. It would be a great expense to the taxpayers to set up and maintain such accounts and to tax officials to audit them.'[32]

The situation is very different in Europe, where certain basic practices and economic conditions differ across Member States. For example, although EU Member States have adopted certain directives designed to bring approaches closer in line with one another, the implementation of these directives varies widely and the directives provide substantial flexibility to accommodate the preferences of Member States. The existence of uniform accounting practices would further the achievement of a uniform tax base, since definitions of taxable income follow accounting concepts more closely in some EU countries (for example, Germany and France) than in others (for example, the Netherlands and the UK).

There is no supranational tax base to which the members of the EU must conform, or on which they can rely. Attempts to define common standards have been unsuccessful, as shown by the rejection of previous Commission attempts at harmonization (discussed below). Finally, contrary to the situation at the subnational level in the US and Canada, taxpayers in the EU are currently required to determine income attributed to operations in each of the Member States using SA/ALS.

Formula apportionment can be problematic in the absence of a common currency.[33] For example, suppose that exchange rates are such that

---

[31] NTA proceedings (1922, p. 202).

[32] As reported in the NTA proceedings (1932).

[33] This discussion is based on OECD (1995a, p. III-22). The SA/ALS has techniques to deal with the artificial impact of exchange rate changes on profits that could perhaps be modified for use under FA/UC until a common currency is introduced.

50 per cent of the income of a given multinational enterprise would be attributed to each of two member states, A and B. Suppose now that the exchange rate of state A strengthens, so that 60 per cent of the apportionment factors, and thus the profits of the enterprise, would be attributed to that state. The fact that the income attributed to those operations would rise when the exchange rate strengthens runs counter to the normal presumption that a stronger exchange rate makes it more difficult to export (and to compete with imports), creating downward pressure on profits. As long as tax rates are uniform, fluctuations in exchange rates would affect only the division of the tax base among member nations of the EU. If tax rates differ, aggregate tax liability would also be affected.

The creation of Economic and Monetary Union (EMU) in the EU and the adoption of a single currency by nearly all EU members makes this currency problem only temporary for those members. With use of a common currency, many of the obstacles that now lead companies to maintain individual accounts for their operations in various Member States will disappear. By the time the common currency is fully introduced, Member States' economies are likely to have converged significantly, since one condition of joining EMU is becoming financially more similar.

Progress is also occurring in creating a standard international accounting system, at least within the EU. The European Commission has decided not to create its own accounting standards board; rather, it will defer to the International Accounting Standards Committee (IASC) for these purposes. The Finance Ministers of the major industrialized economies are encouraging progress in this area.[34]

2.3   Technical problems

If the EU is to move to a system of FA/UC, it will need to resolve a number of technical issues, in addition to the definition of the tax base (a topic too large to discuss here and not unique to the issue of formula apportionment) and the achievement of greater co-operation in tax administration (discussed briefly below). Some of these issues are primarily political, but some are primarily technical, and many may be intractable. The technical issues include, among others, the definition of a unitary business, the choice of apportionment formula (which has political overtones), and the measurement of factors.[35] The US Treasury conference

[34] The IASC is composed of 142 accounting organizations in 103 countries.

[35] This is not intended to be a comprehensive discussion of other issues; among issues not discussed are taxation of non-business income, transition rules, and interaction with SA used in other countries.

held in December 1996 discussed these issues at length; thus they are only briefly analysed here.[36]

2.3.1 Defining a unitary business

If the EU decides to adopt a system based on FA, it may be forced to make a difficult choice. If it chooses to limit the spread between tax rates in the Union (perhaps by imposing minimum or maximum rates as has been suggested in the past), it will reduce the scope for tax planning and may avoid the need for combination and the difficult problems of defining a unitary business. But, in the process, it would have limited the autonomy of Member States over the most important of fiscal choices—the tax rate. If it allows wide latitude in the setting of tax rates, it probably must determine how to define a unitary business, i.e. which of the separately incorporated affiliates should be included in a combined report.

What constitutes a unitary business is arguably primarily a technical issue, but a difficult one.[37] To apply the tax on a unitary basis, it is necessary to draw a circle around the part of the total income of a group of related firms that is to be apportioned. In general, when formula apportionment is applied on a unitary basis, the US states attempt to determine which operations of a group of affiliated entities contribute to or depend upon the operations of the business as a whole. Given this vague notion, some have argued it may be impossible to define a unitary business, since a narrow definition creates an 'intractable' problem, while an overly broad definition creates 'immense distortion'.[38] Nevertheless, it is worth while briefly reviewing US experience on this score, even though the US states face constraints in their ability to tax out-of-state income (for example,

---

[36] In particular, Weiner (1999) provides a detailed discussion of these, and other, technical issues.

[37] Miller and Campion (1996), updating Miller (1984), analyse the unitary approach and discuss California's implementation of unitary combination. It should be noted that most US states have developed their own rules for defining a unitary business, subject to constitutional limits noted below. As Miller and Campion explain (p. 30), the New York approach might be preferable for federal (international) purposes because it requires a threshold evaluation under an arm's-length approach.

[38] Coffill and Willson, 1993. It would be desirable for the EU to attempt to craft a common definition of a unitary business for use in all the Member States. Failure to adopt a single definition of a unitary business would lead to gaps and overlaps in the tax base, complexity, and inequity, as it has in the US.

various US constitutional prohibitions), not all of which would be relevant at the international level.[39]

a. US legal tests Over the years, the US courts, including both state-level courts and the US Supreme Court, have decided cases that help describe what will be deemed to constitute a unitary business from a legal stand-point. These decisions, however, have not settled on a single definition, and many decisions have been controlled by restrictions imposed by a state's underlying legal statute. To help resolve this unsettled issue, the Multistate Tax Commission has begun working on developing standards for defining a unitary business.[40]

Three unities. In 1941, a California court, in *Butler Bros.*, set forth a test based on the three unities of ownership, operation, and use, providing a list of possible indicia of unity to be considered under each.[41] (Unity of operation is indicated by sharing of what are normally called 'staff' functions in administrative theory, including shared or common purchasing departments, advertising, accounting, legal representation, and employee benefits. Unity of use is found in common executive forces ('line' functions) and

---

However, what constitutes a unitary business is necessarily driven by the facts of the business relationship; thus, desirable as a 'bright-line test' would be, the discussion below suggests that, for all practical purposes, it would be difficult to establish a single unitary-business definition, even in one country. At best, the EU can hope for uniform guidelines to follow when determining the elements of the unitary business. Such broad guidance is consistent with the practice in the tax laws of all developed countries.

[39] These restraints result primarily from the provisions of the US Constitution that guarantee due process and reserve to the US Congress the power to regulate foreign and interstate commerce (and implicitly deny the states' power to interfere with it). For example, the fact that the Supreme Court rejected one state's use of an ownership test to determine the taxable unit (see *Allied-Signal, Inc. v. Director, Division of Taxation, 504 U.S. 768 (1992)*) would not be relevant at the international level.

[40] State guidelines for the taxation of multi-state business are outlined in the Uniform Division of Income for Tax Purposes Act (UDITPA) (Multistate Tax Commission, 1996), a model statute adopted by the National Conference of Commissioners on Uniform State Laws in 1957 and since adopted by more than twenty-five states. UDITPA provides standards for many elements of the FA method, such as the apportionment formula, factors, and allocation issues, but does not provide details on the unitary-business concept. States generally adopt the UDITPA through adopting the Multistate Tax Compact.

[41] The following discussion draws on Weiner (1994), Miller and Campion (1996), and Miller (1984).

operational systems, as indicated, *inter alia*, by inter-company transfers of products, shared officers and directors, a uniform theory of management, and a common public image.) Some of these (especially indicia of unity of operation) could easily be corrected by application of arm's-length prices— or simply ignored, without greatly affecting the division of income given by SA / ALS.

Contribution and dependence. Another early California state court case—*Edison Stores* (1947)—provided an intuitively appealing, but subjective, definition of a unitary business. Unity exists 'if the operation of the portion of the business done within the state is dependent upon or contributes to the operation of the business without the state...'. The California Franchise Tax Board later adopted this definition, which was drawn from Altman and Keesling (1946).

Centralized management, functional integration, and economies of scale. The US Supreme Court supplied a much more substantive and objective elaboration in *Mobil* in 1980. In that case, it focused on 'functional integration, centralization of management, and economies of scale' as keys to the existence of a unitary business, and it has since repeated these key words numerous times.

Flow of value. In *Container*, decided in 1983, the US Supreme Court responded to the claim that unity should be reflected in a flow of products between related entities (mentioned below) by announcing that it is a 'flow of value' that characterizes a unitary business. In this decision, the Court rejected the argument that there need be a flow of goods between related parties for a business to be unitary. This decision also highlighted that there must be an element of control in the relationship between the parent and the related entities.

b. Possible 'bright-line tests' Even the brief descriptions provided above make it obvious that, under US state law and practice, a great deal of uncertainty attends the claim that a given group of affiliated companies is engaged in a unitary business. There have thus been several suggestions that there should be a 'bright-line test' of what constitutes a unitary business. While the search for this particular Holy Grail has intuitive appeal, each objective test proposed has important flaws.

Ownership. Perhaps the simplest test is that of ownership; more than 50 per cent common ownership would be deemed dispositive proof of a unitary business and trigger combination (see Corrigan (1980)).[42] This test has the advantage of administrative simplicity, but it has the disadvantage

---

[42] In the US states, the unitary group may differ from the group consolidated for federal tax purposes. At the federal level, the activities of all corporations that

of allowing a company to arrange its business structure so as to avoid taxation. Furthermore, a business can be controlled by another without being majority-owned. Thus this definition would exclude many unitary operations from the unitary principle. (See also McLure (1981).)

Basic operational interdependence. A second objective test of unity is that of 'operational interdependence', which would normally be exhibited by a flow of goods or services between affiliated firms (Hellerstein, 1982). Despite the appeal of simplicity, this approach is also flawed because it is easy to find situations where a unitary business exists (as exhibited by the impossibility of using separate accounting to isolate the income of affiliated firms) where there is arguably no operational interdependence (see McLure (1983a and 1983b)). Hellerstein (1983) has responded that broad tests of 'contribution or dependency' lead only to burdensome and expensive compliance and administration and severely distort and misattribute income.

c. An economist's view   The earliest attempts to define a unitary business were framed primarily by lawyers. Thus, for example, while 'contribution and dependence' had intuitive appeal, it lacked economic substance. What activities gave rise to the contribution and dependence? One suggested approach is to ask (a) whether there is common ownership, (b) whether there are significant amounts of transactions or economic interdependence within the group, and (c) whether these could be so important that separate accounting could not be expected to give a reliable result (at least compared with formula apportionment). (See McLure (1984a).) In contrast to the bright-line tests mentioned above, this approach has the major disadvantage that it is not objective. Thus it can lead to uncertainty, which may, in turn, lead to economic inefficiency if that uncertainty distorts business investment decisions.

2.3.2   Choosing the apportionment formula

In principle, the choice of apportionment formula should be guided by the objective of determining the geographic source of income of a group

are at least 80 per cent commonly owned are consolidated into a single return that treats all the affected corporations as a single taxpayer. Consolidation differs from unitary combination in that it is based solely on ownership and does not consider whether the companies are part of a unitary business. The Supreme Court's decisions have generally precluded states from applying federal consolidation rules, since the entities included in a consolidated group may not have the requisite connection with the state—as would theoretically be true for a combined group.

of companies operating in more than one jurisdiction. Unfortunately, theory does not provide much technical guidance precisely where (and precisely because) it is needed—where SA/ALS does not work because of economic interdependence. Beyond that, the choice of apportionment formula may depend on a pragmatic consideration—that is, the availability of data. Finally, the choice may be heavily influenced by political considerations, related especially to the division of the tax base among jurisdictions.

Musgrave (1984) provides a useful way to look at this problem. First, assuming that corporate taxation is motivated by an effort to attribute the tax base to the taxing jurisdictions that are 'entitled' to tax it, she asks whether entitlement is to be based solely on 'supply' (production) considerations or is also to reflect 'demand' (consumption) considerations. If the former, the apportionment formula should, as nearly as possible, replicate the effects of SA/ALS. This it can do, provided there are no economic rents and no economic interdependence and provided production functions are identical in all jurisdictions. Of course, under these conditions, there would be no need for FA, aside from the prevention of income shifting.

Inclusion of payroll and property in a supply-based formula will adequately capture the contribution of a sales force and sales-related capital; there would be no reason to include sales as a separate factor. Musgrave suggests the only role for sales in the apportionment formula is to reflect demand considerations, issues on which economists have little to say. (The US Congress's only foray into this area proposed a formula based on payroll and property, although for administrative, not economic, reasons.[43] Since most states used the three-factor formula at that time, this proposal seemed doomed to fail, and it did.)

A formula based on only property and payroll does not seem to be correct where economic rents can be traced to market power instead of to other factors. Sales clearly play a different role in these cases and in highly competitive situations. Yet it would be impractical to attempt to consider market power in designing apportionment formulas.

In short, beyond recommending that the factors reflect what generates income, economists have relatively little to say about the design of apportionment formulas.[44] As long ago as 1922, the National Tax Association seems to have correctly concluded that 'there is no one right rule of

---

[43] See the Willis Report (US House of Representatives, 1964).

[44] In commenting on Musgrave (1984), McLure (1984c) has noted, however, that it is theoretically incorrect to use the capital stock in an apportionment formula, as the states do, instead of the flow of capital services (which is what enters a production function), as measured by the user cost of capital (interest plus depreciation). Consider the example of a company that owns new property in state A that

apportionment ... The only right rule ... is a rule on which the several states can and will get together as a matter of comity.[45] Such a statement could apply equally to many elements of an EU tax system based on FA/UC.

Competing forces have influenced the states' choice of factors. First, in theory, the factors should reflect how income is generated and perhaps recognize the contributions to income made by the manufacturing and the marketing states. In the early years of corporate income taxation, the states attempted to craft a formula that included the many factors that are responsible for generating income. In 1929, for example, the formulas used by the sixteen states that then levied the tax included property, payroll, sales, manufacturing costs, purchases, expenditures for labour, accounts receivable, net costs of sales, capital assets, and stock of other companies.

Attempting to gain this precision, however, significantly complicates the apportionment process. It may also lead to substantial multiple taxation (or undertaxation). Thus a second force leads to adoption of a simple, common formula. A formula that assigns equal weight to property, payroll, and sales, commonly known as the Massachusetts formula, became this standard from 1940 until the mid-1980s when the trend toward assigning greater (or sole) weight to sales took off.

Recent analyses have recognized the competing objectives that influence the choice of apportionment factors. On the one hand, there is a tendency to maximize the tax base by increasing the weight on factors that are located within the state. This approach also incorporates the notion that the location of the factors provides a good indication of the location of income. But this tendency must be balanced against the desire not to discourage economic activity, which is achieved by reducing the weight on factors of production located in the state. This conflict (which also arises in deciding whether to provide tax incentives to encourage economic development) is usefully illustrated by the experience in the US, where the number of states that give double weight to the sales factor (and make

is worth $1 million and lasts fifty years and property in state B that also costs $1 million but lasts only one year. The approach used by the states would apportion income equally between the states. Assume that the interest rate (either the cost of borrowed funds or the opportunity cost of equity) is 10 per cent, so interest is $100,000 per year in both cases. Assuming straight-line depreciation, depreciation would be $20,000 in state A but $1 million in state B. Thus the user cost of capital would be $120,000 in state A and $1.1 million in state B, implying a theoretically correct allocation of more than 90 per cent (1.1/1.22) of profits to state B.

[45] See National Tax Association (1922, p. 202). That it is important to get countries to agree on the same rule is, of course, also true of the decision to use formula apportionment in the first place.

corresponding reductions in the weights on property and payroll so that the sum equals 100 per cent) rose from three in 1976 to eight in 1986 and to twenty-five by 1996 (for details, see Weiner (1996)].[46] Since sales of tangible personal property are commonly attributed to the state of destination, this shift presumably reflects a desire to reduce taxation of in-state production, compared with taxation of in-state consumption. However, as offsetting rate changes that affect all companies are often made to preserve revenue, its success has been questioned.[47]

2.3.3   Measuring the factors

In principle, the measurement of the factors in the apportionment formula should be primarily a technical issue. For administrative reasons, however, the definition may be strongly affected by the availability of data. UDITPA defines the three standard factors, which are used below for discussion.

a. The property factor   Property is measured as the historical cost of real and tangible personal property. Severe measurement problems can occur in the property factor. In theory, the value of property in the apportionment formula should be the discounted value of the income flow the property produces. Of course, if one knew the income flow on a geographical basis, one would tax that, instead of using an apportionment formula. Thus it may be necessary to retreat to the use of the historical cost of property. But, in attempting to preserve simplicity, the US states make two serious errors in their treatment of costs. Apart from New York, which does attempt to use fair market value, they do not recognize either depreciation or inflation in the valuation of property.

The use of costs as a surrogate for the value of property may be particularly problematic in two areas: natural resources and intangible assets, areas where economic rents may constitute an important fraction of the

[46] In addition, three states employed only sales in their formulas and one placed a weight of 70 per cent on sales; see Duncan (1996). Florida began the move to double-weighting sales; when it adopted the corporate income tax in 1971, it introduced this formula. Iowa had, however, previously adopted an apportionment formula containing only sales.

[47] See Pomp (1987) for a discussion of the ambiguous effects of New York's move to a double-weighted sales factor. (New York increased its rate at the same time as it changed its formula.) Pomp uses this evidence to defend New Jersey's decision to stick with the Massachusetts formula (New Jersey changed its mind in 1995 when it adopted a double-weighted sales formula). See Weiner (1994 and 1996) for empirical evidence that, after controlling for changes in the tax rate, states that moved to the double-weighted sales factor increased their share of investment relative to states that remained with the Massachusetts formula.

return to capital. First, if natural resources can be discovered and developed with relatively little investment (or if their prices rise dramatically after they are discovered and developed, as happened during the energy crisis), costs will not reflect value. Second, it is notoriously difficult to value intangible assets or to assign a *situs* to them. Indeed, UDITPA does not include intangible property in the property factor, primarily because it is difficult to assign a location. Given that such assets constitute a sizeable fraction of the value of major corporations, this is a major chink in the armour of formula apportionment. (See also McLure (1997a).)

b. The payroll factor The payroll factor accounts for the contributions of labour to the generation of income. It is measured by employee compensation, including salaries, commissions, and bonuses. This factor should be the easiest to measure, given the similar definitions of payroll, or the relative ease of adjusting for differences, available across countries, and the fact that standardized measures already exist at the international level. Instead of payroll, the number of employees could be used. This measure would avoid the valuation differences, which might be quite large between the industrialized and less-industrialized countries, but at the cost of considerable conceptual purity and potential distortion of the division of taxable income. This distinction, however, would not seem to be tremendously significant within the EU.

c. The sales factor Sales generally include sales of tangible personal property and receipts from sales of services. In principle, it should be relatively simple to determine sales to ultimate consumers in a jurisdiction that imposes a conceptually attractive retail sales tax (RST)—one that exempts sales to business.[48] (In fact, the US states do not make a serious attempt either to exempt sales to business from their RSTs or otherwise limit sales at destination in their sales factors to sales to consumers.) It would be much more difficult where value added tax is the sales tax of choice, as in the EU, since value added tax applies to all nonexempt sales. Because the location of sales may be especially difficult to pin down, it is the easiest factor to use for 'profit' shifting. It would also be necessary to decide how to treat sales that occur where a company lacks taxable nexus. To avoid a case where the sale would not be subject to tax in any jurisdiction, many states have adopted a 'throwback' rule

[48] This is not necessarily true in the burgeoning world of electronic commerce in 'content' (intangible products and services sold over the Internet); see McLure (1997b) and literature cited therein.

that attributes such sales to the state of origin, where they would be taxed.

These problems of factor definition may be transitory. Efforts to achieve uniformity (for other reasons) are already under way. For example, the OECD has created a standardized database for comparing productivity, payroll costs, and unemployment rates across countries (Pilat, 1996; OECD, 1995b). Similarly, although data on capital stocks (which could be utilized in constructing a property factor) are not now measured in the same way across nations, the OECD has also published accounts of flows and stocks of fixed capital that are fairly comparable (OECD, 1994). Sales figures may already be comparable, due to the relative uniformity of value added taxes in the EU. However, the concept of sales used in implementing the value added tax may not be conceptually appropriate for the purpose at hand.

2.4 Political problems

The political structure of the EU has inhibited adoption of a common company tax system, and it is hard to see this issue going away. The individual Member States are not ready to give up their fiscal sovereignty; they are certainly not contemplating creating a 'United States of Europe' (a 'United Europe of States' may be more likely). The EU's 'Constitution'—the Treaty of Rome (as amended)—restricts movement toward harmonized direct tax policies. These restrictions include, but are not limited to, the need to preserve subsidiarity and to reach unanimity in tax matters. (Taxation is one of the three exceptions to the general rule of qualified-majority decision-making mentioned in Article 100A of the Single European Act amendments to the Treaty of Rome. See Vanistendael (1994).) Removing these barriers may require a 'constitutional' amendment and all the difficulties that process entails.

Experience suggests that Member States of the EU are likely to be reluctant to surrender control over the important prerogatives of income definition, the choice of apportionment formula, and tax administration. Thus the requisite degree of uniformity, or, more likely, co-ordination, will be difficult, and perhaps impossible, to achieve. However, there is a growing recognition that greater co-ordination of company tax policies may improve the functioning of the European Single Market. This is illustrated by the adoption, in December 1997, of a code of conduct in the area of business taxation and the recent release of a directive on withholding taxes. Thus some of these obstacles may not be as formidable in the future as they are now.

Even though the Single Market created in 1992 enshrined the free movement of capital, labour, goods, and services, cross-border mobility is still much lower within the EU than within Canada or the US. This lack of movement is due not only to the barriers rooted in public policies (for example, to lack of portability of pensions), but also, *inter alia*, to significant cross-country differences in culture, languages, and customs, all of which the Member States desire to preserve even as they move to a closer economic and monetary union.

3. The impact of European integration

As economic integration proceeds in the EU, SA/ALS will become increasingly problematic.[49] While the Ruding Committee reaffirmed the use of transfer pricing as the key to determining the source of income, despite the trends noted, others, speaking of the use of SA/ALS in the broader international context, where economic integration is much less pervasive than it soon will be in the EU, have drawn very different conclusions. For example, Vito Tanzi, head of the Fiscal Affairs Department of the International Monetary Fund, has expressed the following view:

It may not be too far-fetched to predict that in a technologically evolving world, the allocation of income by the use of transfer prices may be subject to increasing challenges and may thus become progressively more controversial. Other allocation principles based on formulas may acquire more legitimacy than now. (Tanzi, 1995, p. 139.)

Munnell (1992) noted that the growing importance of multinational companies in the EU makes it increasingly difficult to administer and enforce efficient and equitable tax systems and suggested that co-ordination of these changes could take two forms. One form is to maintain the current system and improve the mechanisms for avoiding double taxation and preventing tax evasion. The other form is for the Europeans to consider the apportionment system used in federal countries.[50]

3.1 European Union efforts at tax harmonization

The European Commission has attempted, largely without success, to bring about corporate tax harmonization among the Member States.[51] For example, in 1975, the Commission (Commission of the European Communities, 1975) proposed a directive to harmonize the systems and

[49] See Cnossen (1996) for a discussion of a broad range of alternative options.

[50] McLure (1989) and Weiner (1991) also suggest that the EU may be forced to adopt FA. Similar studies have evaluated FA for use in the integrated economies of the North American Free Trade Area. See McDaniel (1994).

[51] For details, see Weiner (1994 and 1997).

rates, but not the bases, of company taxation. In 1988, to correct the failure to harmonize bases in the 1975 directive, the Commission prepared a draft directive providing rules for determining corporate tax bases, but this draft directive was never issued, because of Member States' opposition to the proposed definitions of the tax base.[52]

The European Commission and Commission-sponsored study groups have also examined what type of company tax *system* would be best for the Single Market. However, although each study has proposed harmonizing EC (now EU) company tax systems, each study has proposed a different system. The 1963 study called for a split-rate system, the 1967 study called for an unspecified single corporate tax system, and the 1970 study called for a classical system. In 1975, in its only formally issued directive, the Commission proposed a nearly uniform partial imputation tax system.[53]

Fifteen years later, the European Commission formally withdrew its 1975 proposed directive, proposing, instead, to take a fresh look at determining, among others, what type of company tax system would be appropriate for the Single Market. The Commission (1990) stressed a longer-term need to determine the most appropriate basis for the common company tax system viewed as necessary within the Community.

3.2 The Ruding Committee and Report

The Ruding Committee believed that adoption of a common corporate tax system was a desirable long-term objective, but did not specify a particular system. It did warn, however, that, because market forces were unlikely to be strong enough to bring about this convergence, action would likely be necessary at the Community level.

The Ruding Committee examined whether apportionment could be considered for companies operating within the Community, on the understanding that the arm's-length system would continue to be used in transactions with countries outside the EC (Commission of the European Communities, 1992, p. 130). In doing this analysis, it looked to the experiences in the non-EC federal countries of Canada, Switzerland, and the US.[54]

---

[52] See Commission of the European Communities (1988). The Commission has not officially published this preliminary draft directive. However, it was reprinted in Kuiper (1988).

[53] For details of these studies, see Commission of the European Communities (1980). For details on the directive, see Commission (1975).

[54] See Annexes 9A (Canada), 9B (Switzerland), and 9C (the US) of the Ruding Report (Commission of the European Communities, 1992); i.e. see Daly (1992), Thalmann (1992), and Weiner (1992).

The committee rejected global formulary apportionment when the tax systems of more than one country are involved. It noted that the integration of the Community remained incomplete, citing, in particular, the lack of a common currency, company law, accounting standards, and expertise in tax administrations. Other reasons centred on the need to integrate the Community's apportionment method with the arm's-length method used in other countries and the difficulties that this integration would entail; for example, tax treaties would need to be renegotiated and two tax systems would have to be maintained. For these reasons, the committee found 'no case for introducing a system of formula allocation within the Community in the foreseeable future'.[55] However, the report did indicate that an allocation system could be introduced on an elective basis when the Community has reached a much greater degree of integration and when enterprises located in different Member States may treat their operations as a single group.[56]

3.3 The Monti Report

In March 1996, the European Commission, via the taxation Commissioner, Mario Monti, turned broadly to the issue of taxation policy for the first time in four years. This report (Commission of the European Communities, 1996a) identified tax policy challenges the EU now faces and suggested possible initiatives, all of which would respect the principle of subsidiarity. As with the run-up to the Single European Market in 1992, a chief concern is that the Member States adopt policies that ensure the smooth functioning of the Single Market. Doing this may require co-ordination at the EU level.

The new forces of international tax competition that have emerged with the elimination of barriers to cross-border capital flows seem to have spurred the Commission to finalize its 1996 proposal to achieve greater co-operation in corporate and other tax matters. This document (Commission of the European Communities, 1996b) refrained from endorsing any specific proposals (noting a lack of support for minimum corporate tax rates or bases at this time, but also a need to develop common tax definitions), focusing, instead, on how to achieve greater

---

[55] One participant in the ISPE conference observed that this statement should carry little weight, as it was, in part, political posturing intended to convince California to eliminate world-wide unitary combination (the *Barclays* litigation was active at that time).

[56] The SE (*Societé Européenne* or European Company) mentioned earlier is a step in this direction.

co-operation at the EU level in restraining the harmful effects of individual Member States' tax policies. Thus, in 1997, the Economic and Finance Ministers of the EU adopted a 'code of conduct' in business taxation for purposes of restraining harmful tax competition.[57] Through the Code of Conduct, Member States agree to undertake a political commitment to remove the features of their tax systems that distort the location of investment. As part of this agreement, the Member States also agreed to establish a 'Taxation Policy Group' that will continue the discussions on taxation policy in the EU. These efforts by the Commission and the individual Member States make it plain that action is necessary at the European level to reduce distortions to the Single Market, to prevent significant losses of tax revenue, and to reverse the trend of an increasing tax burden on labour as compared with more mobile tax bases (Commission of the European Communities, 1998).

3.4 Market forces

The EU's more recent approaches appear to derive from the view that market forces may succeed in areas where formal proposals fail in bringing about greater uniformity in corporate taxation. The well-known market-induced income tax reforms of the mid-1980s in the UK and in the US seem to have ignited a widespread movement to lower tax rates and a convergence of tax structures. This spontaneous realignment may not have been possible if company tax systems had been locked together by directive.

Actual tax reforms in the Member States support the Commission's approach. Since the mid-1980s, every Member State has reformed its company tax system, generally by reducing tax rates and broadening the tax base. For example, the average tax rate on retained earnings in the Member States (excluding Greece) fell from 46 per cent in 1980 to 39.7 per cent in 1992. The spread in tax rates also converged, as measured by a decrease in the standard deviation of tax rates. In addition, four out of five countries that offered unconditional investment credits significantly reduced them during the 1980s.[58]

---

[57] The Code of Conduct was approved at the ECOFIN Council Meeting on 1 December 1997. The package is discussed in Commission of the European Communities (1997). It was published in the *Official Journal* on 6 January 1998 (Commission of the European Communities, 1998).

[58] OECD, 1991. The measure of convergence of tax rates reflects the standard Irish statutory rate, not the special manufacturing rate. The four countries that reduced their investment credits are Belgium, Denmark, Spain, and the Netherlands. Luxemburg did not change its policies.

Examining rate changes independently of base changes may hide a pattern of constant, or even rising, effective tax rates. For example, effective tax rates can often rise after tax reforms that cut statutory tax rates due to base-broadening measures, such as the elimination of investment incentives and the reduction in the value of depreciation allowances and interest write-offs. Moreover, effective tax rates also take into consideration inflation and interest rates. For this reason, much of the convergence in effective tax rates is due to convergence in inflation and interest rates and not to changes in tax regimes.

Thus, even if inflation and interest rates tend to converge with EMU, continued differences in effective tax rates are not surprising. For example, Member States exhibit, *inter alia*, a substantial *mélange* of practices in their depreciation and loss-offset provisions, taxation of company groups, treatment of losses of branches and subsidiaries, and valuation of inventories, among other factors. Among other differences (in 1990) were at least six different definitions of company residence, fifteen different means of taxing groups of companies, and six different degrees of company tax integration with the personal tax system among the Member States.

In sum, certain features of company taxation have converged, but substantial variation is likely to be a permanent feature of company taxation in the EU. Several factors support this conclusion, not least among them the fact that corporate tax revenue accounts for nearly four times as much of total tax revenues in Luxemburg as in Germany. Thus the Member States face different constraints on their ability or desire to cede corporate tax issues to the EU level. Given these wide variations, any feasible tax reform proposal must consider the demonstrated reluctance of countries to give up the company tax as an instrument of fiscal policy, as well as the possibility that market forces may be sufficient to bring about enough approximation of tax systems for the individual countries involved.

4. European Union tax policy objectives

The Ruding Report (Commission of the European Communities, 1992, pp. 196–9) prescribed certain principles that should guide deliberations on tax policy in the EC (now the EU). These principles include neutrality, fiscal autonomy, administrative independence, and equitable distribution of the tax base. This section appraises FA/UC in the light of these and other principles.

4.1 Neutrality

In the absence of uniform rates, source-based taxation inevitably distorts locational choice.[59] (But, in some countries, differences are ameliorated by residence-based taxation, wherein foreign tax credits are granted for source-country taxes.) Because of the way the two systems operate, the locational distortions created by SA/ALS and by FA/UC are not identical. For example, SA/ALS may affect the location of accounting profit, with no change in real investment, as well as the location of real investment. Since it does not require use of transfer prices, the FA/UC system avoids distorting the location of accounting profits (at least within the 'water's edge' as presumed here); however, it may distort the location of real investment, because, as explained below, the formula acts as a tax on whatever factors are included in the formula. Any time an economic activity is taxed more heavily in some jurisdictions than in others, companies will have an incentive to locate that factor where tax rates are lowest to minimize their tax burden. For this reason, the definition of the apportionment formula is vitally important in achieving neutrality.

4.1.1 SA/ALS

To the extent that it achieves its intended purpose, SA/ALS determines the accounting profit arising in a given jurisdiction. In the long run, accounting profit consists of the normal return to capital and economic rents. (We ignore quasi-rents, which, by definition, exist only in the short run and are thus not of great interest in the discussion of locational neutrality.) The effects of taxation on the location of economic activity are somewhat different under SA/ALS depending on the nature of taxable income (normal returns or rents from various sources).

Economic rents may be specific to the location of either production or sales in the taxing jurisdiction, but they may not be. Examples of locationally specific rents include those associated with exploitation of natural resources and those that result from tapping local markets—for example, for soft drinks, entertainment (for example, movies and music), and computer software. By comparison, economic rents earned from manufacturing (for example, of pharmaceuticals) that could be produced elsewhere

---

[59] In making this statement, we make the common and reasonable (but often implicit) assumption that company income taxes are not benefit taxes. (Under US law, foreign tax credits are available only for income taxes that are not benefit taxes in disguise.) If, contrary to this assumption, differentials in taxation reflected differences in the value of services provided to companies, tax differentials would not necessarily cause locational distortions.

are not locationally specific. Taxation of locationally specific rents should have little impact on production and marketing decisions.[60] By comparison, taxation of the normal return to capital and of economic rents that are not locationally specific presumably does affect production and marketing decisions.

4.1.2   FA/UC

A tax levied on a base apportioned by formula can usefully be understood as a set of taxes levied on each of the factors in the apportionment formula, imposed at rates that depend on the nation-wide profitability of the taxpayer (relative to the individual factors), as well as the statutory tax rate.[61] Thus the locational distortions created by a tax based on FA/UC will be those associated with taxes levied on the apportionment factors, and not those of a tax based on SA/ALS. Moreover, distortions will be related positively to the profitability of the taxpayer, and not just to the statutory tax rate. But it is the profitability of the taxpayer throughout the domain covered by apportionment (for example, the entire US or the entire EU), and not the profitability within the taxing jurisdiction (the individual US state or Member State of the EU), that matters. As suggested earlier, both normal profits and economic rents are apportioned, without regard to where they actually originate. This suggests that the 'sales-related' portion of a tax based on FA/UC (that is, the portion that is apportioned according to sales) will have roughly the same locational effects as a sales tax and that the 'property-related' and 'payroll-related' portions will have roughly the same effects as property and payroll taxes. (The effects are only 'roughly' the same, because firms with no profits will pay no tax on these factors and those with high profits will experience high taxes on these factors.)

There have been few studies of how the variations in tax bases and rates in an apportionment system affect factor and location choices. Weiner (1994) examines the above two potential distortions caused by the formula apportionment system in the US.[62] The first distortion is to the factor choice of multi-state companies. Weiner finds no evidence that

---

[60] Economic theory might suggest that a tax on economic rents has no effect on the location of economic activity. This is probably an exaggeration, at least if tax rates are quite high.

[61] See McLure (1980) for the argument that a tax that is levied on a base that is apportioned by use of a formula can usefully be seen as a set of taxes levied on each of the factors in the apportionment formula. Empirical evidence from Weiner (1994 and 1996) is discussed below.

[62] These results from Weiner's dissertation (1994) are summarized in Weiner (1996 and 1998).

the cross-state variation in rates and bases has affected the relative choice between capital and labour. With respect to the location choice, however, changes to the formula, such as the move to the double-weighted sales formula, do influence the cross-state location of business investment, at least temporarily. Evidence from the Canadian provinces shows that reductions of tax rates within a relatively uniform origin-based system of apportionment can lead to increased provincial investment.

4.2 Subsidiarity and fiscal autonomy

European Union policy is guided by subsidiarity, a notion introduced with the Maastricht Treaty amendments to the Treaty of Rome (Article 3B), which takes a decentralized approach to fiscal matters. Subsidiarity requires that Member States should be able to determine their own fiscal policies unless those policies have negative spillover effects on the entire Union. The Commission (1991b, p. 7) explained that subsidiarity requires that 'Member States should remain free to determine their tax arrangements, except where these would lead to major distortions'. The Commission has been granted authority only to provide broad guidance to establish tax policy in the individual Member States. Article 100 of the Treaty provides for the approximation of laws, including tax laws, to establish the Common Market. Although indirect taxes have been subject to harmonization since the creation of the Common Market, direct taxes are not subject to such restrictions. The main restriction on direct taxes is to avoid double taxation (Article 220).

Thus, in the context of company taxation, the subsidiarity principle requires that certain conditions must be met before the Community would take over certain policies. Van Heukelen (1990) summarized these conditions as follows. First, differences in corporate tax systems across countries must cause significant distortions. Second, Community action is necessary to prevent these distortions. And, third, Community rules should not cause distortions in the Community-wide allocation of resources. When these conditions are not met, as now, the focus is on co-ordination and approximation of policies, rather than strict harmonization. Although co-ordination of policies at the EU level is needed to eliminate double taxation of cross-border activities while ensuring effective taxation at least once, harmonization of corporate tax systems is not seen to be essential to a successful Single Market.

Adoption of FA/UC with a uniform definition of income, a uniform apportionment formula, and uniform measurement of apportionment factors (and perhaps uniform tax administration) would entail a serious loss of fiscal autonomy and would appear to violate the subsidiarity principle.

(But, as suggested in the Monti Report (Commission of the European Communities, 1996a), the violation may be more apparent than real.) Given the jealousy with which the members of the EU have guarded their prerogatives in this area, as evidenced by the requirement of unanimous approval of tax measures and the relative inability to reach agreement on minor issues in this area, prospects for agreement to move to a uniform system of FA/UC appear dim.

It is, none the less, useful to examine why (and what kind of) fiscal autonomy matters.[63] This can be done by distinguishing among the following four distinct elements of fiscal autonomy: (a) the choice of taxes to be levied; (b) the definition of tax base(s) (which includes the choice of apportionment formula in the present context); (c) tax rate(s) and credit(s); and (d) tax administration. It can be argued that the choice of tax rates (and tax credits) is by far the most important for fiscal autonomy—that it is this choice that primarily determines the amount of revenue that will be raised and thus the size of the public sector.

By comparison, autonomy over the definition of the tax base (and the apportionment formula) can, at the very least, lead to gaps and overlaps in the definition of income, to lack of transparency, and to needless complexity. Worse, it can result in uses of tax policy that run directly counter to the concept of a single market—for example, when tax policy is used to provide incentives that would not be allowed if achieved by tariff policies. (In general, the Commission and the Ruding Committee have stated that certain tax incentives are acceptable, but they should be transparent; that is, they should take the form of tax credits or rate reductions rather than the form of special tax rules and regulations concerning the tax base.) The question, then, is whether these costs of independent action exceed the benefits of autonomy in this area.

The Canadian provinces appear willing to forgo control in these areas, in part because Canada has an ambitious system of fiscal equalization and in part because provinces are allowed to provide special tax credits (which reduce tax liability) for certain activities conducted within their boundaries, but not tax deductions (which would affect apportionable income). Moreover, in exchange for provinces agreeing to adopt the federal tax base and use the same formula, the federal government has agreed to incur all of the collection costs for the provincial corporate tax. Even the provinces that have not entered the agreement use the same formula and essentially the same tax base.

---

[63] This type of analysis has been presented earlier in McLure (1995 and 1997c).

4.3 Administrative independence

In the area of tax administration, the challenge is to reconcile uniformity with subsidiarity, providing Member States operational control over day-to-day administration without sacrificing uniformity. Administrative co-operation would seem to offer substantial benefits: uniformity of interpretation (of a tax law that is assumed to be based on a uniform definition of income and a uniform formula) and avoidance of duplication of administrative and compliance effort.

There appear to be several ways, in theory, to achieve uniformity in administration of company taxes in the EU. The most obvious is a centralized administration subordinated directly to the European Commission. This approach is sometimes opposed on the grounds that it implies that there would be an EU company tax. This conclusion does not follow; one need only consider the hypothetical model of centrally administered surcharges imposed by the members on their part of a common EU base, which would be divided using a single formula but with an EU tax rate of zero. Of course, if the central administration were to be created, the temptation also to create an EU-level company tax might be irresistible. (Given the high mobility of the corporate tax base, principles of fiscal federalism suggest that the company tax properly belongs at higher levels of government than the individual states. See, for example, McLure (1995).)

In a much less centralized system, the tax authorities of the various members would continue to have primary responsibility for tax administration, but subject to mandatory and close co-operation with their counterparts in other members. Similar agreements have been reached within the OECD and in the EU, itself, for example, through the Mutual Agreement and Associated Enterprises procedures.

4.4 Distribution of the tax base

Despite the rather pessimistic view of achieving tax harmonization revealed above, we now ask what issues may influence the contours of an EU unitary tax system. To evaluate this possibility, this section discusses revenue and income distributions under various formulas and identifies the interest groups that might favour a particular formula.

The distribution of the tax base among members of the EU is not likely to be the same under FA/UC as under SA/ALS. The most obvious changes would arise from differences in the profitability of economic activities conducted in various members (as defined by SA/ALS) and the extent of shifting of income between members through the manipulation of transfer pricing (which, of course, would be reflected in the measure of taxable income under SA/ALS). More generally, the reallocation of tax base depends on the definition of the tax base and especially on the formula chosen to apportion that tax base across countries under FA/UC.

Studies both in the EU and in the US indicate that the division of tax base among jurisdictions is relatively insensitive to the apportionment formula chosen.[64] A major point of contention in the development of the apportionment formula within the US states centred on the elements that would be included in the formula. Previous studies conducted on the US states have, however, revealed that the revenue distribution is relatively insensitive to variations in apportionment formulas. (This does not, of course, imply that the choice of apportionment factors has no effect on investment decisions.)

Table 10.2, based on the distribution of manufacturing activities in the EU, shows that the choice of formula is not all that important. Actual distributions will differ from the figures in the table, but these data show that variations in the formula definition have minor effects on the distribution of tax revenues. For example, Italy would be apportioned 13.7 per cent of EU profits with a formula based on value added, payroll, and sales, 14.4 per cent of profits with a formula based on investment, payroll, and sales, and 13.8 per cent of profits with a formula based on payroll and sales. A similar consistency appears across the other Member States.

Although the shares are not very sensitive to the formula chosen, Member States may, nevertheless, have an incentive to advocate a particular formula. For example, Italy would increase its share of total revenues with an investment, payroll, and sales formula. Germany's revenues would rise with a payroll and sales formula. In general, countries with a high manufacturing base but a low sales base might prefer to reduce the weight on the sales factor to maximize their revenues. Or they might pursue the opposite approach to reduce the tax burden on their manufacturers. Evidence from the US suggests that states may reduce the burden on the

---

[64] For example, working on data from the early 1960s, the Willis Committee found that state revenues were not highly sensitive to the formula. For thirty-seven of thirty-eight US states, less than 1 per cent of state tax revenue would be affected in the choice between the best and worst formula. (See US House of Representatives (1964, vol. 1, ch. 16).) For the EU, where operations are less broadly diversified, Weiner (1991) found that revenues would change by somewhat larger amounts. None of these studies, however, was able to use *tax* data, as these data are not publicly available. Thus they represent mere conjectures. But the results in Sheffrin and Fulcher (1984), based on data from California tax returns, are consistent with them.

productive factors of labour and capital located in the state by increasing the weight on the (destination-based) sales factor.

Some countries may step out front and adopt a formula early on, hoping to establish their chosen formula as the EU standard. The four largest countries may be able to exert the strongest influence on the definition of the formula. Table 10.2 shows that these four countries—Germany, the UK, France, and Italy—account for 90 per cent of manufacturing activity. Germany itself makes up over one-third of manufacturing activity, including nearly 40 per cent of gross wages and salaries (in 1983). Not surprisingly, these large countries would be likely to try to define an apportionment formula most favourable to their interests (whether that interest was in maximizing revenue or minimizing the tax burden on producers located in the country). As just noted, however, these Member States may not have the same goal and may not prefer the same formula; it is thus likely that, if these countries acted individually, a non-uniform system would arise.[65]

Table 10.2 Distribution of manufacturing operations under three apportionment formulas in nine EC Member States, 1983 (%)

	Value added + Payroll + Sales	New investment + Payroll + Sales	Payroll + Sales
Belgium	3.5	3.5	3.4
Denmark	1.5	1.4	1.7
France	19.4	19.3	19.6
Germany	35.0	34.5	35.7
Ireland	0.8	0.9	1.0
Italy	13.7	14.4	13.8
Luxemburg	0.2	0.2	0.3
Netherlands	4.2	4.5	4.5
UK	21.8	21.2	20.4

Notes: These figures illustrate potential consequences of apportionment and should not be interpreted as indicating the actual share of corporate tax revenues that would arise under apportionment, which would depend on the industry mix, taxable income, and profitability within each country. A lack of data on manufacturing profits in the Member States prevented estimating actual corporate tax revenues under apportionment. Value added and new investment are used as proxies for unavailable capital stock data.

Source: Eurostat, 1983.

[65] It is possible that the Member States may co-operate in choosing a formula. Precedence exists with the co-operation of several Member States in forming the Schengen group to establish common policies among the individual countries.

One should not be too pessimistic about the Europeans' ability to agree to some basic definitions of the important parameters of a tax system. Experience suggests that, when market forces and business pressures have developed to the point that the present systems are no longer workable, attention will turn toward a replacement system. At that time, the Europeans may not be the only ones who view FA/UC as a reasonable replacement for SA/ALS.

5. What the EU should not do

If the EU decides to adopt formula apportionment, there are several things it should not do. First, if wide variations in tax rates continue to exist, it would be inadvisable to adopt formula apportionment without requiring combination of firms deemed to be engaged in a unitary business, as the conceptual problems and the temptation for income shifting would be too great. The SA/ALS could continue to be used to divide the income of such groups among their constituent parts, but that would largely defeat the purpose of adopting FA.

If unitary combination were to be adopted, it should be limited to the 'water's edge' of the EU; it would be a mistake to apply combination on a world-wide basis, at least in the first instance. World-wide combination should be adopted only in co-operation with other countries, following a multilateral decision (taken, for example, in the OECD) that SA/ALS is not working satisfactorily. There is currently little sentiment for such a multilateral shift to FA/UC.

It would also be a mistake to adopt FA/UC without substantial conformity of definitions of tax bases, apportionment formulas, measures of apportionment factors, and the definition of a unitary business (if combination is to be employed). The result would be complexity, gaps and overlaps in the tax systems of Member States, and inequity.[66]

Finally, it seems unlikely that an evolutionary process, in which first one member of the EU and then another adopts FA/UC, is the optimal way

---

[66] The tax treatment of dividends raises important problems that cannot be discussed adequately in this chapter. Under a system of unitary combination, dividends flowing within the unitary group from unitary income should be ignored. The question is how to treat dividends received by EU payees from EU payers that are not members of the same unitary group. (Dividends received from non-EU payers would presumably continue to be taxed as now.) The correct answer depends on the scheme adopted to provide relief from double taxation of intercorporate dividends. In principle, the US states should exempt non-unitary dividends from their source-based taxes, on the assumption that they are paid from

to go about moving to FA/UC in the EU. While competitive pressures might eventually force convergence to a single, sensible system, particularly if one large country or group of countries were to take the lead, there appears to be little reason for such optimism. While such an evolutionary process is occurring, two different methods (SA/ALS and FA/UC) would be in operation, creating complexity, gaps and overlaps in tax bases, economic distortions, and inequities. Even those members that followed a lead to FA/UC might not adopt systems sufficiently similar to those of the leader to avoid the problems identified earlier. It seems that the only way to make a move to FA/UC, if one is to be made, is multilaterally, by all members of the EU.

Appendix: Formula apportionment in the US: Chaos to be avoided[67]

If one writes the formula for tax liability under an apportioned state profits tax, as it is commonly applied in the US, one finds that virtually everything is up for grabs. Thus

$$(10.1) \qquad T_i = \frac{t_i \, P[f_w \, (W_i/W) + f_a(A_i/A) + f_s \, (S_i/S)]}{f_w + f_a + f_s},$$

where T_i is the company's tax liability in state i; t_i is the tax rate in state i; P is the company's taxable profits; W_i, A_i, and S_i are the company's payroll, property, and sales in state i; W, A, and S are the company's total payroll, property, and sales; and f_w, f_a, and f_s are the weights given to payroll, property, and sales.

The tax rate and the ratio of in-state to out-of-state payroll are the only parts of the right-hand side of this formula that have not been subject to considerable controversy. (The law determining the location of employment for the purpose of unemployment compensation is commonly used to define the latter; this is not required.)

income that has been taxed by the source state or foreign nation, but many do not do so. (On this issue, see McLure (1986). Weiner (1995) evaluates various options used in the states.) Depending on the degree of common ownership, intercorporate dividends may be taxed or exempt, when paid within a single country. It seems that all such non-unitary dividends should be exempt. To the extent that EU source countries provide imputation credits to foreigners (or eliminate tax via a split rate), dividends received should be taxed. But if, as is more common, foreign companies do not receive imputation credits, the dividends they receive from payers in other Member States should be exempt.

[67] This appendix appears, with slight modifications, in McLure (1995).

Within extremely broad limits, each state can adopt its own definition of tax-able profits; although nearly all states have substantial conformity with the federal definition of the income tax base, there is no requirement of conformity with the federal definition or the laws of other states. At times when the federal govern-ment has significantly narrowed the tax base—say through greatly accelerated depreciation—states have chosen to decouple their tax-base definition to avoid extreme revenue losses. Similarly, states need not treat sales in the same way. Most measure sales at destination, but may define destination in a particular fashion. Nearly all of the states that measure sales at destination apply a 'throwback' rule, whereby they also include sales originating within their boundaries that are made to the federal government or to a state in which the firm does not have taxable nexus (one of the few issues on which the law is relatively clear, thanks to a 1959 decision of the US Supreme Court[68]). No effort is made to distinguish between sales made to final consumers and sales to business; thus the tax on the portion of profits apportioned by the sales factor resembles a turnover tax. Double-weighting sales increases this tendency. States may apply whatever weight they wish to each factor, as long as the weights sum to 1. Many states are moving toward a formula with half the weight on sales and 25 per cent on each of the other two factors—payroll and property—and some use only sales to appor-tion profits.

Nor is there agreement about the entity to which the formula is to be applied. Some states adopt a strict legal-entity approach. This approach opens the door for abuse through manipulation of transfer prices. It also fails to recognize difficulties inherent in isolating the income of related enterprises where economic inter-dependence exists. This defect is especially problematic in light of the increasing importance of income from intangibles. Other states prevent this transfer pricing problem by combining related companies deemed to be engaged in a 'unitary business' into a single, taxable entity; but there is no accepted definition of what is a unitary business. Some states have applied unitary combination on a world-wide basis, whereas others have restricted the use of combination to the 'water's edge', apportioning only profits deemed to be earned in the US. The possibilities for multiple taxation and undertaxation are endless.

The treatment of intercorporate dividends by many states is particularly trou-blesome. Dividends flowing between firms filing combined reports are eliminated from the calculation. Some other dividends are taxed, but others are exempt; this practice varies from state to state (see McLure (1986) and Weiner (1995) for a dis-cussion of the particular problem of foreign-source dividends).

The results of this chaotic situation are inequity, distortion of economic choices, excessive costs of compliance and administration, protracted litigation, annoyance of the trading partners of the US, and taxpayer uncertainty. The con-stitutionality of certain features of the system are under review by the Supreme Court—and have been for over a decade.

---

[68] *Northwestern Sates Portland Cement Co. v. Minnesota, 358 U.S. 450, 79 S. Ct. 357 (1959).*

Much of the problem could be eliminated by choosing a common definition of profits (ideally, the definition used by the federal government), a common apportionment formula, common ways to measure the factors in the formula, a common definition of the taxable entity, and uniform treatment of dividends. Given all this uniformity, it would make no sense to have totally decentralized administration.

These problems are essentially avoided in Canada, because the taxes of most of the provinces are administered by the central government, using a uniform definition of the tax base and a single formula based on payroll and sales. The Canadian approach (though not necessarily the Canadian apportionment formula) is the only one the EU should consider.

References

Altman, G. T., and Keesling, F. M. (1946), *Allocation of Income in State Taxation*, New York: Commerce Clearing House.

Avi-Yonah, R. S. (1995), 'The rise and fall of arm's length: a study in the evolution of US international taxation', *Virginia Tax Review*, 15: 89–159.

Cnossen, S. (1996), 'Company taxes in the European Union: criteria and options for reform', *Fiscal Studies*, 17(4): 67–97.

Coffill, E. J., and Willson, P., Jr. (1993), 'Federal formulary apportionment as an alternative to arm's length pricing: from the frying pan to the fire', *Tax Notes*, 59 (24 May): 1103–17.

Commerce Clearing House (various years), *State Tax Review*, various issues, Chicago.

Commission of the European Communities (1975), 'Proposal for a Council Directive concerning the harmonisation of systems of taxation and of withholding taxes on dividends', *Official Journal of the European Communities*, C253.

——(1980), 'Report on the scope for convergence of tax systems in the Community', *Bulletin of the European Communities*, Supplement 1.

——(1988), 'Preliminary draft proposal for a directive on the harmonisation of rules for the determination of taxable profits of enterprises', Brussels.

——(1989), 'Proposal for a council regulation on the Statute for a European Company', COM(89) 268 final, Brussels.

——(1990), *Guidelines on Company Taxation*, SEC(90) 601, 20 April, Brussels.

——(1991a), 'Amended proposal for a council regulation on the Statute for a European Company', *Official Journal of the European Communities*, C176/1, 8 July.

——(1991b), 'Removal of tax obstacles to the cross-frontier activities of companies', *Bulletin of the European Communities*, Supplement 4/91.

Commission of the European Communities (1992), *Report of the Committee of Independent Experts on Company Taxation*, Luxemburg (the Ruding Report).

——(1996a), *Taxation in the European Union*, SEC(96) 487, 20 March, Brussels (the Monti Report).

——(1996b), *Taxation in the European Union: Report on the Development of Tax Systems*, COM(96) 546 final, 22 October, Brussels.

——(1997), 'A package to tackle harmful tax competition in the European Union', Communication from the Commission to the Council and the European Parliament, COM(97) 564 final, 5 November, Brussels.

——(1998), 'Conclusions of the ECOFIN Council Meeting on 1 December 1997 concerning taxation policy', *Official Journal of the European Communities*, 98/C 2/01, 6 January.

Corrigan, E. F. (1980), 'Toward uniformity in interstate taxation', *Tax Notes*, 11 (15 September): 507–14.

Daly, M. (1992), 'Tax coordination and competition in Canada', Annex 9A in Commission of the European Communities, *Report of the Committee of Independent Experts on Company Taxation*, Luxemburg.

——and Weiner, J. (1993), 'Corporate tax harmonization and competition in federal countries: some lessons for the European Community?', *National Tax Journal*, 46: 441–61.

Devgun, D. (1996), 'International fiscal wars for the twenty-first century: an assessment of tax-based trade retaliation', *Law and Policy in International Business*, 25: 353–421.

Dexter, W. D. (1976), 'Taxation of income from intangibles of multistate-multinational corporations', *Vanderbilt Law Review*, 29: 353–421.

Duncan, H. T. (1996), 'Taxing multijurisdictional businesses: the state approach', in US Department of the Treasury, *Conference on Formula Apportionment*, 12 December, Washington, DC.

Eurostat (1983), *Structure and Activity of Industry, Annual Inquiry: Main Results 1983/84*, Brussels: Statistical Office of the European Communities.

Ferguson, F. E. (1986), 'Worldwide unitary taxation: the end appears near', *Journal of State Taxation*, 4: 241.

Harper, J. B., and Lewis, C. L. (1988), 'Recent federal and multistate developments affecting state taxation', *Journal of State Taxation*, 7: 29–30.

Hellerstein, J. (1982), 'Allocation and apportionment of dividends and the delineation of the unitary business', *Tax Notes*, 14 (15 January): 155–68.

——(1983), 'The basic operations interdependence requirement of a unitary business: a reply to Charles E. McLure, Jr.', *Tax Notes*, 18 (28 February): 723–31.

——(1993), 'Federal income taxation of multinationals: replacement of separate accounting with formulary apportionment', *Tax Notes*, 60 (23 August): 1131–45.

——and Hellerstein, W. (1993), *State Taxation: Corporate Income and Franchise Taxes*, second edition, Boston, MA: Warren, Gorham & Lamont.

Hellerstein and Hellerstein (1989), *State Taxation: Corporate Income and Franchise Taxes*, 1989 Cumulative Supplement.

Kuiper, W. G. (1988), 'EC Commission proposes a directive on the harmonization of rules for the determination of taxable profits of enterprises', *European Taxation*, October.

McDaniel, P. (1994), 'Formulary taxation in the North American Free Trade Zone', *Tax Law Review*, 49: 691–744.

McLure, C. E., Jr. (1980), 'The state corporate income tax: lambs in wolves' clothing', in H. J. Aaron and M. J. Boskin (eds), *The Economics of Taxation*, Washington, DC: Brookings Institution.

——(1981), 'Toward uniformity in interstate taxation: a further analysis', *Tax Notes*, 13 (13 July): 51–63.

——(1983a), 'Operational interdependence is not the appropriate "Bright Line Test" of a unitary business—at least not now', *Tax Notes*, 18 (10 January): 107–10.

——(1983b), 'The basic operational interdependence test of a unitary business: a rejoinder', *Tax Notes*, 21 (10 October): 91–100.

——(1984a), 'Defining a unitary business: an economist's view', in C. E. McLure, Jr. (ed.), *The State Corporation Income Tax: Issues in Worldwide Unitary Combination*, Stanford, CA: Hoover Institution Press.

——(1984b), 'Unitary taxation: the working group's contribution', *Tax Notes*, 24 (27 August): 879–83.

——(1984c), 'Comments' on P. B. Musgrave, 'Principles for dividing the state corporate tax base', in C. E. McLure, Jr. (ed.), *The State Corporation Income Tax: Issues in Worldwide Unitary Combination*, Stanford, CA: Hoover Institution Press.

——(1985), 'Federal law and state corporate income taxes', *Vanderbilt Journal of Transnational Law*, 18: 275–310.

——(1986), 'State taxation of foreign-source dividends: starting from first principles', *Tax Notes*, 30 (10 March): 475–89.

——(1989), 'Economic integration and European taxation of corporate income at source: some lessons from the US experience', in M. Gammie and P. W. Robinson (eds), *Beyond 1992: A European Tax System*, London: Institute for Fiscal Studies; also *European Taxation*, 29: 243–50.

——(1995), 'Revenue assignment and intergovernmental fiscal relations in Russia', in E. Lazear (ed.), *Economic Reform in Eastern Europe and Russia: Realities of Reform*, Palo Alto, CA: Hoover Institution Press.

McLure, C. E., Jr. (1997a), 'US federal use of formula apportionment in the taxation of income from intangibles', *Tax Notes International*, 14 (10 March): 859–71; also in US Department of the Treasury, *Conference on Formula Apportionment*, 12 December 1996, Washington, DC.

—— (1997b), 'Taxation of electronic commerce: economic objectives, technological constraints, and tax law', paper presented at a conference on Taxation of Electronic Commerce, New York University, May.

—— (1997c), 'Topics in the theory of revenue assignment: gaps, traps, and nuances', in M. I. Blejer and T. Ter-Minassian (eds), *Macroeconomic Dimensions of Public Finance: Essays in Honour of Vito Tanzi*, London: Routledge.

Miller, B. F. (1984), 'Worldwide unitary combination: the California practice', in C. E. McLure, Jr. (ed.), *The State Corporation Income Tax: Issues in Worldwide Unitary Combination*, Stanford, CA: Hoover Institution Press.

—— (1993), 'A reply to "From the frying pan to the fire"', *Tax Notes*, 61 (11 October): 241–56.

—— (1995), 'None are so blind as those who will not see', *Tax Notes*, 66 (13 February): 1023–35.

—— and Campion, E. (1996), 'California's unitary accounting method: AKA worldwide combined reporting or unitary tax and case studies of formulary apportionment', in US Department of the Treasury, *Conference on Formula Apportionment*, 12 December, Washington, DC.

Multistate Tax Commission (1996), *Model Regulations, Statutes and Guidelines: Uniformity Recommendations to the States*, updated May, Washington, DC.

Munnell, A. H. (1992), 'Taxation of capital income in a global economy: an overview', *New England Economic Review*, September–October: 33–52.

Musgrave, P. B. (1984), 'Principles for dividing the state corporate tax base', in C. E. McLure, Jr. (ed.), *The State Corporation Income Tax: Issues in Worldwide Unitary Combination*, Stanford, CA: Hoover Institution Press.

National Tax Association (NTA) (various years), *Proceedings of the Annual Conference*, Washington, DC.

OECD (1979), *Transfer Pricing and Multinational Enterprises*, Paris: Organization for Economic Co-operation and Development.

—— (1991), *Taxing Profits in a Global Economy*, Paris: Organization for Economic Co-operation and Development.

—— (1994), *Flows and Stocks of Fixed Capital, 1967–1992*, Paris: Organization for Economic Co-operation and Development.

——(1995a), *Transfer Pricing and Guidelines for Multinational Enterprises and Tax Administrators*, Paris: Organization for Economic Co-operation and Development.

——(1995b), *Labour Force Statistics, 1973–1993*, Paris: Organization for Economic Co-operation and Development.

——(1996), *Model Tax Convention on Income and on Capital*, revised, Paris: Organization for Economic Co-operation and Development.

Pilat, D. (1996), 'Labour productivity levels in OECD countries: estimates for manufacturing and selected service sectors', Organization for Economic Co-operation and Development, Economics Working Paper 169.

Pomp, R. D. (1987), 'Reforming a state corporate income tax', *Albany Law Review*, 51: 375–788.

Sheffrin, S. M., and Fulcher, J. (1984), 'Alternative divisions of the tax base: how much is at stake?', in C. E. McLure, Jr. (ed.), *The State Corporation Income Tax: Issues in Worldwide Unitary Combination*, Stanford, CA: Hoover Institution Press.

Smith, E. H. (1976), 'Allocating to provinces the taxable income of corporations: how the federal–provincial allocation rules evolved', *Canadian Tax Journal*, 24: 545–71.

Tanzi, V. (1995), *Taxation in an Integrating World*, Washington, DC: Brookings Institution.

Thalmann, P. (1992), 'Tax coordination and competition in Switzerland', Annex 9B in Commission of the European Communities, *Report of the Committee of Independent Experts on Company Taxation*, Luxemburg.

US Department of the Treasury (1984), *The Final Report of the Worldwide Unitary Taxation Working Group: Chairman's Report and Supplemental Views*, Washington, DC: US Government Printing Office.

——(1996), *Conference on Formula Apportionment*, 12 December, Washington, DC.

——and Internal Revenue Service (1988), *A Study of Intercompany Pricing under Section 482 of the Code*, IRS Notice 88–123, 1988-2, C.B. 458, 475 (the White Paper).

US General Accounting Office (1992), *International Taxation: Tax Effects of Intercompany Prices*, GAO/GGD-92-89, Washington, DC.

US House of Representatives (1964), *Report of the Special Subcommittee on State Taxation*, 1: 'State taxation of interstate commerce', 88th Congress, 2nd Session, Washington, DC: US Government Printing Office (the Willis Report).

Van Heukelen, M. (1990), 'The assignment of corporate tax competencies in the European Community', Commission of the European Communities, mimeo.

Vanistendael, F. (1994), 'The limits to the new community tax order', *Common Market Law Review*, 31: 293–314.

Weiner, J. M. (1991), 'A new direction in company taxation for Europe 1992', in J. M. Weiner (ed.), *Company Taxation in Europe 1992: Design and Implementation of Company Tax Reform*, Brussels: Institute of European Studies, Université Libre de Bruxelles.

——(1992), 'Tax coordination and competition in the United States', Annex 9C in Commission of the European Communities, *Report of the Committee of Independent Experts on Company Taxation*, Luxemburg.

——(1994), 'Company taxation for the European Community: how subnational tax variation affects business investment in the United States and Canada', unpublished Ph.D. dissertation, Harvard University. (The empirical evidence from the dissertation is summarized in Weiner (1996 and 1998).)

——(1995), 'Alternative methods available to state tax authorities for taxing non-US-source corporate income', *Proceedings of the 88th Annual Conference*, Washington, DC: National Tax Association.

——(1996), 'Estimates of how the unitary tax affects business investment', paper presented at the Allied Social Science Meetings, San Francisco, California.

——(1997), 'Company tax reform efforts in the European Union', in *Proceedings of the 90th Annual Conference*, Washington, DC: National Tax Association.

——(1998), 'Formula apportionment and unitary taxation: what works and doesn't work', in *Proceedings of the 91st Annual Conference*, Washington, DC: National Tax Association, forthcoming.

——(1999), 'Using the experience in the US states to evaluate issues in implementing formula apportionment at the international level', Office of Tax Analysis, Paper 83, Washington, DC: US Department of the Treasury; also *Tax Notes International*, 13 (23 December 1996): 2113–44; also in US Department of the Treasury, *Conference on Formula Apportionment*, 12 December 1996, Washington, DC. Available in the working paper series of the Office of Tax Analysis at 'www.ustreas.gov/OTA/ota83.pdf'.

Author index

Italic numbers denote reference to illustrations.

Subject index

Italic numbers denote reference to illustrations.